Christianity and Comics

Christianity and Comics

• • • • • • • • • • • • • • • • • •

Stories We Tell about
Heaven and Hell

BLAIR DAVIS

Rutgers University Press
New Brunswick, Camden, and Newark, New Jersey
London and Oxford

Rutgers University Press is a department of Rutgers, The State University of New Jersey, one of the leading public research universities in the nation. By publishing worldwide, it furthers the University's mission of dedication to excellence in teaching, scholarship, research, and clinical care.

Library of Congress Cataloging-in-Publication Data
Names: Davis, Blair, 1975- author.
Title: Christianity and comics: stories we tell about heaven and hell / Blair Davis.
Description: New Brunswick: Rutgers University Press, 2024. | Includes bibliographical references and index.
Identifiers: LCCN 2023032533 | ISBN 9781978828216 (paperback) | ISBN 9781978828223 (hardback) | ISBN 9781978828230 (epub) | ISBN 9781978828247 (pdf)
Subjects: LCSH: Comic books, strips, etc.—Religious aspects—Christianity. | Comic books, strips, etc.—Social aspects—United States. | Bible—In comics. | Superheroes—Religious aspects—Christianity. | Christianity and literature—United States. | LCGFT: Comics criticism.
Classification: LCC PN6712 .D38 2024 | DDC 741.5/3823—dc23/eng/20230814
LC record available at https://lccn.loc.gov/2023032533

A British Cataloging-in-Publication record for this book is available from the British Library.

Copyright © 2024 by Blair Davis
All rights reserved

No part of this book may be reproduced or utilized in any form or by any means, electronic or mechanical, or by any information storage and retrieval system, without written permission from the publisher. Please contact Rutgers University Press, 106 Somerset Street, New Brunswick, NJ 08901. The only exception to this prohibition is "fair use" as defined by U.S. copyright law.

References to internet websites (URLs) were accurate at the time of writing. Neither the author nor Rutgers University Press is responsible for URLs that may have expired or changed since the manuscript was prepared.

⊖ The paper used in this publication meets the requirements of the American National Standard for Information Sciences—Permanence of Paper for Printed Library Materials, ANSI Z39.48-1992.

rutgersuniversitypress.org

Dedicated to the teacher who banned me from Sunday school when I was twelve.

I'm sorry for drawing the poster to *Return of the Living Dead Part II* when you asked for an image of what resurrection meant to me.

Contents

	Introduction	1
1	The 1940s: From Superheroes to *Picture Stories from the Bible*	11

The Spectre; *Samson*; *The Spirit*; Madam Satan; *Pocket Comics*; *Suspense Comics*; *The Life of Christ Visualized*; *Picture Stories from the Bible*; *Catholic Comics*; *Marvels of Science*; *Lots "O" Fun Comics*

2	The 1950s and 1960s: Sunday Schools, Secularism, and *Seduction of the Innocent*	57

The Case against the Comics; *The Teacher and the Comics*; *Heroes All*; *Topix Comics*; *Treasure Chest of Fun and Fact*; Catechetical Guild Educational Society; *Bible Tales for Young Folk*; *Martin Luther King and the Montgomery Story*; *Oral Roberts' True Stories*; EC Comics; *If the Devil Would Talk*; *Hot Stuff*; *Zap Comix*; *The Book of Genesis Illustrated*

3	The 1970s: Comix, Jack Chick, *Archie*, and Spire Christian Comics	107

Wimmen's Comix; *Binky Brown Meets the Holy Virgin Mary*; *Sacred and Profane*; *Eternal Truth*; *Holy Ghost Zapped Comix*; Logos; Chick Tracts; Crusader Comics; Spire Christian Comics; *Archie*

4	The 1970s and 1980s: Marvel, DC, Saints, and Sinners	151

The Bible; *House of Mystery*; *House of Secrets*; *The Phantom Stranger*; *The Spectre*; *Blue Devil*; *Mephisto Vs.*; *Ghost Rider*; *Son of Satan*; *Cloak and Dagger*; *Daredevil*; *X-Factor*; *Francis, Brother of the Universe*; *The Life of Pope John Paul II*; *Mother Teresa of Calcutta*

5   The 1990s: Vertigo, *Hellboy,* and Marvel's *Illuminator*   189
Batman: Arkham Asylum; *Batman: Holy Terror*; Marvel/Nelson;
Illuminator; *Grendel*; *Hellboy*; *The Sandman*; *John Constantine,*
Hellblazer; *The Mystery Play*; *Preacher*

6   The 2000s: Genres and Auteurs   229
A Contract with God; *Blankets*; *Hot Comb*; *Boxers*; *Saints*; *King*;
March: Book One; *Nat Turner*; *Mary Wept over the Feet of Jesus*;
The Spectre; *Daredevil*; *Hellstorm: Son of Satan*; *Testament*; *Lucifer*;
Punk Rock Jesus; *Jesusfreak*; *American Jesus*; *The Goddamned*;
Lake of Fire; *Loaded Bible*; *Battle Pope*; *Second Coming*

Acknowledgments   263
Notes   265
Selected Bibliography   289
Index   295

Christianity and Comics

Introduction

• • • • • • • • • • • • •

The Bible is full of stories. Whether those stories hold any personal spiritual meaning for you is one thing, but most people—be they Christian, Jewish, Muslim, Buddhist, Hindu, atheist, agnostic, or otherwise—can agree that it contains a lot of thrilling tales. Tales about battles with giants and a war among angels. About devastating plagues, floods, and fire. About deadly curses, human sacrifice, dismemberment, and genocide. About torture, death, and resurrection.

The Bible's accounts of heaven and hell, God and the devil are stories. You might believe in some or all of them as literal events that happened in the past. Or you might not, perhaps preferring to read them through the lens of allegory or myth. But no matter how you choose to interpret them, the fact that such stories shaped Western civilization remains undeniable. We need not personally believe in the spiritual teachings of Christianity to grasp the ways they have shaped societies across numerous eras and nations. Many people use the Bible's stories as a way of finding meaning in their lives and to make sense of the world, including its history and its origins. Who we are, how we got here, and what our role is in our universe are questions that many find the answers to in Christianity and its teachings.[1]

Because their historical, social, and cultural implications are so widespread, the ways the Bible's stories are told are vitally important to us all as human beings. Sometimes they are passed down orally from parent to child or from pastor to congregation or in printed text via poetry or prose. But they have also increasingly been retold through visual media in the twentieth and twenty-first centuries in the form of movies, television series, and comic books. If we think of the Bible and Christianity through the framework of storytelling, then the ways its stories (which we might have faith in, be skeptical about, or reject entirely) get retold across various media shape how people understand them. Even those who are not regular churchgoers often know many of the Bible's lessons and anecdotes because of how they are retold outside the walls of the church through various forms of popular culture. The fragmented ways many people now come to understand particular Bible stories via their retellings and reworkings across numerous media forms even echoes how the Bible was originally conceived. As anthropologist Claude Lévi-Strauss noted in *Myth and Meaning*, "It seems that [the Bible's] raw material was disconnected elements and that learned philosophers put them together in order to make a continuous story."[2]

By the 1940s, comics had become a burgeoning format for telling stories about Christianity, not long after the comic-book format first arrived on newsstand shelves in the mid-1930s. Often, the tales featured in Christian-oriented comic books were faithful ones about the lives of famous figures from the Bible or the Catholic Church, especially at first. Or they strategically applied Christian concepts such as heaven and hell as a way of enhancing otherwise nonreligious adventures in genres such as superhero, horror, and humor comics (even if such stories weren't explicitly Christian in their intent). But by using Satan as a supervillain, for example, such stories adhered to and upheld the larger traditions and morals of Christianity.

While many early comics creators approached the Bible as source material to either be adapted (in series such as *The Life of Christ Visualized Picture Stories from the Bible*, and *Bible Tales for Young Folk* in the 1940s and 1950s) or merely alluded to via devilish, God-like and/or Bible-inspired characters (in 1940s series such as *Pocket Comics* and *More Fun Comics* and decades later in *House of Mystery* and *Son of Satan*), more recent creators are now just as likely to use comic books as a forum for reexamining Christianity's role in Western civilization. Moral panic concerns arose in the 1950s as parents, politicians, and psychiatrists alike viewed the medium as a dangerous one for both children and adults, but in later decades comics creators used their work to confront some of the most serious social, cultural, ideological, and spiritual questions of our time.

As the decades passed, more and more comics began using aspects of Christianity in increasingly complex ways. By the cusp of the twenty-first century, writers such as Neil Gaiman and Garth Ennis were offering readers a more challenging approach to Christian themes, tropes, and images in series such as *The Sandman* and *Preacher*. Many subsequent creators also took a more overarching approach to the role of Christianity in the history of world religions, such as in the 2006 DC/Vertigo series *Testament* by Douglas Rushkoff and Liam Sharp. Issue 6 of *Testament* begins with the statement that "every god has a creation story," then explains that "each story is only as true as the number and intensity of those who believe. For their devotion to a god writes history itself."[3]

Similarly, when an old woman tells a monk about how Christianity has been maintained circa AD 1000 in issue 6 of *The Department of Truth* by James Tynion IV and Elsa Charretier, she tells how "the ground is not solid beneath our feet" due to how "the belief of the people in great numbers shapes the truth of the world."[4] And in Jonathan Hickman, Mike Costa, and Di Amorim's *God Is Dead*, one character responds to a question about the value of studying ancient spiritual traditions and "centuries-old mythology that's been distorted by thousands of retellings and of dubious veracity in the first place" with a trenchant answer: "All a God *is*, is a story . . . a story that spills the banks of fiction and begins telling itself."[5]

Stories shape culture and cultural practices, and a story gains influence as it gets retold. But this process is also reciprocal: culture also influences how stories are retold (some might say distorted) in different ways based on how "the belief of the people" evolves. This reciprocity lies at the heart of how comics have told Christian stories since the 1940s.

Methods and Meanings

The eight decades' worth of comics examined in *Christianity and Comics: Stories We Tell about Heaven and Hell* are the basis for a historically driven narrative about how comics have approached Christianity. While most comics fans would name superheroes, funny animals, cowboys, and detectives as the most recurrent subject matter of comic books in past decades, Christian-oriented comics have had a steady presence on newsstands and in comic-book shops throughout most of the medium's history. In recent years, new generations of comics creators have examined Christianity in complex and increasingly critical ways via publishers such as Marvel, Dark Horse, Image, and DC Comics, reflecting changes in the role of religion in society and in popular culture overall.

My exploration of how Christianity was represented for churchgoing and secular readers alike over the past eight decades of American comics is framed around several questions. How and why did the different approaches to representing Christianity in the pages and panels of comics books emerge and evolve in the United States? How did publishers initially envision the potentials of the medium for using Christian tropes for the purposes of both education and entertainment in the 1940s? How did new generations of creators reimagine these aspects in later decades? How did changes in where comics were sold and who read them affect what kinds of stories could be told? And how did these changes parallel larger shifts in the social and moral roles of religion in America across eras?

My methodology is centered first and foremost on building a historical narrative as I seek answers to these questions. In shaping the chapters that follow in the form of a decade-by-decade exploration, my hope is that patterns of representation (such as how notions of heroism, morality, and faith are represented) can be weighed against the changes taking place in different eras in the comic-book industry itself and in American society overall.

This historiographic approach means that this book is itself telling a story, so it is important to note from the outset that I am framing this historical narrative via my experience as both a comics scholar and a media historian. The story I am telling showcases the industrial roles, processes of adaptation, and creative practices used to bring the Bible and its themes, figures, and imagery to comics. While I use strategies that analyze the industry (such as how various production and distribution models have affected how comics are published and purchased) as well as textual analysis (for example, by examining thematic patterns and character tropes, such as how Satan has been characterized as a supervillain in various decades), these approaches are ultimately in service of a larger overall goal: to trace the conceptual patterns behind how and why comics use the Bible across numerous eras, genres, and publishers for a wide array of readers, some devoutly religious, others not.

One of the key ways I delve into the specifics of how comic-book writers, artists, and publishers construct their discourses about Christianity is by using a medium-theory approach that stems from the work of Marshall McLuhan and the larger scholarly tradition of media ecology. Medium theory examines the specific codes and conventions of any particular medium— the "fixed features" that make it "physically, psychologically and socially different from other media," as communication scholar Joshua Meyrowitz tells us.[6] With comic books, this involves a concrete analysis of the particularities of the comics medium and how it formally constructs its content (for example, how elements such as panels, artwork, captions, and word balloons handle biblical material differently from other media) as a way of determining specific qualities of and potentials for representing Christianity.

It is also important to note that although the medium of comics encompasses many different forms of publication, the vast majority of examples studied in these pages are *comic books*. As a format, comic books gained mass popularity in the mid-1930s with titles such as *New Fun Comics, Famous Funnies*, and *Popular Comics* that regularly contained sixty-four pages of content (although page count varied, especially as time went on), measured 7¾ inches wide by 10½ inches long (which again changed in subsequent eras), and were distributed to retail outlets such as newsstands (and later to supermarkets and specialty comic-book shops). Many of these early series reprinted previously published newspaper comic strips, but I am largely setting the latter and other earlier traditions of comics aside as a way of setting some limits on the scope of what I can tackle here. Analyzing eighty years of comic books is already a wide-ranging agenda, as rewarding as studying the religious dimensions in comic strips such as *Prince Valiant* and *The Family Circus* or the work of Rudolph Töpffer, James Gillray, and other creators from earlier centuries might be. I also largely limit my analysis to American comics and the role of religion in the United States, also out of a necessity to keep the scope of the patterns I'm looking at more manageable in this study.

As this book unfolds, I do sometimes address other formats such as graphic novels, webcomics and comic tracts (the latter including those from Jack Chick) when warranted, especially when those realms begin to increasingly intersect. Jack Chick released a line of comic books at the same time as he did minicomics in the shorter tract format. Graphic novelists such as Gene Yuen Lang often write serialized comics for Marvel and DC, while webcomics such as *Coffee with Jesus* and *Adventures of God* are frequently published in paperback form. But for the most part, what I am looking at here is serialized comic books, some of which were eventually collected into trade paperback formats that some fans and commentators also call graphic novels.

The scope of this book also means that as we move closer to the twenty-first century, there are far too many cases of comics that depict Christianity for me to cover in as much depth as I do in earlier chapters. This is a symptom not only of the industry's growth and the increase in the number of titles published each month from a rising number of independent companies by the 1980s but also of the growing number of ways that such titles began to depict Christian elements. Social commentary became commonplace in comics by the end of the twentieth century in a way that was rarely there in the first few decades, allowing for shaper critiques of religious institutions in many titles.

So please be assured that the examples I cover herein are not exhaustive but are rather indicative examples of the patterns I am tracing. By the time I arrived at the 1980s and beyond in my research, I had to leave out nearly as many titles as I included because of how prolific these trends and tropes had become in modern comics. This also means that as the chapters progress, you will find more and more examples introduced, but with less and less room to dive as deeply into each case study as some readers might have hoped. Examples include *The Sandman* and *Preacher*, which other scholars have covered from alternative perspectives that I would point curious readers to.[7]

While some of the comic books I look at feature superheroes, most do not. Much has already been written about the spiritual parallels between superheroes and various religious figures. Ben Saunders examines the mythic nature of superheroes in *Do the Gods Wear Capes? Spirituality, Fantasy, and Superheroes*,[8] while Danny Fingeroth sees heroes such as Superman as extensions of Judaism in *Disguised as Clark Kent: Jews, Comics, and the Creation of the Superhero*.[9] Other books equate Superman with Jesus Christ, such as John T. Galloway's *The Gospel According to Superman*.[10] But while the story of how comic books have depicted Christianity must address superheroes to some extent, I have chosen to cover a wider range of genres and approaches in each chapter in aid of charting the less-explored corners of comics history.

Beginning with 1940s comic books such as *Picture Stories from the Bible* and *Catholic Comics*, then moving on to such titles as *Bible in Life Pix* and *Treasure Chest of Fun and Fact*, early chapters examine how some titles were distributed in Sunday schools and parochial schools as a way of teaching the gospel to young people while other comics were sold to the general public (sometimes on newsstands or by mail order, but increasingly in Christian bookstores) in the hope of inspiring them to learn more about Christ's teachings. In the 1950s, comics featuring televangelists Oral Roberts and Billy Graham appeared, along with titles encouraging children to become nuns and priests from the Catechetical Guild and the comical adventures of a diapered devil-child in *Hot Stuff*, while in the 1960s and 1970s, the rise of underground comix led to new directions in spiritual subject matter in the pages of *Zap Comix* and *Wimmen's Comix*.

Subsequent chapters examine how by the 1970s and 1980s, numerous Christian-oriented Archie comic books were created specifically for sales in Christian bookstores, while Marvel Comics created titles about such prominent figures as Mother Teresa and Pope John Paul II. Marvel also reimagined Satan and Jesus Christ in the pages of *Ghost Rider* and the Four Horsemen of the Apocalypse in the *X-Men* spin-off series *X-Factor*, while DC balanced humorous approaches to spirituality in *Blue Devil* with menacing ones in series such as *House of Mystery* and *House of Secrets*.

The final chapters explore how series in more recent decades have taken increasingly unconventional approaches to Christianity in comics such as *Preacher, Lucifer, The Goddamned, Loaded Bible, Battle Pope,* and *Second Coming*. In contextualizing how comics of the past few decades have moved away from directly adapting the Bible to more metaphoric takes on biblical themes and figures, this book examines how the lines have become increasingly blurred in modern comics between traditional understandings about heroism and hell, salvation and damnation.

Audiences and Aspirations

Christianity and Comics was written with a wide array of readers in mind: Christians, non-Christians, atheists, agnostics, and everyone else. It is not written from any particular spiritual or ideological position, at least not deliberately. When I use the word "Christianity" throughout the book, I am aware that this term means different things to different people. *The Concise Dictionary of Christianity in America* notes that "the meaning of Christian has fluctuated over the centuries," although it originally was used to define those who believe in Christ's teachings.[11] In *The Meaning and End of Religion*, esteemed religious scholar Wilfred Cantwell Smith distinguishes between Christianity as "an ideal" connected to a tradition of theology and understood in spiritual and transcendental terms, on the one hand, and as "an empirical phenomenon, historical and sociological" in connection to human beings, on the other.[12] In the former meaning, Christian faith is rooted in its intent and in the latter meaning, Christianity is expressed in a variety of protocols and practices.

I alternate when required between the use of the term "Christianity" as it applies to the notion of personal, spiritual faith and a broader set of diverse institutional practices grounded in historical and social contexts. Christianity is not marked by a unified group of practitioners—there are dozens, if not hundreds of practicing denominations across America. The 2018 edition of the *Handbook of Denominations in the United States* accounts for such categories as Orthodox, Catholic, Episcopal, Anglican, Lutheran, Reformed,

Presbyterian, Congregationalist, Mennonite, Anabaptist, Brethren, Pietist, Baptist, Methodist, Holiness, Pentecostal, Restorationist, Adventist, Unitarian, Latter-day Saints, and fundamentalist churches. Each of these categories contains numerous denominations, up to a dozen or more for a grand total of more than 200 entries.[13]

But specific denominations such as the Roman Catholic Church are rarely specified in the comic books I am looking at. Some publishers specified whether they were addressing a Catholic or Protestant audience, as in *Catholic Comics*, but more often publishers took a generic approach—not only in the hope of being all-encompassing in how spirituality was envisioned (and could be interpreted by the reader), but also, and more important, so they could sell more copies to a wider readership. So my goal is to be specific as I can whenever a certain comic is created with a specifically Catholic or Protestant audience in mind. But in many cases, this isn't possible or practical when creators took only a general approach to such subjects as Christian faith, Jesus Christ, the Holy Trinity, and the Bible.

I should also note that while the Old Testament plays a large role in the content covered in this book, I do not examine it in any significant detail through a Judiac lens in terms of such factors as the Torah's role in the creation of the Bible. When such connections do arise, my goal is to help explain the ways that Christianity is understood and applied by comics creators and readers instead of using comics as a forum to enter into theological inquiries. And for what it is worth, the version of the Bible that I am primarily using in my research is the New International Version, for the simple reason that my Mum gave it to me before she died.

Also, on the subject of audiences, this book is written for both comics fans and comics scholars. While comics studies is a relatively new scholarly discipline, it has quickly become a rising area of focus in academia. In 2002, esteemed cultural theorist Arthur Asa Berger asked the question "Is This the Kind of Thing That Serious Academics Do?" as the title of an article for the *International Journal of Comic Art*. The answer has increasingly proven to be "yes, it is." A growing number of scholars have committed themselves to the study of comics, and the amount of comics-related essays and manuscripts published by academic presses and journals has grown tremendously in recent years. The medium of comics spans a range of historical, epistemological, and technological perspectives, but its representations of religious and spiritual discourses are still in dire need of further examination. I see this book as a larger mapping of the terrain that offers paths for future study rather than any kind of final word on the subject.

Previous books such as the edited collections *Graven Images: Religion in Comic Books and Graphic Novels*, and *Comics and Sacred Texts: Reimagining Religion and Graphic Narratives* have taken approaches to religion in general.[14] Both contain wonderful essays about numerous religious traditions, although Christianity does not make up a majority in either book. As I write this introduction, a forthcoming work of feminist scholarship called *The Bible and Comics: Women, Power and Representation in Comics* by religious scholar Zanne Domoney-Lyttle will soon add to our understanding of how comics represent biblical figures such as Eve and Sarah in a range of titles (including works of manga, which I do not cover here).

Few of the creators who made Christian-related comics, at least those I encountered in my research, were women or people of color or people who identify as queer. For every creator such as Trina Robbins who used a series such as *Wimmen's Comix* as a forum for telling a story about the potentials for feminist identity in Christian history, there are far more male creators interested in tales about sexual repression during Catholic school. I have attempted to confront the implications of race, gender, class, and sexuality in the examples I study whenever possible—consciously, but not always extensively, given the wide scope of this project. Further work applying theories of postcolonialism, intersectionality, and other aspects of cultural studies to these comics is much needed.

A book like this one, or any book that analyzes how media approach Christianity, could take any number of approaches to the topic. My entry point is as a comics scholar, not as someone trained in religious studies, so my emphasis is rarely on issues of theology and more about patterns to do with questions about medium specificity and about comics creators, publishers, and audiences as I assess how and why these comics were made and consumed. This is a history of comics across decades, much as my earlier books *Comic Book Women* and *Movie Comics* were, so I am approaching things as a comics historian first and foremost.

But while I am not writing this book with any particular theological, spiritual, or ideological agenda, I am not hesitant to call out abuses of power, intolerance, and hatred when I come across them. Whether it is stereotypical images or hate-filled rhetoric directed toward immigrants, queer people, Muslims, women, people of color, or any other historically marginalized group, I denounce hate in comics that are hateful, as a lot of the work of Jack Chick is.

Some readers will applaud this position while others may belittle it. But *Christianity and Comics* is written for religious and nonreligious readers alike, just as it is written for both scholars and nonscholars and for comics fans as well as those who don't regularly read comics. So if this turns out to not be the book you were hoping to read or if you take issue along the way with the level of critique (or lack thereof) about a certain issue or idea or even if you just wish that I had looked at a particular example with greater or less scrutiny, then I encourage you to keep in mind that I'm trying to allow entry points into an incredibly wide-ranging history for a very diverse set of readers—which means that this book was not just written for you and your own set of particular needs and beliefs alone.

There are perhaps more comics available today that explore the themes, images, and teachings of Christianity than there ever were in the earliest decades of comics through the mid-twentieth century, even though many of these modern takes are much more critical than those of past eras. These new comics might not always be reverent toward their source material in the same way that *Picture Stories from the Bible* was, but the steady presence of books about God, the devil, and all sorts of crises of faith signifies that there are still many stories about Christianity that people want to have told, that there are many conversations about the role of organized religion still to be had, and that comics are a vital forum for such stories and discussions.

1

The 1940s

● ● ● ● ● ● ● ● ● ● ● ● ●

From Superheroes to
*Picture Stories from
the Bible*

Comic books seemed an unlikely venue for Christian-oriented stories as the 1940s began. The industry's early years were both cut rate and cut throat. Publishers worked quickly and cheaply to cash in on the rising demand for titles featuring costumed characters, funny animals, and thrilling adventures. The product was squarely aimed at children, but the business practices behind these colorful pages were often marked by schemes as devious as those of the vilest comic-book villains and henchman.

While comic strips had been around in newspapers (along with hardcover reprint editions of popular characters) in prior decades, the modern comic book as we now know it arose in 1933 with *Funnies on Parade*. A promotional giveaway for Procter & Gamble produced by Eastern Color Printing, *Funnies on Parade* featured reprints of well-known comic strips in a new format with a glossy cover. Its success prompted Eastern to create a new title the following year, *Famous Funnies*, also reprinting existing comic strips.[1] It was this physical format that became the comic book, which would soon become a home for the regular adventures of Superman—as well as Satan, Samson, and many other biblical figures.

Numerous imitators emerged over the next few years, including *Feature Funnies*, *Jumbo Comics*, *King Comics*, *Popular Comics*, *Star Comics*, and *Tip Top Comics*, all offering readers various newspaper strips in a new package. Perhaps the most notable of these early titles was *New Fun Comics*, created by Major Malcolm Wheeler-Nicholson in 1935. Unlike the reprinted efforts of *Famous Funnies* and others, *New Fun* specialized in all-new characters (albeit many who had already been turned away by newspaper strip syndicates) such as Jack Woods, Buckskin Jim, Don Drake, Loco Luke and Sandra of the Secret Service.[2] Dr. Occult, written by Jerry Siegel and Jerome Shuster, soon emerged in the series. Siegel and Shuster eventually sold a new character (who was faster than a speeding bullet and more powerful than a locomotive) for the first issue of *Action Comics*. Dr. Occult continued when *New Fun* changed its title to *More Fun Comics*, a series that later birthed such superheroes as The Spectre, Aquaman, Doctor Fate, Green Arrow, and Superboy. But Wheeler-Nicholson wouldn't profit from the success of those characters or from how he launched the title that would soon deliver the Dark Knight—*Detective Comics*.

Shortly before the release of *Action Comics* in 1938, the major faced forcible removal from his own company after he struck a deal with printer-distributor Harry Donenfeld and accountant Jack S. Liebowitz the previous year due to financial struggles. Before moving into the comics business, Donenfeld had found success with pulp magazines such as *Ginger Stories*, *Hit Stories*, *Juicy Tales*, *Spicy Detective Stories*, and *Spicy Mystery Stories*. Many of these magazines crossed over into pornography—known as "girlie pulps," "sex pulps" or "smooshes" in the industry for their exploitive images of women and lurid stories built around sexual imagery.

Unsurprisingly, Donenfeld was charged with obscenity in 1934 for the nudity on his covers, but he avoided jail time by having his colleague Herb Siegel "take the rap for him" and go to prison in his place in return for a full-time job when he got out.[3] By vastly overprinting copies of *Detective Comics*, his new partners scammed Wheeler-Nicholson into believing that the title wasn't selling well in order to convince him to sign over the company. When that didn't work, they changed the locks on his office door and forced the cash-strapped major into bankruptcy court, where he faced a judge who was friends with Donenfeld.[4] Underhanded business moves were nothing new for

Donenfeld—he was rumored to have worked for the infamous crime boss Frank Costello, using his publishing ventures to help aid racketeering and bootlegging.[5]

The origins of DC Comics are rooted in Donenfeld's corrupt business practices, so it is ironic that the story of Christian comic books begins with DC, their spiritual-themed superhero The Spectre, and one of the first-ever religious comic books, *Picture Stories from the Bible* (1942). As the comic-book industry found its footing, two parallel, perhaps even contradictory trends emerged in the early 1940s about how Christianity was represented through the panel and the page: for the purposes of genre-driven spectacle as well as for educational aims.

"I Want Eternal Peace!": 1940s Superheroes and the Supernatural

As comic-book publishers experimented with new genres such as superhero stories in the format's early years, many strove to make their heroes mean more to readers by introducing religious parallels and imagery—sometimes subtly, more often overtly. The comparisons between Superman and Jesus Christ flourished in later decades with books like John T. Galloway Jr.'s *The Gospel According to Superman*. "Superman," says Galloway, is a hero people "wish existed. He is a hero with a direct link to the inner world. When people allow their minds to drift . . . they find images of their saving hero and ethical ideal."[6]

Films like *Superman* (1978) and *Superman Returns* (2006) have included Christian themes and images,[7] while the origin story of a young Kal-El's parents placing him in a rocket to escape the exploding planet of Krypton echoes the story of Moses being set forth along the Nile river in a papyrus basket. Communication theorist Marshall McLuhan argued that Superman is "the comic strip brother of the medieval angels," citing Thomas Aquinas's explanation that angels are "superior to time and space, yet can exert a local and material energy of a superhuman kind. . . . Like Superman," posited McLuhan, angels "require neither education nor experience, but they possess, without effort, flawless intelligence about all things. Men have dreamed of becoming like these beings for a quite a while."[8]

The early adventures of the angelic "Man of Tomorrow" in comics revolved mainly around secular concerns, however. Before he battled the likes of Mr. Mxyzptlk, Bizarro, and Brainiac, Superman faced off against crooked union bosses, corrupt politicians, con men, foreign agents, and racketeers. While in later decades the Man of Steel regularly battled an array of superpowered and intergalactic villains, in his initial years the emphasis was on righting the wrongs of evil men who lie, cheat, and steal (ironic, given Wheeler-Nicholson's fate).

Following his success with Superman, writer Jerry Siegel created a new costumed hero in 1940, but one with a distinctly spiritual slant. Introduced as a "supernatural being whose mission on earth is to stamp out crime and enforce justice" with his "weird powers,"[9] The Spectre debuted in *More Fun Comics* issue 52 and remains a significant character in DC Comics to this day. Murdered detective Jim Corrigan is brought back to life with strange new powers granted to him by an unseen force known only as "the voice." Moments after his death, the story's narrator describes how Corrigan's body streaks upward into "the streaming light" with "infinite speed." Finally reaching the source of the celestial light, Corrigan hovers among the clouds: "Only one thing can explain this experience," he exclaims, "I—I'm dead! But for some reason I'm not passing through the gates of eternity! Why?" A disembodied voice echoes through the clouds: "Listen Jim Corrigan and you will learn... your mission on earth is unfinished.... You shall remain earthbound battling crime on your world with supernatural powers, until all vestiges of it are gone!!!" Corrigan pleads, "But I don't want to return to earth! I want eternal peace!" but he is quickly cast down to Earth again.[10]

While the voice is never overtly identified as a heavenly one, religious rhetoric is often used at key moments throughout the series. Corrigan is described in the opening narration of each story as "the earthbound Spectre," beginning each appearance by invoking the character's inability to reach the afterlife.[11] In one story, our hero battle the devilishly named Dr. Mephisto, who is secretly a villain called The Blue Flame (a symbol commonly connected with Satan).[12] Another villain is described as having "a face as evil as Satan" with "fiery eyes as foreboding as a flaming pit."[13] In another tale, The Spectre confronts a criminal for information, compelling the man to look into his ghostly eyes: "Those eyes are boring into my soul!" cries the crook.[14]

The idea that as human beings "we are embodied souls" with "more to us than our physical bodies" is prevalent in many religious traditions, including Hinduism, Judaism, Islam and Christianity.[15] Modern Christian beliefs about the soul are influenced by what religious scholar Eliezer Gonzalez describes as "a Descartian ontological body/soul dualism."[16] This stems from how the seventeenth-century French philosopher René Descartes described the distinction between the mental and the physical: "mind and body are completely

FIGURE 1 The Spectre's mission prevents him from achieving eternal rest in *More Fun Comics* 53 (March 1940), page 10.

different kinds of substance," with the soul being distinct from the human body and capable of "immortality."[17] Thus, when the criminal describes The Spectre's gaze as piercing his soul, writer Jerry Siegel clearly positions his ghostly hero as a spiritual force whose powers extend beyond the physical realm of existence.

The voice only ever appears to The Spectre as a ray or a burst of bright light, evoking the Bible's descriptions of the Lord in the same terms (such as John 8:12, "I am the Light of the world" and Psalm 27:1, "The Lord is my light and my salvation"). The Spectre even possesses a "ring of life" that can defeat evil spirits by "caus[ing] the darkness to be split asunder by a blinding light."[18] When he is engulfed by a black cloud in one adventure, his ring causes "the forces of darkness [to] shrink back to reveal The Spectre surrounded by a protective glow of pure light!"[19] Although he was never directly acknowledged as a servant of the Lord in his early adventures, The Spectre's adventures regularly suggested that the character was akin to a biblical force sent from Heaven to rid the world of evil. Seigel and DC weren't concerned with using The Spectre as a vessel for teaching about theology or faith, but the character's easily understood spiritual connections add thematic depth to what might otherwise have been rather routine adventures.

Other publishers offered their own heroes based on the supernatural and the spiritual, some more direct in their use of Christianity. Several series emerged starring Samson, a character descended from the powerful Israelite described in the book of Judges. Possessing the same enhanced strength and agility as his biblical antecedent (as well as the same weakness: haircuts), Samson debuted in the first issue of Fox Feature Syndicate's *Fantastic Comics* in 1939 and gained his own title from the publisher the following year. "Out of the mists of history comes The Mighty Samson to save America!" his first issue's cover proclaimed. But despite this national focus, Samson quickly proved to be an international hero in the series, although other cultures and faiths were represented in problematic ways. Superman may have been dedicated to the "American way" in his quest for truth and justice, but Samson was able to "see events all over the world," thanks to a special invention.

In *Samson* issue 1, his first adventure is spurred in response to "someone in the East praying for a mighty man of valor." While we are never given any specific location other than "the East" (a generic term used in this era in Western countries to encompass the continents of Asian and India, among other areas), we are shown a turbaned man praying atop a tall stone tower. "Hear ye!" the man prays. "A strong man is needed to combat the forces of evil and injustice rioting loose in the world!"

FIGURE 2 Samson heeds the prayer of a man of "real faith" in *Samson* 1 (Fall 1940), page 2.

Samson quickly acts on the man's prayer: "That man in the East has real faith. I must see to it that his prayer is answered. I leave for the East at once," he pledges, adding "It won't take me long. But that prayer must get results!"[20] Postcolonial theorist Edward Said describes in *Orientalism* how terms like "the East" or "the Orient" reduce diverse cultures and their religious beliefs to an indistinct sameness. He cites political scientist Anwar Abdel Malek's view that such terms serve to stamp human beings "with an Otherness—as all that is different, whether it be 'subject' or 'object.'" Such conceptions of "the East" mark the inhabitants of this vague realm with a "constitutive otherness" and "an essentialist character," Malek argues.[21] Samson's adventures devolve into colonialist stereotypes as he battles the brown-skinned "fanatics of a murder cult" who perform a ritualistic human sacrifice called the "blood ceremony." As he sets out to find the cult, Samson tells his young ward, "Remember our oath, David! We've got to stop these demons!"

Within only a few pages, the indistinctly "Eastern" inhabitants that Samson encounters are treated in both humane and demonized ways. They are "mad thugs" who refer to Samson and David as "unbelievers" to be burned in a sacrificial fire, while elsewhere in this foreign land we see Samson free innocent men from prison and offer protection for some oppressed townsfolk ("You can't ride poor, weak people down without paying for it!" he warns). Yet when Samson returns to the "wise man" whose prayer initially summoned him, the series' representation of cultural otherness becomes more complex. "As long as evil and injustice live, you will fight them!" the wise man tells Samson.[22] While the series clearly draws on biblical history, it does *not* position faith and morality as exclusively Christian. His turban suggests that the man is most likely Muslim or Sikh rather than a Christian (although some eighth-century Christians did wear them),[23] but the fact that his prayers demonstrate "real faith" inspires Samson to action, regardless of the God he prays to.

Renowned religious scholar Wilfred Cantwell Smith describes in *The Meaning and End of Religion* how faith had become a denominational concept by the twentieth century: "It is no longer easy or even possible to have a religious faith without selecting its form," says Smith. Faith cannot be equated "to some abstraction of religiousness in general," but rather to a "unique tradition—or even [to] one unique section within that," he argues.[24] Samson was drawn to the wise man's prayers not because they signaled a devout Christian faith or the abstract "religiousness" that Smith describes, but simply because the man's (unspecified) faith was devout to his own religious tradition. To be devout, then—according to *Samson* issue 1—means that you are deserving of justice regardless of your particular religion, but only if you aid the poor and oppressed rather than slaughter and sacrifice them.

Yet the story soon upholds Orientalist stereotypes in another way, by introducing mysticism as a way to advance the plot. Lest Samson grow "lonely" in his fight against injustice, the wise man foretells "a youthful helper—a young David."[25] Samson indeed goes on to adopt a young orphan named David, whose skill with a lariat is meant to align the boy with the young biblical shepherd (and future king) who slew the giant Goliath with a sling. The wise man's prophetic ability marks him as a mystic figure, another symptom of how American popular culture of this era represented non-Western faiths. Religious scholar Richard King describes how "once the term "mystical" became detached from the specificity of its original Christian context and became applied to "the strange and mysterious Orient," the association of the East with "mysticism" became well and truly entrenched in the collective cultural imagination of the West."[26] After prophesying David's debut, the wise man is never returned to in the story; he serves only to pair Samson with a young sidekick, much as Batman had Robin. The stereotypical trope of a mystical wise man from "the East" is used primarily to serve a narrative need to add a preteen partner.

Samson also appeared in the pages of Fox's *Big 3 Comics* alongside Blue Beetle and The Flame. Both series were short lived, however, ending in 1941 and 1942, respectively. Many stories featured the same gimmick of having Samson use his mighty strength to tear down various pillar-like structures (despite the fact that this action led to his death in Judges 16:30). Samson was overshadowed by the wealth of colorful costumed characters in the early days of superhero comics, but other publishers tried new versions in later decades, most notably Gold Key's *The Mighty Samson* from 1964 to 1969 and again from 1973 to 1976. In each case, the main goal is entertainment rather than religious pedagogy, but with the strategic intent to use a biblical character whose strength is so well known among casual readers that his adventures transcend the confines of Sunday School enough to aid sales among nonchurchgoers.

Although the 1940s version of Samson may be little remembered today, another heroic character inspired by the Bible remains one of the most critically acclaimed characters in comics: The Spectre in Will Eisner's *The Spirit*. Featured as a special comic-book section of Sunday newspapers, *The Spirit* used a distinctly biblical premise for the character's origin. Detective Denny Colt is killed in the line of duty but returns from the grave (thanks to the experimental chemicals soaking his corpse) to fight crime as a self-proclaimed "spirit of good."[27] Eisner stated, "I don't know whether it really occurred to me, a Jew, that the Spirit's origin was a Christlike idea, like the Resurrection," yet he admitted in retrospect that the connection was a strong one.[28]

Eisner, like Siegel, was a Jewish creator, as were many pioneering comic-book writers and artists of the era. But the connections to tropes such as the resurrection with The Spirit and the Holy Trinity with Superman demonstrate the fact that many early tales in a range of genres reflected Christian principles and figures, consciously or not. From The Spectre's auxiliary role as the wrath of God to Samson's mighty strength, the earliest comic-book heroes often drew on biblical heroes and concepts for inspiration—but in ways that still allowed room for enjoyment by religious and nonreligious readers alike, who might appreciate the thematic depths of these spiritual elements or simply enjoy the ways they added layers of spectacle. While many writers see superheroes as a distinctly secular phenomenon, the origins of these powerful characters are steeped in a wealth of religious traditions, themes, and images.[29]

"The Further Adventures of Satan"

Not all biblically themed characters were holy in nature. Many were downright devilish. As the 1940s began, publishers introduced a growing number of colorful villains as recurring foils for their costumed heroes, pitting characters such as Superman and Batman against foes who were more distinctive than the generic criminals and corrupt politicians they often faced. DC offered up hideous foes like Two-Face and the Joker while Timely introduced Captain America's nemesis, the Red Skull. Other publishers instead turned to a familiar figure who was already widely recognized as evil personified—Satan. In using the devil as a supervillain, comics publishers could add an instantly recognizable fantastic foe while drawing on long histories of Christian iconography and morality, loosely straddling the lines between entertainment and edification, much as heroes such as Samson did.

Satan's literary pedigree was centuries old by the 1940s, from Dante Alighieri's *Inferno* to John Milton's *Paradise Lost* and *Paradise Regained* to Charles Baudelaire's *The Litanies of Satan* to Mark Twain's *The Mysterious Stranger*. Literary scholar Harold Bloom described Satan as a complex figure open to the reader's interpretation in works such as *Paradise Lost*, in which "it was clear that Milton's Satan as a moral being was far superior to Milton's God." Bloom argued that "each reader of Paradise Lost must find for himself the proper reading of Satan, whose appeal is clearly all but universal."[30]

This "universal" interest in Satan saw him as a main or supporting character in the output of numerous comics publishers, such as in MLJ's adventures of Madam Satan. Beginning with issue sixteen in 1941, *Pep Comics* depicted the character as a servant of the Devil who seduces men with her deadly kiss. Readers are told of how her unholy reign began when "the Devil searched far and long for an ally to wreak havoc amongst mortals.... Then, the black, corrupt soul of a beautiful woman, a victim of her own fiendish plan on earth, left its bodily habitation to stand before the king of purgatory... and his search was at an end.... The Devil had found himself a fitting mate, and called her..... Madam Satan!"[31] Her first appearance opens with the Devil atop Bald Mountain, "the mythical mountain on whose peak, Satan and his imps hold revelry while the winter passes. Then the king of the fiends makes his unholy plans of death and destruction for his mortal enemies!"[32]

Bald Mountain had been popularized only the year before in Disney's *Fantasia* (1940), in an animated segment using Russian composer Modest Mussorgsky's *Night on Bald Mountain* as a musical score for its depiction of the

FIGURE 3   Madam Satan is ready to serve the Devil in *Pep Comics* 16 (June 1941), page 51.

devil Chernabog (referred to as Satan in the film) as he calls forth countless spirits from their graves. Satan's depiction in *Pep* has many similarities to that in *Fantasia*, from his massive size and muscular form to his long and pointed ears and giant horns. Missing from *Pep*'s rendition are a pair of large wings, and the comic also changed his skin to red in keeping with the devil's traditional color palette. Most comic-book depictions of Satan used the majority of these design elements throughout the 1940s and 1950s. Some added a headpiece while still keeping the horns, and most emphasized long, pointy facial features and a red color scheme, preserving stylistic traditions to do with the devil's appearance that dated back centuries through such other artistic traditions as painting and woodblock carvings.[33]

In each issue, Madam Satan uses her seductive charms in her attempt to capture the souls of unsuspecting men: "There are your next victims, Madam Satan. Do not fail me this time," the devil warns as one story begins. "Once again the maw of Hades spews forth black evil, as Madam Satan, the devil's ally, stalks the earth to do her master's bidding!" the narrator tells us.[34] But this emphasis on fiery rhetoric and wicked deeds became tempered by the appearance of a decidedly heaven-sent figure in later issues. After one unwitting victim is saved from Madam Satan's clutches in *Pep* issue 17, he marvels at the beauty of the rising sun's light. "How beautiful its light is! And I can see clearly I can see things now!" the man says. The story's final panel offers readers a deus-ex-machina appearance of a mysterious figure clad in a brown robe and riding a donkey (much as Jesus did through Jerusalem on Palm Sunday), bathed in the golden sun's rays. "Yes, my dear Carl. I have brought you into the sunlight! Through all your tribulations I guided your destiny," the peculiar man reveals. The narrator then leaves us with these parting questions: "Who is this strange creature of the sunlight, the guiding hand of the good? The next issue of *Pep Comics* contains the answer!"[35]

We soon learn that the glowing figure is a heavenly figure named Brother Sunbeam who has been sent to stop Madam Satan. Once again, light is used to symbolically connect a virtuous character to God, just as it was with The Spectre. "I am the good that exists in all your hearts!" proclaims Brother Sunbeam,[36] who soon confronts Satan on Bald Mountain: "Ho! Satan! I come to deliver a message. Give up your evil plotting against man, for you are doomed to failure. Man is essentially good!" Madam Satan intervenes on her master's behalf, telling the holy figure, "You fool! Once I have become imbedded in man's heart, there is no room for good. Evil will prevail!" Satan responds with his own threat: "Faith in humans and human goodness, hah ha—I'll show that meddlesome Sunbeam how much they mean!"[37] These stories regularly used the larger scope of heaven versus hell for their pulpy adventures, lending a distinctly devotional discourse to tales of the supernatural in a way that series such as *House of Mystery* and *The Phantom Stranger* would do more frequently in later decades.

Madam Satan appeared in only six issues of *Pep Comics*. She was dropped from the series in 1943 to make room for a character who soon became a leading figure in popular culture for many decades to come—Archie Andrews, who debuted in *Pep* issue 22. The shift in tone paralleled the comic-book industry's changing approach to genre throughout the decade. Although superheroes dominated newsstands in the early years of the 1940s, teenage titles like Archie and Patsy Walker took over as top sellers by the decade's latter half as sales of costumed characters declined and horror titles such as *Adventures into the Unknown* became commonplace by 1948.[38] But as short lived as they were, Madam Satan's supernatural adventures were an important precursor in the history of horror comics. The tropes and trappings that represented hell and the devil became common fixtures of horror comics well into the 1950s, but such fire-and-brimstone imagery got its start in a variety of series of the early to mid-1940s that featured Satan in villainous roles across a range of different genres.

The devil could even be considered one of the first supervillains to appear regularly in comics throughout the 1940s, alongside Lex Luthor and the Joker. His visage may have changed from series to series and artist to artist, but in each case, Satan is understood as the ruler of hell. Just as Superman's archenemy and the "Clown Prince of Crime" would pop up in issues of *Action Comics* and *Batman*, so too did the devil show up on occasion in other superhero comics. Satan plays a key role in an issue of *Kid Eternity*, for instance, in which he empowers a new villain who will battle the series titular hero (who in later decades joined the DC superhero group the Teen Titans). Summoning his "true and faithful servant," the devil sends Master Man to wreak havoc upon the world. Throughout the story, hell is described as a "dismal plain," divided from the world by swirling mists.[39] By envisioning hell not as a flame-filled pit but as an empty void, the issue presents a more modern conception of hell, in which the absence of God's presence creates a damnable state. Religious scholars note how the enduring portrait of hell as a realm of tormented damnation emerged in the final years of the fourth century, with Dante Alighieri further crafting a fiery vision of the underworld as Inferno in his fourteenth-century poem *Divine Comedy*.[40] But as literary scholar William C. Creasy notes in his article "The Shifting Landscape of Hell," Dante's influential conception of Hell began to shift in the seventeenth century in work of writers such as John Donne: "The image so solidly established during the Middle Ages and early Renaissance of Dante's burning fires and eternal, unbearable physical torment had slowly shifted to a focus on isolation and despair. The fires still burned in the Pit ... [but] it was primarily spiritual suffering—the *poena damni*—on which eternal damnation rested."[41] While the fire-and-brimstone imagery of hell was common, comic books also served up alternative portrayals of hell that challenged long-standing preconceptions about the afterlife.

Satan also played a starring role in the pages of *Pocket Comics* and *Suspense Comics*, often drawing on traditional images of a fiery hell. At the same time, many tales gave Satan new (sometimes slightly ridiculous) character traits that created new cross-genre permutations while still attempting to uphold conventional morality by ensuring that evil is punished. In 1941, Satan had the lead story in Harvey's *Pocket Comics* issue 1, in which the Prince of Darkness is a "mad underworld dictator," according to the cover blurb, and works as a saboteur who's out to help the Nazis defeat democracy. Written by Otto Binder, who is best known for his work on *Captain Marvel Adventures* in the 1940s and for creating Supergirl in 1959, the first story opens by telling readers just how loathsome its leading man really is: "Satan—Mad dictator of the underworld! Born with an ugly body and a warped mind, filled with hatred toward his fellow men seeks the downfall of civilization. Wherever there is crime, brutality, death in the world, there is Satan."[42]

Forging an alliance with Hitler, Satan calls his "Kraut friend" on the phone after sinking an Allied battleship loaded with munitions. But rather than destroy democracy simply for the fun of it, Satan soon reveals that he is motivated by the same thing most villains are—money. When Hitler announces that he has another job for the Prince of Darkness, Satan protests: "Just a moment, my treaty-breaking friend. First my pay. A million dollars in gold. If you fail me, I'll smash your whole program in America."[43] After arranging for a sneak submarine attack of American naval ships in New York Harbor, the narrator describes how Satan "watches the results of his unholy with malicious glee" from inside the Statue of Liberty's torch. Confronted by guards, Satan jumps. "He's getting away by parachute!" a guard yells. Satan, then, according to Harvey Comics, is a money-hungry, base-jumping supervillain who does contract work for Hitler.

In the second of issue of *Pocket Comics*, Satan does battle with the Spirit of '76 (a patriotic hero in the vein of Captain America) aided by a beautiful blond named Satana, while issue 3 finds him buying a machine that "can control the workers in any factory in the country" from a scientist named Dr. Boneblood.[44] Satan wreaks havoc at a munitions plant on the eastern seaboard by causing employees to "suddenly go insane" and start a "riotous strike" while pledging to "Kill the bosses! Kill!" and "Wreck the factory!" One worker's goals for the strike are much more general: "Down with everything!" he cries while holding a picket sign. "Satan eggs them on," the narrator tells us, as he tells the strikers to "Go to it! Don't be afraid! The power of Satan is behind you!"[45] While the story's moral message clearly constructs Satan as a villain to be defeated, its treatment of labor-management relations is troubling in how it positions striking workers as mindless, murderous thugs doing the devil's

FIGURE 4 Satan, the "mad dictator of the underworld," stars in *Pocket Comics* 1 (August 1941), page 1.

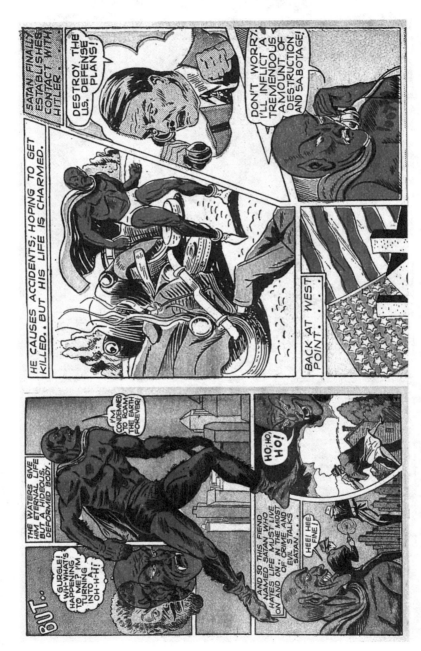

FIGURE 5 The continuing adventures of Satan in *Pocket Comics* 2 (September 1941), pages 4–5.

work in an era of real struggles surrounding strike breaking and union busting.[46]

Confronted by a radio operator at the plant, Satan leaps into a nearby speedboat and escapes to his "secret yacht" headquarters.[47] The fourth and final issue of *Pocket Comics* finds Satan musing about how he "must destroy property as well as lives," which leads him to his next evil scheme: "Ah, I have it! Arson! I'll set fire to the Federal Post Office and burn the nation's mail!"[48] His plan is thwarted, however, by a group of young children who beat Satan up with a barrage of stones, bottles, and tiny fists (it's hard to imagine a fellow supervillain like Lex Luthor being bested by a gang of kids, but the publisher clearly wanted to prove that even the smallest of us has the power to stand up to Satan). Harvey Comics is best remembered for its line of popular children's comics starring such multimedia stalwarts as Richie Rich and Casper the Friendly Ghost, but in the early 1940s the publisher found success in making Satan a speedboating supervillain.

A different iteration of Satan—though only slightly less goofy—began in 1944 with the fifth issue of Holyoke Publishing's *Suspense Comics*. The story, in which the devil locks horns with one of Earth's greatest gangsters to determine the king of the racketeers, begins: "Satan, Lord of the netherworld, overlooks no opportunity to advance his philosophy of evil. He takes pleasure in seeing innocent victims become entwined in his diabolic schemes!" He regularly teamed up with and/or did battle in the series with such fictional gangsters as Woody Malone and Duke Mills ("What chance has a modern gangster got against the king of all racketeers: Satan?" we are asked).[49]

What's most striking about the series is how it uses pulpy rhetoric and tested genre tropes to sensationalize Satan's adventures: "Another episode in this fantastic story of Satan taking a holiday" one story begins, while another proclaims that "due to the requests of many readers, we are continuing the series. . . . When we left Satan, he and Woody Malone, a gangster from the outer world, were engaged in a fierce combat for lasting supremacy."[50] Many stories end with similar gusto, highlighting the serialized nature of these devilish tales: "Watch for the further adventures of Satan in the following issues of Suspense Comics!" one tale ends, while the next concludes with "Satan, the world's greatest master of evil, will return in the next issue of Suspense Comics!!! Watch for him in another different and thrilling adventure!!"[51]

But alongside this sensational tone, readers are also presented with the minutiae of Satan's duties as ruler of the underworld, which at times is directly compared to a bureaucratic job: "Let your imagination run away with you, and pretend you're looking into the office of Satan himself!" the narrator tells

FIGURE 6 Another iteration of Satan stars in *Suspense Comics* 5 (August 1944), page 9.

us. When we first meet Satan, he sits before a large wooden desk that holds a book with the names of the damned, whose arrival he must keep track of like an inventory list ("Hmm, let me see, who's next on the books?" he wonders).[52] When finds that the wrong gangster has arrived, Satan tells him that he cannot return to Earth despite the fact that his death isn't expected for another six years: "Oh, but that's impossible. I can't let you go back. It's against rules and regulations!—Hmm . . . what am I going to do with you?"[53] He may be in charge, but even the Prince of Darkness apparently has to uphold hell's policies and procedures.

Odder still are the sudden shifts in genre. The first story depicts hell as a realm full of skulls, skeletons, snakes, and hellfire, but the final caption ends on a jovial note: "Come with us on one of the most hilarious adventures in comic magazines, as Woody Malone matches brain and brawn with Satan, in the next thrilling issue of: *Suspense Comics*."[54] Other stories stray into romantic territory as Satan attempts to wed different women. In one particularly melodramatic moment, Satan falls in love with a woman named Susan Foster, the fiancée of his earthly rival—policeman Tex Dugan. He looks forlorn, with his head resting on his hand as he stares at the calendar. The narrator tells how "the days roll by for Tex and Susan—but in the lower regions, the time drags slowly for Satan" as he longs for his unrequited love.[55] After kidnapping Susan in the hope of making her his bride, Satan tries to comfort her: "You have nothing to fear—I want to make you my partner—to share my glory with you." When he finds himself unable to gain her consent before daybreak (again, hell has rules and regulations), poor lovelorn Lucifer cries, "Fickle fate is against me—I must return to my domain—but I will be back to wreak vengeance against everything you stand for."[56]

Like a spurned lover, the "king of the lower domain" retreats to his bachelor pad to plot his next moves (which include partnering with a "famous figure" from the Spanish Inquisition, infiltrating Mardi Gras in New Orleans, and manipulating an aging cook into stealing money from the "poor box" before her eventual suicide).[57] In his final appearance in *Suspense Comics*, Satan hightails it back to hell once his schemes are found out. "I'm getting away from here!" he says as a policeman arrives. Still, as the story ends, Satan gives the reader a knowing wink as he welcomes a new arrival to hell: "See what I mean?" he sneers, reveling in his role.[58]

Satan may be a supervillain in this pages of this series, but he is alternately portrayed as a bureaucrat tied to corporate policy, a gangster-wrestling ruffian, a "hilarious" figure, a cowardly crook, a smirking scoundrel, and a lovesick paramour. Satan may have been a natural fit as a comic-book villain in the 1940s, but *Suspense Comics* regularly undercut him by combining horror and crime imagery with emasculating elements from other genres. Comics readers wouldn't see a more sophisticated version of the devil until decades later, in the pages of numerous Marvel and Vertigo series. Superheroes might have evoked Christian themes and imagery in a range of subtle and overt ways, but the use of Satan in a variety of villainous roles in the early 1940s shows that comics publishers were clearly comfortable using hell as an obvious backdrop for stories that served as a lurid updating of the medieval morality plays in which the devil got his due.

The Life of Christ Visualized

While Satan's pulpy adventures continued in various comic-book anthologies, some publishers began using the medium to represent the Bible in more earnest ways. Comics publishers tested out numerous new genres throughout the 1940s, finding success with true crime, horror, and romance titles by the decade's end. The surging popularity of superheroes and funny animals in the early 1940s didn't stop creators from testing out new options for the types of stories comics could tell. In turn, some wondered whether comic books could be used to tell some of the world's oldest and best-known stories to educate instead of just entertaining readers, especially younger ones.

In 1942, Standard Publishing released the first issue of *The Life of Christ Visualized*, a three-part series chronicling events from the New Testament. Formed in 1872 by a group that included future president James A. Garfield, Standard regularly published Christian books, journals, and Sunday School materials dating back to 1866. Magazines such as *Sunday School Standard* and *Girlhood Days* had proved that there was a market need for youth-oriented titles in the early twentieth century, and the publisher saw Christian comic books as a natural fit for school-age readers who were being inundated with secular superheroes.

The three issues of the series were released in 1942 and 1943 before being collected together in a cardboard slipcover case and sold directly to churches and by mail order rather than on newsstands. The slipcover text described *The Life of Christ Visualized* as "a reverent translation of Gospel narrative into continuous pictures." The steady emphasis on the visual nature of the series is noteworthy—few comics of this era focused so explicitly on the fact that they used *images* to tell their stories. Much like the creators of cinema, photographs, and paintings, comic-book creators use visual imagery to

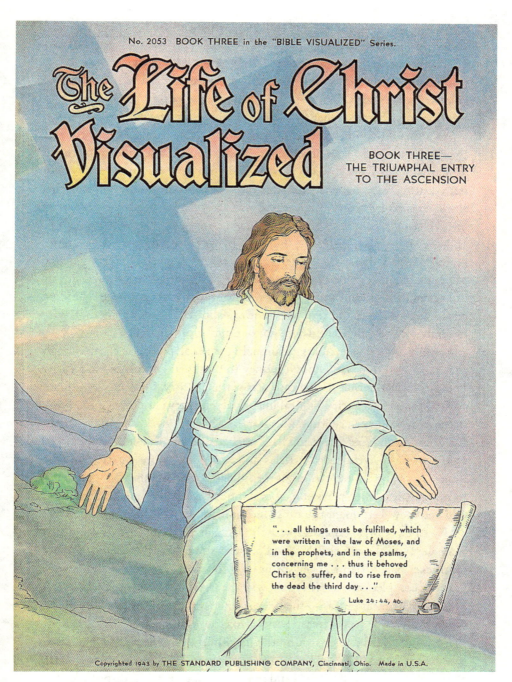

FIGURE 7 The cover of *The Life of Christ Visualized* 3 (1943).

communicate meaning to their audience. Art forms such as paintings and sculptures had been used for centuries to depict Christian imagery but had been limited to a single audience at a time, who could only view the original work in a single, fixed location The printing press allowed religious texts to be distributed widely, but literacy rates limited who could enjoy them and printing costs dictated whether pictures could be reprinted.[59]

As a mass medium capable of reproducing visual images quickly and cheaply for a universal audience, comic books became a significant platform for Christian imagery to reach mass audiences in new ways in the early twentieth century. Yes, there had already been silent and then sound films in this era, such as *The Life and Passion of Jesus Christ* (1902), *From the Manger to the Cross* (1912), *Ben Hur: A Tale of the Christ* (1925), *The King of Kings* (1927), and *The Sign of the Cross* (1932), but such imagery lacked permanence, quite literally. Film audiences could see an actor portray a given biblical figure for a fleeting moment while a projector cast their flickering image on screen, but in the era before home video, there was no way that these images could be paused, scrutinized, and studied. Paintings allowed for such contemplation, but only for those privileged enough to stand before them in a gallery.

Comics, though, are a mass medium. In the 1940s, they were cheap enough that most children had enough money to buy them, and they were easily found on street-corner newsstands across the country. Outside of churches and museums or galleries, biblical images weren't prevalent for common folk in the early twentieth century. Magazines such as *Catholic World*, the *Christian Register*, and *Eternity* might have reached religious readers, but their content was mainly text-based articles and not visual representations of the Bible. Comic-book adaptations of the Bible offered something not regularly seen since the passion plays of medieval times—a distinctly visual account of Old and New Testament teachings meant primarily for the general public.

The Life of Christ Visualized was also a much different product physically than the typical comic book found on newsstands. Each issue was printed on thicker paper than the newsprint used for most comics, not to mention how the complete set was also sold with a cardboard slipcover. Most comic books weren't meant to last—their newsprint pages tore easily and their glossy covers were effortlessly creased and crinkled, especially as young readers shared and traded copies around the neighborhood. The sturdy paper and slipcover case of *The Life of Christ Visualized* marked it as something special, as a comic book to be preserved and reread and not treated as disposable. The better paper quality also made the book's coloring appear more vibrant than that seen in most comics made with newsprint—the images look almost like watercolor paintings, full of pastel tones of powder blue, goldfinch yellow, and violet alongside lush tones of red and orange. On a formal level alone, *The Life of Christ Visualized* was a beautiful product—more akin to modern printing standards than the cheaper-quality efforts of most 1940s comics publishers.

Though the book was not meant to compete with the adventurous comics put out by Fawcett, Fiction House, Quality, Timely and other publishers of the early 1940s, *The Life of Christ Visualized* did use a similar rhetorical strategy on the cover. To the right of the title, in small print, it reads: "Book One—From Bethlehem's Manger to Calling of the Twelve." Similarly, the third issue's cover states "Book Three—The Triumphal Entry to the Ascension." By describing the chronology contained within—from Christ's birth to the gathering of his apostles in the first issue—the covers announced a narrative arc. This strategy not only framed reader expectations about what parts of Christ's life were to be visualized, it also implied that the book was dramatic in nature and not just a sermon; the "from-to" wording served as a tagline with the same function as taglines on adventure comics, magazines, and movie posters—it was used to sell readers on buying the comic by promising that its contents were stirring and compelling. The book's ultimate purpose may have been to enlighten rather than entertain its readers, but the tagline approach was well in keeping with the comic-book format's typical aim of providing thrilling tales that engage and amuse.

The text is credited to Dorothy Fay Foster as editor rather as writer and the artwork was done by William E. Fay and Fred D. Lohman. The writing is pleasantly concise and the artwork often highly detailed. Clearly inspired by Hal Foster's art in his *Prince Valiant* newspaper strip, the drawings in *The Life of Christ Visualized* regularly contain ample linework in the characters' faces and clothing, allowing body language and facial expressions to tell the story alongside the narrative captions.

The artwork also pays close attention to the architecture and landscape. Comic-book artists in this era often used blank backgrounds in their panels (sometimes when rushing to make a deadline), resulting in figures who lack any grounding in a specific location. Nearly all of the panels in *The Life of Christ Visualized* contain detailed renderings of the physical setting, whether it be the stone columns, archways, and stairways of temples or tombs; the rolling hillsides and rocky terrain of Galilee; or the bustling city streets and marketplaces of Jerusalem. Many pages show us these places at great distances, similar to the use of establishing shots in cinema. This attention to space and place along with the minimal use of text allows readers to envision the Bible's

FIGURE 8 *The Life of Christ Visualized* 2 (1943), page 39.

imagery in a way that widescreen, Technicolor films such as *The Robe* (1953) and *The Ten Commandments* (1956) would soon offer film audiences—further evidence of the series' commitment to emphasizing *visual* elements to teach about the life of Christ.

While later biblical comics often used a rigid approach to their layout (commonly a grid of six square panels), *The Life of Christ Visualized* was more graceful in organizing its imagery. Many pages contain only three or four panels, usually of different shapes and sizes. Some panels stretch from left to right across the page while others jut from top to bottom. These larger panels often depict the first glimpses of heavenly or majestic figures, such as when the angel Gabriel appears before Mary and when the three wise men follow the star of Bethlehem. The same pattern is used to depict Jesus performing miracles, such as the long panel of him walking on water and wide panels showing him healing the sick and the disabled. Some images of Christ are even circular insets framed by the rounded edges of surrounding panels, akin to the stained-glass windows found in many churches.

The first issue begins with the birth of Christ, drawing on Luke 2:1–20 and 2:22–38 (skipping over verse 21 in which Jesus is circumcised). After depicting Mary and Joseph's flight to Egypt with the newborn Messiah, the life of Jesus as a young boy in Jerusalem, his first encounter with John the Baptist, the first miracles and the gathering of his disciples, among other events, the first issue ends with the introduction of Judas Iscariot—who we see looking back over his shoulder at Jesus in the final panel. The image serves as somewhat of a cliffhanger ending for those who know the Bible and as foreshadowing for those more unfamiliar with Jesus's life. Much like the cover's "to-from" rhetoric, the strategy behind this final panel draws on an older tradition of serialized narratives to keep readers motivated for the next installment.

While the first issue drew only on the book of Luke—perhaps given how it is the only part of the New Testament to go into detail about Jesus's birth in Bethlehem—the second issue combines verses from Luke with those from the book of Matthew. The two gospels are used to recount Christ's sermon on the mount, the numerous miracles at various cities and regions, as well as his disciples learning the Lord's Prayer. The book of Mark is also used to retell such events as the stilling of the tempest and Jesus being tested at Caesarea Philippi. The book of John is used to depict the feast of tabernacles, Jesus's healing of a blind man, and the return of Lazarus from the dead, while all four gospels are combined in retelling the feeding of the five thousand with only two fish and five loaves of bread. Issue 3 also draws on all four gospels in its accounts of the last supper, Judas's betrayal of Jesus for thirty pieces of silver, Jesus's appearance before Pontius Pilate, and Jesus's crucifixion, burial, and resurrection.

While Matthew, Mark, Luke, and John each recount Christ's life in different ways, there is significant overlap between the four gospels in terms of which events are described. The fact that the first issue of *The Life of Christ Visualized* sticks only to the book of Luke shows an evolution in how the series' creators approached the logistics of adapting the Bible: they either found it easier to start by using only one gospel as their source material or else felt the need by Issue 2 to be more explicit in identifying the parallels between the four gospels in their representations of Christ's life. In either case, this shift in how the gospels were used reflects just how untested the process was in adapting the Bible into a printed form that was both visually and narratively driven in the early 1940s, especially given how comic books themselves were less than a decade old as a publication format by 1942.

The Life of Christ Visualized is significantly different from other 1940s comics that adapted the Bible. Some panels include dialogue, but most feature short descriptive passages. In many cases, these descriptions drew on direct language (either in whole or in part) from the Bible, but in other cases the writer paraphrased or summarized the events. As an adaptation of the Bible, many parts of the original text were omitted, condensed, or conflated because of how much shorter the new version is. The comic omitted the first chapter of the book of Luke entirely, which chronicles both the appearance of the angel Gabriel before Mary to foretell the birth of the Son of God as well as the birth of John the Baptist, among other events. This moment of the Annunciation (Gabriel's announcement to the Virgin Mary) is a seminal image in Christian artwork, depicted in paintings by Leonardo da Vinci, Titian, Fra Angelica, Jan van Eyck, Sandro Botticelli, and Peter Paul Rubens.

The Life of Christ Visualized used this image on the cover of the first issue, pairing it with a passage from Luke 1:35. Even though the moment was not included in the issue, the publisher smartly aligned the series with centuries of artistic tradition: even as the subtle "from-to" tagline positions the book for comics fans using a common pattern from sensationalistic storytelling practices, the choice of cover imagery sets it apart from secular comics as a way to preemptively quell potential criticisms about using the same medium that came up with Superman, The Human Torch, and Sheena, Queen of the Jungle to adapt the Bible.

Pages one and two of the first issue move swiftly from Caesar Augustus's decree for a census to be taken to Joseph and Mary's journey from Nazareth

FIGURE 9 *The Life of Christ Visualized* 2 (1943), page 12.

to Bethlehem to the birth of Jesus in a stable to the angel's appearance before a group of shepherds. Each panel depicts a separate moment, and significant passages of time occur between each panel—we see Mary and Joseph being turned away by the innkeeper in one panel, for instance, while in the next panel Mary is already holding the newborn baby with the caption, "And in a stable the Christ child is born. Mary lays him in a manger." For any readers unfamiliar with the story, the comic efficiently introduces the major events surrounding Christ's birth. But in accomplishing the goal its title announces of offering a visualized account, the book foregoes lengthy explications of certain details. For example, it is not explained in these first two pages that Mary is a virgin, that Joseph is not her husband (but they pledged to be married), and that the innkeeper offered the stable to the couple.

In contrast, the 1992 Marvel comic *The Life of Christ: The Christmas Story* spends twenty pages covering what the first issue of *The Life of Christ Visualized* does in only two pages plus the cover. The Marvel book details the Annunciation, an angel's foretelling of John the Baptist's birth, as well as an angel's appearance to Joseph in a dream. It also chronicles how the three wise men passed through King Herod's palace, spends time establishing Mary and Joseph's relationship before their journey to Bethlehem, and uses two pages to detail how there was no room for them at the inn. The ways comics creators tell stories is a continually evolving process: five decades later, Mary and Joseph being turned away by the innkeeper was encompassed in ten panels across two pages as opposed only one panel in *The Life of Christ Visualized*. Neither approach is inherently better or worse—formal and narrative conventions ebb and flow in any medium over time, not just comics.

The Life of Christ Visualized offered readers a concise, largely descriptive version of the New Testament that sticks closely to what is written in the Bible, depicting Jesus's actions throughout his life without evaluation or speculation. Many subsequent adaptations, in contrast, offered an expanded narrative with original dialogue that dramatized the events in greater detail, straying from the Bible's text so that readers could learn about its teachings in an extended narrative form that relied more heavily on literary devices instead of a strictly didactic approach. Even though these comics depicted historical figures rather than fictional ones, analyzing the literary roles of characterization and narrative structure in biblical adaptations offers insights into how and why these books were created. The differences between whether a particular comic does or doesn't explain the motivations behind the actions of Mary, Joseph, Jesus, and others can help us better understand the intended audiences and pedagogic uses for these books in their respective eras.

EC Comics and Picture Stories from the Bible

In 1946, Standard published *The Life of Joseph Visualized* by Foster and Fay as a single issue, focusing on chapters 30 through 50 of the book of Genesis. This was followed by two issues of *New Testament Heroes* in 1947 from Foster and Lohman that adapted the book of Acts. That same year two other single issues appeared, *Parables Jesus Told* and *The Life of Esther Visualized*, both drawn by Anthony Abruzzo and written by Foster. Abruzzo would go on to draw such romance titles for DC Comics as *Falling in Love, Girl's Romance Stories, Young Love*, and *Young Romance* in later decades—panels from which were repurposed by artist Roy Lichtenstein for numerous pop art paintings, including *Drowning Girl* (1962), *Hopeless* (1963), *Oh, Jeff, I Love You Too . . . But . . .* (1964) and *M-Maybe* (1965). Where some saw comics as a venue for religious discourse, others saw potential intersections with the realm of fine art.

The *Visualized* series was quickly joined in the mid-1940s by another biblical adaptation—Maxwell Charles Gaines's *Picture Stories from the Bible*. Even though he played a seminal role in the rise of the superhero genre, Gaines also believed in the power of comic books to educate and enlighten readers as well as to entertain. Gaines had been involved with comic books from their start, working as a salesman at Eastern Color Printing in the early 1930s and organizing the 1933 promotional comic *Funnies on Parade* for Procter & Gamble. Later that year, he helped Dell Publishing launch *Famous Funnies: A Carnival of Comics* for newsstands sales, heralded as the birth of the modern comic-book format.

In 1938, Gaines partnered with Harry Donenfeld and Jack Liebowitz, who were fresh off the success of issue 1 of *Action Comics* and their successful ousting of Major Nicholson from their company. Having worked with Donenfeld in printing *Detective Comics* at Eastern the year before, Gaines (now working for the McClure newspaper syndicate) convinced Donenfeld that Jerry Siegel and Joe Shuster's story about a costumed hero from the planet Krypton was worth publishing.[60] Trusting Gaines's instincts, Donenfeld agreed to partner with him on a new publishing line, All-American Publications. In this new line, heroes such as The Atom, The Flash, Green Lantern, Hawkman, Hawkgirl, and Wonder Woman debuted in series such as *All-American Comics, Flash Comics*, and *Sensation Comics*. As a sister company to Donenfeld's National Periodical Publications and Detective Comics lines, All-American's titles bore the common DC logo, and superheroes such as Hour-Man, The Spectre, and the Sandman published by National were also part of the Justice Society of America in the All-American series *All-Star Comics*.

But while superheroes proved immensely popular, Gaines also wanted to use comics to tell stories that emphasized history, science, and religion instead of just spectacle. In 1939, All-American published six issues of *Movie Comics*, testing the market for non-superhero titles by adapting current films such as *Gunga Din*, *Stagecoach*, *The Man in the Iron Mask*, and *Son of Frankenstein*.[61] In 1942, Gaines turned to the Bible, publishing the first issue of *Picture Stories from the Bible* in September. Comics historian Qiana Whitted notes that Gaines's motivation was both monetary and moral, describing how he "turned to educational comics for children in the belief that they would be a better investment than superheroes, though his background as a school principal also factored into his decision."[62]

That same year, perhaps as a way of validating comics for any potential business clients, Gaines wrote an article for the graphic arts journal *Print* entitled "Narrative Illustration: The Story of the Comics." In it, he traced the history of sequential art back to ancient cave paintings and Egyptian hieroglyphs in a way that anticipated Scott McCloud's same comparisons in *Understanding Comics* five decades later as a way of establishing a longer cultural pedigree for the way comic books tell stories. Gaines also describes "a ninth-Century Carolingian manuscript, known as the Bamberg Bible" with its "picture story of Adam and Eve in the garden of Eden," along with block books from the fifteenth century "bearing a remarkable resemblance to the modern comic book" such as "the *Biblia Pauperum*, a sort of harmony of the gospels done in pictorial form." Gaines used such comparisons to show the natural fit between the comics medium and religious discourse, benefiting his efforts to sell a modern take on the Bamberg Bible and block books with *Picture Stories from the Bible*.[63]

Gaines is listed as the series editor and the scripts were written by Montgomery Mulford (who had only previously written for religious magazines, but who went on to write issues of *Blue Beetle*, *Real Hit Comics*, and *Sparkling Stars* for Holyoke Publishing). Artwork was done by Don Cameron (not to be confused with Donald Clough Cameron, who wrote various issues of *Action Comics*, *Batman*, *Detective Comics*, *Superboy*, and other DC titles throughout the 1940s). Four issues were published on a quarterly basis that adapted the Old Testament. These were collected into a hardcover edition at the end of 1943. The New Testament was adapted in three issues in 1944 to 1946, with another hardcover collection released in 1946.

Although the first issues of both *Pictures Stories from the Bible* and *The Life of Christ Visualized* were released in the fall of 1942, the two series took

FIGURE 10 Adam and Eve in *Picture Stories from the Bible* 1, Old Testament Edition (1942), page 5.

distinct approaches to how they approached their subject matter. To begin with, each framed their openings differently. *The Life of Christ Visualized* contained no editorial material other than a map of Israel showing where Jesus traveled, while *Picture Stories from the Bible* opened each issue with a lengthy editor's introduction.

The first issue began with a history of how the Bible was written: "The Bible is the most popular book in the world—and one of the oldest. Its beginnings go back thousands of years, when America was a forest covered wilderness." The editorial introduction went on to detail the Bible's connection with different writing techniques:

> When the Bible was written, there were no printed books. The story of Noah and his ark, of lovely Esther and her loyalty, of Jonah and his submarine ride inside a live whale, of sweet-faced Ruth gathering barley and winning a

husband, were all lettered with brushes or quills on sheepskin, in the strange characters of both the old Hebrew and Aramaic languages. Instead of pages such as our modern books have, the pieces of sheepskin were fastened together, top to bottom—yards and yards of them—and the whole was rolled up into a scroll like a small bolt of cloth, and tied together with leather strings. But the Bible did not really come into general use until the invention of printing by Johann Guttenberg about the year 1450. When books had to be written out by hand, they were both scarce and costly. No one but a very wealthy person could own a book. But Gutenberg's printing press changed all that. The very first thing he did with it was to print many copies of the Latin Bible. Of all these, only a few are left in the world today, and each one is worth a fortune. In their time, they helped to make the Bible live for the people and to instill in them the desire for individual liberty and national freedom.[64]

This opening clearly emphasized how new printing technologies can create more affordable versions of established texts, subtly implying that comic books are the next extension of this centuries-old trend. It then went on to differentiate various versions of the Bible printed in English over the last few centuries, from the King James Version used by Protestants to the Catholics' Douay-Rheims Bible and the Leeser version of the Hebrew Old Testament: "All three have been consulted in planning *Picture Stories from the Bible*," we are told. The emphasis in this introduction was on the *materiality* of how God's word has been spread in written form over the centuries. It described how from the scroll to woodblock-printed books to paperbacks to comic books, the Bible's teachings have reached readers in a variety of forms in different eras. It implied that new interpretations of the Bible were also necessitated as it was translated from Latin to Aramaic to English, just as comics become a reinterpretation of words into images when adapting textual material.

To further establish the authority of the series, each issue listed members of a multidenominational Editorial Advisory Council, including Rabbi Ahron Opher, *Christian Herald* editor Frank M. Mead, minister (and author of *The Power of Positive Thinking*) Norman Vincent Peale, and Prof. Samuel Hamilton, chair of the Religious Education Department at New York University. The first issue also opened with a full-page table of contents, aligning it further with the centuries-old tradition of the book as a material form.

While the terms "picture stories" and "visualized" both emphasize visual storytelling, the adaptation strategies of the two series were very different.

Where *The Life of Christ Visualized* used minimal text (sometimes only a single sentence or less), Gaines emphasized narrative in his books in much more detail by relying on a range of textual devices common to non-Christian comics such as narrative captions, word balloons, and thought balloons. While the captions in *The Life of Christ Visualized* are placed within each panel as straight text, whether in the third person or as dialogue that is directly spoken by the figures in the panels, Gaines largely separated his narrative captions in their own boxes, usually at the top of the panel. These are accompanied by either word or thought balloons in each panel, giving the reader a more direct account of the participant's inner beliefs and outer assertions than the descriptive or contextual accounts in the captions.

Indeed, one of the biggest appeals of Gaines's adaptation strategy lies in how the various biblical figures are literally given a voice—we hear directly from them in a way that doesn't occur in the Bible itself. As comic scholar Barbara Postema describes in *Narrative Structure in Comics*, word and thought balloons "are conventional shortcuts into characters' minds, showing what characters are saying or thinking."[65] Such additions often serve to develop characterization beyond the Bible's text: we hear from Jesus's father, Joseph, for example, in a way that we don't get in any of the gospels. Joseph is not mentioned in the gospel of Mark and is never referred to in any of the gospels after Jesus attends the Passover in Jerusalem at age twelve. But in *Picture Stories*, Joseph and Mary have numerous conversations together, showing us their relationship in a new way.

While much of their dialogue is expository as it chronicles the various destinations of their travels, some offer insights into their love for their son. After they escape to Egypt and return to Nazareth, Mary and Joseph watch young Jesus as he plays with some local boys. Luke 2:40 describes how "the child grew, and waxed strong in spirit, filled with wisdom: and the grace of God was upon him." *Picture Stories* presents this strength as bodily as well spiritual, with a caption telling the reader, "Jesus grew up strong in mind and body" as Joseph watches his son win a footrace against his peers. "Our boy Jesus is a born leader—there he is winning the race—some day soon he should go with us to the feast of the passover!" he says to Mary.[66] Joseph's dialogue not only shows him as a proud father, it also sets up Jesus's role as a future shepherd of his disciples.

While some figures such as Joseph and Mary have new dialogue written for them, Jesus's words are taken directly from scripture (with minimal editing). Rather than face questions about why they presumed to know Jesus's inner beliefs, Gaines and his team used an almost entirely literal approach to

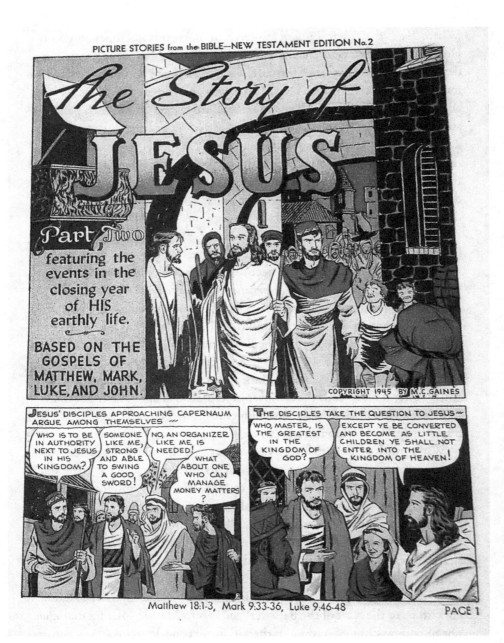

FIGURE 11 *Picture Stories from the Bible* 2, New Testament Edition (1945), page 1.

Jesus's words as found in the King James Version of the Bible. (The editorial introduction also states that "the revised Catholic New Testament translated from the Latin Vulgate was also consulted.")[67] Thought bubbles are skipped entirely for Jesus. His word balloons contain a reddish-pink tinge in their outer edges, in keeping with how his words are commonly printed in red in the Bible for emphasis. When Louis Klopsch, publisher of the *Christian Herald* newspaper, produced a "Red Letter Version'" of the Bible in 1899, the format's popularity led to the technique becoming a widespread publishing practice. In turn, when the *Christian Herald*'s editor joined Gaines's advisory board for the series, it was only natural for *Picture Stories from the Bible* to carry this printing technique over into how word balloons render speech.[68]

While *Picture Stories from the Bible* contains far more words (whether newly created or taken literally from the Bible itself) than the snippets of text found in *The Life of Christ Visualized*, Gaines's goal was to be faithful to the Bible's events and utterances. In any adaptation of a text from one medium to another, creative decisions must be made in accordance with the new medium's formal limitations and possibilities. This is especially true when moving from a textual medium to a visual one, since words and images are inherently different entities. In his 1957 book *Novels into Film*, the first major study of media adaptations, George Bluestone noted how the adaptation process is often misunderstood. He describes a "lack of awareness that mutations are probable the moment one goes from a given set of fluid, but relatively homogenous, conventions to another; that changes are inevitable the moment one abandons the linguistic for the visual medium."[69]

Though he is writing about the way novels are turned into films, his insights about adaptations resonate across media and are highly applicable to the visual medium of comics. In their introduction to *Comics and Adaptation*, David Roche, Isabelle Schmitt-Pitiot, and Benoît Mitaine extend the call to examine adaptations by way of "consider[ing] the various media in context" and seeking "to avoid a binary approach that would involve assessing the gap between the source and its adaptation in terms of the quality or even the 'dignity' of the adaptation compared to its original work."[70]

While Gaines felt strongly that the medium of comics could offer readers more than just costumed heroes and thrilling adventures, he recognized that some parents and critics might consider his biblical adaptations to be substitutes for the source material, much like how some teachers feared that their students might only be reading issues of *Classic Comics/Classics Illustrated* rather than the original novels on which they were based. Beginning with the second Old Testament issue, *Picture Stories* ended its editorials with a plea for its young readers to turn to "the Good Book" to learn more. With a header stating "Read the Bible Itself," the last paragraph on the inside back cover states that "a book which has endured for so many centuries and has so powerfully affected the lives of so many people must commend itself to every American boy and girl, and it is the hope of the publisher and the Advisory Committee that after reading and enjoying "Picture Stories from the Bible," you will extend your acquaintance by turning to the grand old Book itself—and so to a whole new world of inspiration and understanding."[71] The spectacular adventures of The Spectre, Samson, and a speedboating Satan could get away with offering only allusions to biblical content, but Gaines knew that he needed to be more direct in how positioned the relationship between *Picture Stories* and the Bible itself. Readers had to be encouraged to compare his version to original for themselves.

The same plea is found in the third and fourth Old Testament issues, while the New Testament issues ask readers to turn to the specific books being adapted in each issue: "And so we urge you, after you have finished reading these New Testament Picture Stories From the Bible, to turn to and read the original of the four gospels, on which they are based," the second issue concludes, while the third announces, "So we feel sure that after reading these Picture Stories From the Bible, you'll want to turn to the Acts of the Apostles in your Bible and enjoy them again as originally written."[72] These statements sought to frame the series as an earnest teaching tool and a potential stepping-stone to reading the Bible itself rather than as a poor substitute or a desecration.

The series was indeed welcomed by many religious educators and commentators. When it was used as the basis for a package of color filmstrips by Filmfax Productions for educational use, a review in *Educational Screen* praised how the Bible was adapted into comics form: "The scenarios are generally good, and one is pleased to see that the treatment squares with biblical scholarship. This is a gain over the biblical literalism and historical confusion to be found in some materials intended for use in the church school."[73]

Despite his pedagogical intent, Gaines used certain well-tested publishing strategies from his experience with superhero comics to draw readers to the series. As comics historian Dale Jacobs notes, the cover to the first Old Testament issue spotlights a fistfight, "using both the visual and gestural modes" of traditional adventure-oriented comic books "to convey action that is designed to make an audience of comic book readers (who are used to kinetic action) notice the book and pick it up from the newsstand."[74] Don

FIGURE 12 Panels from *Picture Stories from the Bible* 2, Old Testament Edition (1943), page 47 (top row) and page 64 (bottom row) feature artwork similar to that found in other DC and All American Comics titles.

Cameron's artwork also clearly aligned the visual style of *Picture Stories from the Bible* with Gaines's line of All-American Comics superhero titles. Cameron drew the adventures of amateur radio enthusiast Les Watts (changed to Les Sparks after four issues) in issues 12 through 28 of *Flash Comics* beginning in 1940.

Much like that series and others from DC and All-American at the time, Cameron used a six-panel grid layout for most pages. Characters' faces in *Picture Stories* are drawn similarly to those in *Flash Comics*, and the coloring is just as vibrant as that found in *Action Comics*, *Sensation Comics*, and their peers. But while the *Educational Screen* article praised *Picture Stories'* handling of the Bible, it took issue with its artwork: "Many religious education people, especially the children's workers, are going to be very unhappy about the general lack of artistic quality. The drawings are too much in the manner of the comic cartoon. The colors are exaggerated. Many frames carry too much material."[75] In other words, the very fact that *Picture Stores from the Bible* looked like any other comic on newsstands turned this particular reviewer off. (Admittedly, most of the nonbearded male characters look more like Clark Kent or Bruce Wayne than not!) Yet it is this very quality that would have captured the attention of young readers at the time and that makes the series so enjoyable to read for comics fans even today.

In 1944, with two years of successful sales from *Picture Stories*, Gaines was convinced that the superhero market had already peaked. He sold All-American Publications to Liebowitz, who officially merged it with National Allied Publications. In 1945, while still in the middle of publishing the three New Testament issues of *Picture Stories from the Bible*, Gaines launched a companion series—*Picture Stories from American History*, which ran for four issues over the next two years. He published two issues of *Pictures Stories from World History* and two issues of *Picture Stories from Science* in 1947, using both the EC logo as well an imprint called School Comics Inc. for direct sales to educators. Gaines also began planning new series such as *Picture Stories from Geography*, *Picture Stories from Mythology*, *Picture Stories from Natural History*, and *Picture Stories from Shakespeare*, but he never got the chance to make them. On August 20, 1947, Gaines was killed in a motorboat accident at Lake Placid, New York. His twenty-five-year-old son Bill took over the company, reluctantly.[76]

Conventional comics wisdom has it that *Picture Stories from the Bible* never sold well because it was a boring product. In his introduction to *The EC Artists*, Ted White describes how *Picture Stories* "was earnestly done" and say that Gaines and his staff had "the best intentions," but that the result "was pretty dull going for a comic book, and it did not sell out. But Gaines believed in it and pushed it."[77] EC's business manager Sol Cohen recalled the company "going down the toilet. The Picture Stories weren't selling."[78]

But several sources contradict this sentiment. In *Of Comics and Men: A Cultural History of American Comic Books*, Jean-Paul Gabilliet notes how Gaines's "educational line" of comics "sold several million copies by the end of [World War II]" and "were constantly reprinted until the end of the 1950s."[79] In the final issue of *Picture Stories from the Bible* in 1946 (the third New Testament installment), the opening editorial reported that the collected editions of the Old Testament and Life of Christ issues had already sold more than 1,250,000 copies combined.[80] Gaines's son William confirmed in a 1985 interview that *Picture Stories from the Bible* sold well initially: "That was very successful, for a while. He sold an awful lot of those, but to try and get back into newsstand comics, he found very difficult. And at the time of his death, he had been losing money because the titles that he was putting out weren't successful."[81] The series might have stopped selling well, but initial sales seemed strong.

In 1946, Gaines launched three youth-oriented comics for newsstand distribution: *Animal Fables, Land of the Lost Comics,* and *Tiny Tot Comics.* The next year, he added four more kid-friendly books: *Animated Comics, Dandy Comics, Happy Houlihans,* and *Fat and Slat Comics.* But while he was an innovator in the realm of nonfiction titles, Gaines was merely chasing a popular trend with his humor titles, a market that was dominated by Dell and its Disney comics in the mid-1940s. When he died, EC Comics was $100,000 in debt—because of Gaines's humor comics, not his religious ones.[82] When looking back at the state of the company at the time of death, commentators often lump *Picture Stories from the Bible* together with his poorer-selling books to imply that the biblical books never sold well when in fact they were relatively successful in their own right. The biblical titles sold well for several years, but poor sales from Gaines's new line of children's titles dragged the company's bottom line down.

His son William shifted the focus away from educational and kids" comics to sterner genre fare. First it was westerns such as *Gunfighter* and *Saddle Justice* and crime comics such as *International Crime Patrol* and *War against Crime!.* Next came the infamous horror titles *Tales from the Crypt, Crime SuspenStories, The Haunt of Fear,* and *The Vault of Horror* and science fiction books such as *Weird Fantasy* and *Weird Science.* He later called his father's line of *Picture Stories* comics "dry stuff," and once even wrote a letter to the *New Yorker* staunchly disavowing that EC Comics published educational titles alongside their horror comics. The letter, however, was merely a promotional stunt to differentiate his two product lines, as he recounted in a 1983 interview:

> When we started putting out the type of material that we put out, it seemed absurd to call it "Educational Comics." In fact, one of the funniest things I ever did was write two letters to The New Yorker, which they published, because they got a kick out of them. One was as President of EC Publications complaining that they had credited us with putting out such dry stuff as

Picture Stories from the Bible and another one from Educational Comics saying we had nothing to do with horror comics and so on and so forth and I signed both of them as president. I thought it was very funny and they ran it and sent me 50 bucks, which, as I recall, [Al] Feldstein and I spent at the Moroccan Village, a nightclub which is now defunct.[83]

But without the continued sales of *Picture Stories from the Bible* and EC's other educational titles throughout the late 1940s, the younger Gaines might have been less confident about the risks he was taking by moving into new genres targeting older readers. Both the individual issues and hardcover editions of these *Picture Stories from the Bible* comics went through multiple printings, featuring both DC and EC comics logos, depending on when they were released.

Most tellingly, despite attempts to distance his new line of crime and horror comics from his father's educational comics, Bill Gaines still advertised *Picture Stories from the Bible* in his new crime and horror books. The first issue of *Tales from the Crypt* (no. 20) features an ad for the collected editions of both the Old and New Testament editions plus single issues from each series, which could be ordered directly from the publisher. "Here under one cover, in full color continuity, re-edited and arranged in chronological order, are all the stories of the Old Testament heroes from the four issues of the magazine. Printed in four colors throughout and bound with brightly varnished heavy board covers" the ad read. It described the New Testament edition as "collecting the complete story of the Life of Christ and Peter and Paul and the founding of the early Christian Church. Included are maps showing Palestine at the time of Jesus and chronological indexes of principal events and Scripture references to episodes illustrated."[84]

Considering how readers would have contemplated purchasing these religious titles after reading such stories as "The Thing from the Sea," "Fatal Caper!" and "Rx...Death" in this first issue of EC's most infamous horror series, William Gaines clearly had no qualms about selling his father's line of educational comics alongside his new brand of lurid tales about murder, adultery, and other plot details that broke the Ten Commandments. Whitted notes in *EC Comics: Race, Shock & Social Protest* how the younger Gaines went on to use his company's comics as a forum for socially conscious tales of "allegorical fantasy" about white supremacy and racial discrimination in numerous stories.[85] Like his father before him, William Gaines knew that the medium of comics could do more than just entertain readers, even though he changed the company's name from Educational Comics to Entertaining Comics in 1950.

Lots "O" Fun with *Catholic Comics*

With a proven market for Christian comics by the mid-1940s with series such as *Picture Stories from the Bible* and *Life of Christ Visualized* numerous imitators emerged as the decade progressed. Most offered churchgoing readers exciting stories about biblical figures, real-world Christian heroes, or fictional characters who upheld Christian values. But a few were more hastily produced, intended only to make a quick buck from a new market of comic-book readers.

In 1945, three issues of *The Living Bible* were published in 1945 and 1946 by the appropriately named Living Bible Corporation. The first issue is about the apostle Paul, while the second looks at Joseph as well as Jonah and the whale. The third issue, however, departs from the Bible to offer a modern tale of "Chaplains at War," about four real-life chaplains who died heroically in 1943 when the military ship SS *Dorchester* was sunk by a Nazi submarine ("Bravery favors no religion . . . bravery is in the heart!" the cover tagline read).[86]

In 1946, a new series called *Catholic Comics* offered the adventures of Father O'Malley ("genial guide and adviser to St. Cecilia's Catholic Youth Association") as he helped steer young minds in a positive direction, articles such as "October Is Rosary Month," plus a regular "Catholic Crossword Puzzle Contest."[87] The series also featured Christian-themed tales of King Arthur and Sir Galahad along with humorous morality plays featuring talking animals. The 1940s was a period of growth in American church attendance: 76 percent of people claimed some religious affiliation by 1947 and 57 percent of Americans declared a church membership by 1950.[88] Such growth meant that publishers could afford to target Catholic readers specifically, whereas Gaines and others had taken a more open-ended approach to their audience earlier in the decade.

Despite the word "Catholic" in the title, the origins of the series were actually grounded in science, not religion. The first issue of *Catholic Comics*, listed as number 5, was a rebranding of the canceled nonfiction series, *Marvels of Science*, from Charlton Comics by the newly formed publisher Catholic Publications, Inc.[89] *Catholic Comics* number 5 contains such science-driven offerings as "The Romance of Radiophoto" and "You'll Ride an Autoplane Soon!" which had clearly been intended for a fifth issue of *Marvels of Science*. Numerous stories from the first four issues of that series were later reprinted in various issues of *Catholic Comics*, including "Jet Plane, the Aircraft of the Future," "Young Scientist's Home Experiments," "The First

Trip to the Moon," "Wonder World of the Present and Future," "Helicopter Boy Wizard," "Railroads Go Modern," "Synthetic Quinine," "Plant Wonders," "Be Weather Wise," and "New Inventions."

Catholic Publications, Inc. apparently saw an overlap in stories about science and those centered on Christian themes—a pairing that became less natural to some in later decades. In the early months of the COVID-19 pandemic in 2020, Dr. Anthony Fauci, head of the U.S. National Institute of Allergy and Infectious Diseases, lamented the anti-science bias in America. "One of the problems we face in the United States is that unfortunately, there is a combination of an anti-science bias that people are—for reasons that sometimes are, you know, unconceivable and not understandable—they just don't believe science," said Fauci.[90] By reprinting these stories in an obvious cost-cutting move, the publisher combined faith with science in a way that has rarely be seen in any medium since. (The two forces were pitted against one another in later Christian comic books by Al Hartley in the 1970s, as chapter 3 will show.)

Along with science, sports was a major emphasis in every issue of *Catholic Comics*, starting with the leading role of fictional football hero "Bill Brown of Notre Dame" in *Catholic Comics* number 5. Bill Brown went on to appear in all twenty-nine issues of the series from 1946 to 1949, balancing his role as a sophomore star on the football team with his faith and his studies. When he falls short on his Latin and trigonometry exams, he soon passes them by praying hard and studying even harder: "I prayed hard enough, now for more football!" he exclaims after learning his exam results.[91] Sports, including football, baseball, basketball, track and field, skiing, soccer, boxing, fencing, high diving, and roller-skating, are featured on the majority of the series covers. To the publishers, being a strong Christian meant developing the capabilities of one's body and well as the mind by participating in organized sports (something that, again, Hartley argued against in his later books for Spire Christian Comics).

Catholic Comics is sought after by modern collectors not so much for its unique blend of science, sports, and spirituality but because it features some of the earliest work by artist Joe Orlando, who went on to draw such popular series as *Haunt of Fear*, *Incredible Science Fiction*, *Tales from the Crypt*, and *Weird Science* for EC Comics; *Creepy* and *Eerie* for Warren Publications; *Boris Karloff's Tales of Mystery* and *The Twilight Zone* for Western Publishing; *House of Mystery*, *House of Secrets*, and *Metamorpho* for DC Comics; and *Daredevil*, *Journey into Mystery*, *Marvel Tales*, and *Strange Tales* for Marvel Comics. Orlando was joined on *Catholic Comics* by artist Sol Brodsky in 1947, who also drew issues of *Heroic Comics* and *Archie*, plus covers the same year for such titles as *Famous Crimes*, *Captain Kidd*, *Murder Incorporated*, *Western Killers*, *Western Outlaws*, and *Women Outlaws*.

The fact that so many artists who worked on Christian comics also did work in such genres as crime, horror, humor, superhero, and westerns demonstrates how Christian comic books were not produced in isolation from larger industry trends in the 1940s. Some publishers offered exclusively Christian titles and had their own in-house artists, while others hired freelance artists to create a range of religious and nonreligious titles. For many artists, work was work. For many editors at Christian publishers, quality and professionalism outweighed personal belief. An artist might draw a tale about murder in a series for one publisher and a story of sainthood for another in the same month. Most young comic-book readers would have consumed Christian titles the same way—alongside issues in a variety of genres that were traded with friends and around the schoolyard.

This capricious quality of how many creators came to work on Christian titles and how readers consumed them is also reflected in one of the most unusual comics of the era, *Lots "O" Fun Comics*. Not so much an actual series as it was a repackaging of other comics to be sold under a new guise, *Lots "O" Fun Comics* was the unique product of the Robert Allen Company (which sold mail order goods like watches and jewelry by catalogue and later became involved in radio/television broadcasting).[92] Removing the covers from remaindered issues of various comics from recent years, the company then added a new, generic cover with the *Lots "O" Fun* title to be sold anew to unsuspecting buyers. *Lots "O" Fun* was the ultimate metaphor for the shady side of the comic-book industry, and its publisher was not above dragging Catholicism into its unethical business practices.

The series' new cover features four young faces—three of which try to convince potential readers to buy the issue ("Raise the Lid for Your Favorite Comics!" / "The Show is on the Inside!" / "A Whole Hour of Laughs for 5¢") while a fourth inexplicably gossips about one of her peers ("Oh, Jimmy! Did you See Sally?"). No dates or publisher information appear on the new covers. In addition to such repackaged efforts as an issue of Fox Feature Syndicates' *Crimes by Women*, Fiction House's *Planet Comics*, *Detective Comics* number 147 (1949, in which Batman and Robin defeat a water-skiing villain named Tiger Shark) and *Superman* number 64 (1950, which sees Superman defeat a swarm of giant insects and Lois Lane become a professor), readers of *Lots "O" Fun* might find an issue of *Catholic Pictorial* number 1 (1947). The latter issue features such stories as "The Life of Saint Joseph," "Lives of

FIGURE 13 The cover of *Lots "O" Fun Comics* (1949).

the Great Catholic Scientists," "The Miracle of Our Lady of Guadalupe," plus tales of adventurous Catholic schoolboy Johnny Donald and "Father Pat Hannegan, Missionary" (the latter two drawn by Alex Toth, best known for drawing such DC series as *All-Star Western, Batman, House of Mystery, Justice League of America,* and *My Greatest Adventure* and his animation work for Hanna-Barbera).

Along with sales of the actual comic itself, the creators of *Lots "O" Fun* used the inside front and back covers to sell various products to their readers. The contents of *Catholic Pictorial* were framed by ads for the Spartus Box Camera ("the easiest picture taker you've ever seen") and a Hopalong Cassidy Official Trail Knife complete with "clip, pen and screwdriver" for only eighty-nine cents, which could be ordered directly from the company.[93] The Robert Allen Co. had no qualms about using Christianity in aid of capitalism. Superman and St. Joseph were interchangeable figures in between the same indistinct *Lots "O" Fun* cover that surrounded each repackaged issue of other series.

While it may have been legal for the Robert Allen Co. to repackage these remaindered comics, the practice was ethically dubious. The indeterminate, interchangeable covers bear no relation to the contents within. Regular comics readers might have already purchased the issue being resold. Parents purchasing the title without examining its interior pages might have been giving their children an issue of a crime comic they would not have otherwise bought. And that issue of *Catholic Pictorial* was certainly not everyone's idea of lots "o" fun.

But the comics business was not one marked by a long tradition of ethical behavior—quite the opposite, given its roots in pulp magazines. Publishers such as Donenfeld and Goodman built their comic-book empires from the profits generated from tales that exploited women. Pulps such as *Spicy Detective Stories* and *Marvel Science Stories* reveled in stories about sadistic violence committed against half-nude (and, in the case of *Spicy*'s Sally the Sleuth, fully nude) women.

Comic books seemed to be a natural home for the crime-fighting exploits of Batman, Captain America, and their contemporaries. The question then became what *other* kinds of stories comics could tell and whether young readers (and their parents, educators, and other controlling forces) would approve of using comics as a way of learning about the world, its history, and the Bible's role therein. For a time, entertaining titles and educational ones seemed like they might be able to find a place side by side. But by the early 1950s, a growing number of critics were determined to set fire to the industry's entire output.

2

The 1950s and 1960s

● ● ● ● ● ● ● ● ● ● ● ● ●

Sunday Schools, Secularism, and *Seduction of the Innocent*

By the early 1950s, an anti-comics movement was well under way in several corners of American society. Parents worried about the influence of crime and superhero books on their children. Teachers decried the impact of reading comics on student literacy. Psychiatrists feared for the mental health of young readers exposed to an array of violent and sexualized imagery. In response, some pressed for boycotts. Others encouraged fierier solutions.

On October 26, 1948, children from the town of Spencer, West Virginia, were urged by parents and teachers to burn their comic books in a public display of contempt for the medium. Students went door to door for several weeks, gathering enough issues from the neighborhood to form a pile of comic books that stood six feet high. Hundreds of children gathered behind the school to watch their comics burn, publicly vowing to never read them again.

At the front of the crowd stood a boy named David Mace, holding a pack of matches. "Do you, fellow students, believe that comic books have caused the downfall of many youthful readers?" Mace asked before lighting a match and setting the comics ablaze. Mace, who had worked closely with teacher Mabel Riddel to organize the event, further asked: "Do you believe that you will benefit by refusing to indulge in comic book reading?" To each question came the rote response from the young crowd: "We do."[1]

Two months later, *Time* magazine reported on a similar burning in Binghamton, New York, for which "students of Saint Patrick's parochial school collected 2,000 objectionable comic books in a house-to-house canvas, [and] burned them in the school yard."[2] Similar book burnings were held at parochial schools in prior years, placing Christian institutions at the forefront of the anti-comics movement in the 1940s.

In 1945, a Catholic school in Wisconsin celebrated "Catholic book week" by hosting a bonfire fueled by comic books "classed as 'undesirable.'" Rev. Robert E. Southard compiled a list of comics "under the headings 'harmless,' 'questionable,' and 'condemned,'" with parents and students "urged to contribute those on the questionable and undesirable lists to the bonfire." According to Southard, "comic book addiction is a symptom which indicates lack of balance in the child's home and school environment, especially in the line of entertainment. With comic addicts, good comics should be substituted for bad, but more important still the child should be trained in the art of self-entertainment."[3]

In 1947, over 3,000 comics were burned in a schoolyard bonfire at Chicago's St. Gall Catholic school, followed up with a petition from 600 students "requesting the banning of 'indecent comics'" by Congress. The *Chicago Tribune* reported that among the titles burned "were such comic magazines as 'Batman,' 'Archie,' 'Crime Busters,' 'Miss Marvel,' 'The Spirit,' 'The Phantom,' 'Superman,' and 'Mandrake.'" The children defined an "indecent comic" as "any comic that plays up crime or sex, that portrays life in a fantastic way, or ridicules the law.'"[4] But even though *Archie* made the list of "questionable" entertainment for children in the 1940s, Spire Christian Comics would use it three decades later as a regular vehicle for teaching the gospel.

The most famous moment of the anti-comics crusade arrived in 1954, when psychiatrist Fredric Wertham testified about the negative effects of comics on children before the U.S. Senate Subcommittee on Juvenile Delinquency. That year, Wertham published his book *Seduction of the Innocent*, escalating his previous critiques of comic books in articles for the *American Journal of Psychotherapy* as well as popular publications such as the *Saturday Review of*

Literature, Ladies Home Journal, and *Readers Digest.* Wertham decried the negative effects of comics on the "mental hygiene" of young readers, seeing his work as part of larger movement in "scientific public-health thinking for the protection of children's mental health."[5]

Although Wertham's concerns were often tied to societal morality, he did not take an explicitly Christian stance against comics in his work. Although he interviewed Rev. Shelton Hale Bishop for *Seduction of the Innocent*, Bishop was just one of many figures quoted in the book. Wertham referred to himself at one point as a "devil with two horns" in the eyes of the National Cartoonists Society for his research,[6] and also referred to "the mark of Cain" with regard to certain beliefs about child rearing.[7] But overall, *Seduction of the Innocent*'s approach toward the perils of comics was not born out of any religious concern for young readers, even though its critiques often matched those promoted by Christian critics of comic books.

While Wertham's efforts have been the most publicized example of how cultural critics fought to keep comics out of children's hands, many of the earliest attempts were born out of a concern for the soul as well as the mind. But the issues raised weren't always the simple fear that comics embodied a "fantastic way of life." In 1942, Margaret Frakes published an article entitled "Comics Are No Longer Comic" in the *Christian Century* in which she argued that the caricatures of Japanese soldiers drawn "literally as beasts with fangs for teeth and bright yellow skin" in World War II–era titles were racist and damaging to society. Such images, she argued, promoted hatred rather than the Christian ideal of love for one's fellow human and instilled "a color prejudice which will make post-war tolerance and understanding a practical impossibility."[8] Wertham also critiqued the racism found in American comics, making it hard to dismiss these mid-century moral critiques of comics outright.

Other anti-comics articles from Christian publications in the early 1940s included Thomas F. Doyle's "What's Wrong with the Comics" in the February 1943 issue of the *Catholic World*, as well as a column by Rev. Frank E. Gartland in the June 20th edition of *Our Sunday Visitor* a few months later. Gartland decried comics as "a many-sided tragedy" for their damaging effects on the morals of young readers:

> The chief ill effects are mental and emotional; sometimes the harm is physical also. Instead of filling the children's minds with a balanced understanding of life-as-it-is and life-as-it-could and-should-be, the "comics" gear the kids to an impossible unrealistic fantastic life. But the bad effects on the moral and religious life of the youngsters is something far worse. The "comic" books

specialize these days in filling innocent minds and hearts with hate. Considering that the children in the lower grammar school grades are with their "comics" much more than with books proper for youngsters—and this goes for Catholic children as well as non-Catholic—what chance do Our Lord and His Gospel stand of becoming the dominant Person and the governing force in the lives of our boys and girls?[9]

Gartland's insistence on regularly offsetting the word "comic" in quote marks is meant to signal that he was not amused by them and that anyone who read should not them take them lightly. Also in 1943, Sister Mary Clare, SND, published a pamphlet with Our Sunday Visitor Press called *The Comics* (subtitled *A Study of the Effects of Comic Books on Children Less than Eleven Years Old*) that, like Gartland's article, sought to warn parents and teachers of the immoral influence and powerful sway that comics have over children. In it, she wrote that "it does not take an experienced teacher long to see that these 'comics' are being written by 'intellectual hucksters' who have ideas to sell and that they are poisonous and fatal ideas which are wide open to social and moral and personal suicide."[10] Whereas Wertham largely avoided religious rhetoric in his studies of comics, Clare clearly positioned comics in opposition to Christian values: "Decent-living, God-loving parents will not sit back complacently and let hare-brained money-mad pagans carry moral disease germs into the souls of their children. Such parents will redouble their efforts to train their children in self-mastery and self-sacrifice, knowing that only through self-discipline can there be true freedom," she wrote.[11]

Many religious leaders, particularly those in midwestern Catholic churches, worried about the fast-growing popularity of comics among young readers. They feared—or saw the value in fear-mongering about—the fact that comics might replace the Bible and traditional works of children's literature as a key conduit for teaching moral lessons. The same fear had driven the efforts of the Payne Foundation a decade earlier. Led by philanthropist (and later Republican Member of Congress) Francis Payne Bolton, the foundation commissioned numerous studies in the 1920s and 1930s decrying the moral effects of cinema on young viewers.[12] Titles included *Movies and Conduct*, *Motion Pictures and the Social Attitudes of Children*, and *Movies, Delinquency and Crime*. Moral panic surrounding the effects of media content on young minds was a prominent concern among many Christians in this era and was a key factor in how the anti-comics crusade, Christian comic-book publishing and the demise of EC Comics developed in the 1950s.

The Catechetical Guild, *Topix Comics*, and *Treasure Chest of Fun and Fact*

While some critics of comic books decried the medium and others burned the object of their scorn, one publisher took a unique approach, not only criticizing what it saw as the potential dangers of comics but also creating its own titles for pedagogic purposes. In 1942, Father Louis A. Gales launched the Catechetical Guild Educational Society as a forum for a wide array of Catholic material such as pamphlets, books, and comics. Gales had founded the monthly magazine *Catholic Digest* in 1936 as an assistant pastor at St. Agnes Church in St. Paul, Minnesota. Early Catechetical Guild pamphlets were included in issues of *Catholic Digest*, while later editions such as *The Stations of the Cross*, *Mary Talks to Us*, and *Blessed Martin de Porres* were sold individually. In 1944, Catechetical Guild staff writer Gabriel Lynn wrote a pamphlet called *The Case against the Comics* that was included in the September issue of *Catholic Digest*. In it, Lynn highlighted numerous concerns, including how comic books glorified violence, how promoting vigilantism was non-Christian, and how the regular display of sexual images was antithetical to chastity.

Describing comics as "pornographic material" and publishers as "filth-peddlers,"[13] he quoted Judge J. M. Braude from the Chicago Boys' Court in aid of warning parents about the dangers that comic books pose for young readers: "As long as parents continue to let their youngsters read them just so long will comic books and newspaper strips continue to instill in children a distorted and depraved conception of the meaning of real life and living."[14] Lynn also took issue with the fantastical nature of the stories in most comic books and the fact that Christian figures, beliefs, and institutions were rarely featured: "The world of the comics is an unreal world. It is, moreover, an almost totally irreligious world. Moral and Christian values are rarely to be found identified in such comics. Night clubs, gang hideouts, worldly scenes are to be seen with wearying frequency, but the church is practically never seen or referred to. The world of the comics is an irreligious world. It is, in the main, a Godless world."[15]

The cover to *The Case against the Comics* attempted to convey this "Godless" quality in visual terms and to depict the harm the medium did to children. A group of four kids gather around a fifth as he reads a comic book. His mouth hangs open and his eyebrows are arched in surprise as he reads. Two other children read over his shoulder, their faces also conveying a sense of curious disbelief. Two more children linger farther behind, not reading the comic book themselves but still exhibiting a look of quiet suffering on their faces. Four different scenes in the background suggest tales from a quartet of genres: crime (as we see one man shoot another), horror (a Mr. Hyde–like creature with test tubes and a poisonous vial), superheroes (a masked crusader), and science fiction (a flying ship attacks a city as buildings burst into flames). The implication is that the four tableaus are part of the sights these seemingly distressed children are reacting against. One boy wears a shirt and tie and two girls wear frilly dresses, and parents picking up the pamphlet are meant to realize that these are clean-cut children—potentially *their* children—and not just any average youth off the street.

Lynn followed up *The Case against the Comics* with another pamphlet in 1946, *The Teacher and the Comics*, that was aimed at parents and teachers. In it, Lynn warned against comics that glorify violence but still praised the medium's pedagogic potential. He described comics with "laugh-producing qualities" such as Disney titles as harmless so long as they were part of a well-balanced reading diet. However, he scorned superhero titles for their fascist qualities, given how their heroes act "without regard to established law-enforcement procedure," often bestowing their judgment and penalty of wrongdoers in the form of death. "This," says Lynn, "manifestly, is the vigilante procedure, the Hitlerian method. It is Ku-Klux terrorism in the new garb." By asserting the hero's law in place of "government by law," superhero storytelling "creates disrespect for and impatience with constitutional methods, reveals regularly constituted law-enforcement agencies in an unflattering light, and . . . surely conditions the youthful mind for acceptance of those ideologies upon which dictatorships are built."[16]

Lynn extended this comparison between superheroes and the white supremacy of Hitler and the Ku Klux Klan by describing a group of midwestern teenage boys who were supposedly inspired to form a terrorist group after reading too many superhero titles. Having "organized a subversive, anti-religious society which they called 'The State,'" the boys committed numerous robberies as a means of arming themselves "with an arsenal of firearms, ammunition, knives, blackjacks, handcuffs and police badges." The group also used a stolen printing press to create "literature designed to create anti-Jewish and anti-Negro prejudice, contempt for religion, and defiance of the government of the United States," and devised plans to systematically assault Black men and women in order to "provoke a city wide race riot." The attacks were prevented when police raided their headquarters, at which time they seized "'a huge library' of comic books of 'the superhuman variety.'"[17]

Lynn described how the group's leader confessed to police that "he and his associates had based their whole mad scheme upon their 'systematic study' of the comic books, numbering several hundred, found in their headquarters. The youth was specific in fixing the responsibility upon these books, from which the society had pieced together the plan."[18] Superhero comics, in the eyes of the Catechetical Guild, were not only symptomatic of an irreligious world, they were also platforms for intolerance, hate, racial violence, and domestic terrorism.

For Lynn and other anti-comics proponents of the era, most comic books were harmful to children and in turn to society, fit only for the trash bin. The back cover of the pamphlet depicts a scene in which a group of fifth grade students stage a "mock funeral" for the "trashy comic books [that] are a detriment in the lives of children. A photo shows the children standing before two graves dug outside their school while holding two caskets. A headstone reads "Here Lies Trashy C. Book R.I.P." Lynn tells us how the trashy comics "were torn to bits, placed in caskets, lowered into graves, a match applied and after the books had burned, the children covered the remains with dirt. They hope other schools throughout the country will follow their example and thus aid in curbing juvenile delinquency caused by comic books."[19]

But while Lynn deemed superhero comics and other action-oriented titles to be harmful, he found value in comic books that featured "true stories based upon the lives of great historical characters, biblical figures, and the like," viewing them as "useful adjuncts to academic and religious text material," adding that "their use by children may with propriety be encouraged."[20] Lynn's recommendation inferred that wise teachers would use comics that presented historical and biblical topics such as *Picture Stories from the Bible* and *The Life of Christ Visualized* "whenever possible" in order "to stimulate interest in the persons depicted so that the child may go on naturally to reading history and Bible study." He saw biblical comics as a way to wean children away from harmful comics by fostering an interest in other reading material: "The growth of appreciation of literary quality thus encouraged will in due course serve as a most effective antidote to the poison of an all-comic diet."[21]

Because of the belief that comic books could become a positive tool in the right hands, several publishers used the medium as a way to provide teachers with material that might entertain as well as educate children. In 1942, the Catechetical Guild began publishing a series called *Timeless Topix* for distribution primarily to parochial schools. The Catholic Publications Company did the same with *Heroes All: Catholic Action Illustrated* in 1943. Many schools

FIGURE 14 The back cover of the Catechetical Guild's 1946 booklet *The Teacher and the Comics* features a mock funeral for "trashy comic books."

purchased religious comics for classroom use, heeding the advice of voices such as Lynn's that advocated for the pedagogic value of religious comics. Many Christian publishers had already added sections with comics material to their youth magazines, such as Catholic Publications' *The Catholic Boy, The Catholic Miss*, and *The Catholic Student*, so the move toward full issues of Christian comics was a natural one.

Early issues of *Timeless Topix* were eight pages long and lacked a cover, as did *Heroes All* at first, making them appear similar to a Sunday newspaper comic insert such as those that featured Will Eisner's *The Spirit* in the 1940s. Later issues of *Timeless Topix* doubled in size to match the sixteen pages of *Heroes All*. In 1946, the series changed its name to *Topix Comics*. The new iteration came with a cover and fifty-two pages of material, similar to most other comic books of the time. Whereas *Picture Stories from the Bible* specialized in adaptations of the Old and New Testaments, *Heroes All* and *Topix Comics* regularly presented short biographies of notable Catholic missionaries, martyrs, and other luminaries. The first issue of *Timeless Topix* chronicled the efforts of Saint Maurice to lead the Theban legion in the third century in defiance against the emperor Maximian, while the second issue featured "The First Christian Martyr," St. Stephen, who was stoned to death in AD 34.[22]

When the series moved to its new title and format in 1946, the covers were often conspicuously non-Christian in their rhetoric and imagery. A wide range of genres were included in the first ten covers of the revamp, from knights, Vikings, and pirates to funny animals and hockey players. Issues eleven and twelve spotlighted the life of Christ on their covers, but these were followed by baseball players, a newsboy in Times Square, and more anthropomorphic animals. A new tagline—"Timeless / Truthful / Telling"—hinted that the series offered historical tales but not necessarily religious ones. This strategic rhetoric continued in advertisements for subscriptions: "You will always find entertaining, instructive and inspirational stories in *Topix*."[23] The new covers were clearly designed with an eye toward reaching non-Christian readers, even though the series was primarily distributed in parochial schools. Because comics were regularly traded among children in the 1940s, many issues of *Topix* would have circulated around the local neighborhoods of Catholic schoolchildren across America and made their way into the hands of young secular readers.

This strategy continued inside the rebranded series as well; stories about famous Catholic martyrs and missionaries frequently crouched within the structure of adventure tales about crusading knights and murderous pirates.

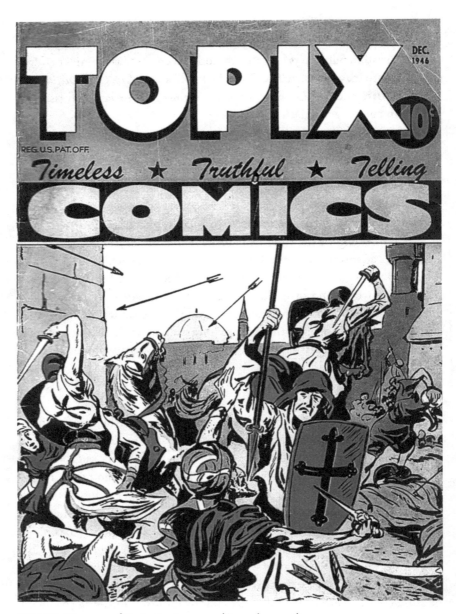

FIGURE 15 The cover of *Topix Comics* 5, no. 3 (December 1946).

Comics scholar Dale Jacobs describes how "rather than simply presenting the Bible as [a] foundational cultural text," as *Picture Stories from the Bible* and *Life of Christ Visualized* did, "Topix instead used the multimodal form of comics to reinforce and strengthen a specifically Catholic faith."[24] Comical animals offered morality plays for younger readers, for instance, in such stories as "Foxy Rabbit and Dopey Fox" and "The Wise Old Owl" in the December 1946 issue and "It Pays to Cooperate" in the June 1947 issue.[25]

While few of the creators who worked on *Topix Comics* are remembered today, two issues in 1947 featured a humor strip entitled "Just Keep Laughing" done by someone who would soon become one of the biggest names in comics—*Peanuts* creator Charles Schulz. When he returned home to St. Paul, Minnesota, after serving overseas in World War II, Schulz took a job as a letterer for the Catechetical Guild in 1945, where he continued to work while also creating the strip *L'il Folks* for his local newspaper, the *St. Paul Pioneer Press* in June of 1947. The cartoonist recalled this early work fondly in interviews, as he did for one in the *Washington Post* in 1985: "'This was the first page I ever had,' Schulz says with some pride, opening a bound scrapbook to a yellowed newspaper clipping of four cartoons under the heading 'Just Keep Laughing.'" They are sweet, single-gag cartoons: a small boy presents a vase to his mother and says, 'Happy Birthday, Mom, and if you don't like it, the man said I could exchange it for a hockey puck!'"[26]

By the time he started *Peanuts* in 1950, Schulz had been drawing the humorous exploits of young children for several years, beginning with the February and April 1947 issues of *Topix*. Given how Schulz became a devout Christian after World War II and regularly embedded spiritual themes in *Peanuts*, it's easy to trace an auteurist line with regard to how comics and Christianity intersected throughout the entirety of his comics career. "Everything that you know becomes part of this comic strip. Of course, I do have an interest in spiritual things. I do like to study the Bible. It is fun to throw in some of these items now and then," Schulz said of *Peanuts*.[27]

While *Topix Comics* was canceled in 1952, publisher George A. Pflaum had an even longer run with the similar series *Treasure Chest of Fun and Fact*, which began in 1946 and lasted until 1972. Pflaum had already found success with Catholic magazines for young readers such as *Young Catholic Messenger*, *The Junior Catholic Messenger*, and *Our Little Messenger*, so the comic-book market was a natural extension by 1946, given the success of *Picture Stories from the Bible* and *Topix*. The first issue contained a mix of overtly Catholic material devoted to the upcoming observance of Lent, facts about animals and about how table salt is made, and an adventure story featuring a character named Skee Barry, Salvage Diver. The latter tale is entirely secular, but the underwater scenes of Barry in his diving gear are dramatic and visually engaging. Issue two similarly featured facts about the history of April Fool's Day and how pepper is made along with features about Joan of Arc and how Maryland was founded (plus the continuing subaquatic salvaging adventures of Skee Barry).

Much like how the artwork in *Picture Stories from the Bible* was akin to that in DC series like *Superman* in how its faces were drawn and pages were colored, series such as *Heroes All* and *Treasure Chest* sought to resemble the art quality of secular comics. Artist Vee Quintal Pearson said of her work for *Heroes All* that "I enjoyed making my characters more exciting, like muscular super-heroes, though it wasn't kosher for me to draw St. Peter quite that way."[28] The second issue of *Treasure Chest* contained a parting editorial that sold readers (and, more important, their parents and teachers) on how the series was a superior title not only because of its "well-rounded variety" and the "tradition of quality" from its Catholic publisher but also because its "superior illustrations make *Treasure Chest* stand out from the usual type of comic magazine. They are excellently drawn, in four colors, by skilled illustrators."[29]

Some of these artists, such as Violet Moore Higgins, had previously worked for magazines that were not comics, while others, such as Earl Lonsbury, drew titles for other comics publishers alongside their work for Pflaum. Lonsbury simultaneously drew *Crime Smasher* for Fawcett Publications and stories about Skee Barry and "Steeltown, U.S.A." teenager Chuck White for *Treasure Chest* in the 1940s.

Similarly, artists Reed Crandall and Joe Sinnott drew *Treasure Chest* throughout the 1960s in addition to working for Marvel, DC, and other publishers. Crandall drew such titles as *Journey into Mystery*, *Kid Colt Outlaw*, *Love Romances*, *Navy Tales*, *Strange Tales*, and *Two-Gun Western* at Marvel's previous incarnation, Atlas Comics, in the 1950s, along with stories for nearly every title EC Comics published in that decade. While drawing *Treasure Chest* in the 1960s, he also worked for Warren Publications on such horror series as *Creepy* and *Eerie*. Sinnott drew *Captain America*, *Fantastic Four*, *Nick Fury*, *Silver Surfer*, and *Sub-Mariner* in that 1960s along with drawing a range of war stories, westerns, and fantasy tales.

When Stan Lee offered Sinnott work in the late 1950s, he accepted under the condition that he be able to keep up his work for *Treasure Chest*. "At that time, along with the romance work, I was working on this comic called Treasure Chest for a publisher in Ohio someplace," Sinnott recalled.

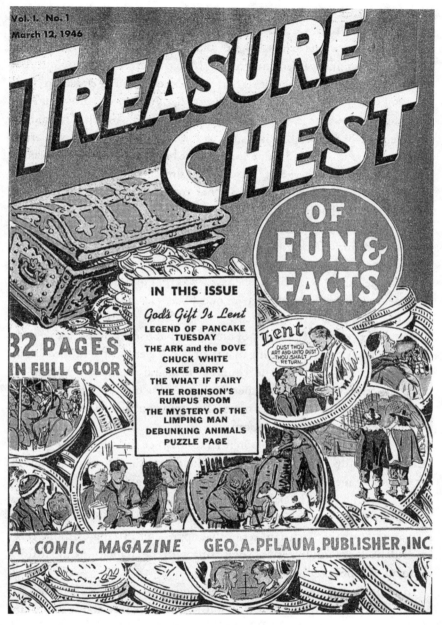

FIGURE 16 The cover of *Treasure Chest of Fun and Fact* 1, no. 1 (March 12, 1946).

"When Stan called up, I told him I could only promise him a book a month, because by this time we were getting into the bigger stories, you know, twenty or twenty-one pages long. I told him I had got this account at Treasure Chest and I liked the type of work they were doing... and they paid very well. So, that's how it started out, but sometimes I ended up doing two books for Stan, two twenty-one page stories! And covers! The stuff I was doing for Stan was mostly monster books, and a lot of westerns," he said.[30]

Given the pedigree of artists such as Crandall and Sinnott, the art in *Treasure Chest* was indeed "superior," in part because Pflaum was evidently unconcerned about whether its artwork was similar in style to that of crime, horror, and tales in other genres. What mattered was connecting with readers in a way that helped them "become perfect Catholic American citizens." Religious historian Anne Blankenship notes that unlike other Christian comics, *Treasure Chest* was not meant as a forum for biblical adaptations or stories about heroes of the Catholic church. "The most prominent theme" of *Treasure Chest*, she says, "was that of American citizenship. Repeatedly, stories modeled behavior or explicitly stated what children must do as responsible American citizens."[31]

An advertisement at the back of one of the publisher's other titles overtly describes this strategy, promising that their books were geared toward "training good citizens for God and country" first and foremost: "Among the main objectives of Catholic teachers is the training of today's boys and girls to become tomorrow's good citizens." Pflaum promised that its titles "are among the most effective classroom aids designed to help in this important work." Such books offered the potential to instruct children in the value of "Christian family living," "civic responsibility," "spiritual growth," "moral values," "wholesome fun," and "interracial unity" (the latter ideal illustrated by a panel showing a multiracial group of children conversing).[32] Pflaum's strategy was to offer parents and teachers a wholesome alternative to other (both secular and overtly Christian) series that appealed to young Catholic readers of all backgrounds instead of competing with the adaptations and historical focus of other publishers.

In addition to its ongoing titles *Topix Comics* and *Treasure Chest*, the Catechetical Guild and Pflaum often published single issues about important Catholic figures and subjects. Pflaum offered the 1954 title *Behold the Handmaid* about the life of Mary, combining the visual strategies of *Picture Stories from the Bible* and *The Life of Christ Visualized* in using both the former's multipanel grids and the latter's full-page illustrations. Artist Paul Eismann moved deftly between six-, three-, two-, and one-panel pages, a strategy that allowed the most iconic images from Mary's life to be rendered in fewer, larger panels and often without any text or dialogue. In so doing, *Behold the Handmaid* harnessed the power of comics' potential for visual storytelling to convey Mary's journey to Bethlehem, the birth of her child, and the arrival of the three magi. Through silent, sequential images, Eismann captured the grandeur of these pivotal scenes in an appropriately large scale without using text that might overexplicate the well-known events.

Pflaum also published *The World Is His Parish* in 1954, a one-shot publication about the life of Pope Pius XII, and Mary Fabyan Windeatt's *Of Such Is the Kingdom*, in 1955, about Christ's teachings. The Catechetical Guild similarly published numerous one-shot titles in the 1940s through early 1960s. Many profiled Catholic rituals and duties such as *Call from Christ* (1952), about the steps young men take to enter into the priesthood; *In Love with Jesus*, about how young women prepare for life as a nun; *The Great Sacrament* (1953), about preparing for marriage; and *Know Your Mass* (1954), *The Sacraments* (1955), *Our Family Catechism* (1955), and *Catechism in Pictures* (1958).

Other Catechetical Guild titles chronicled the lives of famous Catholic figures, including *Joan of Arc* (1949); *The Truth behind the Trial of Cardinal Mindszenty* (1949), about the Hungarian cardinal József Mindszenty, who was arrested for treason and beaten until he made a forced confession in 1948; *Blessed Pius X* (1950); *Padre of the Poor* (1952), about Father Nelson Henry Baker; *Pope Pius XII* (1952); *The Life of the Blessed Virgin* (1951); and *Jude: The Forgotten Saint* (1954), about St. Jude Thaddeus. The guild devoted two comic books to the life of St. Vincent de Paul: *Father of Charity: The Life of Saint Vincent de Paul* (1950) and *Vincent de Paul* (1960), both of which depicted his efforts to serve the poor in seventeenth-century France. Martyrs throughout history were the subject of such titles as *Men of Battle* (1945), *Firebrands of Christ* (1947), *New Men of Battle* (1949), *Men of Courage* (1950), and *God's Heroes in America* (1956), which profiled Father Isaac Jogues and José Ramón Miguel Agustín Pro Juárez, a Jesuit priest in Mexico.

The latter tale illustrates how the Catechetical Guild occasionally took steps to be somewhat inclusive for Hispanic Catholics. It chronicled how Father Miguel Pro was executed after being accused of the attempted assassination of Mexican president Álvaro Obregón. The miracle at Fatima, Portugal, in 1917 is portrayed in both *Fatima . . . Challenge to the World* (1951) and *Our Lady of Fatima* (1955), each depicting how the Virgin Mary appeared before three children named Francisco, Jacinta, and Lucia on the thirteenth day of May, June, July, August, September, and October of 1917. It was rare for Hispanic children to see young people who looked them themselves in the pages of a Catholic comic book in this era, when Hispanic Catholics accounted for approximately 5 percent of the Church's demographics (compared to the 40 percent they accounted for by 2014).[33]

Most comic-book publishers of the mid-twentieth century, whether they produced secular or religious material, targeted white readers and only occasionally created material with others in mind. Latinx characters were frequently relegated to supporting roles in western comics while Black characters were found in jungle comics, often as villains, and regularly reinforced racist and colonialist stereotypes. Comic books produced for nonwhite readers were extremely rare and rarely endured. In 1947, a single issue of *All-Negro Comics* was released, but a planned second issue never emerged because of systematic discrimination from retailers (many of whom refused to shelve the first issue), distributors (who returned numerous unopened boxes) and even paper suppliers (who refused to sell the publisher the newsprint it needed to print the issue).[34] A relatively more successful effort arrived three years later with *Negro Romance* (1950) from Fawcett Comics. Featuring love stories about Black characters, the publisher released three issues before it was canceled.

Nonfiction series about famous Black figures also had some success in the 1940s and 1950s, such as *Negro Heroes* (1947). The first issue featured biographical stories about scientist George Washington Carver, actor Paul Robeson, and educator-activist Mary McLeod Bethune, while the following year's second issue spotlighted baseball legend Jackie Robinson, author Booker T. Washington, and lawyer Sadie Tanner Mossell Alexander, among others. A comic-book series devoted solely to Robinson, *Jackie Robinson*, was published in 1952 that lasted for six issues.

These biographical issues about Black heroes, along with the success of the Catechetical Guild's titles about real-life figures, inspired the creation of a comic book about Martin Luther King Jr. in 1957. Published by the Fellowship of Reconciliation, "a pacifist Christian organization" that worked with King during the civil rights movement, *Martin Luther King and the Montgomery Story* was distributed in American churches, schools, and civil rights organizations as well as in South Africa, Vietnam, and throughout Latin America in a Spanish-language edition.[35]

Martin Luther King and the Montgomery Story was meant to educate readers, especially younger ones, about the ways they might participate in civil rights action. As literary scholar Joanna C. Davis-McElligatt notes, the issue "pushes African American readers to see themselves as a potentially vital part of the movement."[36] At the same time, the book frames itself as an explicitly

Christian approach to activism. The issue concludes with the statement that "this booklet is published by the Fellowship of Reconciliation, whose thousands of members throughout the world attempt to practice the things that Jesus taught about overcoming evil with good."[37]

Chronicling Rosa Parks's arrest and King's work in organizing the subsequent bus boycott by Black passengers in Montgomery, Alabama, as a form of protest against segregated seating, the issue also contains a step-by-step guide to using nonviolent action as a way of achieving social change in a section entitled "How the Montgomery Method Works." The section begins: "In Montgomery we used this nonviolent Christian action to get Jim Crow off the buses. It can be used anywhere though, against any kind of evil." Readers are advised that they can take action through individual agency because "God says *you* are important. He needs *you* to change things." Empathy and the Christian adage of "love thy neighbor" is invoked as the reader is reminded about how "God loves your enemy too, and that makes him important to you. You have to see him as a human being, like yourself. You have to try to understand him and sympathize with him."[38]

King's faith is highlighted throughout the issue. The first images we see of King are of him as a boy in his father's church, reading a Bible and listening to a sermon. As his father tells him to "love thy neighbor as thyself," a narrative caption tells of how Martin "learned Jesus's teachings about love and its power."[39] A later panel shows King describing the connections between his faith and nonviolent protest at a 1956 meeting: "This is a spiritual movement.... Violence will defeat our purpose. Violence is not only impractical but immoral".[40] The issue's final image depicts King as he tells the reader, "When the going gets hardest, if you remain true to Christian love, you'll find God waiting there for you, holding you and supporting you, giving you a victory far beyond what you had hoped."[41]

Martin Luther King and the Montgomery Story was given away for free in various "churches, trade unions, colleges" and civil rights organizations in the late 1950s. The Fellowship of Reconciliation felt that the book had mixed success, however. The comic "was not embraced among poor, rural African Americans or among working class union members," but it did find a welcome audience among "young activists and college students in the South and abroad."[42] In *Graphic Memories of the Civil Rights Movement: Reframing History in Comics*, Jorge J. Santos Jr. critiques the issue for how it "inadvertently slights the contributions of countless actors whose sacrifices were invaluable to the civil rights movement's successes" and for the ways "the comic's hopeful, even lighthearted tone masks the daunting amount of violence faced by

FIGURE 17 The "Montgomery Method" of nonviolent resistance is taught in *Martin Luther King and the Montgomery Story* (1957).

civil rights activists at the time (and anticipated to come)."[43] That hopeful tone was central to King's message, of course, and a key part of both his own faith and the book's integration of activism and spiritual conviction.

One young reader of the period found considerable inspiration in the comic book—John Lewis, a future Member of Congress. He later said that *Martin Luther King and the Montgomery Story* "was part of learning the way of peace, the way of love, of nonviolence" and that the issue "set me on the path that I'm on today."[44] That path eventually led him to collaborate on comics of his own, the *March* trilogy (2013–2016) that he created with Andrew Aydin and Nate Powell about his own experiences with his civil rights movement.

Martin Luther King and the Montgomery Story remains one of only a handful of comic books to feature a recognizable Black face on its cover in the 1950s. As comics scholar Qiana Whitted explains in *Desegregating Comics: Debating Blackness in the Golden Age of American Comics*, the legacy of how Black people have been represented "in comic art has long been tied to caricatures of grinning minstrels, devious witch doctors, and vicious criminals" and notes that this makes the medium of comics "deeply connected to legacies of racist objectification."[45] Comics from Christian publishers such as the Catechetical Guild rarely addressed nonwhite readers or spotlighted notable people of color and often portrayed other cultures and nations in stereotypical ways.

But some readers did occasionally push back against the stereotypical depictions of other cultures in Christian comic books. Complaints about representation led Catholic Publications Company to cancel *Heroes All: Catholic Action Illustrated* in 1948. Vee Quintal Pearson recalled that the series "folded because of a lawsuit concerning another artist's portrayal of certain ethnic group,"[46] although further details about the lawsuit and the group in question remain elusive.

In keeping with this emphasis on white readers and a colonialist-informed history, Christian comics depicting missionary work in North America regularly framed Indigenous peoples as savage aggressors while presenting missionaries as peaceful intermediaries who bring what the narration often described as "civilization" to new lands.[47] In *God's Heroes in America*, readers were told of how a priest named Father Jayme "had tried to win over a warlike tribe" and saw him shot with an arrow as he approached them. "Love God, my children—ugh!" he cries as the arrow pierces his chest. "Kill! Kill all! Burn mission!" shouts a tribesman in a panel that reduces the colonization of North America's Pacific Coast to a simplistic skirmish between seemingly peaceful and brutal forces.[48]

Issues of class were often handled with more care than historical representations of race. In *Saint Vincent de Paul* (1960), which chronicles Vincent de Paul's devotion to helping those in need, the issue opens with an editorial reminding Western readers that their current era is one built on a capitalist ideology: "Living as we do in a prosperous nation, we often associate success with wealth. For this reason our story is doubly amazing because in it we find a penniless youngster rising, not from poverty to riches, like the Count of Monte Cristo, but from poverty to voluntary destitution, and then on to the heights of success precisely because he was poor and remained poor."[49] St. Vincent de Paul was one of the Catechetical Guild's most prominent figures; he was also the subject of its 1951 comic *Father of Charity*.

For churches seeking material that wasn't explicitly Catholic, *Sunday Pix* debuted in 1949 from publisher David C. Cook. Billed as "America's favorite Sunday school weekly for Juniors,"[50] *Sunday Pix* was similar to early issues of *Timeless Topix* in its short (usually eight or twelves pages), all-newsprint format that featured serialized Bible stories and adventure tales as a way to keep kids coming back to church each week. The series changed its name to *Bible in Life Pix* in 1968 and then to simply *Pix* in the 1990s. Its flimsy format favored disposability, but the editors encouraged readers to make their copies collectible. When a new round of adaptations of Old Testament stories began in 1964, the publisher suggested, "Why not make a scrapbook of each story so that you will have your own personal picture story of the Bible."[51] While David C. Cook had published Christian material since 1875, the company had branched into comics with the serialized strip *Tullus* in 1943 about a young Christian boy in Rome in AD 1. The strip appeared in the Sunday school periodicals *Boy's World*, *Girl's Companion*, and *What To Do*, all three of which were later merged to form *Sunday Pix* after educators saw the potential of the comics medium for religious instruction thanks to success of *Tullus* and series such as *Topix* and *Treasure Chest*.

While newsstand series such as *Picture Stories from the Bible* were no longer around by the early 1950s, other publishers soon took advantage of the growing viability of religious titles by adding Christian comics to their roster. Atlas (formerly Timely and soon to be Marvel Comics) launched *Bible Tales for Young Folk* in 1953, while Eastern Color Printing Co. debuted *Tales from the Great Book* in 1955. Together, the two series were widely distributed across the nation's newsstands, alongside popular titles such as Eastern's *Famous Funnies* and Atlas's *Apache Kid*, *Marvel Tales* and *Patsy Walker*.[52]

Both *Tales from the Great Book* and *Bible Tales for Young Folk* (which became *Bible Tales for Young People* after two issues) took a similar approach to that of Max Gaines a decade earlier, adapting specific Bible tales such as the creation of the world from book of Genesis and the Nativity story as well as spotlighting major figures such as Noah, Samson, Joshua, and David.

While Gaines didn't live long enough to see the success of series such as *Bible Tales for Young Folk*, *Treasure Chest*, and *Sunday Pix*, those comics are indebted to his efforts to raise the profile of comics created for educational purposes. As Gaines wrote in his 1942 article "Narrative Illustration: The Story of the Comics," comic books arose from a long lineage of graphic art forms whose creators use "ingenuity, imagination and an unerring control of the pen in communicating ideas."[53] Gaines noted how from hieroglyphs to mosaics to picture scrolls and block books, "the idea of picture sequences" for the purpose of cultural and religious expression had been used for centuries before the arrival of comics.

Using comic books to tell spiritual stories was simply a natural extension of an age-old instinct to use a "series of pictures" to tell stories of importance.[54] Gaines's words made an immediate impact on Wonder Woman co-creator William Moulton Marston, who described in a 1943 article for the *American Scholar* how the pages and panels of *Picture Stories from the Bible* were part of a long tradition of using the art forms of one's era to create "visual histories," whether they were done by ancient civilizations using shells and limestone to create mosaics or a 1940s artist using "ink, zinc plates, and a four-color printing process."[55]

But as Christian comic books grew in popularity throughout the 1950s, some in the religious community saw the format as a venue for attracting attention to the efforts of individual religious figures—or what we would now call a branding exercise. A year after beginning his popular radio program *Hour of Decision* in 1950, Pastor Billy Graham created a comic book for his younger followers with the show's host and musical director, Cliff Barrows. The 1951 issue of *Billy Graham with Cliff Barrows Presents The Story of Naaman the Leper* was followed in 1953 with *The Story of David and Goliath*, with Barrows narrating both books. The first issue's cover depicts Graham reading from the Bible, while the second issue features Goliath towering above the young David. The comics were primarily focused on adapting biblical content, with just a brief introduction of Barrows and the other men on Graham's "team" on the inside front cover before the story begins.[56]

In 1956, evangelist Oral Roberts took a different approach with his new comic book *Oral Roberts' True Stories*, inserting himself not only as the host of the series but also as its subject. Roberts was a media-savvy preacher who would go onto become one of the most famous Christians of the twentieth century as a forerunner of the televangelist movement. In stories such as "The Miracle Touch" and "A New World," Roberts introduces biblical accounts of how Jesus healed the sick and the lame before shifting to modern-day tales of his own efforts to heal followers of his ministry.

After depicting how Jesus cured a paralyzed man in Capernaum in "The Miracle Touch," Roberts addressed the reader directly: "Now let me tell you the true, thrilling story of Willie Phelps, who was healed by Jesus of Nazareth through my prayers."[57] The issue tells of Roberts's efforts to heal Phelps, who suffered from Perthes disease, a crippling bone disorder affecting children that limits hip movement. Willie is teased by schoolmates who steal his crutches, but the boy's parents soon discover a newspaper ad for Roberts's traveling ministry. Attending a meeting at a packed auditorium, Willie is seemingly healed through the power of prayer after Roberts lays a hand on him: "I felt God's power in my body! Mom! I'm healed! I'm going to walk to you!" shouts Willie, discarding his crutches and walking to his mother. Perthes disease actually resolves itself without treatment in many young sufferers, but as Willie tells it, "When Mister Roberts touched me, I felt God touch me too, and I was instantly healed!"[58] The story concludes with Willie telling his teacher that Roberts's meetings are free to attend before the recess bell prompts him to run off with his friends into the schoolyard.

Alongside his radio and television appearances, Roberts used the medium of comics as part of a multimedia approach to building his ministry in the 1950s. Jacobs notes how Roberts and his associates "saw comic books as a tool to communicate with their partners, elicit testimonials from readers, reinforce the power of the live, radio, and television ministries, spread the Gospel, effect conversions, and solicit dollars to support every facet of the Oral Roberts Evangelistic Association."[59] As a way of soliciting such testimonials, Roberts offered children the chance to join his Christian Adventure Club at no cost, which got them a membership card and a button: "Write me today. If you have a spiritual problem, tell me about it. I want to help you," he said.[60]

Roberts further solidified his role as a cross-media personality by depicting himself on television in his comics, tapping into the perceived legitimacy of the new medium among his audience to expand his reach across multiple media. In "A New World," a young deaf woman named Nancy Imel watches Roberts's show after a co-worker tells her in sign language, "Nancy, you don't *have* to be deaf. God will heal you. Have you ever watched the Oral Roberts program on television?" As Nancy watches that Sunday afternoon,

Roberts tells his audience, "This is Oral Roberts. I'm coming into your homes today to tell you that God wants to deliver you. Soul, mind and body."

By stressing the intimacy of the television medium's presence in the home and by offering enlarged panels of Roberts on Nancy's television screen, the comic presents Roberts as having a personal connection with Nancy and in turn with the reader. His message about the healing power of prayer is meant to be amplified by the fact that it has a television network and not just a comic-book publisher behind it. The narrator tells readers that "as Nancy watched the program from Sunday to Sunday, her faith not only increased. But it inspired the rest of her family to believe. She was deeply moved as she saw Oral Roberts pray for the sick."[61] Nancy then attends one of Roberts's sermons and is healed by the preacher, which is recorded for television. One panel depicts a cameraman filming Roberts and Imel ("The cameras in the huge auditorium caught the remarkable story of Nancy's healing that night," the narrator tells us), while the next shows a family watching the event on their set at home ("In thousands of homes throughout America, families witnessed on television the healing of Nancy Imel").[62]

While Roberts's series positions itself as a modern-day updating of biblical stories, each issue devotes ample space to promoting Roberts's ministry, whether it is his personal appearances or television program. Unlike other Christian comic books of this era, *Oral Roberts' True Stories* is about a personality, first and foremost. The "true stories" place Roberts at the center of the conclusion of each issue. Other series offered biblical adaptations, historical tales, and/or allegorical characters as a way of building a connection between young readers and their church, their school, and the Bible itself. Roberts used his comic books as a way of drawing attention to his appearances on television and at local gatherings, ultimately building a multimillion-dollar ministry in the decades that followed.

Wertham, EC, and the Comics Code Authority

As publishers such as Atlas and personalities such as Oral Roberts used Christian comics as a way to reach new segments of their respective markets in the 1950s, cultural critics such as Wertham escalated their attack on the medium and its content, regardless of whether the intent was to entertain or to educate. In *Seduction of the Innocent* (1954), Wertham decried comic-book adaptations of literary sources:

Comic books adapted from classical literature are reportedly used in 25,000 schools in the United States. If this is true, then I have never heard a more serious indictment of American education, for they emasculate the classics, condense them (leaving out everything that makes the book great), and [are] just as badly printed and inartistically drawn as other comic books and, as I have often found, do *not* reveal to children the world of good literature which has at all times been the mainstay of liberal and humanistic education. They conceal it.[63]

Despite Gaines's editorial statements in *Picture Stories from the Bible* about his hope that young readers could use his comics as a gateway to enjoying the Bible in its original form, Wertham described how his own studies "have shown us conclusively that children who read good books in their comic-book deformation do not proceed to read them in the original; on the contrary, they are deterred from that. Librarians all over the country have borne that out."[64]

While he didn't directly weigh in himself on whether reading biblical comics might lead children to pick up a Bible, Wertham followed up a quotation from someone described only as an "expert" who argued for how comics "may be used as an introduction to reading of the originals—especially of the Bible" by undercutting their argument with its counterpoint: "Another team-expert will inadvertently admit the opposite, that 'one of the most unfortunate things about comic books is that ... children are not so apt to read better books which might of course influence them to higher ideals.'"[65] In arranging these two 'expert' quotes in the order that he does, Wertham deliberately weakened the pro-comics argument while also implying that any seeming expert would eventually reveal, if only 'inadvertently,' the ways comics harm young readers.

Wertham's key role in the anti-comics crusade helped establish the Comics Code Authority (CCA) in 1954, through which the comics industry adopted a standard set of rules that regulated the types of content permissible in comic books. While the code's limitations on the amount of violence and lawlessness permitted on the page meant that the number of crime and horror titles quickly declined by the mid-1950s, even some Christian titles found themselves on the wrong side of the code at times. Pflaum's *Treasure Chest of Fun and Fact*, whose covers bore the Comics Code seal of approval to signal their supposed virtue to any skeptical parents or teachers, was not immune to the CCA's scrutiny. According to Pflaum's son Bill, the CCA asked the publisher to revise an issue of *Treasure Chest* depicting Christ nailed to the cross. Christ's hands, it seemed, had too much blood on them, and Pflaum had to tone down how gory the wounds were drawn.[66]

Along with explicitly barring "all scenes of horror, excessive bloodshed, gory or gruesome crimes, depravity, lust sadism, [and] masochism" among other lurid aspects, the Comics Code also specified that "ridicule or attack on any religious or racial group is never permissible."[67] The emphasis on preventing horror and crime comics affected publishers who specialized in those genres such as EC particularly hard. EC publisher Bill Gaines felt strongly that the code's language was deliberately crafted to prevent his titles in particular from gaining CCA approval. But the code's point about ridiculing race and religion was certainly not a factor in EC's poor standing among cultural critics. EC regularly advocated for racial equality in its comics, using genre stories as allegories for equity and tolerance, sometimes even using Christian symbolism in direct aid of this goal.

The most direct allusion to Christ is found in the tale "He Walked among Us" from *Weird Science* issue 13 (1952). In the story, an astronaut from Earth named Kraft is stranded on another planet in the year 2963, where he finds himself worshiped by the locals as a savior when he seemingly performs a series of miracles. In actuality, he uses antibiotics to cure a boy's illness and turns water into nourishment using "dehydrated food pills," but he is still praised as "our savior . . . our deliverer!" by the impoverished masses. Centuries later, when new space explorers finally visit the planet again, they learn that an entire religion has been built around Kraft, who was executed on a stretch rack by the planet's rulers for the ways he "favored and helped the poor, rather than the high caste" with his seeming miracles. A square wooden symbol representing the method of Kraft's death has become the symbol of this religion, much like how the cross symbolizes Christ's death by crucifixion. "Rather a familiar story, eh, Commander?" says one of the visiting explorers about the ironic parallel with Earth's own religious traditions.[68]

But in most cases, Christian images and allusions to Christian themes appear only in passing in EC titles and rarely as more than surface elements that serve to establish a setting or advance the plot or are there for other pragmatic narrative purposes. Most of the time, Christian imagery is limited to the use of a few iconic symbols such as crosses, but only as a way to aid tales about death and evil creatures. In a tale called "Vampire" from *Haunt of Fear* issue 16 (July–August 1950), a character brings a cross and wooden stake with him into a Louisiana bayou as protection against vampires, pulling out the cross as a bat approaches. Several horror tales in *Tales from the Crypt* use crosses as tombstones, for example "Death Suited Him" in issue 21 and "Last Respects" in issue 23. But such imagery is used only to establish the deathly confines of a graveyard setting for the ghastly tale, not to comment on the hallowed nature of the symbolism involved.

Rhetorical nods to Christianity are also sporadic and are often used in place of curse words. In "Last Respects," a man trapped inside a mausoleum with his wife's casket breaks one of the ten commandments as he takes the Lord's name in vain while seeking to escape: "Locked! Good Lord! How'll I get out of here?" he cries. He seems to pray to God for reprieve as he collapses before the door while sobbing, "I . . . I'll starve to death. . . . Please . . . God . . . someone."[69]

Given how his invocation seeks both divine and human intervention, it's clear that the story doesn't position the man as an especially religious figure (which is cemented by the fact that he eventually eats his wife's corpse in the hope it will enable him to survive). Other characters exclaim "Good Lord!" in issues of *Tales from the Crypt* ("None but the Lonely Heart," issue 33, December 1952–January 1953), *Crime SuspenStories* ("Private Performance," issue 14, December 1952–January 1953), but not out of any religious devotion. Instead, these words are gasped in the face of extreme terror, such as when someone is trapped in the first tale by a raving madman or in the latter when a man's wife returns from the grave as a decaying corpse.

A more overt use of Christian images is found in the story "The Catacombs" from *The Vault of Horror* issue 38 (August–September 1954), in which two thieves named Pietro and Gino attempt to hide their stolen goods deep within the cavernous recesses of what we are to presume are Roman catacombs. Gino uses wine from a flask to create a trail for the pair to follow back out, but we soon learn that he has a solo return trip in mind. Planning to keep the riches for himself, Gino stabs Pietro with a switchblade. The injured man runs off into a darkened passageway, blood droplets trailing behind him. As Gino searches for the trail again, he passes by huge paintings of various Christian saints as well as a large image of Christ with his right hand raised and his fingers signaling the blessing gesture as "a sign of divine benevolence."[70]

Christ's blessing appears behind Gino just as he appears to pick up the trail once more, but he is soon lost again when it turns out to made from Pietro's blood. As his lantern dies out, Gino recedes into the darkness as the story ends—presumably to die. Christ's blessing is a deceptive one, arriving at a turning point in the narrative that leads to one of EC's infamous twist endings—the trail that he discovers is the one that his violent actions caused

FIGURE 18   EC Comics uses Christian imagery in aid of a horror story with a twist ending in *Vault of Horror* 38 (August–September 1954).

rather than the one made with wine, a mistake that costs him his life. The fact that Christ's blessing appears to at first coincide with what Gino and the reader believe to be his road to salvation is a deliberately ironic choice on writer Carl Wessler's part. As one of the few moments in any EC comic book that uses Christ's image as a direct part of the narrative, the scene can be read either as a moral condemnation of murder and betrayal or as a sardonic comment on the empty value of following Christ's path.

While it might seem counterintuitive for a company that once published a series called *Picture Stories from the Bible* to be disparaging toward Christianity, EC's stories often did use Christian iconography toward critical ends as it infused many of its tales with social commentary. The 1954 story "Blood

Brothers" from *Shock SuspenStories* issue 13 (February–March 1954) opens with the image of a burned cross and a narrative caption that reads, "A last faint whisp of smoke curled upward from the blackened and charred cross that still stood grotesquely upon the singed lawn as they brought the body out." Cross burning became a regular practice among the Ku Klux Klan in the early twentieth century after being featured in Thomas Dixon Jr.'s 1905 novel *The Clansmen*, which was infamously adapted into *The Birth of a Nation* by director D. W. Griffith in 1915.[71] One branch of the KKK in Kentucky declared that as a symbol of Christ and "of Faith, Love and Hope," the fiery cross is "used to rally the Forces of Christianity against the ever increasing hordes of the Anti-Christ and the Enemies of America."[72]

The reader soon learns that the burning cross was the work of a man named Sid to scare his next-door neighbor into moving after he learns that the man's grandmother was Black. Burned or burning crosses appear in nine of the story's forty-five panels, signaling on a visual level what Qiana Whitted describes as "the cognitive implications of EC's visual representation of shame and contrition as a challenge to white power structures."[73] EC's use of Christian iconography was occasional at best, but it was often used in aid of powerful commentary about ongoing concerns of social justice.

Dueling Devils: *If the Devil Would Talk* and *Hot Stuff*

While EC's comics were frequently strategic in the use of Christian imagery, unlike other publishers in the 1950s, it rarely made mention of the devil in their horror comics. There were occasional passing references to Satan in stories about witchcraft such as "The Purge" in *The Vault of Horror* issue 39 (October–November 1954), but even here we only see a figure with the conventional visage of the devil (i.e., red skin and clothing, pointy beard, horns) in an opening panel that seems to have only a thematic connection to the story instead of a direct narrative role.

Compared to EC's sparse use, the devil got his due far more often at other publishers such as Ace Magazines and Toby Press in such series as *Web of Mystery* and *Tales of Horror*. In such comics, the cartoonish appearance of Satan as seen in 1940s comics is typically continued and the devil is thwarted in his attempts at all manner of evil schemes. Much like how Satan switched roles with a gangster in his 1940s adventures, in a 1953 issue of *Voodoo*, an "infamous, power-crazed, rising gang leader" named Johnnie Grotz steals the devil's trident and crowns himself the new "King of Hades." He then forces Satan to shine his shoes and installs an air conditioner to cool things down in Hell.[74]

One issue of *The Unseen* in 1954 even included a special section called "The Devil's Puzzle," offering readers a crossword puzzle with such clues as "Satan's Home," "He Teaches It," and "It Cooks Bones" (the answers being Hades, hate, and vat, respectively). A narrative caption warns readers that "If you can't solve this puzzle, it's too bad! Look what happened to the creatures that failed!" alongside the image of two skeletal ghouls.[75] Clearly, not all horror comics were as tonally sophisticated as those from EC in the 1950s. Uses of Christian themes and images were far more complex in stories such as "The Catacombs" and "Blood Brothers."

But it wasn't all fun and games for Satan. In 1950, the Catechetical Guild published *If the Devil Would Talk*, a controversial title that divided members of its own ranks with its heavy-handed approach. A story of juvenile delinquency, socialism, and suicide, *If the Devil Would Talk* used Satan not as a sinister boogieman or a comical despot but as the reader's guide through a series of complex moral issues. The story was written by Rev. Demetrius Manousos (who also wrote such Catechetical Guild publications as *Know Your Mass* and *The Life of the Blessed Virgin Mary*), with art by occasional *Topix* artist Addison Burbank.

Readers are greeted on the inside front cover with a large image of Satan from the shoulders up as he delivers some extended opening remarks. Introducing himself as the "Prince of hate," Satan tells the reader of his hatred for God, "and because I hate God, I hate all that he has made! I hate myself! I hate the world! I hate man!" He tells of how because he has brought himself to ruin, he feels compelled to bring "eternal ruin" upon humanity and has already found success in winning many of the world's souls: "I have forged a weapon. It is more terrible than the atom bomb, more destructive than the hydrogen bomb. These bombs can destroy man's body. My weapon blasts his soul—his mind—his spirit. My enemies have called it secularism—from *saeculum*, the Latin word for *world*."[76]

Secularism was not a new concern among Christian leaders in the mid-twentieth century. Publisher George Holyoake developed the term in 1851 as an alternative to the concept of atheism, contrasting how atheism rejects religion with how secularism allows for religion and government to function separately. The devil reminds readers in the opening of *If the Devil Would Talk* that secularism and atheism are not synonyms for one another, as someone need not disavow God's existence to live a secular lifestyle: "Secularism isn't

FIGURE 19 The cover of the Catechetical Guild's *If the Devil Would Talk* 1 (1950).

only for the atheist. It's deep in the life of anyone who acts as if God were not first and all other things second."[77]

Holyoake viewed secularism as a way for both church and state to function autonomously and for each institution to play its own appropriate role in society. He saw secularism as placing trust in "reason" rather than scripture, using methods from "science and philosophy" to stress "the common sense of mankind" through evidence that can be measured via real-world "experience."[78]

Satan echoes the notion that secularism is a system of belief based on considerations of real-world values at the beginning of *If the Devil Would Talk*, describing secularism as "an attitude, a philosophy of life, a way of thinking, speaking and acting which makes things of this world more important than the things of God."[79] The distinction made here about the role of "this world" in secularist belief is key to understanding the idea regardless of whether one takes a side on the issue. Holyoake defined secularism as "giving the precedence to the duties of this life over those which pertain to another world."[80] Secularists, then, emphasize "things of this world" as a basis of moral and rational judgment. Satan may be known as the "father of lies," but he accurately assesses the foundational principles of secularism in his opening remarks of *If the Devil Would Talk*.

As the narrator of the story, Satan introduces us to a young boy named Legion and his parents: "Legion was the son of average parents in a modern world. They paid their income tax. They liked movies and baseball and comfort."[81] While the family were regular churchgoers who did charity work, we are shown how they did not put God first because they chose not to have second child. When Legion asks why he doesn't have any brothers or sisters, his mother reminds his father about a recent church sermon on the subject. "Listen. We're not rich, are we? And your health isn't too good, is it?" his father asks his wife. When she agrees, Legion's father tells her that they can reassess having another child later on. Satan takes this as a sign of secularism at work: "So God is not first! Once that is established, the rest is easy. Watch!" We jump ahead two years in time to the dissolution of their marriage due to adultery. "Oh no, no. What's happened—what's happened to us?" asks the mother. "I can tell you, lady," Satan answers. "You're going my way! You didn't expect your husband to put you before himself, did you? After you put yourselves before God!"[82]

Satan regularly appears at the beginning or final panels of most pages to comment on the events. We learn that Legion's mother (referred to only as "lady" by the devil throughout) got divorced several times while her son joined

FIGURE 20 Satan describes secularism as his ultimate weapon in the opening page of *If the Devil Would Talk* 1 (1950).

a gang and committed numerous robberies. Satan guides the reader through the numerous supposedly wrong choices that Legion and his parents make throughout their lives as they choose secular over spiritual matters.

Along the way, the devil also places hefty blame on worldly institutions such as government-run education and the entertainment industries. Legion signs up for a public high school rather than a parochial one, which his mother approves of: "I'm glad you decided to go to the public high school. It's much nicer than St. John's. They have all the facilities and a nicer class of boys go there," she says. "Yeah, there are no foreigners there," Legion adds. Not only are we apparently meant to be critical of the modern facilities offered by public schools, but Manousos's phrasing here also positions public education as exclusionary while Catholic schools are seemingly inclusive.

But the casual racism on display from Legion and his mother feels less admirable given how little context readers are given. In the next panel, Legion has already arrived at his new school and is complaining about public transportation ("I guess I got to go here. I live 'way out of town and you can't use the bus unless you go to the public school").[83] Satan never comments on the racist behavior, leaving readers to process the issues of class and race in play in the mid-century American educational landscape on their own. Modern readers might hope that a 1950s audience understood Legion's racism as yet another tragic character flaw, but these comments were just as likely brushed aside given how they are expedited in the narrative.

When he arrives to register for school, he meets a boy named Mahoney who is concerned that they don't offer any classes on religion. "This is a public school, young man. We have excellent classes in all important branches. You can study religion at home in your spare time," an administrator tells him. Satan then explains why education no longer has room for God: "I've been working on scholars for six centuries—first making man's thought more important than man's revelation—then blinding philosophers to the reality of God's teaching—finally coaxing them to deny the whole world of the spirit! It's easy to trip up the thinkers once they put their own minds in the place of God's. And every error of the philosophers eventually filters down to the people through schools, press, and entertainment."[84] Manousos draws a line straight through the roles of education, journalism, and show business in the lives of the general public, blaming all three for inculcating secularist ideals among the masses.

Manousos then turns his ire toward Hollywood, much as the Payne Fund studies had done decades earlier. After high school, Mahoney joins the seminary while Legion goes on to college, graduates with honors, and then lands a job in the "theatrical industry" (although it's unspecified whether that means the movies or stage plays). Thanks to some shady business dealings, he rises through the ranks to become president of Entertainment Enterprises, Inc., a generically named company that Satan describes as allowing Legion to "control a large part of theater, radio, movies and television." Mahoney serves as the story's moral compass by asking his former schoolmate, "Don't you see what you're doing to the people? What has become their chief interest in life? Pleasure! They can't have enough of it. It's not recreation to refresh the body, or art to raise the spirit. It's just pleasure—a drug in their minds and hearts!" When Legion counters with the fact that pleasure pays well, Mahoney retorts, "It's turning a nation of courageous, enterprising, freedom-loving men into a mob of pleasure addicts worried only about good time and security.... Ninety percent of what you produce is harmful to souls."[85]

The role of government in society is also a target, as Satan tells the reader how "as soon as I've convinced a strong man that he needs no God and can rule his own destiny, he starts dreaming about ruling the fate of others." Legion becomes a campaign manager to an aspiring politician named Mr. Small who is soon elected governor and then president using a platform based on Mahoney's warning about the perils of pleasure and security. Using a slippery-slope argument, the Catechetical Guild equates secularism with socialism: "We'll offer them security. Let the government control the things that touch the lives of the people most closely—the utilities, coal, medicine, oil, housing, eventually the basic foods!" Legion says. "Sounds like socialism," Small points out. "Call it what you will. It's security," replies Legion. "Of course, we can't do it all at once. But we can guarantee people government aid all the way through life. We'll take care of everything. The more people get, the more they want."[86]

In the eyes of the Catechetical Guild, the public is willing to trade liberty for security and amusement, even if it means giving up on democracy: "Small was elected—not once, but again and again," says a grinning Satan, who takes delight in the abolition of term limits. "The country went socialist. I had it where I wanted it. Security was God, and God was forgotten." When the country faces an economic depression, Legion devises a plan by which workers must take on extra hours for the same pay each week. When a reporter complains that "totalitarianism is here!" Legion has him detained by the police and shuts down the freedom of the press by limiting newsprint supply and broadcasting access.[87]

Once the public learns of the government's plan thanks to Father Mahoney's grassroots actions, large-scale riots ensue. When a mob of rioters

FIGURE 21 Secularism leads to suicide in the finale of *If the Devil Would Talk* 1 (1950).

(whose ranks even include police officers) shouting "Lynch them! Kill them!" storms what is presumably the White House, they smash the windows of what appears to be the Oval Office and shoot the secretary of state. Legion passes the president a revolver and says "Here. We played our game and lost," urging him to kill himself. When the president refuses, Legion shoots him and then himself. "That's right—suicide," says Satan. "Suicide and revolution, depression and discontent, hatred and bloodshed!" He boasts, "Secularism hits everything in society from the family to the government. No one wins in the end but I!"

"Legion and his suicide are only symbols—symbols of modern man and the suicide of society being brought on by secularism. I have found no greater weapon for my hate. I never shall. Unless God is first, all else is chaos!" Satan concludes, offering readers a final, parting warning that secularism leads to hatred, chaos, and suicide.[88] The issue ends with a page of quotations printed on the back cover, taken from a 1947 statement on secularism from American bishops linking the rise of secular life to the moral downfall of the family, the rise of juvenile delinquency, the lack of religion in the classroom, economic downturn, and the fraying of the international community.

But the book's overt warning of the how the faithless masses of American society may soon slide into a readily desired socialist lifestyle did not sit well with everyone in the Catholic community or even in the Catechetical Guild itself. The book was printed but never sold. When the publisher's board members saw the final product, they deemed it too controversial to be released. A handful of copies exist today, but the rest were presumably destroyed.[89] A version in black and white also exists that may have been circulated as an unauthorized reprint among comics fans.

In 1958, an updated version of the book was commissioned with a few key changes. The first was to attribute it to a new publishing imprint called Impact Press rather than put the Catechetical Guild's name on it. References to secularism throughout the issue were changed to "materialism" instead. On the back cover, the American bishops' comments about secularism were replaced by a new statement with the headline "The Enemy within the Gates" condemning materialism and godlessness while appealing to the reader's sense of patriotism as a way of promoting the importance of preserving America's religious heritage: "Many well-informed citizens plead for a moral revival. They are convinced that military strength alone will not save the United States if Godlessness is permitted to destroy us from within. The aim of this book is to present the philosophy of materialism which attempts to push God out of His world and leave man without any basis on which to build freedom, justice and peace." The final text says that "a nationwide survey shows that 98% of the American people say they believe in a Supreme Being," so therefore "America's religious heritage must be saved."[90]

The new version still stirred readers' fears even though it replaced language about secularism with the more abstract notion of materialism. But while the

Catechetical Guild had an issue with the focus on secularism of the original version, it apparently had no problem allowing suicide to remain as a concluding plot point. Legion still kills himself at the end, and materialism is now to blame instead of secularism. Early Catechetical Guild artist Charles Schulz would also place materialism at the heart of his message in the animated *A Charlie Brown Christmas* television special of 1965, but Schulz wisely avoided having a despondent Charlie Brown kill himself as a way out of his problems at the end of the episode.

If the Devil Would Talk was not the only instance when the Catechetical Guild took a strong political stance in their comics. That same year, the guild published *Blood Is the Harvest* (1950), about the Communist martyr Pavlik Morozov. The book is a straightforward biography of young Pavlik, who was killed by his own family in 1932 at age thirteen after turning in his father as an enemy of the state. The Catechetical Guild presented his story as a way of offering American readers what they call "a devastating condemnation of Communism" in their concluding editorial. "We are sure you will appreciate the complete hopelessness of the situation where the state is totalitarian. Let us work and pray that such a system never comes to America!"[91]

But as direct as their message is in these final words, the Catechetical Guild had been even more heavy-handed in its anti-Communist approach in *Is This Tomorrow* (1947), the cover of which depicts an American flag in flames and the subtitle *America Under Communism!* while three presumably Russian agents restrain a priest, choke a woman, and punch a Black man in the face. As unsubtle as the message of the front cover is, the opening editorial of *Is This Tomorrow* declares to its readers that the book was "published for one purpose—*To Make You Think!* To make you more alert to the menace of Communism." Communists, we are told, "are working day and night—laying the groundwork to overthrow *Your Government!*"[92] Much like how the Catechetical Guild posited the role of popular media in the rise of secularism, *Is This Tomorrow* implicates radio and newspapers in helping to spread Communist values throughout the 1940s: "We've been training writers and editors for years to follow the party line. They will be ready to take complete control of radio and publishing once we get in," a Communist leader says of their plans to spread propaganda.[93]

The comic blames Communism for increased racial animosity and for religions that are pitted against one another. Education is taken over by Communist teachers who disavow Christianity: "I defy anyone to prove that there is such a thing as a God!" says one instructor. "Capitalists invented God to keep the workers satisfied. You can't get anywhere as long as you believe that pie-in-the-sky story," he warns his young students.[94] Book burnings are held to incinerate Bibles and churches are taken over by the military as the country slides into absolute Communist rule.

The story's final page offers a concluding editorial warning to readers: "If you want to keep living in freedom, you must know who the Communists are—and their methods of working." This sentiment would soon be echoed by Senator Joseph McCarthy, who took office the same year as *Is This Tomorrow* was published. "Knowing who the Communists are" would soon take on a more ominous tone in Washington and in the entertainment industries as McCarthyism took hold. The threats of Communism, secularism, and materialism raised by the Catechetical Guild in comics such as *Is This Tomorrow* and *If the Devil Would Talk* show just how much the Catholic Church was concerned with preserving the traditional values of churchgoing Americans as the 1950s began.

Satan may have seemed like a potent adversary to use as the host of a comic book that warned young readers about the dangers of secular life at the start of the decade, but by the late 1950s another publisher offered children a very different devil—one who was much cuter and wore a diaper. In 1957, Harvey Comics debuted the character Hot Stuff the Little Devil in the pages of *Hot Stuff* issue 1. Harvey had found so much success with comics based on the Paramount animated film star Casper the Friendly Ghost that it knew the market was right for another kid-friendly supernatural character. Harvey artist and art director Ken Selig notes how the company's owner, Alfred Harvey, was initially hesitant about creating the character because he was "suspicious whether we should print it, because we were very much concerned about the Bible Belt [of southern American states] being one of our principal areas of sales." But Selig recalls such hesitation lasting only a few weeks before "Alfred saw that it still had a potential in spite of him being nervous about it" and asked artist Warren Kremer to create potential character sketches for *Hot Stuff*.[95]

Although not meant to be Satan himself, Hot Stuff is a young demon child who was drawn in what was by 1957 the well-worn visual shorthand for rendering the devil: red skin, a pointed tale and ears, horns, and pitchfork. But writer-artist Warren Kremer, who had created Richie Rich for Harvey Comics in 1953, added a distinctive piece of costuming to Hot Stuff to set him apart from all the other versions of devils in American comics—a white diaper. While Casper is apparently shapeless enough in his spectral form to preclude the need to cover his genitals, all of the demons in *Hot Stuff* wear

FIGURE 22 *Hot Stuff, The Little Devil* 75 (December 1966), page 9.

diapers—young and old alike—as a way of maintaining their decency for young readers. Alfred Harvey, who was a Lutheran, did ask Kremer to redesign one aspect of Hot Stuff's visual design, however: he "had hooves, rather than toes on his feet" at first, recalls Selig. "By putting hooves on him, you had a character that might be a wrong character for the Bible Belt," he says of the apparent line that could not be crossed when designing a satanic children's character for a potential religious readership.[96]

Whereas earlier comic-book incarnations of Satan set his exploits in the underworld, Hot Stuff's adventures took place on Earth rather than in Hell; the young demon lived by himself in a cave in the woods. The character may have embodied a long spiritual tradition of hell-born figures, but his exploits were almost always secular in nature. He used his heat power to stir up some excitement across a wide range of earthly settings—such as local farms, fishing holes, the circus, and other locations that kids would recognize. Other demons occasionally make appearances, often extended family members such as the dimwitted Cousin Demo, Uncle Scorchy, and Uncle Smokey (whose long, curly white beard makes him akin to a visual hybrid between God and Satan).

The character was so popular that several additional series were soon launched, including *Hot Stuff Sizzlers* in 1960 and *Devil Kids Starring Hot Stuff* in 1962. In many of his stories, Hot Stuff stirred up trouble, such as in *Hot Stuff* issue 23 (1960), in which he asks himself "Now what kind of mischief can I make today?" while envisioning three possible scenarios: eating watermelon in front of a "Keep Out" sign in a watermelon patch, taking a nap in a kangaroo's pouch, and frightening a moose. After some consideration, he decides against all three options, rationalizing, "Naw! I did all that yesterday."[97]

On a visual level, the young character is a literally infantilized version of the ways Satan was characterized in various 1940s and 1950s adventure and horror tales. Uncle Scorchy even resembles a less-dressed version of the Catechetical Guild's Satan from *If the Devil Would Talk*, replete with cape and goatee. Hot Stuff can certainly be read in several ways simultaneously. For many readers, he is simply a funny little fellow whose hijinks are meant to amuse. He is also clearly meant to be a caricaturized version of Satan, albeit in a way that lets the devil become a symbol of fun rather than as a figure who embodies a moral warning about the collapse of a secular society.

Ironically, many *Hot Stuff* stories offer lessons about kindness, friendship, and repentance that are entirely in keeping with Christian morality. In the tale "Cold Stuff," the Little Devil protects a rabbit and bear cub from a "mean ogre" who has been teasing them,[98] while in "Snow Bawl" he helps build a new snowman for two children after accidentally their original one. "Hmmm! That was my fault!" Hot Stuff thinks to himself contritely after realizing the destructive power of his flaming trident.[99]

The ways representations of the devil shifted from the 1940s to the 1960s is in keeping with how popular culture handled all manner of menacing figures. Ghouls such as Dracula and Frankenstein's monster were no longer a potent force by the 1950s, having been reduced to comedic foils in films such as *Abbott and Costello Meet Frankenstein* (1948). The first comic-book version of Frankenstein began as an ongoing horror tale in 1940 in *Prize Comics* issue 7 but shifted into comedy in 1945 with *Frankenstein* issue 1 from writer-artist Dick Briefer (who did both versions). Horror hosts such as Vampira and Zacherley offered mocking commentary while presenting monster movies to television audiences in the 1950s, while the early 1960s brought comedic takes on classic monsters and horror tropes in the form of sitcoms such as *The Munsters* and *The Addams Family*.

In the context of these larger trends in popular culture, a comedic take on the devil for younger readers such as *Hot Stuff* seemed only natural in the late 1950s, an era when parodic titles such as *Mad* and *Cracked* thrived with their satirical look at society and entertainment. By the late 1960s, satirical comics would take on new dimensions with the rise of underground comix—a forum in which religious imagery took a bold, subversive new turn.

Into the Underground

Mad began as a comic book in 1952 from EC Comics before shifting to a magazine format three years later. The change came after the publisher canceled its line of horror, crime, and sci-fi comics in the wake of Wertham's efforts and the rise of the Comics Code Authority. Although M. C. Gaines had created EC with pedagogical purposes in mind, the publisher's legacy is ultimately best encapsulated by two figures, one ghastly, the other jovial—the Crypt Keeper and Alfred E. Neuman.

But as far removed as both characters seem from the pious material found in Gaines's biblical adaptations, the first issues of both *Mad* and *Tales from the Crypt* contained advertisements for *Picture Stories from the Bible*. *Tales from the Crypt* issue 20, the first of the series after the prior series *The Crypt of Terror* was retitled, features a half-page ad complete with mail-order form with which readers of EC's new horror series could send away for copies of both the collected editions or single issues of both the Old Testament and New Testament series of *Picture Stories from the Bible*. *Mad* issue 1 contains a similar mail-order ad for *Picture Stories from the Bible*, alongside copies of *Picture Stories from Science* and *Picture Stories from World History*. The advertisement even contains a note for educators: "Write for special school prices."[100]

The fact that EC assumed that reader interest in the biblical adaptations would overlap with fans of the publisher's new line of horror tales is amusing enough, but the juxtaposition is made even more comical by the fact that the ad in *Tales from the Crypt* issue 20 appears alongside a text-based story about a man who drowns to death after trying to kill his wife's dog. On the right side of the page, the reader can ponder purchasing the New Testament edition of *Picture Stories*, which we are told contains "the complete story of the Life of Christ and Peter and Paul and the founding of the Early Christian Church. Included are maps showing Palestine at the time of Jesus and chronological indexes of principal events and Scripture references to episodes illustrated." On the left side of the page, the reader learns the fate of the would-be dog murderer: "He opened his mouth for a last scream for help ... and there was a bruising impact of his head striking the cement ceiling! There was no air left in the flooded room ... even the surging sound of the water had stopped! All he could hear was a thin bubbling sound ... which seemed to start deep in his strangling throat."[101]

By the early 1960s, young readers had fewer Christian comics to choose from as publishers such as the Catechetical Guild and its competitors reduced their output. *Topix Comics* had folded in 1952. Oral Roberts released his final issue of *Oral Roberts' True Stories* in 1959. The Catechetical Guild published another anti-communist title in 1960 called *The Red Iceberg* (the cover depicted Uncle Sam atop an ocean liner seeking to steer clear of the titular crimson mass emblazoned with a hammer and sickle), while one of their final releases was the 1964 comic "*... To Speak of God*" about cardinal Marcantonio Barbarigo's path to sainthood in seventeenth-century Italy. The publisher's output had been marked by wide range of topics across eras and nations since the 1940s, from the life stories of saints of past centuries to how-to guides for young people seeking to become nuns and priests to the perceived dangers of certain modern ideologies to American life. The demise of these one-shot issues about a variety of sacred subjects happened at the same time as the success of serialized storylines in 1960s series such as *Sunday Pix* and *Treasure Chest*, which continued to be given out to children in Sunday schools and/or parochial schools throughout the decade.

But although images of Christian figures such as Satan could no longer be found in didactic-minded titles such as *If the Devil Would Talk* by the 1960s, they were more prominent in mass-market children's titles such as *Hot Stuff* as the decade continued. The devil was no longer simply a stern figure to take moral warnings from; now he was also a figure of mirth and merriment. And as a new generation of comics artists emerged in the 1960s, religious imagery increasingly became subject to parody.

This shift was also occurring as the rise of the underground comics movement (often called comix) began to offer alternative approaches to the content and the target audiences of comic books by the late 1960s. Comix typically rejected traditional mainstream genres and artistic norms while frequently offering adult readers images of sex, drug use, and other issues that were specifically banned by the Comics Code Authority. Comics scholar Charles Hatfield notes in *Alternative Comics* that comix creators were regularly "in tune with the radical sensibilities of the Vietnam-era counterculture."[102] Media scholar Nicholas Sammond similarly describes how underground comics "celebrated nonmarital reproductive sexuality, unlimited freedom of speech, drug use (and the expansion of consciousness it was meant to promise), and a communalism that challenged the hegemony of the white, suburban, nuclear family."[103]

Artwork typically matched the subversiveness of the content in tone and design, often drawn in a deliberately less polished style than traditional comic art. Sammond describes comix artists as "breaking the aesthetic norms for mainstream comics," while Hatfield points out how their "broad, exaggerated style" was used for the purposes of "parodic grotesqueness."[104] Comix, in sum, were not meant for younger readers and could offer very different interpretations of religion than other comics had to date.

While underground comics gained ground throughout the 1960s in various forms, the first major success in comix was *Zap Comix* (1968), created by Robert Crumb. The first issue was published in February of that year, with a backdated issue 0 appearing by year's end. Crumb wrote, drew, and edited issue 0 and issue 1, while other artists such as Rick Griffin, Victor Moscoso, and S. Clay Wilson joined Crumb starting with *Zap* issue 2. The series distinguished itself from other comic books by placing a tagline across the top of the first issue's cover: "Fair Warning: For Adult Intellectuals Only!" while later issues contained the more succinct label of "Adults Only." Wilson notes how he enjoyed drawing provocative images as a way of expressing himself creatively: "I have this morbid fascination with deviancy and I like drawing it. I find it entertaining. I'm sure a shrink would have a field day trying to figure out why I did it. I just find it fun. People can take it or leave it."[105]

The origins of the term "comix" are usually attributed to Crumb and *Zap Comix*. Sammond notes how "the new spelling was a rejection of the North American comics industry and its restrictive and prudish Comics Code.... A potent signifier, the *x* invoked a rejection of the code in favor of unbridled, libidinous, and uncensored expression. It foreshadowed the X-rating for movies, which was instituted in November 1968, only months after Crumb released *Zap Comix* issue 1. Like X-rated movies, comix repudiated the notion that a vernacular art form, comics, had to be 'family friendly,' embracing traditional standards of morality."[106]

The first issue featured nudity, profanity, drug references, and surrealism—along with exaggerated racial caricatures that, while intended for the purposes of parody and social commentary, are hard to read as anything other than racist.[107] In *The Content of Our Caricature: African American Comic Art and Political Belonging*, Rebecca Wanzo describes the "language" of caricature as "excessive and indeterminate" because it "reduce[s] people to real and imagined excesses in order to represent something understood as essential about their character."[108] She notes that while Crumb "has claimed that his comics can be read as embedding antiracist critique because the representations are so transparently egregious," the cartoonist ultimately "offers an early form of allegedly 'post-race' humor to his implied comics reader, one who is a white subject outside of these political passions and the seriousness of revolutionary politics."[109] Crumb saw himself as willfully subverting the taboo in his work, but admits that he went too far at times: "The problem with it is that people get hurt: you hurt people with that kind of thing. So you really have to know what you're doing. There have been times I have regretted things that I've done because I realize that I did hurt people with my comics."[110]

Alongside their divisive themes and images, early issues of *Zap* also contained a range of approaches to Christianity—some blatantly blasphemous, others more contemplative. Religion often proved to be a prominent subject in the early days of comix. Frank Stack's independent comic strip *The Adventures of Jesus*, which "satirized stories from the New Testament," was collected for a small print run of fifty copies in 1964. That same year, Jack Jackson released a thousand copies of a forty-two page, self-published comic called *God Nose* in which God uses "a magic sinus wand" in order to "clear up quandaries about birth control, racism, and love."[111] Building off of these early forays into satirizing Christian figures, *Zap Comics* offered an ongoing forum for such explorations—one that reached an even wider audience as the series' notoriety grew. Issue 0 offers a tale called "City of the Future" that chronicles numerous inventions that will transform society in the years ahead. Along with machines that will eliminate workplaces, warfare, and going to the bathroom, Crumb concocts a "fantasy" machine called the Fantazoom that allows you to "have the whole spectrum of experience at your fingertips," much like a modern virtual reality headset does. The Fantazoom lets users adopt any number of personas: "Be a locomotive engineer! Be a secret agent! Be a whore! Be Jesus Christ! Create your own masterpieces!"[112]

We might be tempted to see this reference to Christ as a throwaway gag, but Crumb's personal history with the Catholic church adds an autobiographical dimension to his use of Christian imagery in his comics. Crumb was raised Roman Catholic and began attending Catholic school at age six in 1949. He describes himself as being a devout Christian in his younger years before turning away from the Church by his adolescence: "I guess I wasn't cut out to be a true believer," says Crumb. "I learned about dogma from experts. I started Catholic school in the first grade and got a heavy dose of it. In fourth grade the nuns used to tell us, 'Some of you will abandon the Church.' I always said, 'No, I never will, not me.' I was fanatically Catholic, praying all the time.'" he says. Crumb recalls how he began to struggle with his faith at the age of fifteen: "One day it just became clear to me that the truth about reality is actually something that is beyond our comprehension. Nobody knows the truth. It's something to be curious, not dogmatic about."[113]

Crumb worked through his spiritual struggles in his comics, often in the form of Christian allegories. *Zap Comix* issue 2, for instance, features a story called "Hamburger Hi-Jinx" starring a character named "Cheesis K. Reist" who constantly craves burgers. After talking to his burger and telling it that "it is not without malice that I tell you, baby, you must die so's that I may live!" the burger and condiment bottles come to life. The tale revolves around death and metaphorical resurrection, offering readers a condiment-based passion play about Christ's persecution, suffering, and resurrection using a character named for the phonetic equivalent of Jesus Christ. Even hamburgers can be used as religious allegory in hands of an underground comix artist, forcing readers who might not otherwise contemplate spiritual concerns to engage with them in a highly mischievous form.

While some Christians might take offense to a character named Cheesis K. Reist, *Zap Comix* issue 1 also features a spiritual quest undertaken by a more universally named character. Crumb introduces Schuman the Human by telling of how he "goes forth with his fine mind to find God! And believe me, he took a long lunch!" Dressed in a fedora and trench coat, Schuman scours the city late at night, looking for God. "After months of intrigue, I believe I finally have a hot lead!" he says. "There are those who consider me unstable... the fools! They are not aware of the seriousness of my efforts ... in fact, this could be the night!" At ten minutes after two in the morning, Schuman notices a patrol car passing by and is in the middle of describing it to the reader when he is interrupted. "AHEM!" says a loud voice booming from out of the sky.

Schuman, unprepared for such an acknowledgement of God's presence, tugs at his collar nervously. "Gulp!" he exclaims, before sticking his hands in his pockets and replying, "Er ... uh ... heh heh. Never mind."[114] He runs off, his head shrinking more and more in successive panels as a visual symbol of his unpreparedness for finding God. Searching for God became a theme in many later comics for older readers, as we will see, such as in Garth Ennis and Steve Dillon's 1990s series *Preacher* (in which a much more forceful confrontation occurs when God is finally located).

Looking back at his career more than thirty years after the debut of *Zap Comix*, Crumb noted in a 1999 interview that he remained influenced by his religious upbringing as an adult, even though he was no longer a practicing Catholic: "I realized that I'm not past all that Catholic crap at all. Even though I think it's stupid, it's still there."[115] He said that he did "actually believe in God, to tell you the truth. I believe in a superior force in the universe" and that he still prayed. "I turn to God when I'm really desperate. It's sometimes the last hope you have, to pray. ... It's the last resort to call out to the universe to help you in some way."[116]

In light of such confessions, Crumb's work in *Zap Comix* can be read as early attempts at working through personal spiritual struggles. He went on to learn about Buddhism and other religions throughout his life, becoming a proponent of meditation and other spiritual practices. As literary scholar David Stephen Calonne writes in *R. Crumb: Literature, Autobiography, and the Quest for Self*, Crumb "is preoccupied with finding the truth of the inner self, which has led him to consider a variety of spiritual traditions including Buddhism, Hinduism, existentialism, Gnosticism, and voodoo as well as theosophical, esoteric and occult sources."[117] Like Schuman the Human, Crumb has been on a quest throughout his life to find the center of his own spiritual universe, one that started with Catholicism as a child and led him to consider many new directions later in life.

Crumb returned to examine certain aspects of Catholicism closely again with *The Book of Genesis Illustrated* (2009), an adaptation the first book of the Bible in comics form. The book's cover contains several disclaimers alerting readers to the fact that even though it is a faithful adaptation of Genesis, the literalness with which Crumb presents the material means that it is both sexually explicit and full of graphic violence. "The First Book of the Bible Graphically

FIGURE 23 Robert Crumb's Schuman the Human searches for God in *Zap Comix* 1 (1967).

Depicted! Nothing Left Out!" one tagline proclaims, while another states, "Adult Supervision Recommended For Minors."[118] Crumb notes that while he "did not adapt it reverently," he "respected the text insofar as I did not want to ridicule it."[119]

Among the literal or graphic depictions are such moments as Adam and Eve's nudity, Cain's killing of Abel resulting in copious bloodshed, the destruction of Sodom and Gomorrah leading to charred bodies from the rain of fire and brimstone, the daughters of Lot each having sex with their father in panels that explicitly depict their intercourse, Jacob's daughter Dinah being abducted and raped across multiple panels, the murder of Judah's sons Er and Onan rendered with ample amounts of blood, and the death of Jacob showing a graphic disembowelment during his embalming.

Anticipating criticism of his approach to the Bible, Crumb wrote in the book's introduction that he has, "to the best of my ability, faithfully reproduced every word of the original text" in his adaptation. "If my visual, literal interpretation offends or outrages some readers, which seems inevitable considering that the text is revered by many people, all I can say in my defense is that I approached this as a straight illustration job, with no intention to ridicule or make visual jokes. That said, I know that you can't please everybody."[120]

Crumb's position here seems aloof, in keeping with his ideas in prior decades about how those who criticize the racist and sexist elements of his work are simply being too sensitive: "[It] never ceases to amaze me [how] touchy and humorless people are about these things," he said in a 1980 interview.[121] But in his commentary at the end of *Book of Genesis Illustrated*, Crumb mentioned an awareness that he had approached the Bible from a predominantly "male, patriarchal point of view" before he began the project, an indication that he does have some self-awareness about how his approach to representing various racial, cultural, and gender identities impacts others.[122]

Literary scholar David Stephen Calonne points out in *R Crumb: Literature, Autobiography, and the Quest for Self* how Crumb "emphasizes throughout the patriarchal theme in his illustrations" for the book.[123] Calonne concludes that those able to "read between the lines" of *Book of Genesis Illustrated* will find Crumb "advocating for an alternative and more tolerant view of human possibility than that advocated by traditional interpretations of Genesis."[124] Many will question whether Crumb's work advocates 'tolerance,' however, given the sharp criticism of his work throughout his career.

In between this later work on *Book of Genesis Illustrated* and his early years on *Zap Comix*, one publisher compiled much of Crumb's most sexually explicit material from the latter series for reprint in a 1986 release entitled

Bible of Filth. With a cover bound in black leather, the book physically resembled a Bible complete with a yellow-ribbon bookmark. Its contents, however, were driven by horniness rather than holiness, such as "Horny Harriet Hotpants" from *Zap Comix* issue 4 (1969), which ends with Harriet's marriage to Jesus Christ. A 2017 reprint edition of *Bible of Filth* also includes more recent sketches, including an ejaculating cloven-hoofed demon with a caption that reads "Go and F-ck Thyself," as well as a self-portrait of Crumb in his boxer shorts straddling a character called Devil Girl with the caption "I was raised to be a Christian. But somehow the Devil got me. I don't know how it happened. Lord help me!"[125]

Crumb has used sexuality as a way of exploring his Catholic upbringing throughout his career. Using comics for personal exploration in the 1960s was a radically different approach to that seen just a decade earlier, when storytellers used the medium for the primary purpose of entertainment (and for both ideological and pedagogical purposes at publishers such as the Catechetical Guild). Cultural critics such as Wertham who decried comics as largely unwholesome for younger readers in the 1950s could not have envisioned how they became a counterbultural forum for decidedly adult interests.

There had certainly been pornographic comics in earlier decades in the form of short booklets commonly called 'Tijuana Bibles" that often depicted well-known (but not officially licensed) characters in sexually explicit situations. Yet those were intended primarily for the purposes of arousal, not artistry or self-expression, let alone to explore spiritual faith and doubt. Where the Catechetical Guild used their comics for religious community building, Crumb and his underground contemporaries used comics as a way to embed religious themes and tropes in ways that prioritized personal meaning.

The role of the individual creator took on greater importance in the comics industry in the decades ahead. Few writers and artists had their work credited in the pages of their comic books in the industry's early years. But by the 1960s and 1970s, fans knew who made their favorite comics and often followed the work of artists such as Jack Kirby and Neal Adams as they moved from publisher to publisher. And in the world of Christian comics, the 1970s would be dominated by two men: Jack Chick and Al Hartley.

3

The 1970s

● ● ● ● ● ● ● ● ● ● ● ●

Comix, Jack Chick, *Archie*,
and Spire Christian Comics

The 1970s was a transitional period in American history. Although 49 percent of Americans reportedly attended a church service in 1955, that number had fallen to 40 percent by 1971. Young adults under the age of 30 accounted for much of the decline.[1] Not coincidentally, the countercultural efforts of young students, protestors, and artists that began in the 1960s continued to change social perceptions about sex, gender, race, and politics throughout the 1970s.

Popular culture reacted in turn. Hollywood introduced a new ratings system in 1968 that allowed older audiences to experience violent and sexual content previously prohibited on screen. Both the film and television industries began to recognize the need for more diversity in their programming, and more movies and programs appeared that were tailored to Black audiences. There was also some recognition of the progress being made by women in what was then termed the women's liberation movement.

Comic book publishers were arguably slower to react to social change, although small increases in the number of titles starring Black and female characters were seen at Marvel and DC by the end of the decade with characters such as Luke Cage, Black Lightning, and Ms. Marvel. Although superhero comics slowly embraced social change in their storytelling, many Christian publishers such as Chick Publications and Spire Christian Comics took an opposing strategy. They used their titles to warn readers about what they saw as the dangers of cultural change and secular life in ways that took the proselytizing strategies of older publishers such as the Catechetical Guild to new levels.

Comix in the Early 1970s: *Wimmen's Comix* and *Binky Brown*

But as Spire and Chick's work gained traction, underground comix continued to flourish in the early 1970s, extending the creative and subversive approaches toward Christian tropes Crumb and his contemporaries had popularized in the mid to late 1960s. Some creators were more explicit than others in their work. Artists such as S. Clay Wilson explored combinations of sacred and sexual imagery in stories such as "Angels and Devils" (in which the Ten Commandments are recounted via numerous sexual acts among angels and demons) and "Wanda and Tillie Featuring Jesus Christ" (in which Christ performs oral sex on Satan) in *Zap Comix* issue 6 (1973). Jim Osborne's 1971 story "The Harbinger" offers a nude angel destroying a city of orgiastic revelers with an atomic explosion in *Slow Death Funnies* issue 3.

Male comix creators regularly used their work as a pulpit for exploring sex and Christianity in tandem, albeit with ranging levels of subtlety. But women made underground comic books too, and their work also frequently used sexual and religious imagery (mostly without tying them together as directly as their male peers did). Similar to *Zap*'s anthology format of a variety of artists and content, the one-shot issue *It Ain't Me Babe* by editors Trina Robbins and Barbara "Willy" Mendes was an underground comic done entirely by women creators in 1970. It was followed by the ongoing anthology *Wimmen's Comix*, which published seventeen issues in the period 1972 to 1992.

Although male creators such as Wilson depicted Christian figures in compromising sexual positions for the shock value, Robbins offered a more earnest tale of religious love in 1984 with the story "Liadan and Curithir" in *Wimmen's Comix* issue 9. The titular couple are seventh-century Irish poets whose union is prevented when Liadan becomes a nun. "Though it is hard for me to tell you, let me see you no more, do not destroy me; since I cannot escape from death, come not between me and the love of God," Liadan tells Curithir.[2] The story is a serious exploration of a woman's personal power in a pre-medieval era, using religion as a forum for commentary about gender roles and women's agency.

Other creators used *Wimmen's Comix* as a space to explore their own faith, much like Crumb did. Both Judy Becker and Penny Moran wrote stories about growing up in Catholic school. Becker's tale from issue thirteen of 1988 is about a young girl named Monique's relationship with her guardian angel. The story explores sexual development in sincere ways rather than gratuitously: "Sometimes she saw the angel, a vague figure in the shadows, watching her and judging her actions. Monique's major sin was masturbation. She pleaded with the angel to help her overcome the temptation to touch herself down there, but evil often prevailed," the narrator tells us. After Monique's mother catches her masturbating in the shower and hits her daughter in the face at the exact same time as Monique has her first orgasm, we are told how "Monique's guardian angel was gone. She didn't know if her mother had killed the angel, or if it had abandoned her because she was a hopeless sinner. She said the entire rosary, but it didn't help. She got her first period a few days later."[3]

In issue fifteen of 1989, Moran narrates her story "Catholic School" in the first person, describing her time at Catholic school in the period 1959 to 1966. We learn of how the nuns "wore black habits, bonnets and long black rosary beads that hung from their waists like a ball and chain," and about how Moran was disciplined by her instructor for disrupting the class. "Go up to the front of the room . . . and apologize to the Blessed Virgin Mary!!!" the angry nun tells Moran after pulling on her hair. "I was sent to the shrine of the B.V.M. . . . There was a snake around her feet. I was not sorry," says Moran, as her youthful visage glowers before the snake-strewn statue.[4]

Much like Crumb, Becker and Moran use comics to examine their childhood relationships with Catholicism, Moran doing so in an explicitly autobiographical form. Crumb says that many of his stories are about "left-over hang-ups from catholic school where the nuns were these big scary women who liked to pick on little boys so I developed this obsession to 'conquer' these big scary women and I'm still like that. . . . I never grew up."[5] Unlike Crumb's desire to "conquer" the women who shaped his spiritual upbringing, Becker's story depicts a young girl's confusion about the role faith can play in her burgeoning sexual desires and pubescent development, while Moran's reminiscences convey her childhood feelings about punishment and repentance in a way that does not sexualize her aggressor. Both stories show the power and potential of the comics medium to offer readers narrative and autobiographical accounts of Catholic school life, especially for readers who were not male. Although the constant parade of pulsating penises in *Zap Comix* were often used for their shock value (especially in Wilson's work), the women behind *Wimmen's Comix* regularly used religion an opportunity for exploring personal identity and sexuality in ways that not all underground comics creators did.

One underground artist who took a more thoughtful approach to exploring Catholicism in his work was Justin Green, whose 1972 book *Binky Brown Meets the Holy Virgin Mary* has been heralded as a classic work from this era. Whereas *Zap Comix* and *Wimmen's Comix* were anthologies featuring shorter works by numerous creators, *Binky Brown* was a full-length book at over forty pages long. The extended format of both *Binky Brown* and Green's 1976 follow-up effort *Sacred and Profane* allowed for more in-depth reflections about the author's personal faith and parochial school upbringing than any prior comic book, underground or otherwise. Crumb was especially encouraging of the confessional nature of Green's work: "He was the first guy to really just get down and reveal himself in a very personal way," he says.[6]

The cover of *Binky Brown*—which featured the tagline "Youngsters Prohibited" beneath its price tag—features the title character kneeling on the front lawn of a suburban home while a nun attempts to pry his jaw open: "Speak, my son," she commands. "But—my thoughts / No! / Impure thoughts / No!" Brown exclaims as he grabs his crotch.[7] A young woman wearing a plaid skirt hula-hoops behind him, and a long serpent winds its way down a tree and between Binky's legs. The scene combines imagery from the garden of Eden and middle America, but it also highlights the book's sexual themes through Green's rhetorical (" impure thoughts") and visual choices (the phallic snake slithering between Brown's legs as it slides past a jiggling schoolgirl).

Chronicling his younger years as a Catholic student as well as his obsessive-compulsive disorder, Green introduces himself to the reader as the book begins by confessing that the tale was created out of his need for autobiographical catharsis just as much as any desire to inform or entertain. Dangling naked from the ceiling while chained to a pulley, with a pen held tightly in his teeth as the song "Ave Maria" bellows from a record player, Green declares:

> O, my readers, the saga of Binky Brown is not intended solely for your entertainment, but also to purge myself of the compulsive neurosis which I have served since I officially left Catholicism on Halloween, 1958. You may deem my material as being too indulgent, morbid, and obscene. I daresay that many of you aspiring revolutionaries will conclude that instead of focusing on topics

FIGURE 24   Justin Green's *Binky Brown Meets the Holy Virgin Mary* (1972), page 8.

which would lend themselves to social issues, I have zero-ed in on the petty conflict in my crotch! My justification for undertaking this task is that many others are slaves to their neuroses. Maybe if they read about one neurotic's dilemma in easy-to-understand comic book format these tormented folks will no longer see themselves as mere food-tubes living in isolation. If all we neurotics were tied together we would entwine the globe many times over in a vast chain of common suffering—Please don't think I'm an asshole, Amen.[8]

The story begins with Green's stand-in, Binky, shattering his mother's statue of the Madonna while playing ball in the house, symbolically foreshadowing his eventual departure from the Catholic church. We learn about Brown's obsessive-compulsive tendencies as a young man and of how his developing sexuality gets intertwined with it. He also explores his burgeoning desires through his Catholic upbringing, such as his fantasies about one of the nuns at school: "The strands of hair that occasionally jutted from the tight white dome that bound Sister Virginia's forehead were as thrillingly illicit as those that might sneak out of a little nymphet's bikini!"[9]

Along the way, Green offers numerous observations about Catholicism, such as how countless young Catholics seem to envision the soul as resembling a set of lungs. "Maybe the reason why so many f-cked-up Catholic youngsters envision the soul in this semi-lung shape is that the sign of the cross spans the upper torso, which houses this vital organ. Also when the lungs cease to function, one 'gives up the ghost.' There are no holy signs below the waist, folks. . . . This lung-shaped soul accumulates sin like a smoker's lungs collect tar and nicotine. However, in most cases a trip to the confessional cleanses the soul," Green posits (sarcastically, we assume).[10]

Throughout *Binky Brown*, Green explores various Catholic practices such as Holy Communion, saying the rosary, penance, and confession as well as the connections between his sexual desires and obsessive-compulsive tendencies in such rituals. Green questions the seeming arbitrariness of what he calls Catholicism's "holy regulations," such as how one's sins become a kind of "debt [that] can be fulfilled with celestial coupons and/or sweat" or how the priest ends Binky's confession by saying "Hocus Pocus . . . you are absolved of your sins. Go now."[11]

At the end of the book, Binky Brown confronts the relationship between his religious childhood and his sexually motivated neuroses, with Green concluding (via evolutionary-themed language): "At long last, Binky has crept out of the primeval morass of superstition and guilt fostered by well-meaning institutions such as the Catholic church! While you may think his victory is a puny one, don't forget that just such desperate leaps as his were taken by our brave ancestors, the fish."[12]

Green followed up *Binky Brown Meets the Holy Virgin Mary* with *Sacred and Profane* in 1976, which collected the story "We Fellow Travelers" that was originally featured in the 1974 series *Comix Book* (a *Zap*-inspired anthology featuring work by Howard Cruse, Kim Deitch, Trina Robbins, Art Spiegelman, and Basil Wolverton that was published by a surprising entry into underground comic books—Marvel Comics). "We Fellow Travelers" continued the themes of neurosis and religious skepticism from *Binky Brown* and even brought back Binky's favorite nun, Sister Virginia. Centered on a "Saw-Church of Profanity," the story features a fake film called *The Cuss-Cross and Its Saw*, which begins, "As you know, Jesus, a nice Jewish boy from Nazareth, was framed a couple of thousand years ago. It's an old story, but it's always been big box office. To this, folks cry out his name when they're under stress," the film's narrator tells us (as we see a businessman cry out "Jesus Christ! I could've saved $14!!")[13]

Binky Brown himself also returns in a story called "Sweet Void of Youth" in which his "tormented antics" and "sexual/religious turmoil" are on further display as Green chronicles his early years as a cartoonist. Describing the tension between balancing artistic ambitions with hard work, Green notes in his narration, "Though Bink fancied himself as quite the rogue in his new role there was no getting away from ye olde puritan work ethic: if thou does not toil then thou art as a booger in God's eye" as we see Brown hard at work crosshatching his drawing of an "adulteress."[14]

The tale ends with Brown as a new father holding his child in his arms while debating whether to pursue a career as a cartoonist or a commercial sign painter. In weighing "the demands of survival" in his choice of artistic career paths,[15] Green uses Binky as an avatar for both childhood concerns surrounding his personal and spiritual development and the dilemma most artists (comics creators or otherwise) face as they mature surrounding how to provide for themselves financially while staying true to their artistic sensibilities. The fact that Green did so using the autobiographically inspired figure of Binky Brown in the 1970s points out that when comics creators began to use longer-form comics narratives (like those of the graphic novel) as a way of tackling more mature themes and topics, spiritual concerns were among the very first subjects to be explored in depth.

Comics scholar Hillary L. Chute describes *Binky Brown Meets the Holy Virgin Mary* as "the first work of autobiographical comics,"[16] although numerous cartoonists such as Milton Caniff, Al Capp, Chester Gould, and Ham

Fisher had done shorter autobiographical pieces in the 1940s.[17] "Binky Brown was powerful because it set the space for comics to be a realm of the intensely personal—a space to reveal, through words *and* pictures, what one might consider the purview of the especially private," says Chute.[18]

Artist Aline Kominsky-Crumb was an immediate fan of *Binky Brown*, describing how she saw it as "the first comic that directly regurgitated life into comic art." She says that Green's work inspired her to make her own comics: "The way that Justin portrayed his own tragic-comic life made it clear to me how I could approach the comic form directly and how the truth as I saw it could be more surreal and intense than anything I could ever fabricate."[19] *Binky Brown* was not just a major work in the history of Christian comics, it also plays a pioneering role in the burgeoning history of both autobiographical comics and the graphic novel.

Green was also instrumental in the development of the early career of Art Spiegelman, whose graphic novel *Maus* is the only comic to ever win a Pulitzer Prize to date. Spiegelman took his first step toward *Maus* with a three-page story by the same name for *Funny Animals* issue 1, a comix anthology edited by Green and Terry Zwigoff and featuring work by Green, Crumb, Bill Griffith, and others. As Chute notes, "there would be no 'Maus,' or *Maus*, without Green's *Binky Brown Meets the Holy Virgin Mary*," a sentiment that Spiegelman also expressed in his introduction to a 2009 edition of *Binky Brown*.[20]

Christian Comix: *Eternal Truth, Sammy Saved,* and *Holy Ghost Zapped Comix*

As underground comic books grew in popularity by the early 1970s, other publishers became aware of how titles such as *Zap Comix* and *Wimmen's Comix* reached an adult readership that comic books had not traditionally catered to. In turn, Christian publishers and independent creators alike saw an opening to use the tropes of comix as a way of spreading the gospel to an untapped group of young adults more interested in countercultural pursuits than in traditional religious or cultural institutions. One small publisher, Sonday Funnies Comic Corporation (note the pun), offered several titles that borrowed their look from series such as *Zap Comix*, including *Eternal Truth* and *Sammy Saved and Al Most*. The covers echoed the visual design strategies of various *Zap* issues, while their linework paralleled Crumb's "rubbery, polymorphous characters."[21] Both might be mistaken at first glance for the work of Crumb and his contemporaries, which is exactly the point. Christian comix deliberately imitated their sexually explicit counterparts as a way of getting new readers (and potentially new converts to the flock) to pick them up.

Eternal Truth was created by artist Jim Phillips in a style highly influenced by Crumb's artwork. Phillips would go on to become a major artist in the surfing and skateboard communities, designing art for numerous skateboard decks as well as the 1988 skater comic book *Road Rash*. Phillips also designed concert posters for musicians such as Gregg Allman, James Brown, George Clinton, Jerry Garcia, and Tom Petty.

Although *Eternal Truth* is an attempt to reach a new generation of comics readers, it also draws on some of the earliest work that used comics to spread the gospel—literally quoting from one of Max Gaines's *Picture Stories from the Bible* editorial advisory council members, Dr. Francis C. Stifler (who both Gaines and Phillips credit as the editorial secretary of the American Bible Society). Phillips cites Stifler's praise for the pedagogic potential of comics and the idea that "since the comic strip is the language of many millions of boys and girls in America, why not let God speak to them their own tongue."[22] The quote is used unironically even as the issue as a whole evokes the satirical tradition of underground comix, uniting Phillip's approach in that subversive tradition with the earliest examples of Christian comics three decades earlier. In each case, both Phillips and Gaines saw the value of linking their attempts at proselyting in comics form to larger authoritative institutions, thereby lending their work a greater sense of legitimacy in the eyes of those who might doubt its value.

Sammy Saved was written and drawn by Craig Yoe and featured various characters sharing their personal experiences with Christ as they encounter various strangers, a practice known as "witnessing." Yoe also includes a parody of the famous Charles Atlas ads for his strength-training program ("Wanted! Spiritual Weaklings to Become He-Men"),[23] lampooning advertising practices in mainstream comics in a way that models the sardonic spirit of other comix of the era.

But Yoe's work in Christian publishing did not last long. He went on to work as a toy designer and then for Jim Henson before later launching his own publishing imprint that specialized in reprinting some of the most lurid works in comics history. In 2009, *Secret Identity: The Fetish Art of Superman's Co-Creator Joe Shuster* collected the erotic artwork done by Shuster in the 1950s for a sadomasochistic series of comics called *Nights of Horror* that centered on bondage and discipline.

Yoe also edited such collections as *Clean Cartoonists' Dirty Drawings*, which featured risqué work by popular artists such as *Beetle Bailey*'s Mort

Walker, *Archie*'s Dan DeCarlo, and *Joe Palooka*'s Ham Fisher as well as more provocative images from Shuster. Yoe has also edited reprints of various pre–Comics Code Authority horror comics and published a collection of stories about Satan from various 1950s horror series entitled *Devil Tales* under his Yoe Books imprint. Several of the stories featured in *Devil Tales* (including ones discussed in the previous chapter from such series as *Voodoo* and *The Unseen*) illustrate how the interests of some Christian comics creators evolved considerably in their later careers.

Comix were also coopted by the Christian publisher Logos, which released four issues of *Holy Ghost Zapped Comix* (*HGZC*) beginning in 1973. Initially created by cartoonist Steve Gregg in 1971 as an independent release, Logos printed new versions of the series starting in 1973. Each issue has an *HGZC* insignia in the top left corner, although issues 2, 3, and 4 all feature new titles on their covers: "The Growthbook," "New Creature Comix!" and "Jews for Jesus," respectively. The first three issues all feature a similar cover design strategy, while the fourth features a full-page image of a group of Jews holding signs proclaiming their support for Jesus Christ (including one that reads "Jesus Makes Us Kosher"). The tagline of issue 4 promises tales about such biblical Jews as Abraham, Lot, David, and King Saul, along with "Baruch Zimmerman & His Wonderdog Ignatz!"

Gregg had previously worked on a series of comics with writer Robert Forester in a smaller booklet format in 1971—"You're Invited," "Confessions of a Wise Guy" and "God Leads a Sheltered Life"—under the company name Three Jesus People Comics. *HGZC* issue 1 is much less stylized than Phillip's *Eternal Truth* and also far less satirical than Yoe's *Sammy Saved*, making it far less memorable than those issues aside from the obvious ways it draws on Crumb's *Zap Comix*. Gregg includes allegorical stories such as "Lazarus and the Rich Man" in the first issue as well as a retelling of the book of Genesis in "The Continuing Story of Man & God Act 1." These tales are told simply and seem like they would be a good fit for younger readers. He also includes a story about a young man who wants to "go get loaded" and runs into the devil after fleeing from a "Jesus freak." There is also an editorial that draws on countercultural rhetoric as well as that used by anti-secularists:

> I'm here, basicly [sic], to tell you how to "escape the system" and I'll tell you right now that your problem isn't, in fact, parents, the pigs, pregnancy, the president, dope, etc. These may be "symptoms" . . . you know what symptoms are . . . they are not the problem! They are the evidence that a problem exists! Now I'll tell you what the problem really is: it's the world! That's right! The

FIGURE 25 *Holy Ghost Zapped Comix* 1 (1973).

Greek word is "cosmos," which also means "the system." Now the only reason this "world system" is a problem at all is that it is run, according to Jesus, by the Devil! And this is a problem because human beings are born into the system and are under the tyranny of the system ... which is the Devil's domain! In other words every human is born a mind slave of Satan's! Because of this, we see war, murder, rape, addiction, etc. Everyone is doing what Satan wants.[24]

Although it uses the lingo of its day, the message here directly echoes that found in *If The Devil Would Talk* two decades earlier. *HGZC* strikes several different tones and appears to be aimed at several different audiences: both younger ones with its simplistic biblical tales and more mature readers who might be questioning society and their role in it. The Catechetical Guild found the anti-secularist message of the heavy-handed *If the Devil Would Talk* too controversial for distribution in the 1950s, but when that message was delivered in the gentler form of *HGZC* it seems Logos was less concerned two decades later.

Logos was an established publisher of such nonfiction Christian books as *The Holy Spirit and You*, *Hear My Confession*, *The Real Faith*, and *Prison to Praise*. The latter is an autobiography by Rev. Merlin C. Carothers about his work as an army chaplain in World War II that was published in 1970. It was turned into a comic book in 1974 along with adaptations of other Logos titles such as *Run Baby Run* and *Ben Israel*, all of which were based on true stories of finding Christian faith under difficult circumstances. *Run Baby Run* chronicled the life changes of Puerto Rican gang leader Nicky Cruz, while *Ben Israel* recounted Jewish author Arthur Katz's transformation from atheist to Christian. The comic-book versions were not written specifically for children but rather for a reader of any age, indicative of a new strategy that previous Christian comics publishers had not attempted: offering the same story in different publishing formats as a way of reaching a wider range of readers.

Run Baby Run and *Prison to Praise* were adapted by veteran comics artist Tony Tallarico, whose work for publishers such as Harvey, Dell, and Charlton included a wide range of genres on such titles as *Texas Rangers*, *Mysteries of Unexplored Worlds*, *Eerie*, *Fightin' Army*, *Hot Rods and Racing Cars*, and *Just Married*. Tallarico had also adapted several popular television series to comics in the 1960s, including *Bewitched*, *Bozo the Clown*, *Car 54 Where Are You?*, and *F-Troop*. Much like how Reed Crandall and Joe Sinnott were hired to work on titles such as *Treasure Chest*, Logos saw value in using an established creator such as Tallarico to give their comics a style that matched many mainstream books currently on the market, even if he had more experience adapting *Bozo* and *Bewitched* than biblical tales.

Chick Tracts

In the early 1970s, there was a major shift in comics from Christian publishers. *Treasure Chest* released its last issue in 1972 after more than twenty-five years of bringing scripture-inspired stories to generations of parochial school students. New companies such as Logos and Spire filled the gap, but they were distributed in retail outlets such as Christian bookstores instead of classrooms, meaning that readers had to seek them out rather than get them for free as so many schoolkids had.

But an entirely new type of Christian comic was gaining widespread distribution—often showing up in the unlikeliest of places. Jack Chick found success with his line of Chick Tracts, small pamphlet-like comics measuring 2.8 by 5 inches. The format parallels the longer history of text-based tracts that had been used to spread Christian ideas for centuries; missionaries had been using small pamphlets to spread the gospel in new ways since the eighteenth century.[25] Chick updated the idea to use comics for similar purposes, hoping to gain a new audience by using panels instead of paragraphs to reach new converts.

The origins of Chick's work were in the late 1950s, when he did church outreach work with prisoners. Chick took a flipboard into prison and used his own drawings to teach inmates about the gospel, inspiring one of his first tracts, *This Was Your Life*, which was published in the early 1960s.[26] The tract features a skull-faced grim reaper holding a scythe (an image that predates Christianity, stemming from the figure of Chronos in Greek mythology)[27] and claiming a man's life. The man is buried and an angel takes his soul to heaven for judgment. Scenes from his life are replayed in which he committed various sins and turned away from God ("Bunk—I don't need Christ! There's nothing wrong with me! I'll make it *my* way!" a younger version of the man says as he rejects a pastor's outstretched hand).[28] When the man's name is not found in the Book of Life, his soul is taken to hell and cast into a lake of fire. The panel includes a passage from the book of Revelation: "And whosoever was not found written in the Book of Life was cast into the lake of fire. Revelation 20:15."[29]

The tract's final page is entirely prose text describing the steps that anyone can take to get into heaven, starting by admitting that you are a sinner

FIGURE 26   Advertisement for Jack Chick's line of tracts.

and accepting Jesus Christ as your personal savior. Chick wrote and drew a few more tracts through late 1960s, including *Why No Revival?*, *The Beast*, *Somebody Goofed*, and *A Demon's Nightmare*, but his publishing business had grown by 1972, when he hired artist Fred Carter to draw his scripts.[30] The output of tracts increased steadily throughout the 1970s. In 1972, he tackled topics such as evolution in *Big Daddy* and popular culture in *Bewitched?* (decrying witchcraft and the occult in shows such as *Bewitched* and board games such as *Ouija*). There were also stories set in the future and distant past, such as *The Last Generation* (1972), about a dystopian America in which the government bans Christianity, and *Humbug!* (1975), which retold *A Christmas Carol* as an explicitly Christian allegory of Scrooge's salvation.

In keeping with how Chick's work began with inmates, prisons soon became one of many places where his tracts were found, reaching a literally captive audience who might be receptive to a different kind of proselytizing. Actor Danny Trejo, who spent time in numerous prisons before his Hollywood career, recalls how finding a Chick Tract comic while in solitary confinement started him on a spiritual path toward asking God for help to change his life.

Trejo recalls how prisoners often exchanged pornographic letters. He received one from a convict named Bambi "with a comic book that been used as a weight. I glanced at it, then turned my attention to the love letter. Bambi had written a graphic description of sex. It was *dirty* dirty—it didn't sit right with me. So instead I turned my attention to the comic. It was one of those small pamphlets with Christian themes that floated around the prison. This one was called "Joe's Woes." It was about a guy named Joe who had an alcohol problem. Joe couldn't get on top of his problem and was resistant to the idea that there was a spiritual solution."[31]

Although there is no Chick Tract called "Joe's Woes," the title Trejo describes is similar to one named *Happy Hour* about a man who turns to the church instead of alcohol for fulfilment. Trejo recalls how the comic made him remember the advice from an Alcoholics Anonymous meeting he attended at age fifteen: "In that cell God killed the old me, made a new Danny Trejo, and said, 'Now let's see what you do with him,'" the actor says.[32] The tract had a major impact on his life, achieving Chick's desired effect of using a randomly accessed comic to reach those who might not otherwise be open to a spiritual message.

The randomness through which Trejo encountered the tract is a key part of Chick's distribution strategy for his comics. The publisher encourages Christian readers to leave their comics in places where the general public might find them as a form of missionary outreach to non-Christians. The Chick Publications catalogue even offers instructions on the best places to leave the tracts, such as airports, restaurants, grocery stores ("Leave Chick tracts on shelves and bulletin boards. Hand one to the cashier"), hospitals, park benches, vending-machine trays, photocopiers ("Leave a tract under the flap"), gas-station washrooms, arcades ("Leave tracts on the games"), clothing-store dressing rooms, libraries ("Place tracts in returning books"), bowling alleys ("In rented shoes, at the lane"), with checks to pay bills, and at drive-through windows ("Place money inside a tract and give it to the cashier).

The publisher also encourages giving tracts away at Halloween to trick-or-treaters even though its tracts decry the supposed evils of the holiday and recommends giving them to police officers in the hope of avoiding a ticket or arrest while driving ("If you get pulled over, cheerfully hand one to the officer").[33] Religious studies scholar James R. Lewis describes how the smaller format of the comics lend themselves to surreptitious distribution: "Small and cheap, any evangelist could buy a few hundred Chick tracts and leave them wherever the casual passerby might pick them up—laundromats, telephone booths, bus station benches, etc."[34] The strategy presumes that many such encounters with these comics will be unwanted ones, but it also places faith in the pattern of how mainstream comic books were passed along by one reader to another in earlier decades. Those who pass out these tracts hope that eventually they will reach a receptive reader, even if the majority of those who pick them up might reject their message.

But that message is often seen as more than just an evangelical one. Chick Tracts have been deemed hate literature by several groups. The Southern Poverty Law Center has declared Chick Publications a hate group and the Canadian government has banned certain tracts from being imported into the country.[35] Jack Chick defended his work against the label of "hate literature" in a 1996 column of his *Battle Cry* newsletter, stating: "The term 'Hate Literature' has been used by Satan as far back as the time of Martin Luther. It is supposed to shake the confidence of those proclaiming the gospel." He saw those who accused him of spewing hate as "the enemy" who "must increase his attacks" in the face of Chick's ever-growing success in reaching the unsaved.[36]

Chick noted that he wasn't accused of spreading hate until he released *The Gay Blade* in 1972, one of several tracts that are excessively cruel in how they treat homosexuality as a sin.[37] Warning that a "Gay Revolution is Underway!" *The Gay Blade* pits queerness against society: "out of Satan's shadowy world of homosexuality, in a display of defiance against society, they come forth—those who suffer the agony of rejection, the despair of unsatisfied longing—desiring—endless lusting and remorse crying that gay is good—their tragic lives prove that there isn't anything gay about being 'gay.'" Chick reminds readers that God punished the Sodomites in the Old Testament "to keep the filth and brutality from spreading."[38] He warns readers that in the current era, "New laws are encouraging the Sodomites (homosexuals) to take the offensive" by claiming that anyone who opposes homosexuality is a bigot. "Only Christ can overcome this demonic power that controls them," says Chick, who ranks queerness as "one of many sins" alongside "murder, lying, adultery, drunkenness, etc."[39] He extends this notion of queerness as a demonic force on a visual level in the tract *Home Alone?* in which a babysitter (Coach Brad: "26 years old. Everybody likes Brad, and women are nuts about him") looks after a ninth grade boy named Charlie. As they "watch late-night cable TV" together, Brad apparently rapes Charlie, although the act is not directly shown. We are told that "Charlie knows nothing about God or morals. His teachers were no help. He has no defenses. To oppose the coach would be 'intolerant.' This made it easy for Brad to destroy his innocence. The spirit that oppressed Brad now invaded Charlie," Chick's narration tells us, accompanied by an image of a demonic, fork-tongued spirit moving from out of Brad's body to wrap its hands around Charlie.[40]

Chick continued his condemnation of queer people in other tracts such as *Doom Town* and *Sin City*, both of which use the story of Sodom and

Gomorrah to frame homosexuality as a deliberate choice and as rebellion against God: "Rebellion is as the sin of witchcraft. *All* who rebel against God will be cast into the lake of fire," Chick writes, quoting from the book of 1 Samuel as we see an angel towering high above a lake of hellfire. *Sin City* also features a gay character named Reverend Ray who has a change of heart once he learns more about the Sodomites: "Oh God, I'm in trouble.... How many young people have I enticed into the gay lifestyle?" cries Ray, with Chick again framing homosexuality as a lifestyle choice rather than in biological terms. "I'm facing God, covered with the responsibility of *ruining* their lives. I've held rallies and gay pride parades. I've cursed pastors as being bigots! I've even preached that *Jesus* was gay! Will *that* put me into hell?" he asks.[41]

The emphasis on Christians being falsely accused of bigotry is a repeated pattern in Chick's work. But along with overtly condemning queer people, his comics also regularly reinforce numerous racist tropes, especially in how they depict Arabic and Latinx people. In *Is Allah Like You?*, Chick depicts domestic violence as a man's right according to the Qur'an, even though many Muslim communities and scholars have reinterpreted the verse (chapter 4, verse 34) to preclude such violence.[42] The same interpretation condoning violence against women has been used by some Christians regarding the passage from Ephesians 5:22–23 ("Wives, submit to your husbands as to the Lord").[43] The artwork in *Is Allah Like You?* distorts the facial features of male Muslims, making their noses and ears unnaturally large as a way of demonizing them visually. As cultural scholar Jack G. Shaheen notes, large noses are a visual stereotype used to villainize both Jews and Arabs in popular culture, such as the "hook-nosed" villains in Disney's animated *Aladdin* films.[44]

The same pattern occurs in *Camel's in the Tent*, in which a Muslim man's nose takes up half of his face (which is not the case in how non-Muslim figures are drawn in the same tract). Chick describes how Muslims intend to "invade" various nations, stating that England is currently "losing control" and is getting "closer to accepting Sharia law." He describes a five-point "pattern of conquest" at work in how Muslims are attempting to bring the Qur'an's Sharia law to new nations: "Infiltrate (Move in) / Populate (Grow large families and recruit others) / Legislate (Make laws against converting Muslims) / Decimate (Take over the country little by little, one city at a time) / Eliminate (Destroy those who do not submit to Sharia law)." This five-point list comes alongside an image of a machine-gun-toting figure—face fully covered—and the declaration that "America's next!"[45] The vilifying rhetoric ("infiltrate," "take over," "destroy") matches that used by various anti-immigration forces as a fear-mongering tactic and is doubly emphasized when paired with the image of what we are clearly meant to assume is a gun-toting terrorist.

This visual distortion is also seen in how Chick Tracts depict Latinx people. The facial features of Latinx characters are often drawn in exaggerated ways that emphasize various stereotypes. Chick created relatively few tracts with Latinx characters, yet most revolve around stereotypes of poverty (*Tiny Shoes* about a rural Mexican family and a boy named Juanito whose only wish is to own a pair of shoes), and violence (*Gomez Is Coming*, about gang violence). Latinx characters in those two tracts are regularly drawn with more cross-hatching and shading techniques than white characters are in other tracts in ways that make such characters appear unkempt, emphasizing their lower-class status and reinforcing stereotypes for some readers.

Even Chick's defenders occasionally admit to such racist tropes. In *The Art of Jack T. Chick*, Kurt Kuersteiner describes the excessive use of tattoos on the gang members in *Gomez Is Coming*: "Speaking of tattoos, check out some of the stereotypical Mexican styles: Gomez has tear drops etched next to his eye and a spider on his neck. One of his henchmen has a web tattooed next to his eyes."[46]

Lewis notes that "although many people who have seen them are appalled by the tracts, the theology of Chick Publications is squarely aligned with the mainstream of fundamentalist Christianity"; the comics format and "the focus on the enemies of 'Real Christians' make Chick Publications appear more offensive than other ministries."[47] Regardless of the specific subgroup being represented and/or confronted, Chick's tracts revolve around several recurring themes: the notion that all human beings are horrible sinners who need to repent and accept the Lord in order to achieve salvation, that a fiery hell full of endless torment and insufferable brimstone awaits us if we don't accept Jesus as our personal savior, that there is only one true God and we must turn away from any and all earthly pursuits that distract us from believing otherwise, and that affairs of the heart are no match for that which benefits the soul. Chick's work generally adheres to a Christian fundamentalist world view, stemming from a conservative Protestant belief in older, established moral and social values over progressive ones.[48] It rejects evolution in favor of creationism, and it portrays gender (and its associated social roles) and sexuality in traditional ways, in keeping with the fundamentalist belief that the Bible must be understood in a literal sense instead of allowing any reinterpretation that fits with social advances.

Much of the imagery depicting Satan and hell in various Chick Tracts matches that found in comic books of earlier decades and in the religious artwork of earlier centuries—from the burning pits and the lake of fire to the hooved and horned red devils inhabiting that fiery realm. Chick also draws God as a robed, glowing, and faceless entity sitting on a giant throne, towering above all others in heaven. Such imagery would later be seen in the 1990s Vertigo series *Preacher* by Garth Ennis and Steve Dillon, albeit in a far less reverent way than Chick's.

Many Chick Tracts use a slippery-slope argument in warning against the supposed dangers of popular culture, such as how listening to rock music (in the tract *Angels?*) and playing Dungeons and Dragons (*Dark Dungeons*) can put you on a path toward Satanism. The tracts also deem music festivals a forum for "drugs, alcohol and immoral sex [designed] to keep you away from the Savior." Satan organizes one in *Party Girl*: "Master, we've loaded the city with drugs and alcohol," a demon tells Satan. "Your music is also ready. We've booked the hottest groups in the world. Your warehouses are packed with low-grade condoms. And hundreds of volunteers are ready to give them away." Satan replies, "The Souls of *all* these party-goers belong to me. And I don't intend to lose a single one!"[49]

Even reading *Harry Potter* books leads to satanic ends, according to Chick: "The Potter books opened a doorway that led untold millions of kids to hell" (*The Nervous Witch*).[50] Celebrating Halloween leads to the same fate, according to several tracts (*Happy Halloween, The Trick, Spooky, Boo!*), which declare that "Halloween opens the door to Satanism" and that "Satan loves Halloween because it glamorizes the powers of darkness, drawing little kids into his camp." In turn, glamorizing Halloween could lead to a rise in human sacrifices, because "to satanists and witches, Halloween is not joke. It is their most solemn ceremony of the year. As we get closer to the Second Coming of Jesus . . . Satanism will increase. So will human sacrifice!"[51]

Chick regularly uses an elaborate approach to cause and effect to describe the consequences of rejecting God. In *Titanic*, it is implied that the famous ship sank because a character named Chester rejected his aunt's efforts to convert him: "Ha! Ha! Ha! . . . Doesn't she know that God Himself couldn't sink this ship?" he laughs.[52] Chick also sees a connection between not taking Thanksgiving seriously enough and the decline of Christian belief in America: "Thanksgiving was once our most honored day. But today it's a joke. . . . We're not thankful for *anything*. And this offends God. When any nation stops being thankful and forgets God, it's headed for judgement," says a character in *The Missing Day*.[53]

Many of Chick's stories use the fate of children in highly manipulative ways. In *Trust Me!*, a young boy is lured off of the street and given a pill to try, which leads to a life of crime to support his burgeoning drug habit and then to becoming a dealer. He gets arrested and locked up, where he is raped, contracts AIDS, and dies in prison (but not before repenting his sins and accepting the Lord, which gets him into heaven). Chick also uses sick kids as a recurring focus; *Cathy* and *The Little Princess* are both about young girls on their deathbeds whose families find peace in their deaths because the girls have accepted Christ.

Perhaps the most indefensible tract was *Lisa*, which takes a callous approach toward sexual abuse as a way of preaching about salvation. When a neighbor confronts a father named Henry about abusing his daughter, he tells the dad, "I'll keep quiet, old buddy, if we can share and share alike." When a doctor confronts him about the abuse after Lisa is diagnosed with herpes, Henry blames his wife for "pulling away" and his neighbor for conspiring with him: "I can't even make a decent friend. I guess I'm a total failure."[54]

Instead of reporting the crime, the doctor uses it as an opportunity to convert Henry, who soon repents his sins and accepts Jesus as his savior. The story ends not with any arrests but with a reconciliation between Henry his wife and a promise to never hurt Lisa again—turning child abuse into a sermon about repentance and forgiveness. "Oh, Henry, God has forgiven both of us. I feel like a new person. I love you and I love Lisa. Will she ever forgive us? We must never hurt her again" says his wife, Linda, who admits to physically abusing her daughter. "We've got wonderful news, Lisa. Your daddy and I will never hurt you again," Linda says as the story concludes.[55] Created in 1984, *Lisa* proved so offensive that it was no longer distributed by 1991.

Chick's defenders and apologists shrug off the extreme aspects of his work, often claiming that those who take offense to it are just promoting a liberal sense of political correctness or simply lack a sense of humor. Kuersteiner prefaces *The Art of Jack T. Chick* with the warning that "if you have no sense of humor about controversial matters, we urge you to avoid this book. Our intent is not to offend or pick on any particular group, but to discuss matters in an entertaining way that some people take very seriously." He states explicitly, "This is not a politically correct book," drawing on the phrase that became popular among conservatives in the 1990s as a way of describing liberals as easily triggered killjoys and the political equivalent of helicopter parents. "It's difficult to enjoy Chick's work if you get upset every time he makes you laugh at someone else's expense," says Kuersteiner, adding that "these are, after all, *comics*, and 'funny books' are meant to be funny. So relax and enjoy yourself."[56]

Similarly, collector Robert B. Fowler opens his book *The World of Jack T. Chick* with the declaration that Chick's tracts "spare no one's feelings" and that "Even if you do not go along with Chick's philosophy (you sinner), you have to respect the commitment and theatrical talents evident in his scripts."[57] These empty reassurances are meant to convince us that Chick's work is all in good fun, that it's not about your feelings and you just need to have a sense of humor about how Chick makes you laugh in his blunt-yet-theatrical condemnation of "any particular group." But usually when you are told to relax or to take a joke, the topic is neither relaxing nor comical.

Some comics readers separate the extreme content of Chick's work from his craft, acknowledging the effectiveness of the tracts for the purposes of propaganda even if they take exception to the message being spread. In a 1979 correspondence with Fowler, Robert Crumb described Chick's work as having "interesting and intense" artwork. He noted that "the guy's world outlook is so psycho and so twisted" and displays a sense of "sick morality . . . that] pervades all his work" (which is quite the assessment when it comes from the creator of *Zap Comix*). "On one level," says Crumb, "it's really stupid and disgusting, authoritarian, fascistic, etc. The way he views humanity is so warped. But the books are really interesting because, sick as his stuff is, it's so *well done*. Like Nazi propaganda or something."[58]

Crumb's faint praise has been seized upon by Chick's supporters as positive peer support, but the founder of *Zap Comix* is clearly admiring the craft while damning the content. Similar assessments have been made of D. W. Griffith's *Birth of a Nation* (1915) and Leni Reifenstahl's *Triumph of the Will*, both of which have been praised for how they advanced their respective art forms (feature filmmaking and documentary cinema) while at the same time they have been condemned for their propagation of the Ku Klux Klan and the Nazi party.

Other comics creators have parodied Chick Tracts in recent decades as a way of decoding their rhetorical and propagandistic strategies. In 1989, Dan Clowes parodied Chick in the first issue of his award-winning series *Eightball* with the story "Devil Doll?" (in which role-playing games, pornography, tarot cards, Ouija boards, and heavy metal music are all paths to Satanism).[59] In 1996, Jim Woodring's *Jesus Delivers* came in the form a mini-comic similar to that of Chick Tracts. Woodring, who has won an Eisner, a Harvey, and an Ignatz for such works as *Jim* and *Frank*, tells the story of an Indian boy named Purna who encounters a Christian missionary from America and then immediately tries to convert his mother: "You see, Ma, it's like this: Jesus is the only true Son of God, and he alone can save us from eternal damnation. All humans are born wicked; only Jesus can save us from hell!" he says. "And how does he do that?" his mother asks. "That's not for you to worry about," replies Purna. "Your job is to recognize the truth and repent! The religion you raised me in is false! It won't save us from hell!" he cries. "Frankly, Purna, I don't believe that. I believe that God is loving and just," his mother tells him. "Don't try to tell me about God! I'm an expert since I became a Christian a few minutes ago! God *is* all-loving! That's why he wants to save you from his terrible wrath!" declares Purna. "Doesn't that seem a little self-contradictory to you?" asks his mother, as Woodring mocks Chick's polemical tactics.[60]

Ultimately, Chick took pride in the fact that his comics made many uncomfortable. As religious scholar Jason C. Bivens notes, Chick's work embodied a "culture of fear" designed to scare readers into changing their lives, reveling in moral panic as a way "simultaneously to raise and symbolically to resolve terrors, establishing normative and behavioral guidelines" in his comics "which fold safety, certainty and sanctity together."[61] Chick saw it as his job to cause distress if it made more readers repent their sins and accept the Lord. In the 1993 tract *He Never Told Us!*, Chick includes testimonials from several apparent readers about how his comics changed their life. "Sometimes Chick tracts make people squirm," reads one caption, followed by the account of one reader, who says, "When I was in the world, I used to pick up your tracts and squirm, but I would read them. They planted some good seeds, which helped me find the Lord."[62]

But Chick's work was intended to do more than just make people uncomfortable. He sought to break down the reader's critical defenses through a frequent combination of extreme emotional pleas and a selective, partisan approach to the facts and ideologies presented. That is the very definition of propaganda.

Crusader Comics

In 1974, Chick introduced a new format in his crusade to inculcate new followers. While the surreptitious format of Chick Tracts allowed them to chisel away at a reader's beliefs, his new series of thirty-two-page comic books functioned like a sledgehammer—offering heavier and more sustained pressure in how their messages were delivered. Published under the Crusader Comics banner (although reprints refer to them as "The Crusaders"), each issue's cover featured a tagline announcing them as "Recommended Reading for Adults and Teens." Although many of the smaller Chick Tracts were intended to find younger readers, Chick's "personal assistant" told the *Chicago Tribune* in 1981 that the Crusader titles were "written for teen-agers and adults who "might not otherwise find Christ's message."[63] The publisher's catalogue explicitly positions the comic books as teen oriented, with promotional rhetoric asking: "What's coming *out* of your teenager? What's going *in*? Their minds are fed 95% of the time with evil from every direction. How do you balance what's going into them? Try Chick comic books that teach godly ideas."[64]

Each issue has a different title and tackles a different subject—from the threats of satanism and communism to the supposed dangers of exorcisms, Druids, and the scientific theory of evolution to depictions of biblical events such as the rapture and Noah's ark. The series features a pair of recurring protagonists who play either a starring or supporting role in each issue, Timothy Emerson Clark and James Carter, who serve as pseudo secret agents for an enigmatic Christian organization. In the first story, "Operation Bucharest," we are introduced to Clark and Carter as they smuggle microfilm into Russia so that new Bibles can be printed on an "underground printing press." Tim, a white man, is described as a former "green beret with the special forces" who "speaks eight languages fluently."[65]

Carter, a Black man, is described as having a less illustrious background as a former drug lord: "He was the head of a narcotics ring—an expert in street fighting trained as a black militant. He has a black belt in karate!" Carter was converted by a local pastor who told him about Christ just as the militant drug trafficker was about to cut the pastor's throat: "Man! That's outta sight! Why didn't someone tell me this before?" said Carter. When told by the pastor that he can become a "new man" if he accepts Christ, Carter replied, "This is heavy, preacher! I'll have to clean up my life first!" The pastor shot back, "No way! You can't clean it up! He wants you just the way you are!" before kneeling to pray with Carter on the sidewalk.[66]

There are clear racial undertones to Carter's origins as a knife-wielding, tough-talking drug kingpin, especially in contrast to Clark's former life as a special forces operative (during which he became the only man to escape a sneak attack during the Vietnam war when he was "dropped behind enemy lines on a top-secret mission"). Carter is a reformed criminal while Clark is war hero. Clark is introduced to the reader as "a radiant Christian" while Carter is positioned as "one bad dude."[67] "Operation Bucharest" directly addresses their interracial partnership. The pair speaks to a Russian crowd that mistakenly believes that Carter is dating a white woman. "It looks like my Black brother made your people unhappy," Clark tells the woman. Chick uses this moment to take a seeming stand against bigotry as Clark describes how "people are all the same the world over—there is bigotry in every country, every town, village and neighborhood."[68]

But accepting a lesson about bigotry from Chick leaves one feeling hollow, given how many different groups of people he attacked and condemned throughout his career. Kuersteiner claims that Chick was doing anti-racist work in the Crusader titles, an absurd idea given how often he targeted and scapegoated racial minorities and made them subject to visual stereotyping in his work. "Chick was among the first to use comics to criticize racism, especially among Christians," says Kuersteiner. "This was not just a fad either: "He jumped into the cause with both feet, making one of his two regular *Crusader* heroes an African-American," he argues.[69]

But while Chick might not have harbored any overt ill will toward Black people in the same way that he targeted LGTBQ+ and Muslim communities, he still resorted to numerous stereotypes in representing Black culture, such as Carter's "street fighting" drug-lord origins. Chick also had Fred Carter redraw numerous existing tracts to—in the word of the publisher's catalogue—"make them more effective for reaching black readers." Referred to as "Black Tracts,"[70] in these new versions, stories such as *Charlie's Ants* became *Kura's Ants* and *One Way* become *The Only Way*, using Black characters to teach the gospel rather than white ones. But many lean into stereotypes, whether in their use of slang (*Best Friend* becomes *Soul Sisters*, while *Hi There!* Becomes *Wassup?*) or in their clichéd depictions of gangs, street violence, and drugs (*The Peace Maker* and *It's a Deal* both center on a different violent character nicknamed Ice Man, for instance).

What *is* laudable is how Fred Carter's artwork does not resort to stereotypical physical exaggerations of nonwhite characters, as it does in tracts such as *Gomez Is Coming* and *Camel in the Tent*. Carter's artwork for the Crusader Comics line is similar in style to that of Marvel and DC artist Neil Adams, who drew *Batman*, *Green Lantern*, and *The Avengers* in the early 1970s. Adams has been praised for bringing a more realistic art style to the superhero genre in this era and for drawing Black characters such as John Stewart in *Green Lantern* in a way that strives for naturalism, especially with facial features.[71] The third Crusader issue, *Scar Face*, set entirely in Africa between the 1930s and 1970s, uses relatively realistic artwork in depicting Black characters from a wide range of classes, from villagers to missionaries to government officials.

But even if we applaud such efforts, much of the content found in the Crusader titles is just as sensationalized as the worst of Chick's tracts—and if anything, Chick and Carter offered more gruesome takes on similar subjects, given the older audiences who read these comic books. The second issue, *The Broken Cross*, finds the heroic team of Clark and Carter taking down a group

FIGURE 27 The second issue of Jack Chick's line of Crusader Comics shows satanism leading to cannibalism; *The Broken Cross* (1974), page 14.

of satanists who have been sacrificing kidnapped hitchhikers. The issue is far more graphically violence than the Chick Tracts, which were apparently written for all ages. Sacrificial blood drips from a knife, a goblet, and a young girl's neck in two panels, for example.

In another scene, Tim and Jim encounter a cannibal wandering the highway while snacking on human fingers (accompanied by sound effects: "Slurp!" / "Chomp Chomp"). "This is satanism in its worst stage," Tim declares.[72] The scene is based on a real-life incident involving Stanley Dean Baker, who confessed to murdering a man named James Schlosser and eating his heart in 1970. California Highway Patrol officers found a human finger in Baker's pocket as well as a copy of the book *The Satanic Bible*.[73] Baker, who was under the influence of LSD, said the killing was satanically motivated, but he also claimed during his trial that he was Jesus Christ and that he had caused Jimi Hendrix's fatal overdose via mind control.[74]

Whether influenced by drugs, Satan, or mental illness, Baker's actions are used only as a brief subplot in the exploration of satanic cults in *The Broken Cross*. Chick explains in a footnote that the finger-chomping scene is based on the reported incident, but the overall agenda of the issue is to stage multiple scenes of young white women being sacrificed by hooded satanists. In the climatic moments, Tim and Jim use the power of prayer to make a group of knife-wielding satanists suddenly convulse and vomit, allowing them enough time to rescue a girl named Jody from death. Jody throws her pentagram necklace into a fiery pile of burning objects (which also include a Ouija board and a horoscope book) and declares, "Lucifer gave me power . . . but the price was terrible depression and constant fear! He tricked me! Thank God for the precious blood of Jesus Christ!"[75]

Like most of Chick's work, *The Broken Cross* takes a blunt approach to its subject matter, emphasizing shock and spectacle over nuance and reason. Chick's writing lacks subtlety, whether he's presenting complex ideas or even just staging action scenes: as Jim bursts into the room to rescue Jody, the black robed satanists shout "Get him! Kill! Kill! Kill!"[76]

Other issues tackled similar subjects as Chick's tracts: *Primal Man?* advocates for creationism over evolution, *Spellbound?* warns against the dangers of rock music and Halloween; and *Angels of Light* denounces Mormons and Masons. And as much as Chick might believe himself to be an advocate against bigotry, the eighth issue—*The Gift* (1977)—contains both racist and homophobic dialogue from a character named Marsha, who Jim and Tim have saved from a suicide attempt. When Jim's girlfriend, Tanya Robinson, allows Marsha to stay at her home to recover, the girl insults Tanya when offered a bowl of soup: "What's in it, Aunt Jemima? Hog jowls and turnip greens?"

Tanya takes the high road in response to the racist remarks, saying, "Marsha, you can't get to me. I love you!"—to which Marsha replies, "Wow! Now I'm stuck with a lesbian!" Tim's girlfriend Lois takes immediate offense to the suggestion that Tanya's words had any queer overtones to them: "That's cruel, Marsha! We're all Christians here!" she snaps back with a disgusted look on her face.[77] Marsha's racism is put on further display when she mocks Tanya's offer to stay: "Praise de Lawd!" Marsha exclaims, in an apparent mockery of Black southern preachers.[78]

After Tanya, Jim, and Tim tell Marsha the story of Jesus's life and answer all of her questions about Christianity, she accepts salvation and tearfully embraces Tanya. "I feel clean and beautiful. My life is changed! Tanya, I *love* you, I really do!" she says. "Am I *still* your Aunt Jemima?" asks Tanya. "No! You" re my beautiful sister in Christ!" replies Marsha in the story's final panel. "Shore nuff?" Tanya asks? "Yeah!" says Marsha, adding, "In fact, now I even like your hog jowls and turnip greens!"

The casual racism on display throughout the issue, especially in these final panels, shows Chick's attempts to critique a white character's racist behavior by showing how you can supposedly overcome bigotry through personal salvation. But by using these racist tropes as a comical punchline (along with anti-gay sentiments to make a point about Christian sisterly love), Chick reinforces bigoted stereotypes instead of tearing them down for those readers who might need to learn about practicing love instead of hate.

The most controversial issues of Crusader Comics, however, are those that take aim at the Roman Catholic church. These are comics that even many Christian bookstores have banned from their shelves. Beginning with *Sabotage?* in 1979, Chick devoted seven issues to a systematic condemnation of Catholicism. Chick calls Catholicism an "occult system [that] has never been a Christian church!" He describes the pope as the figure of the "anti-christ, completely controlled by seducing spirits" and says that the rise of Roman Catholic Church brought an increase in "witchcraft" in the form of "hexes, spells, curses, soul travel, black Masses, sacrificial murders, and drinking of human blood," much of it taking place "in the convents and monasteries throughout Europe." Describing the Roman Catholic Church as "Satan's church," Chick quotes a man named Alberto Rivera as saying that "Roman Catholicism was a mixture of witchcraft, Judaism, paganism and just enough perverted Christianity to make it appear respectable."[79]

Chick promoted the belief that the Roman Catholic Church rose to power by authorizing its own translations of the Bible and outlawing older versions stemming from Antioch. As a result, we are told in *Sabotage?*, "The priests had people under their control again. The Word of God was kept from the people. The stronger the Popes became, the deeper the world sank into the dark ages. Millions went to hell. Satan was delighted."[80] Chick tells us that "Pope Paul III ordered a Spaniard named Ignatius de Loyola to set up the "Order of the Jesuits" in 1534 in order to "stop the spread of Protestantism at all costs."[81]

But *Sabotage?* was only the first shot across the bow for Chick, who followed it with the six-part Alberto series. Those issues drew on the ideas of Alberto Rivera, who claimed to be an ex-Jesuit priest, although this claim has been challenged.[82] Throughout the six issues—*Alberto* (1979), *Double-Cross* (1981), *The Godfathers* (1982), *The Force* (1983), *Four Horsemen* (1985), and *The*

Prophet (1988), Chick promotes a wide array of conspiracy theories involving the Catholic church. These range from Rivera's claims that the Jesuits had him "trained as an espionage agent to destroy protestant churches"[83] and that the Vatican is secretly led not by the pope but by the "Jesuit General [who] is referred to as the Black Pope. He actually runs the Vatican behind the scenes and Satan guides him."[84] The Black Pope, says Rivera, is "also a mason and a member of the communist party in Spain" and was also "closely linked to the Illuminati in London."[85] In turn, he argues, "Rome is secretly united with the Illuminati Masonry, Communism, Zionism and their subsidiaries to control banking and world commerce. They also use the media to manipulate almost everyone on earth."[86] Loyola created the Illuminati, says Rivera, as "a satanic organization to control the minds of European leaders through hypnosis, witchcraft and mind control."[87]

Chick tells us that Communism was actually created by the Catholic Church and that Karl Marx and Friedrich Engels were "coached and directed by Jesuit priests." This, he says, led to the Communist Party being "secretly bankrolled by agents of Rome (the Illuminati) in order to create another major power loyal to the Vatican."[88] Jesuits, Rivera and Chick claim, worked under the order of the Black Pope to bring Benito Mussolini to power in Italy.[89] But Mussolini was not the only fascist leader the Jesuits installed, according to Rivera and Chick. They claimed that Father Bernhard Stempfle helped Adolph Hitler edit his 1925 autobiography, *Mein Kampf*. "This book was the master plan of the Jesuits for Hitler's take-over of Germany," Chick writes. "Hitler was the Vatican's choice." According to Chick, the Third Reich became a forum "in which the Roman Catholics would become the masters."[90]

Rivera and Chick also see Catholics as playing a large role in the Holocaust, citing a conspiracy that had "German Catholics, under orders... joining Protestant churches.... These undercover Roman Catholics worked hard to gain the acceptance and trust of protestant pastors and their church members. And when the anti-Jewish atrocities began... these Catholic agents, pretending to be Protestants, publicly accused the Jews and turned them in to the Gestapo for export to the death camps."[91] Rivera also believed that numerous Catholic priests worked as Gestapo officers and that "one of Hitler's greatest sources of military intelligence came through the Vatican via the Roman Catholic confessionals all over the world." Ultimately, Chick says, Pope Pius XII "was very pleased" by the Holocaust because "enemies of the Vatican were paying a terrible price for not bowing down to his holiness."[92]

Chick used these comics to promote numerous conspiracy theories. One posits the existence of underground tunnels leading to hidden burial sites beneath monasteries in numerous cities across Spain for the murdered love children of nuns and priests.[93] Another contends that Abraham Lincoln's assassination was organized by Jesuit priests.[94] Chick also promoted the conspiracy theory that the Ku Klux Klan was "formed by Roman Catholic Confederate Army officers after the civil war, and [was] led by Jesuits" as a "branch of masonry" designed to make Black people "suspicious of Protestants" and steer them "into the arms of the Vatican, and the new army of black Jesuits who are recruiting them across the U.S."[95] He posited that Roman Catholic monks established the prophet Muhammad as a strategic mechanism for the church. He quotes Rivera as saying that "the Vatican wanted to create a messiah for the Arabs, someone they could raise up as a great leader, a man with charisma who they could train, and eventually unite all the non-Catholic Arabs behind him . . . creating a mighty army that would ultimately capture Jerusalem for the pope."[96]

Chick's comics regularly repeated the message that Roman Catholics were not true Christians, across ten years' worth of Crusader titles and in numerous tracts such as *Are Roman Catholics Christians?*, *Why Is Mary Crying?*, *Things to Come?*, *Is There Another Christ?*, *Last Rites*, *The Awful Truth*, and *The Attack*. The sacrament of the confession, he posited, was invented as a way for priests to "pry into the secrets" of their congregation as a way of wielding power through the threat of blackmail[97] and that the crucifix was an occult symbol stemming from the worship of the ancient fertility god Baal. "The crucifix is the real heart of the occult," Chick wrote. "Behind the crucifix are strong demonic forces giving out tremendous power, as depicted in the vampire movies," he has Rivera tell us. Chick argued that "any crucifix, whether it is in a home or convent, wherever, is charged with the powers of darkness and affects everyone near it because it attracts demons."[98]

The sacrament of communion, Chick said, is a "satanic invention."[99] "Satan, using a combination of Jewish and pagan religious rites, developed the Roman Catholic mass, which keeps repeating Christ's sacrifice over and over again. The Lord's supper was replaced by a deadly counterfeit. During the mass, the priest magically turns the wafer into the body, blood, soul and divinity of Christ. Who gave him the boys in religious costumes in the Vatican."[100] Chick argued that in so doing, Catholics are actually worshipping Baal when they take communion and that the Vatican serves as "a temple of

Satan, taking millions into hell by giving them a false Gospel, a false Christ and another Spirit."[101] This belief was summed up in the title of one tract that referred to the communion wafer—*Death Cookie*.

In summation, Chick wrote, "Satan has tricked almost everyone into believing that the Roman Catholic Institution is Christian. We found out that their 'Jesus' is Tammuz, their 'Mary' is Semiramis, the pope is an antichrist, their 'Host' was stolen from the Egyptians and represents the Sun God and the Catholic crucifix is the heart of the occult. The Bible tells us this system is the habituation of devils. Jesus hates, and has cursed, this evil religion, and warns Catholics to get out of it."[102] Although Chick's line of Crusader Comics started out as a way for him to use a wide range of themes and topics to reach adolescent and adult readers, they eventually became a regular forum for the voice of Rivera and his extreme beliefs about the Roman Catholic Church. In so doing, Chick found himself alienating many Christian comics readers and retailers.

Crusader Comics titles have been sold primarily in Christian bookstores and by mail order since their debut in 1974. Despite their limited distribution forums compared to the comics sold on newsstands and in drugstores, supermarkets, and comic-book shops, they have often sold relatively well—for those retailers who are willing to carry them. Not all Christian bookstores have welcomed Chick's work, as Ronald Yates pointed out in an article in the *Chicago Tribune* in 1981: "I found [Chick's Crusader Comics] very hateful," said Mel Tipton, the new owner of the Inspiration for You Christian Bookstore in Buena Park, California. "What they say about Catholics is disgusting. Christ said we should love one another. That is definitely not the message in Chick's publications. We threw them all out."

Another retailer, Tom White, "owner of the Joy Bells Christian Book Store in Garden Grove, Cal.," removed some Crusader titles ("just the ones he considers offensive") from his store but noted that "he sells as many as 2,000 of Chick's publications each month"—presumably a combination of comics, tracts, and traditional books.[103] Even though he enjoyed the robust sales of Chick's work in 1981, White noted that the publisher's contentious strategy might not actually be a helpful one for sustained proselytizing: "Chick is going full blast.... He seems to be attacking everything. He makes the Moral Majority seem like a bunch of left-wingers. The problem is, being overzealous like that sometimes does more harm than good to the body of Christ."[104]

Adam and Eve and *Archie*: Spire Christian Comics

Chick took a hardline approach to proselytizing in his comics, whether they were full length comic books or tracts. When he wasn't promoting conspiracy theories about the Catholic church or issuing old-fashioned fire-and-brimstone warnings about hell, he was reinforcing stereotypes and advocating hate toward a wide range of minority groups. In his Crusader title *The Force*, Chick described how "Jesus is not a weak fairy like so many would like to picture Him. He had guts and strength, with love for the lost sheep of Israel."[105] This anti-gay rhetoric was typical of Chick's strategy of using belittlement, scare tactics, and fanaticism to spread his often-vicious beliefs. His work has proven offensive and cruel to the majority of Christians and non-Christians alike.

Chick tried to reframe idea that he spewed hate in his 2012 tract *Who's the Real Hater?* "Many times Bible-believing Christians are labeled 'haters,'" he wrote, but "this tract was given to you out of love, not hate."[106] Yet racist, anti-gay, and anti-Muslim attacks are all categorized as hate-crimes in most nations, and Chick's rhetorical and visual patterns across his lines of tracts and comic books regularly belittled, insulted, chastised, and abused non-Protestant, nonheterosexual, and nonwhite people. As Catholic author Jimmy Akin put it in his book *The Nightmare World of Jack Chick*, Chick's comics are filled with "shocking, sensationalist allegations" and spread "messages of hate and paranoia."[107]

In stark contrast to Chick's hate-filled, squirm-inducing comics are the various titles published by Spire Christian Comics in the 1970s. On the surface, Spire's comics appear to preach love and inclusion, but they often hide dangerous messages about gender, science, and culture in ways that were not nearly as overt as Chick's work. Introduced into Christian bookstores in 1972, Spire was an imprint of the Fleming H. Revell Company, which began publishing Christian books in the 1870s. The Spire books were the product of writer-artist Al Hartley, who had worked in comics since the 1940s for numerous companies on titles in a range of genres—from the teen humor titles *Dotty* and *Ernie Comics* at Ace Periodicals to the heroic adventures of *The Black Terror*, various humor books for Better Publications, and romance titles such as *Love Confessions*, *Love Letters*, and *Love Secrets* for Quality Comics.

By 1950 he was working for Timely/Atlas (which eventually became Marvel Comics) on western titles such as *Black Rider*, *The Gunhawk*, and *Wild Western*; war titles such as *Battlefront* and *Combat Kelly*; jungle titles such as *Jungle Action*, *Jungle Tales*, and *Lorna the Jungle Girl*; romance titles such as *Girl Confessions, Love Romances, Love Tales, My Own Romance,* and *True Secrets*; and teen humor titles such as *Miss America, Patsy Walker, Patsy and Hedy,* and *Patty Powers*. In the early 1960s, as Marvel transitioned into the superhero genre, Hartley even drew the adventures of Thor in issue 90 of *Journey into Mystery* and wrote tales featuring Giant Man and The Wasp in issue 69 of *Tales to Astonish* and Iron Man in issue 68 of *Tales of Suspense*. For nearly two decades, Hartley wrote and/or drew comics that he would described as unclean, secular minded, and unwholesome after he converted to Christianity.

After leaving Marvel in the mid-1960s, Hartley worked for Archie Publications from 1967 to 1974, serving as writer and artist on nearly all of the publisher's titles—from mainstays such as *Pep, Laugh Comics,* and *Archie's Pals and Gals* to comics featuring supporting characters in their own titles such as *Jughead, Betty and Me,* and *Reggie and Me*. Since he had worked on teen characters such as Dotty and Patsy Walker for nearly two decades by the time he arrived at Archie Publications, Hartley was an experienced hand when it came to addressing adolescent interests in his comics—a strategy that he soon used to express his faith in very direct ways with Spire.

Hartley describes 1967 as a turning point in his life in his autobiography *Come Meet My Friend!*, crediting the first prayer meeting he attended as not only leading him to become a Christian but also saving his troubled marriage. When he got a call from Archie Publications offering him a job that same year, Hartley saw this as God's plan for him: "I knew that the Archie publishers had not just come to me. God had sent them."[108] A few years later, Hartley was able to use comics as a more direct form of spiritual engagement when Spire asked him to adapt David Wilkerson's autobiography *The Cross and the Switchblade* into a comic book in 1972. Wilkerson's book was also adapted into a film in 1970 starring crooner Pat Boone and future *CHiPS* star Erik Estrada. Hartley did numerous cinematic tie-ins for Spire, including *Born Again* and *Time to Run* (not to mention *Paul: Close Encounters of the Real Kind*, which drew on the Spielberg film's popularity in name only).

Hartley also adapted the autobiographical book *God's Smuggler* by Brother Andrew in 1972, about the Dutch missionary's efforts to transport Bibles into Communist countries. The success of *The Cross and the Switchblade* and *God's Smuggler* enabled Spire to expand the scope of their comics line, allowing Hartley to work in a wide range of fiction and nonfiction genres in the dozens of issues he created for the company from 1972 to 1984. Some, such as *Attack!* and *In the Presence of Mine Enemies*, were war-themed biographies of Christian military men, while *Hansi: The Girl Who Loved the Swastika* chronicled Maria Anne Hirschmann's real-life escape from the Hitler Youth movement. Others focused on celebrity musicians such as Andraé Crouch and Johnny Cash and sports figures such as NFL coach Tom Landry, chronicling how they achieved great success in their careers after accepting Jesus. Hartley notes that *Hello, I'm Johnny Cash* was especially effective for reaching prisoners, given Cash's history of arrests and his relationship with Folsom State Prison.[109]

The funny animal genre was well represented with a series of eight *Barney Bear* comics, which used a family of bears to teach very young readers about the Bible. Crime comics were repurposed in *Crossfire*'s tale of a police officer's efforts to save the souls of various young sinners he encounters ("Some people called me a pig! But God called me his child!").[110] In three issues of *Adventure with the Brothers*, twin brothers Pete and Tom Brothers battle rebel soldiers in an unnamed jungle, cult leaders on an island colony, and drug smugglers who have their own castle on an unnamed tropical isle. The blonde brothers surf, hang glide, and use explosives to take a side against revolutionary forces in a foreign land—all while crediting an escape from their adversaries to the power of prayer ("There's always a happy ending with Jesus! He takes the fear and worry out of life!" says Pete as his brother flees the soldiers' clutches via a hang glider).[111]

Many Spire titles were adaptations of Bible stories, such as *Adam and Eve*, *My Brother's Keeper*, *Noah's Ark*, and *Jesus*. Some, such as *Jesus*, were set in historical context, telling the story of Christ's life, death, and resurrection in a similar manner as comics from the 1940s (except for how Jesus and his disciples are drawn far more muscular than in titles such as *Life of Christ Visualized*, a fact that Chick would have likely applauded given his disdain for "weak" representations of Christ). But other titles offered modernized stories set in the present era, such as *Adam and Eve* (who are dressed in 1970s fashions rather than fig leaves and are cast out of paradise into a neighborhood full of strip clubs resembling Times Square). In an apparent attempt to be more relevant to the lives of young readers, Adam and Eve use modern slang as they discuss spiritual concerns, such as "Sin promises a blast... but it produces a bomb!!!" and "Well, we've seen the light... We want to be *turned on* for Him!!!"[112]

Perhaps the most unusual Spire titles were *Alpha and Omega* and *There's a New World Coming*, which used science fiction as a vehicle for retelling parts of the book of Genesis and the book of Revelation. The latter title begins with three teenagers' experience of the rapture as they are lifted into the sky: "W-we're in some kind of divine time machine!!!" one says, explaining how

FIGURE 28 Advertisement for Al Hartley's line of Spire Christian Comics.

it started when she began reading the book of Revelation in her Bible.[113] The three teens witness the coming of the Antichrist and the world's destruction via nuclear war. They also take a detour to meet Babylon, the "Mother of Harlots," a woman with flowing blonde hair who is depicted wearing a slinky red dress, high heels, and fishnet stockings. While Chick regularly described the Catholic Church as the "whore of Babylon,"[114] Hartley offered a more literal interpretation of a seductive woman who symbolizes "spiritual adultery." She sits on a bed before a bubbling cauldron as the words "astrology / black magic / witchcraft / seances / demon contact / sorcery" seem to emanate from the cauldron's bubbling fumes.[115]

The teens, still floating aloft in the sky, then bear witness to Armageddon and the return of Jesus to earth. They eventually descend into an earthly paradise, in keeping with the book of Revelation's promise of the story's titular "new world." "It all seems like science fiction!!!" one of the teens says. "Or a fairy tale!" says another. "Well, we've read the Book of Revelation . . . and here are today's headlines," the third says, while holding up newspapers with the headlines "Crime" and "War," prompting the response, "It all fits together perfectly!"[116]

Although Christians in many different eras have looked at modern news reports as seeming evidence of Revelation's impending apocalyptic events, religious scholar Gerald L. Stevens warns us to avoid such interpretations: "Eventually, the allure of 'signs of the times' reading of the headlines every week [begins] to show a fool's gold shine."[117] *There's a New World Coming* was based on the 1973 book of the same by Hal Lindsey, whose prophecy that the world would end in 1988 helped him sell more copies (at least until 1989).[118]

In *Alpha and Omega*, the two title characters (a man named Alpha and a woman named Omega) serve as the futuristic equivalents of Adam and Eve who battle Lucifer across time and space. Lucifer travels in his own "laser-propelled" spaceship (the "NOVA 666").[119] Sucked through a black hole into a new dimension after believing Lucifer's lies about the planet Mars—which Alpha and Omega are "not programmed" to visit ("It's so beautiful!!! Like a giant apple!!!")[120]—the pair fight a space dinosaur, among other fantastic creatures; revisit historic atrocities in Earth's history; and eventually meet their creator.

In the end, despite the sci-fi premise, Hartley's message stresses the importance of faith over scientific reason. When council leaders reject Alpha's report about the existence of God as "an insult to our scientific progress," he replies that his spiritual beliefs are "not just ideas—I bring truth and reality!!! Alpha says about Christ's death that "all our intelligence and computers could never conceive of such an incredible way to save man!!!"[121] Released in 1978, *Alpha and Omega* used sci-fi to create new allegories by combining a popular genre with multiple books of the Bible in the wake of the massive success of *Star Wars* the previous year.

But if Spire is best remembered for one series of comics, it is their line of Christian *Archie* titles, featuring the whole Riverdale gang as they learn many scriptural lessons. Hartley had inserted Christian messages into several issues of his *Archie* titles prior to working for Spire and was often chided by his former employer for doing so. When an agreement was reached to use the characters in full-length gospel-oriented stories, Hartley was pleased that he no longer had to sneak in the occasional spiritual message in his Archie stories: "Archie would no longer be limited to an occasional witness as he now was in my secular comics. In the Spire series he would be full blast for Christ on all thirty-two pages," said Hartley.

Although his other Spire series such as *Barney Bear* and *Adventures with the Brothers* were original creations, Hartley saw the value in using a familiar licensed character to reach new followers. "Millions of kids all over the world are conditioned to reading Archie Comics. They love him. They identify with him. In the Christian Comic series, Archie would look the same and act the same, with one big difference: All the laughs and excitement and bloopers would just be hooks to get the reader's attention and lead him to Christ. The books looked exactly like the comics, but they were really supertracts."[122]

The first tract-like *Archie* title was *Archie's One Way* in 1973, in which Jughead joined a Bible study group, Betty and Archie interrupted a make-out session to counsel Big Ethel about having a "love affair" with God, and Archie picked up a young hitchhiker running away from home who learns not to "want things your way—instead of God's way!"[123] This first issue was followed by eighteen more: *Archie and Big Ethel, Archie and Mr. Weatherbee, Archie Gets a Job, Archie's Car, Archie's Circus, Archie's Clean Slate, Archie's Date Book, Archie's Family Album, Archie's Festival, Archie's Love Scene, Archie's Parables, Archie's Roller Coaster, Archie's Something Else, Archie's Sonshine, Archie's Sports Scene, Archie's World, Christmas with Archie,* and *Jughead's Soul Food*. Although some of the titles were overtly religious in their rhetoric, most were not, allowing them to be seen as regular Archie titles by many readers who might encounter them. (One pastor in New York handed out thousands of copies of *Archie's Love Scene* to those standing in line outside Radio City Music Hall one Christmas Eve.)[124]

The series gained the attention of the *New York Times* in 1973 with Edward Fiske's article "Jughead, Archie and Their Friends Get Religion and Help in Spreading the Word." Fiske noted that while comics had been adapting the Bible for decades already, the *Archie* series (which is "aimed at the 10-to-16 age group") was "the first to take a well-known comic character and adapt it for religious themes." Ruby Rhoades, one of the company's representatives, said that Spire's titles updated biblical content for modern readers to specifically compete for the reader's attention with non-Christian titles: "We wanted to get away from the old Sunday School-type material where all the characters wear white robes, move slowly and speak in archaic language.... Our goal is to compete with secular comics," she said. But while Spire may have wanted their comics to compete with the type of secular comics that Hartley had previously done for decades, their licensing arrangement with Archie Publications stipulated that the average comics reader would not easily mistake Spire's books for the traditional line of *Archie* titles. Spire's titles couldn't be sold at traditional retail outlets, just in Christian bookstores and by mail. "The comics are manufactured by Archie Enterprises, which insisted that they not be marketed on newsstands where they would compete with the regular Archie product," noted Fiske. Even so, he said, Archie Publication president John L. Goldwater was pleased with how the Spire books "fit in well with its general policy of promoting wholesome family life."[125]

Hartley certainly saw his work for Spire as a more wholesome alternative to those he had produced for other companies such as Marvel over the past few decades, even going so far as to label that work as "filth" in *Come Meet My Friend!* as he compared Christian and non-Christian comics: "Secular comics, like all literature, reflected a rapid decline in morals and philosophy. The art leaned more toward sadism and sex. The life-styles that were suggested were insidiously destructive. Thus, Spire Christian Comics offered an alternative. More than just offering clean content instead of filth, Spire offered God instead of the devil. The response was simply another confirmation of God's promise: His word would not return a void, whether it was in a pulpit, or a comic book."[126]

Echoing these anti-secular sentiments in a closing editorial that first appeared in *God's Smuggler*, Hartley proclaimed: "You know the heart of a comic is the storyline! That's why I appreciate our reader/artist relationship through Spire Christian Comics!!! We're doing our best to produce the finest comic series available—for enjoyable reading and a graphic art experience, and—through the content and spirit of each book—to bring us closer in the great adventure of life, and certainly to aid our awareness of God's unlimited love—and all he provides for us through His Son, Jesus Christ."[127]

Hartley's rhetoric positioned a comic book's narrative as its "heart," which can allow us to better connect with the concerns of the soul embedded in the "spirit" of Hartley's message. Hartley often emphasized the heart as a vessel through which we can find God. "If you ask with all your heart, God will answer!" he told readers in *Archie's Love Scene*.[128] In *Barney Bear Wakes Up*, he taught children to pray with the words "I want Jesus to live in my heart," while in *Jesus* a similar prayer begins, "Lord Jesus come into my heart."[129]

This was a very different message than the one Chick offered in tracts such as *Heart Trouble?*, in which the heart is pitted at odds with the soul. "There's ugly things down deep in your heart that you can't see.... But God does," a cardiologist tells his patient. "The Lord gives us a picture of what's in the human heart, and it's very real!... It's the fleshly part! These things slither out of us from time to time, and they're really nasty!" says the proselytizing physician,[130] who places the blame for adultery, murder, fornication, theft, blasphemy, and "evil thoughts" on the whims of the human heart (accompanied by an anthropomorphic image of a heart with sinister eyes and huge, pointed teeth that snarls "Grrr").[131] This idea also appeared in the 1983 tract *Bad Bob*, in which Chick quotes a line from Jeremiah 17:9 ("The heart is deceitful in all things, and desperately wicked") in response to Bob's mother's claim that "in his heart, he's such a good boy."[132] In Hartley's view, the heart is what we use to ask for God's love and where that love can reside, while in Chick's view the heart is the sinful source of every wickedness that can keep us from living a godly life.

But as much as Hartley touted his work as a "clean alternative" to the seemingly dangerous "morals and philosophy" served up in mainstream or secular comics, the Spire line displays some concerning patterns regarding Hartley's handling of gender, science, and other subjects—patterns that fell squarely in line with the discourses that Chick promoted about such foundational aspects of society. There was a concerning amount of anti-feminist rhetoric, for instance, as well as moments clearly meant to reinforce old-fashioned gender roles. In one story in *Archie's Family Album*, the Riverdale gang plays out scenes from the past in an unspecified era (what Hartley only refers to as "the old days") when horse-drawn carriages were the dominant form of transportation. Morals were apparently better then as well: "Folks took pride in their neighborhood! No one called a cop a pig!!! And women were treated as *more* than equals!!!"

FIGURE 29 Al Hartley's *Archie's Family Album* (1978) argues that women were "treated as more than equals" in "the old days." This is page 28.

Because these olden days meant that more people read the Bible, we are told that "People seem happier! They enjoy what they're doing!"[133] we see Betty in a full-length dress and bonnet being led by the hand throughout town. This image is then contrasted with all of the Riverdale women who wear pants, sweaters, and T-shirts as the story winds down back in the modern era.. Few women fighting in the suffrage movement in the late nineteenth and early twentieth centuries would have agreed with the assessment that society treated them as "more than equal" in that era.

Traditional gender roles are reinforced for Spire's youngest readers in the *Barney Bear* series, in which Barney's mother takes delight in her domestic routine. In *Barney Bear: The Swamp Gang*, Barney's dad takes him on an early morning jog through the woods as a way of spending some quality time with his son. "As long as we keep talking to each other . . . we'll stay close, Barney!" says the father. "I like following in your footsteps, Dad!" replies Barney. "And I like giving you a helping hand, Son!!!" the father says as they return home. "And *I* like making breakfast!!!" says his mother. as she stands flipping pancakes on the stove with a smile on her face.[134]

Older readers also encountered patronizing and patriarchal rhetoric, such as in *Adam and Eve* when Eve expresses disbelief at the notion that she was created out of a rib from Adam's body. He replies that perhaps God did so "to get us into the right relationship!!! If you were made out of my head— that might have set you above me! If he used my foot—I might have walked all over you!!! But he took you out of my side—to make us equal!!! He took you from something close to my heart—so I'd love you—from under my arm—so I'd protect you!!!"[135]

Hartley also regularly told readers not to trust in science. In addition to *Alpha and Omega*'s disdain for scientific leaders, we find science taking a backseat role to the Bible in *Archie Gets a Job*. After Jughead and Archie open a Christian bookstore on the beach, they sell titles such as Hartley's self-help guide *Update: A New Approach to Christian Dating* to their pals and gals. When Dilton Doiley (Riverdale's resident genius) says "Well I'm not interested in girls or dates!!! Do you have any books on ecology? Or solar energy??? What about sociology???," Jughead replies "Try the Bible!!! Who can tell us more about things than the one who put it all together???"[136]

Such sentiments were well in line with Chick's extreme beliefs about science in such tracts as *The Mad Machine*, *Global Warming*, and *There Go the Dinosaurs* (which posited that dinosaurs existed in biblical times and made their way onto Noah's ark but died off because the flooding destroyed plant life, which changed the oxygen. In the "thinner air," says Chick, it was harder for dinosaurs to breathe and so "they got slower and easier to catch").[137] In *The Mad Machine*, the narrator discusses the role that various forces play in society, asking, "What about the great god, science?" This is followed by a scientist who holds a test tube being asked, "Professor, can science save us from deadly pollution ... population explosion and energy shortages?" The scientist says yes, given enough time and funding. When asked how long until we can solve these issues, he responds "Anywhere from twenty to three hundred years." "Oops ... is there that much time left?" asks the narrator.[138]

Similarly, in the 2012 tract *Global Warming*, the narrator says bitterly, "Brilliant scientists graciously counsel us 'little people' on climate changes and the dangers of global warming. Are they right? Is Mother Earth *doomed* because of us? They must be right, because they're '*scientists*'! Hmm ... but wait! Let's think about this," the narrator says, before reminding us that because Nostradamus's ancient prophecies were wrong, we shouldn't trust modern scientists either.[139] Chick also can't resist dropping in some ugly racism along the way when he cites Dr. Paul Ehrlich's prediction in 1971 that "England will not exist in the year 2000" and then adds, "England still exists. Ask any Muslim" as the text for a panel with a sword-wielding Muslim standing before Big Ben.[140]

Chick further tells us that because God created the Earth, "*He* controls its climate—not mankind.... So when a country claims it can cause (or fix) global climate change ... they're only fooling themselves!"[141] A 2010 poll found that 47 percent of American Christians believed that Jesus "would return by 2050 (27 percent definitely and 20 percent probably)."[142] In turn, Chick's narration describes how according to the book of Revelation, the earth will be "scorched with great heat" and a "third of the earth will go by fire." But this should not be cause for concern, we are told: "When Jesus returns, He'll *restore* the planet and reign over it for 1000 years. So why the panic? Jesus is calling the shots ... not the environmentalists!"[143] Religious scholar Bart D. Ehrman describes such notions as promoting a false belief that "there really is no need to worry about CO_2 emissions, strip-mining, deforestation, massive extinctions, or poisoning of the air, land and water. God is in charge and his will [will] be done. In the meantime, take what you want."[144]

Conclusion

What seems so puzzling about both Hartley's and Chick's insistence that scientists should not be trusted is that just a few decades earlier Christian comics had actively touted the *value* of science to society. Publishers in the 1940s, as chapter 1 demonstrates, found ways to strike a balance between science and faith. *Catholic Comics* was explicitly pro-science, offering readers a regular column full of science-based facts and examples in keeping with how the series was a rebranding of the canceled series *Marvels of Science*. M. C. Gaines published both *Picture Stories from the Bible* and *Picture Stories from Science*. In the 1940s, science had been promoted as a way of better understanding God's world, but by the 1970s it was deemed an obstacle to true faith.

As Christian comics progressed over the decades, publishers shifted from showing the connections between spiritual pursuits and earthly ones (such as sports and science) to using the medium primarily as a forum for evangelical messaging and converting the unsaved. Older series such as *Treasure Chest* and *Topix* were targeted toward existing Christians with the aim of helping them strengthen their faith, but Crusader and Spire titles along with Chick Tracts were usually aimed at convincing nonbelievers to become Christians.

Ultimately, Hartley's Christian, kid-friendly *Archie* titles were successful for about a decade and inspired other publishers to take a similar approach. In 1977, Word Books released ten issues of *Dennis the Menace and the Bible Kids*, aiming at an even younger readership than *Archie*'s ten-to-sixteen-year-old target demographic. But with the Spire and Crusader series filling the void left by the demise of *Treasure Chest* and the Catechetical Guild titles, Christian comics looked radically different by the mid-1970s than they had done in prior decades. Whereas many Catechetical Guild titles were meant to prepare readers for the nunnery or the seminary or teach them about important figures in the history of Catholicism, Chick's comic books attacked the very foundations of the Catholic church. Although *Treasure Chest* used original characters such as Skee Barry and Chuck White to deliver faith-based messages in what were often indirect or allegorical ways, Spire and Hartley used licensed characters such as Archie and Jughead and real-life celebrities such as Johnny Cash and Tom Landry as a way of leveraging their recognizability to connect with readers who might be more open to accepting Jesus Christ as their personal savior if the message was delivered by a character or figure they were readily familiar with.

Christian-themed comics were also marked by a turn toward individual voices in the 1970s rather than the editorial efforts of the Catechetical Guild and similar publishers, regardless of whether that voice was supportive or critical of religion. Creators such as Al Hartley, Jack Chick, and Justin Green each used comics as an in-depth forum to explore their own spiritual beliefs and/or deliver strong messages about religious institutions. Chick and Green were both critical of the Catholic church for different reasons, while Hartley and Chick used their work as a venue for evangelical messaging about the need for salvation and for trust in the Bible instead of science or society.

Chick's work has ultimately endured much longer than Hartley's in both the marketplace and in public memory (as the various parodies of Chick Tracts attest). Chick Publications still sells his tracts and comic books years after Chick's death in 2016. Although Green's *Binky Brown* many have played a pivotal role in the development of graphic novels, with more than five decades of retail and grassroots distribution, Crusader comics and Chick Tracts have reached more people than Green (and Hartley) ever did—and Chick's divisive voice has gained the attention of more readers than the pioneers of Christian comics publishing such as M. C. Gaines could have ever envisioned.

4

The 1970s and 1980s

• • • • • • • • • • • • •

Marvel, DC, Saints, and Sinners

Along with how individual voices increasingly replaced institutional ones and vehement evangelism become the dominant goal in the Christian comic-book landscape, a different transition was taking place in the 1970s among mainstream comics publishers. The superhero genre was well entrenched as the decade began, making up the majority of titles at the top two companies, Marvel and DC Comics. Fans and historians point to the early 1970s as the start of a new era of comic book history—the "Bronze Age" of comics, following the "Golden Age" of the 1930s through mid-1950s and the "Silver Age" of the late 1950s and 1960s. Many point to *Showcase* issue 4 in 1956 with its debut of Barry Allen as the new Flash as the start of the Silver Age and its superhero renaissance. Superhero titles had declined by the end of the 1940s as new genres such as crime, horror, and romance dominated newsstand sales, but the success of *The Flash, Justice League of America*, and *Fantastic Four* led to a new boom in costumed heroes by the early 1960s.

But by the start of the 1970s, this new trend in superhero titles was ten to fifteen years old at Marvel and DC, and as with any genre cycle it evolved to include new subgenres. Superhero comics often became more mature and thematically darker, featuring more street-level and supernatural heroes while also making strides in introducing more diverse characters (including new Black, Puerto Rican, and female superheroes).

Within this frequent emphasis on darker and more supernatural characters came space for stories focused on heaven and hell in ways that hadn't been seen in superhero comics since the 1940s. In some cases, these comics continued to use the well-tested strategies of promoting prominent Christian figures and well-known Bible stories and adding spiritual seriousness to genre-based tales. But along with these familiar tactics came new approaches to faith, damnation, and the afterlife. Many creators used popular culture trends of the 1970s such as the "satanic panic" craze to draw in new readers with their terrific tales of demons and devils.

DC Comics: *The Bible*, *Blue Devil*, and the Two Houses

DC Comics may be best known for heroes such as Superman, Batman, and Wonder Woman, but the company's legacy also includes key moments in the history of Christian-oriented comics. From publishing the first few issues of *Picture Stories from the Bible* before M. C. Gaines formed EC Comics to the allegorical adventures of The Spectre (and the Godlike presence of "the voice") in the 1940s, DC was among the first publishers to offer stories that were either adapted from the Bible or inspired by biblical figures. While such efforts had faded by 1945 as *Picture Stories* switched publishers and The Spectre made his final appearance in *More Fun Comics*, DC made a prominent attempt to revive Gaines's adaptation approach in the 1970s.

In 1975, DC published an installment of their oversized line of Limited Collectors' Edition issues entitled *The Bible*. Measuring ten by fourteen inches (instead of approximately seven by ten for a regular comic book), many titles in the series were reserved for special events, such as *Superman Salutes the Bicentennial* and the Christmas editions *Rudolph the Red-Nosed Reindeer* and *Christmas with the Super-Heroes*; tie-ins to television programs, including issues spotlighting shows such as *Shazam!* and *Welcome Back Kotter*; and the Marvel-DC crossover *Superman vs. the Amazing Spider-Man*. The series was

FIGURE 30   Joe Kubert's Limited Collector's Edition of *The Bible* for DC Comics (1975).

regularly used to tell stories that were bigger in scope than most traditional comics, making it a fitting format to adapt the Bible. Written by Sheldon Mayer and illustrated by Joe Kubert (along with Nestor Redondo), both of whom had been creating comics since the early 1940s, *The Bible* features key moments from the book of Genesis, chronicling the stories of Adam, Eve, Cain, Abel, Noah, and Abraham along with the history of Sodom and Gomorrah and the Tower of Babel across its sixty-two enlarged pages.

In the book's narrative framework, a man is telling stories to his two grandchildren, Hannah and David, as the issue opens and closes, providing a worldly narrator to contextualize the biblical tales that follow. Mayer even has the grandfather hedge his bets as to whether the world began via evolution or creationism, leaving room for the possibility for both in a way that other Christian comics of the era never did. When a skeptical David implies that the book of Genesis is "a fairy tale" and says that his science teacher taught him that the world "began millions of years ago," his grandfather replies: "Well, David . . . scientists would be the first to tell you that they don't have all the answers! Sure . . . they'll tell you that life probably began in the sea! But—if it did—how'd it get there! All the different forms of life . . . how'd they all get there?"[1]

In contrast to Chick's ridicule of scientists, Mayer's inclusive rhetoric acknowledges the potential fallibility of science while not discounting the notion that evolution is "probably" how life on earth began. Many scientists and biblical scholars have argued for ways to unite the theories of evolution and creationism into a common understanding of the world's origins, such as Prof. Dennis O. Lamoureux (who has doctorates in both theology and biology) in his book *Evolutionary Creation: A Christian Approach to Evolution*.[2] Mayer allowed for nuanced duality in ways that Chick and Al Hartley never did, which likely made DC's new version of the Bible relevant to a wider range of readers than it might otherwise have been.

The book is beautifully produced, providing a larger platform for Kubert and Redondo's detailed artwork (which often stretches across two-page spreads, making it the comic book equivalent of an IMAX movie screen). The vice-president of DC at the time, Sol Harrison, described the issue as "the most expensive comic ever produced,"[3] and if that is indeed true, then it is easy to see why while reading the lavishly illustrated tome.

As the grandfather winds down his tale, he promises the children, "Next time I'll tell you more spectacular stories from the world's greatest book!" accompanied by a narrative caption stating, "Don't miss the next issue in our series of 'Stories From the Bible.'" A closing editorial promises readers, "But this is only the beginning—the first of a series depicting stories from the Old and New Testaments into a complete library of 'Stories From the Bible.'"[4]

The intended follow-up issues never arrived. Mayer drafted a script for a New Testament issue, but Kubert's time constraints limited his ability to start it.[5] Low sales may have also played a role. Editor Carmine Infantino has noted, "It was a great book, but sales weren't that good. Maybe it was the distribution?"[6]

But DC still featured a key pair of biblical figures throughout the 1970s—Cain and Abel, the sons of Adam and Eve. In Genesis, Cain kills his brother Abel out of jealousy. Both sons offered sacrifices to God, but only Abel's was looked on favorably. DC saw Cain, history's first murderer, as an opportune lead for a supernatural-themed series centered on the macabre in *The House of Mystery* (although this biblical connection was never explicitly stated). The series debuted as a horror anthology in 1951 and shifted to include superheroes in the 1960s before reverting back to chilling tales again with Cain as host when editor Joe Orlando took over the series. Introducing and wrapping up stories in the same vein as such EC Comics characters as the Crypt Keeper and the Old Witch from the infamous 1950s series *Tales from the Crypt* and *The Haunt of Fear* (which Orlando himself drew numerous issues of in that decade), Cain debuted in 1968 with *The House of Mystery* issue 175 and served as caretaker of the titular dwelling until the final issue in 1983.

In hosting issues of *House of Mystery* and *House of Secrets* for over a decade, Cain and Abel's roles were distinctly reframed from their biblical origins. No longer just an allegory for the necessity of brotherly love, the pair became important figures at DC in their role as storytellers. In *House of Secrets* issue 87 (1970), the opening narration tells us, "Throughout the history of man there have been those who listen, and these are few.... Fewer still are those whose way it is to tell.... Come now, past this flitting shadow men call reality, into the world of a story teller... a very particular story teller... a story teller called Abel, who tells his stories to an 'imaginary' friend called Goldie."[7] DC even positioned these supernatural stories in a multidenominational light. For example, Cain wraps up one story (about a priest and rabbi teaming up to defeat a witch) by telling Goldie, "Yes, I liked that tale—it shows something, I think! We're all the same... we may believe different things—may worship different gods... but we're all alike! We dream, we hope... we pray!"[8]

In his first appearance, Cain greets readers as his "fellow tenants" while warning them of the discomforts that lie within: "Now that you've paid your cheap twelve cent rent for this broken-down hovel, you're stuck! This pad is rent controlled, so I don't have to fix your plumbing, patch up your broken

FIGURE 31 Cain welcomes readers to the *House of Mystery* 175 (July–August 1968), page 1.

rat holes, replace your broken windows. I've got orders to freeze you, and generally make your life miserable! So welcome to the House of Mystery."[9] His playful and sarcastic tone mirrors that of other horror hosts, combining humor and menace, even while his shaggy beard, glasses, and rumpled coat make him appear more human and less ghoulish than his EC counterparts. Cain's appearance was actually modeled after that of DC writer Len Wein, who went on to write numerous issues of *House of Mystery* along with its sister series, *The House of Secrets*.

The latter series starred Cain's brother Abel, who was introduced in *DC Special* issue 4 (1969) and became the host-caretaker (along with his unseen/imaginary friend Goldie) of *The House of Secrets* with issue 81 that same year. Cain's appearance—more smartly dressed and rotund than his taller, skinnier, and scruffier brother—was based on that of Mark Hanerfield, Orlando's assistant editor.[10] Whereas prior comics usually modeled biblical figures after existing images from paintings, in later decades, most publishers gave these characters modern updates—from Al Hartley giving Adam and Eve a groovy van and bell-bottoms to DC basing Adam's sons on current staff members.

The visual contrast between the siblings is mirrored in their dissimilar personalities. Cain is cruel and domineering, while Abel is anxious and submissive, in keeping with their biblical roles as aggressor and victim. Cain regularly abuses his brother, calling him "a quivering coward" and "a milksop," while Cain shirks and stutters.[11] In *House of Mystery* issue 182, Cain describes their relationship as one he's ashamed of, given his hatred for his brother: "I'm looking at that house across the way," he says, eyeing the House of Secrets through his window. "It's a real eyesore! Been complainin' about it to the city council ever since it got here! I don't know he did it ... been tryin' to get away from that creep all my life! But there he is, big as day ... livin' right across the way! I'm ashamed of it ... hate to admit it, but that's my dumb brother Abel! Cutting in on my act, tellin' his stupid stories in that wreck he calls ... the House of Secrets!"[12] The rant hints at a degree of childishness and jealousy toward Abel ("dumb brother" / "cuttin' in on my act"), much as Cain's jealousy surrounding God favoring Abel's sacrifice led to murder in the book of Genesis.

Yet despite such biblical connections, neither *House of Mystery* nor *House of Secrets* used scripture very closely aside from a few passing references. *House of Mystery* issue 184 describes "thirty pieces of silver" as a dead man's treasure in reference to the amount that Judas Iscariot was paid to betray Jesus to the Romans,[13] while a story called "The Gardener of Eden" in *House of Mystery* issue 192 features a doctor named Adam Eden and his wife Eve purchasing a spooky mansion. Prayer is posited as a protective force against werewolves in the story "Deliver Us from Evil" in *House of Mystery* issue 211, evoking the rhetoric from the Lord's Prayer in its title. Some stories feature the devil as their antagonist in the same way as horror tales from the 1950s did. References to Satanism occasionally surface, often in connection with witchcraft or vampires. Issues issue 219 and issue 225, for instance, each feature stories about Satan set in centuries past; the devil's frilly outfit and feathered cap are similar to his attire in the Catechetical Guild's *If the Devil Would Talk*. These outdated depictions contrasted starkly to both the fire-and-brimstone versions of the devil found in Chick Tracts and the more modernized embodiments of Satan found in numerous Marvel series of the same era.

While their employment as caretakers of their respective houses ended in 1978 and 1983 with the respective cancellations of *House of Secrets* and *House of Mystery*, the legacy of each series continued throughout the 1980s. Television horror host Elvira took over for Cain as caretaker with *Elvira's House of Mystery* (1986). *House of Secrets* spawned the popular character Swamp Thing in issue 92 of 1971, and the muck monster earned his own solo series in both 1972 and 1982. (The latter edition was the first American work by esteemed British writer Alan Moore.) At the end of the 1980s, another British writer, Neil Gaiman, reinvented the roles of Cain and Abel in the pages of *The Sandman*, a series that reaffirmed the importance of storytelling in human affairs even further.

DC found success with other supernatural-themed series throughout the 1970s and 1980s, drawing on Christian tropes and images with varying degrees of overtness. The Spectre returned in the pages of *Adventure Comics* issue 431 (1974) as an implied agent of the Lord. While the 1967 series *The Spectre* introduced the hero as "an earth-bound spirit" who "still roams the world, seeking out and eliminating evil in the name of good,"[14] *Adventure Comics* took this mission a step further by having The Spectre play an active role in the afterlives of others: "I have come for you, villain," says The Spectre as he confronts a murderer, "because so long as you remain free, the souls of your victims must writhe in torment!"[15]

The notion of souls in torment implies the Christian concepts of purgatory or perdition. The latter is directly presented a few issues later when The Spectre tells another villain that an "eternity in perdition" awaits him.[16] In later decades, other writers tied the character to God more explicitly, such as John Ostrander in his 1992 series *The Spectre*: "It was The Spectre, the instrument of God's wrath, that rained devastation on Sodom and Gomorrah, who turned Lot's wife into salt. And it would be this Spectre who eventually plagued Egypt and the Pharoah!" a character named The Phantom Stranger says about The Spectre's origins.[17] Biblical scholar R.V.G. Tasker describes how both the Old and New Testaments "reveal God as a God of wrath as well as a God of love."[18] By embodying the former as a ghostly character, DC introduced specific spiritual elements as a way to add depth to The Spectre's characterization along with a larger celestial scope to the publisher's tales of worldly adventure.

The Phantom Stranger had his own series at DC in 1952–1953 and again in 1969–1976 in which he navigated the boundaries between supernatural and earthly realms. His adventures sometimes involved those who summon the devil ("The Spawn of Frankenstein" in issue 25) as well as those who turn against the Catholic Church (a nun is branded a heretic by a manic crowd in issue 38). In later decades, the character was reinvented as different figures from the Bible. In 1986, his backstory was revised to reveal him as the legendary "wandering Jew"—cursed to wander the earth after taunting Christ while on his way to be crucified.[19]

In 2012, the character's history changed again to make him the eternal embodiment of Judas Iscariot, cursed to roam the earth as punishment for betraying Jesus and forced to wear his thirty pieces of silver as a necklace: "My greatest sin was the betrayal of my closest friend," he tells us, describing his coins as "a reminder of my greed, and my greater sin."[20] Like The Spectre, The Phantom Stranger allowed DC to add religious elements to their stories while grounding any spiritual messages in genre-based adventure tales. In this way, readers could apply the themes of these comics to their own faith if desired or just take them on face value as thrilling tales of the supernatural.

While the motifs of wrath and atonement in *The Spectre* and *The Phantom Stranger* were often somber in nature, DC launched a series in 1984 starring a new character whose goal was to make the demonic mirthful instead of melancholy—*Blue Devil*. In his origin story, as Hollywood stuntman Dan Cassidy battles a demon named Nebiros on the set of a film called *Blue Devil*, his technologically enhanced costume permanently fuses to his body. Gaining powerful new abilities but unable to shed his blue-hued demonic visage, the trident-wielding Cassidy battles supernatural threats and gains a young sidekick called Kid Devil (who is dressed in a simple red costume). Along the way, he moves in with Cain at the "House of Weirdness" (renamed because Elvira was the current caretaker of the House of Mystery) and encounters a satanic rock star who resembles a parodic version of a pentagram-powered heavy metal musician from one of Chick's tracts.[21]

Although regularly centered on supernatural threats, the series was explicitly branded as fun and humorous by its editors and in various marketing efforts.[22] In the final issue of *Blue Devil*, the hero encounters a pseudo-Satan in the form of a rookie criminal named Lucifer. The villain sports the usual goatee, pointy ears, and a seemingly disco-inspired costume with a red pentagram, but he also dons a large pair of wings and a halo propped up over his head with a wire to visually position himself as a fallen angel (albeit one who looks absurd).

As the final story of the series begins, Blue Devil escapes from a fiery realm after being attacked by demonic creatures, while Lucifer gains advice from a glowing book on how to defeat the blue-hued hero. "This place of fire and brimstone you've built is but a dull cliche! But my pages are always new ... and in them each man's private hell is waiting to be found!" the book proclaims.[23] As Bart D. Ehrman explains in *Heaven and Hell: A History of the Afterlife*, the concept of what happens after we die is one that has evolved over the centuries, with conceptualizations of hell shifting from a communal inferno to a solitary existence.[24] As comics entered the postmodern era of storytelling by the 1980s, series such as *Blue Devil* provided sardonic commentary on how religious tropes are handled in popular culture.

Instead of being taken seriously as a satanic threat to all that is good and holy, Lucifer is routinely mocked throughout the issue, from kids complaining about the sulphury stench of his headquarters to Blue Devil's admonishment to him: "Look, you potato-head, I don't know what your problem is, but I'm warning you to go work it out somewhere else!"[25] We also learn that Lucifer had tried to make it as an actor before launching his crime career but was told by casting agents that his look was too stereotypical.

By the 1980s, DC was telling readers that older images of Satan—like those perpetuated by comic books of the 1940s and by Chick in later years—were in dire need of modernizing. The publisher would soon update such imagery in various Vertigo series.

Marvel Superheroes in the 1970s and 1980s

As the 1970s dawned, some creators at Marvel tried tackling Christian tropes and figures in increasingly direct ways. But in many cases, they quickly found that the marketplace had its limits in this era. Artists Ross Andru and Mike Esposito—who had worked on such titles as *Amazing Spider-Man*, *Fantastic Four* and *Marvel Team-Up* for the publisher—attempted to sell a

FIGURE 32 Blue Devil confronts an outdated version of the devil who can't get his crime career off to a great start in *Blue Devil* 31 (December 1986), page 13.

comic strip called *Genesis* to newspapers but met with strong resistance. In 2005, Esposito said that *Genesis* "satirized the Bible. It was all about everything that happened before Adam and Eve at the apple, when they were still innocent. I loved it, and I still think it's funny." But newspaper editors in the early 1970s were wary of offending some readers with a satirical take on the Bible. Esposito recalled that "we took it to the New York Daily News. The editor said, 'I love it, but I wouldn't touch it with a ten-foot pole, because the Bible Belt readers would never buy our newspaper again. This okay for New York, but you can't do it for the Midwest.'"[26]

But while newspaper strips proved problematic, Christian imagery—especially in the form of battles between heaven and hell—grew more frequent in Marvel superhero comics in the 1970s and 1980s. One of the first major figures introduced to tell these kinds of stories was Mephisto, who debuted in *Silver Surfer* issue 3 (1968) as a surrogate version of Satan in the Marvel universe. His name an obvious play on Mephistopheles (the demon/fallen angel from Christopher Marlowe's 1604 play *Doctor Faustus*), Mephisto is positioned as the ruler of hell in Marvel's comics. *The Official Handbook of the Marvel Universe*, the publisher's guide to its characters published in 1983, in fact lists Mephisto's aliases as "Satan" and "Mephistopheles," his occupation as "Lord of an extradimensional underworld" and his legal status as the "Ruler of Hell." His true identity may be in doubt, however, as we are told that he "occasionally appears to mortals in the guise of Satan, exploiting mankind's belief in a single supreme entity of evil."[27]

Although Mephisto may not actually be Satan, he serves the same narrative role for Marvel's heroes as an underworldly antagonist in hellish stories about demonic forces. As he boasts (in the third person, as all good supervillains do) in *Fantastic Four* issue 277: "Mephisto is older than humanity—older than time itself! Mephisto *is* evil! . . . Mephisto is the living force of evil, the black heart that pumps its putrid bile into the farthest corners of the universe! . . . As evil grows upon the face of the earth, so is Mephisto enriched! So is he made invincible!!"[28]

While Mephisto bears some physical resemblance to older incarnations of the devil with his red skin and pointy ears, Marvel updated those visual tropes to make the character more menacing by giving him a full-body crimson costume and cloak along with flowing, disheveled red hair and sharp, vampiric fangs. These elements, along with his sharp, angular features and gangly limbs, make him far more visually interesting than the increasingly outdated incarnations of the devil that comics creators had presented in earlier decades (and that Chick unwaveringly offered). Mephisto actually shares many

FIGURE 33 Marvel's surrogate version of Satan, Mephisto, takes on the Fantastic Four in *Mephisto Vs.* 1 (April 1987), page 13.

visual elements (fangs aside) with Neil Gaiman's character Morpheus from *The Sandman*; both sport long, shaggy hair and a long cloak to cover their gaunt anatomy.

Shortly before the latter's debut in his 1989 series, Mephisto earned his own limited series, *Mephisto Vs.*, in which he battled the Fantastic Four, X-Factor, the X-Men, and the Avengers as he sought to capture the souls of numerous heroes. *Mephisto Vs.* served to further integrate the realms of earth and the underworld with the Marvel universe, solidifying the notion that there *is* an afterlife in the publisher's stories. This concept was integral to several series of the 1970s, including *Ghost Rider* and *Son of Satan*, which dealt with the supernatural and the demonic in overt ways that heroes such as Spider-Man, The Hulk, and Daredevil did not in Marvel's first decade of superhero tales.

Ghost Rider debuted in *Marvel Spotlight* issue 5 of 1972 with a cover that proclaimed him to be "The Most Supernatural Superhero of All!" while asking curious readers, "Is He Alive ... Or Dead?"[29] The storyline is that stunt motorcyclist Johnny Blaze makes a deal with the devil in the hope of saving his father's life. In exchange for agreeing to be Satan's cycle-riding "servant," he is given "the power of all hell-fire."[30] When Blaze transforms into the demonic Ghost Rider, his face becomes a fiery skull and he uses hellfire "to form quasi-solid objects," including his motorcycle.[31]

The character was a loose updating of a spectral-themed western hero named Ghost Rider who debuted at Magazine Enterprises in 1949 and then gained a short-lived series at Marvel in 1967. But by the early 1970s, Marvel's modus operandi was to create new heroes in response to trends in popular culture: Luke Cage arrived in the midst of the Blaxploitation film cycle, while Shang-Chi and Iron Fist debuted as the martial arts films of Bruce Lee and television shows such as *Kung Fu* proved popular. Ghost Rider's arrival in 1972 coincided with the rising popularity of student motorcyclist Robert Craig Knievel (aka Evel Knievel), whose daredevil exploits were chronicled in the 1971 film *Evel Knievel*, starring George Hamilton.

But Ghost Rider's origins played into another emerging trend in the early 1970s: tales about the occult, the devil, and satanism. The most popular example was William Peter Blatty's 1971 novel *The Exorcist* and its award-winning film adaptation two years later, while other examples include such films as *The Brotherhood of Satan* (1971), *The Mephisto Waltz* (1971), *Asylum of Satan* (1972), *Daughters of Satan* (1972), *Race with the Devil* (1975), and *The Omen* (1976).

Ghost Rider's relationship with Satan was the centerpiece of his 1973 solo series. "I'm begging you, Satan! Take me ... I'm yours to do with as you

FIGURE 34 *Ghost Rider* 2 (October 1973), page 1.

choose!" he exclaims during a thunderstorm in *Ghost Rider* issue 2 as he embraces his role as Satan's servant.[32] Many Christian groups opposed placing Satan at the center of storytelling in the mass media, concerned that images of demonic summoning and sacrifices would lead to copycats, similar to Jack Chick's slippery-slope warnings that you could soon become a murderous, Satan-worshiping cannibal if you watched a scary movie or listened to Ozzy Osbourne songs.

The moral outrage over Satan's role in popular culture became known as the "satanic panic." Its focus shifted to emergent crazes such as *Dungeons and Dragons* role-playing games and heavy metal bands such as KISS, Judas Priest, and Mötley Crüe.[33] In *Religion of Fear: The Politics of Horror in Conservative Evangelicalism*, Jason C. Bivens describes how "for conservatives specifically, Satan is as historically real as God is; both intervene concretely in worldly affairs, and both are associated with specific pattens of life and behavior. Thus one's actions in the temporal realm associate one with—or tie one to—a specific realm of the afterlife and a particular set of eternal consequences."[34] For many Christians, especially conservative ones, the satanic panic was a battle for the souls of their children.

Some of the animosity aimed at satanism ultimately stemmed from older anti-Semitic conspiracy theories that believed "that secret organizations of Jews were devoted to devil worship and plans for world domination through surreptitious domination of public affairs."[35] Other phenomenon that some see as satanic have been explained as false memories among those allegedly involved in satanic incidents.[36] The methods used to interview the young children at the center of the "McMartin preschool trials" of the 1980s, for instance, were deemed highly suggestive in nature. The result was that the defendants accused of performing satanic rituals at a California preschool were either acquitted or all charges against them were dropped.[37]

Against this backdrop of satanic panic in the 1970s and 1980s, Marvel's devilish tales involving Mephisto, Ghost Rider, and other supernatural characters allowed cultural critics to draw parallels between the stories that people (especially children) consumed and their subsequent behavior. The scholarly "effects tradition" in media studies allows us to examine how specific texts and examples impact their audiences,[38] a method that is prone to abuse by those with particular ideological axes to grind. Concerns over how popular culture influences behavior were nothing new, however, given the Payne Foundation's argument in earlier decades that movies were a bad influence on children.

Some might shudder at Marvel's depictions of the specific steps involved in Johnny Blaze's satanic ritual as he summons the forces of hell. "I used to study these books on satanism as boy.... I've lit the sacred candle, painted the symbol on my chest! Now I paint the symbol on the floor... kneel in the middle of it... go around the symbol with the sacred candle... and all that remains is the incantation which I'll recite" he thinks to himself as we see him handle the various items described.[39] With these steps outlined across a series of panels, Christian critics might label the comic a visual guide to summoning Satan, regardless of the accuracy of the information presented.

In later issues of *Marvel Spotlight* and *Ghost Rider*, Blaze encounters a group of devil worshippers known as the "Church of Satan" preparing for a "black mass,"[40] and faces off against Satan and his demonic minions in hell (a cave-like realm inhabited by snakes, dragons, stalactites, and stalagmites in a unique visual rendering of the underworld).[41] While Satan had regularly been depicted as thin, goateed, and ultimately ineffectual in many 1940s and 1950s comics, Marvel turned him into a fiery, muscular powerhouse in the pages of *Ghost Rider*. Now resembling a bulkier version of The Human Torch—drawn with line work that suggests burning embers and colored in a reddish-orange hue—Satan could easily be mistaken for the Fantastic Four character if not for the addition of horns, wings, and fangs to convey his demonic nature. Gone are the feathered cap and red garments in favor of a figure embodying pure fire, his well-built shoulders and pectorals rendering him an appropriately powerful villain for Johnny Blaze to battle.

Early issues of *Ghost Rider* also introduced a new character named Damien Hellstrom, aka the Son of Satan, who was indeed the offspring of the devil. Hellstrom, who literally bears the mark of the devil, is characterized by a need to reject his heritage and redeem his satanic origins: "I stand determined to stamp out the heritage of my birth... and to rid myself of the stigma of evil attached to this mark of Satan birthmark on my chest!" he muses as we first meet him in the pages of *Ghost Rider* issue 1.[42] He soon took over the starring role in *Marvel Spotlight*, where we learn of his Jekyll-and-Hyde nature in his struggle to control his inner demons. He is described as "a man who is more than man—half-human, half-fallen angel—neither mortal nor immortal—adversary of evil... and sometimes of good," and we learn that Hellstrom trained to be a priest before becoming a demonologist. "Am I always to be both heir to hell—and—man of God?" he wonders.[43]

His own solo series, *Son of Satan*, began in 1975 and introduced a sister named Satana who was also the devil's progeny. But not all of the Christian tropes in the adventures of Hellstrom and Ghost Rider centered on Satan. In *Marvel Spotlight* issue 17, the Son of Satan encounters a disfigured being

168 • Christianity and Comics

FIGURE 35 Damien Hellstrom, the Son of Satan, addresses his dual nature in *Marvel Spotlight* 12 (October 1973), page 2.

who is at first described as the cosmic guardian of "the primal matrix—the 'model' on which all universes are structured" but is soon revealed to be Adam from the book of Genesis. Confronting Hellstrom, Adam inquires, "Hast though guessed that I wert thy father's first mortal victim? Yea, t'was him who made me this monstrosity... and now his son doth attempt to compound the crime!" Hellstrom reminds Adam that even though his father offered the

FIGURE 36 Ghost Rider is saved by "a friend" (Jesus?) in *Ghost Rider* 9 (December 1974), page 16.

temptation, he chose his fate in the garden of Eden and in turn fostered "the same freedom to choose for *all* men!"[44] This sentiment seems like an unabashedly American interpretation of the consequences of eating from the tree of the knowledge of good and evil. The inherent understanding of morality born out of Adam and Eve's actions is framed here as allowing personal choice (a hallmark of democracy) and enabling freedom (a core tenet of the U.S. Constitution).

While much of the biblical imagery in Marvel and DC titles is drawn from the Old Testament—from Adam to Cain and Abel to the wrath of God—some writers found ways to draw on the New Testament in their superhero stories. In *Ghost Rider* issue 9, writer Tony Isabella introduced a new character to aid Blaze's efforts in what the cover tagline calls "The Final Fearful Showdown With Satan."[45] Referred to only as a "friend," a man resembling Jesus Christ arrives at the climax of Blaze's battle with the devil and scares off Satan. Helping Ghost Rider up off the ground in a compassionate gesture, the seemingly messianic man tells Satan that Blaze is "free" and that "no claim" can be made to his soul. And with that, the battle ends, Satan flees, and order is restored. When Blaze inquires "about the identity of his mysterious rescuer, the man replies, "I am . . . a friend." This answer, the narrator tells us, is all we need to know: "Somehow, that is answer enough."[46]

The appearance of The Friend creates a deus-ex-machina ending on multiple levels. In an article for *Back Issue*, David Torsiello notes that "originally, Isabella had written himself into a corner with this storyline, as he was not sure how he would get Johnny out of Satan's clutches. It was [Marvel writer] Steve Gerber who playfully suggested that God could save him, and Isabella decided to run with the idea."[47] The character is never explicitly referred to as Jesus or God, but that identity is indirectly implied. In a later issue, Blaze recalls how he "got a special rescue from above" and say that "the last thing I expected to happen was for 'him' to show up and tell Satan to make tracks."[48]

In a subsequent appearance, The Friend's words resemble those of Jesus from the New Testament. When Blaze attacks a villain called The Orb, The Friend suddenly appears and intervenes. "If you must lash out at a fellow creature, Johnny Blaze—why not lash out at me?" says The Friend, evoking the passage from Matthew 25:40 that asks us to practice mercy ("I tell you the truth, whatever you did for one of the least of these brothers of mine, you did for me"). As Blaze rides off, the friend thinks to himself, "My hand is always outstretched, Johnny Blaze. You have only to take it."[49] His words echo numerous passages from the books of Matthew, Mark, and Luke in which Jesus takes people by the hand to heal them as well a passage from Psalm 73: "Yet I am always with you; you hold me by my right hand. You guide me with your counsel and afterward you will take me into glory."[50]

But the character proved to be short lived. Editor Jim Shooter soon demanded that changes be made after The Friend showed up again to aid Blaze.[51] Shooter had the Christlike character reduced to a mere mirage created by Satan, with another demonic villain revealing, "How wickedly delicious! For is Satan not also the prince of false hopes? The image of your 'Friend' was his most delightful ploy! How totally you immersed yourself in false security! How pleasant to shatter that bubble and drown you in despair!"[52] Shooter was reluctant to allow Jesus Christ to continue in a sidekick-like role in the pages of a superhero series in 1976.

Shooter soon took over as Marvel's editor-in-chief in 1978, remaining in the role through 1987. While he shot down the idea of giving Jesus a recurring role, it became a common practice in the 1980s for writers to incorporate churches and priests in more direct ways in various Marvel series, in smaller-scale stories than the epic battles between heavenly forces and hell-spawned forces found in 1970s titles such as *Ghost Rider* and *Son of Satan*.

In *The Mighty Thor* issue 303 (1981), for instance, writer Doug Moench has Thor rescue a Catholic priest from a mugging and heal his stab wounds. The issue uses Christian images and rhetoric in a combination of blatantly sensational ways (the cover image depicts a giant crucifix about to crush the priest and a young woman while the parish burns down, with Thor seemingly unable to stop it in time from falling) and in more nuanced ways that allow readers the chance to contemplate their own spirituality. When Thor (in his human alter ego of Dr. Donald Blake) finds out that the priest has been questioning his faith, he challenges the notion that his rescue was not "the divine hand of God." Blake replies, "Perhaps I *am* a God . . . an instrument of God. Are we not all touched with divinity?"[53]

A priest also plays a central role in the 1983 limited series *Cloak and Dagger* about a pair of teenagers who gain their respective light-based and darkness-inducing powers after taking a synthetic street drug. A recurring character named Father Francis Xavier Delgado aids the pair, with his 42nd Street Holy Ghost church serving as a place of sanctuary for the young heroes. Writer Bill Mantlo uses Father Delgado as a way of creating metaphors about saving lost souls, both in the urban decay of Hell's Kitchen, New York, and in terms of Cloak and Dagger themselves, as wayward teenage runaways from troubled homes. In the opening pages of the series, Delgado prays, "The wretched of the earth are all about me, and I don't know how to help them! Guide me, Holy Father." As he encounters a shining Dagger sitting atop the parish's altar, he exclaims, "Show me the way! Bring your light into my—darkness?!"[54]

Mantlo described in a 1985 interview how he wanted the characters to offer readers "a chance to watch two people grow, morally, physically and spiritually."[55] The series uses numerous Catholic tropes as a way of building up the religious themes that inform the characterization of its heroes. At one point, Delgado is called away to perform last rites at a police precinct, while in another issue we watch him lead a wake in the church. Another scene shows a police officer hiding in the confession booth, gun drawn, as gang members

FIGURE 37 Cloak and Dagger seek sanctuary in a church in *Cloak and Dagger* 1, no. 1 (October 1983), page 4.

enter the church. When one of the assailants grabs a large crucifix to use as a weapon against Cloak, he takes moral offense. "Your presence has already defiled this church. Would you now defile its symbols?" Cloak says, taking the crucifix from the gang member.[56]

Cloak is then distracted as a bolt of lightning illuminates the church, making him mistake the image of a nun in a stained-glass window for Dagger. The moment adds further thematic connection to the religious motif of light and darkness while also allowing the escalating narrative tension to build further as the gang member strikes a distracted Cloak over the head with the crucifix.

This motif is also seen in how each issue opens with a quote from Psalm 139:14: "The darkness and light are both alike.... I am fearfully and wonderfully made." The full psalm is about God's knowledge and his ability to know each human being in their hearts and minds, but Mantlo strategically combines parts of two different lines together for their thematic impact. Using the King James Version of the Bible, Mantlo draws on the following passage (lines 12–14): "Yea, the darkness hideth not from thee; but the night shineth as the day: the darkness and the light are both alike to thee. For thou hast possessed my reins: thou hast covered me in my mother's womb. I will praise thee; for I am fearfully and wonderfully made: marvelous are thy works; and that my soul knoweth right well."

Mantlo's abbreviated version of the passage from Psalm 139 is also used at the beginning of most issues of the *Cloak and Dagger* series that began in 1985 (albeit now without attribution to its biblical source). By regularly grounding the adventures in *Cloak and Dagger* in the context of scripture and by using Father Delgado's church as the regular setting for the series, Mantlo adds thematic depth to the struggles of his two protagonists by drawing on Christianity in explicit ways. This created points of connection for readers of faith and unique narrative elements for readers who are not Christian without creating such an overtly sacred character as The Friend that some might consider to be either blasphemous or heavy-handed.

At the end of the first issue of the 1983 limited series, for instance, Father Delgado looks in on Cloak and Dagger as they get settled into their new home. The narration describes how "the priest sees that light and darkness have become one" as the pair embrace.[57] The opening passage from Psalm 139 is now echoed both visually and in words as we witness a moment of relief and hope in the lives of these two troubled teens, creating in these characters a new metaphor for the balance between darkness and light, fear and wonder that this Psalm describes as an inherent part of Christian faith.

This thematic balance became complicated as the 1985 series continued, however. At the conclusion of the earlier miniseries, Delgado tells the pair, "It's . . . not my place to judge you. All I can do is pray . . . pray for Cloak and Dagger . . . and for the whole mad human race!"[58] But as the new series commences, the priest offers stern judgment for Cloak in particular when asked if he will offer the two communion. "The word of God is for any who'll hear it, Cloak . . . though I fear nothing can cause you to repent of your sins!" Cloak replies, "You would condemn my darkness, Father, and yet you still offer us sanctuary?" "I curse your demonic darkness, Cloak. I invited the two of you to stay so I could pray for the day I might free Dagger from whatever hold you have over her," Delgado tells him.[59]

The exchange reveals a key difference between long-running serialized comic books and those that tell stories in only a handful of issues or a single issue: in a four-issue limited series, Mantlo uses the priest to create thematic resolution, but an ongoing storyline needs to use its setting to create sustained narrative conflict. Hence, Delgado's relationship with our titular heroes shifts from a primarily supportive role to a more nuanced one that allows for character conflicts and for thematic tension that can be supported across numerous issues.

But this shift also creates new interpretations that put racial identity at the center of how we read these characters. Dagger, a young, blonde white woman, is regularly framed using visual patterns of light and purity in ways that make her look angelic. In contrast, Cloak is a young Black man whose face was disfigured when he gained his powers and whose garments transport people into a realm of personal torment. Both are marked by personal loss and pain, but the white hero literally glows and is a figure of healing and renewal, while the Black hero is condemned as demonic for his ability to transport people into a darkened realm and manifest their personal traumas (which often leads criminals to repent and confess).

By issue four, Delgado tells the pair that he resents how they use his church as a sanctuary in between "dispensing [their] own brand of justice on the city's scum," heightening the stakes involved in how religion is used as a narrative and thematic backdrop. Mantlo's rhetoric from Psalm 139 about the balance between light and darkness may add layers of spiritual depth to these adventurous genre tales, but in making Delgado both an ally and an antagonist, the series inadvertently highlights the obvious racial disparity between how Cloak and Dagger literally embody the forces of good and evil, illumination and darkness, allurement and disfigurement.

Although Cloak and Dagger remain less well-known characters among all but the most regular Marvel readers, the pair earned a short-lived television series on the youth-oriented Freeform network. But some of the publisher's most lauded storylines of the 1980s contained overtly Christian elements that have been adapted into some of the most prominent Marvel film and TV franchises. In 1986, creator Frank Miller ended his acclaimed run of *Daredevil* with the story "Born Again" in issues 227 through 231, in which the hero dealt with the fallout of the heroin addiction his ex-girlfriend Karen Page, her decision to reveal Daredevil's alter ego as attorney Matt Murdock, and the introduction of Maggie Murdock, a nun who is Matt's previously unrevealed mother.

The storyline includes a heavy use of Catholic tropes as it deals with themes of confession and repentance.[60] Catholicism was a brief plot point earlier in the series when a boxer who trained at the same gym as Murdock's deceased father is revealed to have become a priest named Father Gawaine in *Daredevil* issue 119 (1975). Religious faith plays only a tangential role in the story from writer Tony Isabella. For example, Gawaine rationalizes that "the Lord does move in mysterious ways" when he is called on to intervene in a scuffle.[61] But while Isabella offered characters such as Gawaine and The Friend as a way to add spiritual supporting characters for his protagonists, Miller turned the spotlight on a title hero's faith more closely than ever in "Born Again," a storyline whose title suggests a form of spiritual rebirth for the star of the series.

After a villain named the Kingpin destroys Matt's personal life, a homeless, delirious, and injured Murdock is nursed back to health by a nun who is eventually revealed to be his mother, Maggie. Single panels emphasize various visual aspects of Catholicism, from her habit to the golden crucifix Maggie wears around her neck before a full-page panel shows her kneeling down to embrace the fallen, bloodied Murdock. The sharp contrast between her black-and-white garments and rest of the page's color tones visually emphasizes her redemptive actions, while thick pink lines suggesting light from a window streak diagonally across the page to emphasize her purity.[62]

As she treats him in the basement of her church's mission, Maggie and Matt are regularly framed on the page and in panels via cross-shaped borders and individual crucifixes. As Maggie kneels beside his bed to offer praise for Matt's recovery at the start of *Daredevil* issue 230, the negative space of a wall lines up with Matt's white sheets to form the shape of a cross. That wall also holds a small crucifix mounted above Daredevil's head.[63] Matt later clutches his mother's necklace with its gold crucifix as he lays in bed with a high fever.

FIGURE 38 In "Born Again," Matt Murdock is rescued by his mother, Sister Maggie Murdock; *Daredevil* 1, no. 229 (April 1986), page 21.

Maggie, kneeling beside him, offers an extended prayer while grasping her rosary beads: "He will die. But he has so very much to do, my Lord. His soul is troubled. But it is a good man's soul, Lord. He needs only to be shown your way. Then he will rise as your own and bring light to this poisoned city. He will bring a spear of lightning in your hand, my Lord. If I am to be punished for past sins, so be it. If I am to be cast into Hell, so be it. But spare him. So many need him. Hear my plea."[64]

While some observers have labeled Daredevil as an "explicitly Catholic superhero,"[65] Murdock never outright declares his faith under Miller's watch despite the use of overt Christian tropes in the series. But even if Daredevil does not explicitly declare himself a Catholic, Miller (who labels himself as "either agnostic or atheist"[66]) closely aligns the hero with Catholicism as a way of adding depth to his characterization and giving the hero a unique backstory with the addition of Maggie Murdock as a new supporting character.

Along with Miller's use of Christianity to tell a story about personal redemption in his final *Daredevil* tale, in the mid-1980s, the Bible was used as source material for an apocalyptic storyline with the 1986 debut of *X-Factor* (a spin-off of *Uncanny X-Men*). The first two years of *X-Factor* are centered on the character arc of Warren Worthington III, aka Angel. When his feathery wings are surgically removed following an accident, Angel is recruited by the mutant villain Apocalypse to become part of his band of Four Horsemen. Angel's body is transformed and he is given new metallic wings. In addition, Worthington is given the new moniker Death as leader of Apocalypse's band of horsemen, who seek to bring about doomsday on Earth and usher in a new era of civilization for mutantkind. In the Bible, the Four Horsemen of the Apocalypse are key figures in the book of Revelation; according to chapter six, verse eight, the horsemen are "given power over a fourth of the earth to kill by sword, famine and plague, and by the wild beasts of the earth."[67]

Marvel used the epic, biblical scope of Worthington's transformation to tell a multiyear story. Apocalypse was introduced in issue 6 of 1986 and his eventual defeat came nearly two years later in issue 25. The storyline proved so memorable that it was adapted into the 2016 film *X-Men: Apocalypse* and in episodes of the 1992 animated program *X-Men: The Animated Series*. Over the course of several issues of *X-Factor*, Apocalypse gathers recruits for his army of horsemen, transforming them into the new embodiments of war, famine, pestilence, and death. The story blends moments of character development for the newly transformed Angel with a scorched-earth narrative scope. "In his heart smolders a dark anger! I, Apocalypse, will kindle that

FIGURE 39 The villainous Apocalypse gathers his Four Horsemen in *X-Factor* 1, no. 24 (January 1988) pages 9 and 23.

anger and he will scrawl my name across this world in fire and blood!" muses the villain about his new recruit.[68] Vague references to biblical events are made in numerous issues, such as when X-Factor first encounters Apocalypse's murderous minions. "The horsemen of Apocalypse! Holee—! They sure *look* like the end of the world!" exclaims Iceman at one point.[69] After he captures the band of heroes, Apocalypse taunts them: "Heaven or hell? Salvation or destruction? On the side of angels or demons—what does it matter?"[70]

The penultimate installment of the storyline in *X-Factor* issue 24 even ends with the aforementioned passage from Revelation as the four horsemen embark on their final mission. A closer look at the issue's use of the biblical passage reveals some key errors, however, since it misattributes the material from 6:8 as coming from 7:7 and misspells Revelation as "Revelations."[71] The intent to frame the tale as a modern adaptation of the Bible's final, apocalyptic eventsis meant to lend gravitas to its serialized superhero storytelling. But the citation errors clearly show a lack of close reading, echoing how the biblical material is used in a surface way in *X-Factor*. *Cloak and Dagger* took greater strides in extending the central material it quotes in metaphoric ways for the purposes of character development.

The final battle, in which the four horsemen are stopped and Angel/Death finds redemption, was part of a larger Marvel event called "The Fall of the Mutants" that took place across numerous issues of *X-Factor*, *Uncanny X-Men*, and *The New Mutants* in 1988. "The Fall of the Mutants" was followed by another major storyline in 1989 called "Inferno," which also took place across numerous Marvel titles. In the mid-1980s, crossover mega-events became a feature at both Marvel and DC, starting with *Marvel Super Heroes Secret Wars* in 1984 at Marvel and *Crisis on Infinite Earths* at DC in 1985. Such series involved tie-in issues with other series at each publisher that extended the storyline outward and encouraged readers to buy more titles. At Marvel, later events included "The Evolutionary War" in 1988 and "Atlantis Attacks" and "Inferno" in 1989, while DC published "Legends" in 1986 and "Millennium" in 1988.

In "Inferno," New York City was changed into a pseudo hell on Earth by the demonic forces that escape from limbo—which in Catholicism is a metaphysical state of existence proposed by theologians for unbaptized infants after death.[72] Marvel turned limbo into an ethereal realm inhabited by demons in the pages of *The New Mutants*, using it as launching point for pseudo-biblical adventures in *X-Factor*, *Uncanny X-Men*, and other series. In so doing, Marvel vastly expanded the scope of such stories, turning them into longer, multititle sagas with spiritual stakes that went beyond the standard encounters with Satan seen in series such as *Ghost Rider* and *Son of Satan* the decade before. While earlier series such as *Cloak and Dagger* and *Daredevil* used Christianity as a way to add thematic depth and enhance characterization in their stories, *X-Factor* used the apocryphal events of Revelation primarily as a way of revamping the look and powers of an older character and of heightening the spectacle inherent in a crossover event involving numerous titles.

Marvel's Catholic Comics

Even as Marvel employed varying degrees of subtlety in using Christian tropes and biblical passages in their superhero titles throughout the 1980s, the publisher also took a direct approach to telling Christian stories in the decade's early years. Marvel published three one-shot issues featuring biographical accounts of famous figures both past and present: *Francis, Brother of the Universe* (1980), *The Life of Pope John Paul II* (1983), and *Mother Teresa of Calcutta* (1984). Each featured an extended account of the life of their titular figure in ways that were largely comparable to the approaches taken by the Catechetical Guild and Spire Christian Comics in earlier decades. Each issue features an opening framing device (modern-day reporters in *Mother Teresa of Calcutta* and *The Life of Pope John Paul II* and Francis praying for guidance as he asks "Where did I fail?")[73] that leads into a flashback narrative of their life story. Each person's life is then recounted chronologically before returning to the present day for Mother Teresa and Pope John Paul II (Francis's story ends with his death).

The three comics were the idea of Gene Pelc, a Marvel representative working in Japan on licensing and distribution matters. An opening editorial in *Francis, Brother of the Universe* describes how while meeting with Friar Campion Lally, O.F.M., and Friar Flavian Walsh, O.F.M., at the Franciscan Chapel center in Tokyo, the pair asked Pelc if Marvel might do a book about Saint Francis. Pelc replied that "a Franciscan would have to do the storyline and dialogue" in order to ensure authenticity. This led to the involvement of Friar Roy Gasnick, O.F.M., of the Franciscan Communication Office in New York. Gasnick had already consulted on several other adaptations of St. Francis's life, including the 1978 off-Broadway musical *Francis* and the 1972 Franco Zeffirelli film *Brother Sun, Sister Moon*. A longtime fan who had collected comic books in his youth, Gasnick worked with Marvel writer Mary Jo Duffy to create a "story scenario" for the book.[74]

FIGURE 40 In Marvel's 1980 comic *Francis, Brother of the Universe*, artist John Buscema drew on visual elements from his prior work on *Conan the Barbarian*. This is page 9.

While Duffy was early on in her comics career, having previously written issues of *Daredevil*, *Marvel Two-In-One*, *Power Man and Iron Fist*, and *The Defenders*, the artwork for *Francis* was done by two of the industry's most acclaimed talents. Artist John Buscema did the line work while Marie Severin inked and colored the issue. Buscema drew most of Marvel's top series in the 1960s and 1970s, including *The Amazing Spider-Man*, *The Avengers*, *Conan the Barbarian*, *The Fantastic Four*, and *Thor*, and he co-created the devilish Mephisto. Severin had worked as the colorist for EC Comics in the 1950s before joining Marvel to draw such series as *Crazy*, *Not Brand Ecch*, *Tales to Astonish*, and *The Incredible Hulk* and had inked and colored various series.

The work of Duffy, Buscema, and Severin on *Francis* was a continuation of the tradition of work done by creators such as Reed Crandall and Joe Sinnott on Christian titles such as *Treasure Chest* in the 1960s. Christian comic books have rarely been made by creators who were not also doing genre-based work for mainstream publishers such as Marvel and DC. The art style and storytelling conventions used at these major publishers regularly informed the work done on religious-themed titles. Christian comic books typically look similar to secular comic books in their art and narrative structure, fulfilling the expectations of a wider range of comics readers about what comics typically look like and how their stories are told based on dominant marketplace norms.

Buscema's artwork contains many moments reminiscent of his work on *Conan*, given how both are set in the distant past. *Francis* features numerous scenes of knights in battle or heading off to war, while a young Francis longs for "a life of chivalry and glory," only to weep for his fallen comrades on the battlefield.[75] When Francis encounters an Egyptian sultan after a battle, the ruler Buscema draws is very similar in appearance to the Middle Eastern rulers Conan encountered. With its cover images of a sword-wielding Francis on horseback in the midst of battle and a tavern scene in which he and his cohorts raise their goblets, potential readers may have easily assumed that the issue was another installment in the popular sword-and-sorcery genre of the early 1980s in titles such as *Conan the Barbarian*, *Savage Sword of Conan*, and *Kull the Conqueror*.

The issue was distributed by both Marvel and the Catholic publisher Paulist Press, allowing it to reach readers in both mainstream and religious venues (i.e., in both comic shops and Christian bookstores). It remained in print through 2007 and was translated into numerous languages, selling over one million copies worldwide.[76] Its success led to a follow-up effort: *The Life of*

Pope John Paul II, about the life of Karol Wojtyła, with a cover date of January 1983. The issue was done with the pope's approval after members of his team were given copies of *Francis, Brother of the Universe*. Pelc once again worked with Friar Julian to set the issue in motion, arranging a meeting between "the Pope's chosen representative, Fr. Mieczyslaw Malinski" and Marvel editor-in-chief Jim Shooter. Written by Steven Grant, drawn by John Tartaglione, inked by Joe Sinnott, and colored by Marie Severin, the issue was distributed to newsstands, the direct market, and Christian retailers.

The Life of Pope John Paul II ends with the attempted assassination of the pope and his recovery, which the book's creators had to work into the narrative while its production was already under way.[77] The attempt on his life made him a household name even among non-Christians by the time *The Life of Pope John Paul II* was published. Some copies also spotlighted a familiar Marvel figure, albeit inadvertently: issues sold in comic shops featured a box with a picture of Spider-Man's face in place of a UPC barcode, creating a jarring visual juxtaposition between the images of the world's most influential Catholic and one of the world's most popular superheroes. (As a child, I figured that the religious title somehow needed Spidey's seal of approval when I saw it in stores.)

The Life of Pope John Paul II also uses a narrative convention common to both the crime and superhero genres—a reporter trying to get at the true heart of a story as the issue's narrator. "Me? I'm a newspaper man—and the Pope is my beat!" the reporter says, introducing himself to the reader. After investigating why his 1979 appearance at Yankee Stadium proved so popular among both the faithful and those he describes as "hoodlums," the reporter recounts the pope's personal history for the reader ("perhaps that missing element might already be in my grasp, if I only went over the facts once more," he muses before an extended flashback into the pope's early life).[78]

Writer Steven Grant was well versed in the crime genre in the 1980s; he wrote the first solo series starring gun-toting antihero *The Punisher* in 1985 as well as issues of *Master of Kung-Fu*, *Moon Knight*, and *Power Man and Iron Fist*, in which the heroes regularly fight street-level criminals instead of costumed masterminds. Grant wrote the reporter's dialogue with a similar level of streetwise attitude, having him describe how the pope "is in America, on my turf, in New York City" during his 1979 visit.[79]

But despite adhering to certain genre conventions, *The Life of Pope John Paul II* is unique among Christian comics for the way that Malinski provided an insider's perspective to one of the Catholic church's most important figures—offering ideas for Grant to draw on in his script. The issue's

FIGURE 41 Karol Józef Wojtyła's life is chronicled in Marvel's *The Life of Pope John Paul II* (January 1983). This is page 54.

editorial notes: "Providing anecdotes, insights, history and bits of human interest from his 40 odd years of close friendship with the pope, Father Malinski related events that have never before been told to the general public in any medium. True insights and facts about Pope John Paul II are told for the first time in this Marvel magazine."[80] The book sold around half a million copies, making it one of the top-selling titles of the decade. (For comparison, the fan favorite *Daredevil* sold an average of 259,000 copies per issue in 1983.)[81]

In 1984, a final Catholic title was released, *Mother Teresa of Calcutta*. Written by David Michelinie (who co-created the popular character Venom four years later in the pages of *Amazing Spider-Man*), drawn and colored by John Tartaglione, and inked by Joe Sinnott, the book chronicles the life of Mother Mary Teresa Bojaxhiu MC, who was canonized as a saint in 2016, nineteen years after her death in 1997. While Wojtyla had approved of his life story being turned into a comic book, Mother Teresa did not—at first, anyway. Father Roy Gasnick, who helped develop the comic, notes that he "almost immediately learned that I could not use Mother Teresa herself as a source because she was not willing to cooperate with anyone writing a biography about her." Gasnick instead relied on "a close contact" of hers at Catholic Relief Services, Eileen Egan, who "fed me much up-to-date information about Mother Teresa that had not appeared in written resources."[82]

As work began on the issue, Gasnick recalled Egan telling him that she had a phone conversation with Mother Teresa in which Mother Teresa asked her, "By the way, how is that comic book coming along?" Gasnick and Egan were "astounded that she knew about the project." Egan told Mother Teresa "that it was in good hands and not to worry." Gasnick says that the exchange "gave relief to me because I now knew I had her implicit blessing." Gasnick also received a thank-you note from Mother Teresa after the issue was published, confirming her admiration of the project.[83]

As Grant had done in *The Life of Pope John Paul II*, Michelinie used a reporter as his story's narrator. Television journalist Nick Bugatti recounts the events of Mother Teresa's life beginning in the modern-day war zone of Beirut as a way of making the issue more compelling. "I wanted to write an entertaining story, not just a dry 'Mother Teresa did this, and then Mother Teresa did that' kind of thing. Her activities in Beirut [in 1982] against the background of war seemed like a good setting to start with to provide some visual excitement," says Michelinie.[84]

Like other Christian comics before them, from *Treasure Chest* to Spire's *Archie* line, Marvel's Catholic titles were designed to appeal to both readers

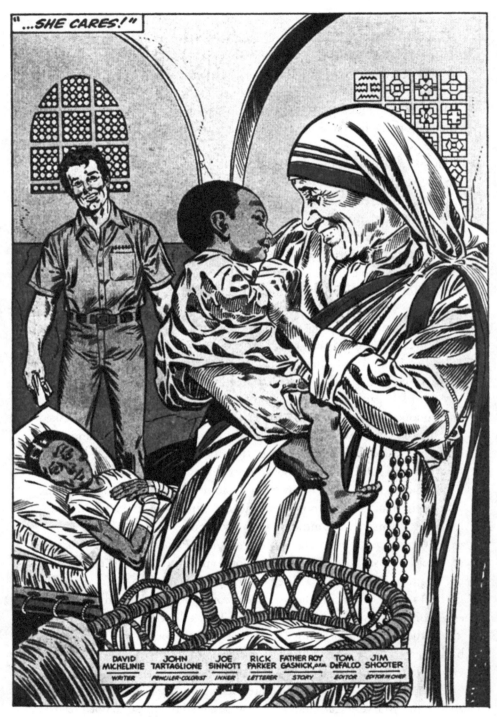

FIGURE 42 Mary Teresa Bojaxhiu's life story is presented in Marvel's *Mother Teresa of Calcutta* (1984). This is page 48.

who believed in the Bible's teachings and those who did not. Whether in their stylistic choices in the artwork, the story structure, and/or cover design, many Christian titles hope to draw in nonchurchgoing readers interested in the subject matter, characters, or presumed genre elements. This leads many publishers to be strategic in how overtly religious their content appears at a glance. Marvel reinforced the message that their Catholic titles were relevant to everyone in the storyline of *The Life of Pope John Paul II*. When a colleague assumes he is Catholic after expressing anguish about the pope being shot, the reporter replies, "I never said I was . . . and this has nothing to do with religion. Pope John Paul II is a voice for justice and wisdom in the world, a voice for hope—and there's not so much hope in the world that we can afford to lose a single source of it."[85]

From superheroes to saints, Marvel regularly embedded spiritual themes, images, and figures in their comics throughout much of the 1970s and 1980s. Many of the creators who worked on their early 1980s Catholic titles saw a distinct parallel between them and their other work for Marvel. Micheline notes that he "was trying to create an entertaining story rather than a dry recitation of facts" in *Mother Teresa of Calcutta*, "so I guess those two factors combined to generate what you might see as a superhero structure."[86] Sinnott saw his work on the two Catholic titles he inked as some of his "most satisfying accomplishments" because they allowed him to do artwork that emphasized realistic likenesses while still drawing on "all of my experiences doing books with a religious theme" in his many years at Marvel on such books with cosmic themes as *The Fantastic Four* and *The Mighty Thor*.[87]

Having worked on those series simultaneously with *Treasure Chest* until its demise in 1972, Sinnott found room to balance overtly Christian projects with those that took more metaphoric approaches to spirituality. With Marvel and DC series such as *Ghost Rider*, *Son of Satan*, *House of Mystery*, and *House of Secrets* that drew on biblical figures such as Jesus Christ, Lucifer, and Cain and Abel in direct and implied ways, comics readers were offered a range of biblically inspired stories throughout the 1970s and 1980s.

Marvel's efforts at using series such as *Daredevil* and *Cloak and Dagger* to explore issues of faith at the level of individual characters became replaced by surface-level nods at biblical events such as the use of the four horsemen in *X-Factor* as a way of aiding larger crossover events. But the publisher would launch a new imprint in the 1990s, not only to adapt some of the best-known Bible stories and works of Christian literature but also to create a new Christian superhero. And while DC's attempt at publishing an ongoing, oversized edition to adapt the Bible proved short lived after the first installment in 1975, the publisher would reinvent how it invoked scripture by the end of the 1980s with the debut of series such as *Hellblazer* and *The Sandman* that eventually helped form its Vertigo imprint in 1993. As the satanic panic of the 1970s gave way to new efforts to embed Christianity in the superhero genre throughout the 1980s, a new generation of creators such as Neil Gaiman, Garth Ennis, and Mike Mignola would soon reinvent how comics could represent heaven, hell, and everything in between as the 1990s dawned.

5

The 1990s

• • • • • • • • • • • • • •

Vertigo, *Hellboy*, and
Marvel's *Illuminator*

By the end of the 1980s, the comic-book marketplace had undergone major changes in readership and distribution from just a few decades earlier. The rise of specialty comic-book stores (aka the direct market) corresponded with declining sales at general retail outlets such as newsstands, supermarkets, and corner stores, creating a shift in where readers bought comics and who was buying them. Direct-market sales skewed toward adolescent and adult comics fans. Younger readers (or their parents) bought titles at their local 7-Eleven or supermarket checkout. As a result of this shift, most publishers increasingly planned their stories with mature readers in mind throughout the 1980s. Creators such as Frank Miller and Alan Moore offered revisionist superhero tales with series such as *The Dark Knight Returns* and *Watchmen*, while Keith Giffen's *Ambush Bug* and Bob Rozkis and Stephen DeStefano's *'Mazing Man* offered satirical takedowns of the genre's tropes for seasoned fans.[1]

With this shift toward catering to older readers came the implosion of titles written for all ages. In 1984, Western Publishing ceased its line of children's titles, including the long-running (and for many years top-selling) *Walt Disney's Comics and Stories*, while Harvey Comics folded in 1982. Although Christian comics never had a significant presence on newsstands, Harvey's demise meant fewer well-meaning morality plays for young readers in series such as *Hot Stuff*. Even Christian bookstores were affected with the end of the Spire line of titles in 1984, as the amount of new product dwindled.

In 1987, Christian publisher Tyndale House sought to fill this void by introducing a line of kid-friendly titles for Christian bookstores. Using the imprint name Cosmics on each cover, Tyndale released four titles featuring well-known biblical figures: *Joseph: The Kid Whose Dreams Came True*, *Samson: The Kid Who Never Got a Haircut*, *Jesus: The Man with the Miracle Touch*, and *Moses: The Man Who Talked to Bushes*. Each was drawn by artist Win Mumma in a loose style reminiscent of various Harvey and Archie series. Two emphasized the childhood of Joseph and Samson, aiding in accessibility for young readers. The stories used humor in their retelling of popular Bible stories, echoing the playful tone of earlier series such as *Richie Rich*: "Heavens t' haircuts!" exclaims Samson's mother at one point, while Samson refers to a discarded jawbone as a "Philistine swatter" while he clobbers his foes with it.[2]

But the marketplace for comic books of all kinds had swung widely away from younger readers as the 1990s dawned, whether it was Chick's Crusader line in Christian bookstores or the rising popularity of writers such as Miller and Moore in the direct market. Tyndale's Cosmics line was discontinued after its 1987 launch, and even Marvel's youthful Star Comics line of original and licensed titles such as *Star Wars: Droids*, *Strawberry Shortcake*, and *Peter Porker, the Spectacular Spider-Ham* lasted only from 1984 to 1988.

As readers began to choose stories about mayhem and menace over mirth, death became a common trope in DC Comics storylines such as "Death in the Family" (1988), in which Batman mourns the loss of Robin (after readers voted for his demise via a phone poll), while in the early to mid-1990s, heroes such as Superman and Green Arrow were killed off, albeit temporarily. The psychology of various characters had also become a regular focal point for DC by the 1990s: Miller's 1987 *Batman* storyline "Year One" explored the character's origins, while trauma and mourning were central to the story arcs of heroes such as Hal Jordan, Kyle Rayner, and Jack Knight in mid-1990s issues of *Green Lantern* and *Starman*.

A rising star at DC in this era was writer Grant Morrison, one of several creators who had started in the British comics industry before working for

American publishers. Known as the "British Invasion," this influx of new talent previously had done adults-only series such as *Warrior* and *2000 A.D.* in Britain.[3] Their output for Marvel and DC was informed by these early experiences; they used darker themes and more violent imagery than was found in most American comics of the 1980s. Morrison's work for *2000 A.D.* was followed by *Doctor Who Magazine* for Marvel and a new series called *Zenith*. In 1988, DC hired Morrison to write *Animal Man*, a series that has been praised as a postmodern take on the superhero genre (in which Morrison literally appeared before the main character as the writer, breaking the narrative's fourth wall).

After the success of *Animal Man*, DC gave Morrison the chance to do a darker take on the Dark Knight in *Batman: Arkham Asylum* (1989). Released as a full-length, hardcover graphic novel in an era when that format was rarely used for superhero stories, the book featured painted artwork by Dave McKean that was visually distinct from the art in other comics of the time. Its subtitle, *A Serious House on Serious Earth*, came from Philip Larkin's poem "Church Going," foreshadowing the story's decidedly somber tone and creating a spiritual allegory out of its central setting.

In aid of this seriousness, Morrison used biblical motifs throughout the book, especially from the book of Revelation, to lend Batman's cast of supporting characters more thematic depth. Early 1980s readers may have envisioned Batman as a friendly do-gooder in line with recent Saturday morning cartoons such as *SuperFriends* and *The New Adventures of Batman*, but Morrison hoped to lend the character a more apocalyptic tone at the end of the decade by going deeper than the surface elements of the Four Horsemen in *X-Factor* in the same period.

In the story, Batman faces escaped supervillains in Arkham Asylum, a psychiatric facility for the criminally insane. This is interspersed with flashbacks of the asylum's founder, Amadeus Arkham, building his institution. As a giant statue of the Archangel Michael slaying Satan is lowered onto the grounds, Amadeus draws a parallel between his work and that of the archangel. Morrison's dialogue draws on Revelation 12:7:

> Michael and his angels fought against the dragon; and the dragon fought against the angels. And the great dragon was cast out, that old serpent called the devil, and Satan, which deceiveth the whole world. Just as the Archangel subdued the old dragon, so shall I bend this house to my will. I will bring light to those dismal corridors of my childhood, I will open up the locked doors and fill the empty rooms. And set above all an image of triumph of *reason* over the irrational.[4]

FIGURE 43 Amadeus Arkham oversees the delivery of a statue of St. Michael slaying the serpent in *Batman: Arkham Asylum* (1989).

The annotated script Morrison gave to artist McKean to guide the illustration of *Batman: Arkham Asylum* reveals just how complex their use of Christian tropes was. Batman becomes a Christlike figure as he battles villains such as the reptilian Killer Croc. Grabbing the spear from the statue of the archangel, Batman impales Croc with it, much like Michael slew the dragon. "What we're evoking here," Morrison's notes to McKean explain," is another series of Christ images—by conquering the unconscious in the shape of Croc, Batman has embraced the unconscious." Morrison adds: "The images here are designed to recall Christ's clearing of the temple and even more importantly, the Harrowing of Hell. This event has no scriptural basis but formed a powerful part of the ritual imagery of mediaeval Christianity. In the story of Hell's Harrowing, Christ descends into Hell, has a confrontation with the devil and his minions and then, at the climactic moment, tears down the Gates of Hell and sets free the tortured souls within." Morrison adds, "Batman transforms from sacrificial lamb to Redeemer here. More Christian mystery biz."[5]

DC soon followed Morrison's allegorical take on the archangel's apocalyptic battle with a more overt application of Christianity to the Batman mythos in *Batman: Holy Terror* (1991). Written by Alan Brennert with art by regular *Detective Comics* artist Norm Breyfogle, *Holy Terror* is an Elseworlds tale (set in an alternate narrative continuity than the one used in regular DC titles). American society is reimagined as a "covenant nation" ruled by scriptural law and the "holy elite," and Bruce Wayne has become a clergyman-turned-vigilante.[6] With his costume redesigned to incorporate a white clerical collar, Batman seeks to avenge the murder of his parents but soon encounters a subdued Superman in a government-run laboratory: "A God-fearing couple in Kansas found him, and turned him over to us," a scientist tells Batman as we see a nude Clark Kent strung up in a pose akin to Christ on the cross.[7]

Whereas DC was relatively coy in its applications of Christianity in earlier years, using characters such as Cain, Abel, The Phantom Stranger, and The Spectre as vessels for the supernatural rather than as a vehicle for social commentary, a new generation of creators had arrived from Britain to bring religion to comics by the late 1980s. Using allegory, satire, provocation, and other literary tactics, writers such as Morrison, Neil Gaiman, Jamie Delano, and Garth Ennis offered challenging stories about Christian figures and the role of Christianity in society throughout the 1990s.

FIGURE 44 Bruce Wayne navigates a dual identity as both a man of the cloth and a caped crusader in *Batman: Holy Terror* (1991).

Marvel and Nelson: Jesus and *Illuminator*

As we will see, DC was reimagining who wrote their comics, who was reading them, and how directly their titles could incorporate religion and mythology—whether as allegory, for the purposes of ideological critique, or even as a major narrative theme. Marvel, however, turned to different strategies as the decade began. New heroes/antiheroes such as Deadpool, Cable, and War Machine tapped into the trend of violent vigilantes with big guns in the wake of the success of *The Punisher*. The serious tone used in the storylines about crises of faith and personal redemption in *Daredevil* and *Cloak and Dagger* in the 1980s was often replaced by shallow displays of violence that sought to evoke on a surface level what writers such as Miller and Moore had explored in deeper ways. Much has been made of Marvel's emphasis on "grim and gritty" heroes in the 1990s,[8] but the result was often merely abrasive in the form of major events such as "Maximum Carnage" and "Heroes Reborn" that placed spectacle ahead of story. *Ghost Rider* returned, but the titular hero was no longer a satanic force, simply a supernatural one. While Damian Hellstrom returned in the short-lived series *Hellstorm: Prince of Lies* (note the different spelling used to give the character a more heroic-sounding name), Marvel seemed largely uninterested in using Christian tropes in their superhero stories throughout the 1990s, leaving them to other publishers such as DC/Vertigo and Dark Horse.

Marvel regularly tested new publishing strategies in the early 1990s. For example, it offered British series such as *Doctor Who*, *Strip*, and *Fantasy Zone* to the American market in those years. It recruited sci-fi novelist Joe Clifford Faust for a series of squarebound books (with spines containing square edges akin to a paperback rather than staples like other comic books) called *Open Space* and adapted Ron Goulart's *TekWar* novels as *William Shatner's TekWorld* in the hope of reaching new readers. It added series such as *Spider-Man* and *X-Men* (known as the "adjectiveless" iterations of the characters, given how they were published in addition to *Amazing Spider-Man* and *Uncanny X-Men*) as vehicles for star artists Todd McFarlane and Jim Lee. It formed a new imprint in 1993 called Razorline in consultation with horror novelist Clive Barker and a new superhero line called Marvel 2099 set well into the future. It picked up an independent series from the small comics publisher Slave Labor Graphics (best known for Evan Dorkin's *Milk & Cheese* and Andi Watson's *Skeleton Key*) called *Tales from the Heart*, continuing it in 1990 as a "one-shot prestige book" called *Tales from the Heart of Africa: The Temporary Natives* under Marvel's Epic imprint.[9] It reprinted works by acclaimed French creator Jean Giraud such as *The Airtight Garage*, translating them into English.[10] It tapped into the growing popularity of hip-hop culture by giving the rap duo Kid 'n Play their own series after the success of their films *House Party* (1990) and *House Party 2* (1991).[11] Marvel even struck a licensing deal with Mattel to publish two series based on one of their most popular toy lines—*Barbie* and *Barbie Fashion*.[12]

But even though Marvel largely left religious-based adventures to others in this decade, the publisher briefly entered the Christian comics market in the 1990s by collaborating with the publisher Thomas Nelson, a centuries-old firm that produced Bibles and various types of Christian fiction and nonfiction. So when Nelson inquired about collaborating in 1992, Marvel did not strike a deal with the publisher out of an overwhelming need to save souls. It was simply another way for them to diversify their product line. After the success of its Catholic titles in the early 1980s, Marvel must have seen little downside to creating a line of titles for Christian bookstores. The result was a short-lived line of titles published in 1992 to 1994, including one about a Christian superhero called Illuminator.

Drawing inspiration from the passage in John 8:12 about Jesus being "the light of the world," Illuminator's powers are light based. The series starred a character named Andy Prentiss who gains his new abilities while at a summer camp in Tennessee. He becomes "illuminated" after encountering bright lights in the sky, gaining the power to fly and emit a glowing form of energy as his body turns into a beacon of pure light.

Although Andy is not depicted as a spiritual character when we first meet him, the debut issue shows him learning about faith as he comes to realize that his powers were heaven sent. After battling a demon named Nick with the power of "night-fire," Prentiss hides out in a church, only to be told by a caretaker that his powers are a way to serve God. "You don't need physical power to be threatenin'. Just will power. The power that comes from faith. From belief in a cause. I believe in the teachings of Jesus... that good is stronger than evil. That those who try to do right must never ignore a wrong. That, if you have the chance to help, you should. That's why I helped you..." says Gus the caretaker,[13] in a Christian variation on Stan Lee's infamous power/responsibility adage from Spider-Man's debut in *Amazing Fantasy* issue 15.

Gus serves as a mentor to Andy, lending him a motorcycle outfit and helmet as a costume and inadvertently providing a heroic moniker in the midst of teaching Andy about the need to find religion: "A man without Jesus is really just a shell, Andy. He's dark and hollow inside. He's got nothing to draw

FIGURE 45 Marvel/Nelson's *Illuminator*, no. 1 (1993), page 36.

from except those he hurts.... It's easy to spread hate, to spread the darkness in this world—it's harder to be an illuminator, to light the way to righteousness." Andy grows more curious about Christianity, asking Gus before heading out to stop the demonic villain, "Um, Gus... do you think I could come back later and talk about this 'faith' thing? If Nick doesn't kill me, that is."[14]

Compared to the hard-sell approach in Al Hartley's Spire titles and the literal fire-and-brimstone warnings of Jack Chick's work, *Illuminator* is relatively low key in how it uses the superhero genre as a vessel for any kind of evangelism. Unlike Hartley and Chick, writer Glenn Herdling's career was not primarily tied to Christian work—he served as an editor at Marvel before writing various issues of *Avengers, Blackwulf, Cable, Daredevil, Deadpool, Namor, the Sub-Mariner* and *What If...?* Herdling's stories for *Illuminator* emphasized the tropes of the superhero genre first and foremost, with proselytizing used to develop key moments of the plot and character development rather than try to brusquely break down the reader's defenses in the vein of Chick and Hartley.

While the second and third issues increased the amount of faith-based rhetoric as Andy learns more about becoming a Christian, the first issue emphasized general moral lessons rather than specifically religious ones. A camp counselor scolds a group of teenagers for hazing a new camper, for instance, while Andy laments how ill he feels after drinking beer at a party: "Never should have given in to peer pressure. I-I'll just go home and sleep it off."[15] But Herdling doesn't preach, often using *Illuminator* to stress acceptance over intolerance. In the third (and final) issue, Gus tells Andy that Christians can still have meaningful relationships with those who don't share their faith: "It's true, our job is to tell people about Christ and how he changes lives.... But it's also a reality that not everyone is going to believe. And we must still love those people, be there for them, and serve as examples," says Gus.[16]

Three decades later, that message is one that Pastor Andy Stanley feels American congregations still do not apply often enough. In his 2022 book *Not in It to Win It: Why Choosing Sides Sidelines the Church*, Stanley argues: "As long as we're content to be believers rather than doers, we will be divided. Reducing faith to a list of beliefs provides us with plenty of margin not to love, forgive, provide for, celebrate, and pray for people we disagree with. Reducing faith to a list of beliefs frees us to slander people we don't align with politically. It gives us license to mock, jeer, and celebrate the failure of people whose views differ from ours. If your version of Christianity leaves the door open to those behaviors, you're nothing like your Father in heaven. And you're nothing like his Son. You are an instrument of disunity," he tells us.[17] *Illuminator*'s lesson of love and unity, then, is a valuable one.

In keeping with *Illuminator*'s nuanced approach to faith, the back covers of the series feature different taglines aligning the hero with his faith while still emphasizing the bombastic for marketing purposes. Issue 1 proclaims, "Like a nuke from heaven—Illuminator,"[18] while issue 2 declares, "He's not a hero from another planet! He's not a grim avenger of the night! He's not a radioactive mutant! Illuminator—The hero that keeps the faith!"[19]

While the series only lasted three issues, its artist Craig Brasfield noted in a response to a blog post about *Illuminator* that "the book actually sold very well for the price, but having 2 different editorial depts made it a headache for scheduling. The Nelson approval process was arduous compared to Marvel-style and the two houses didn't meld well. 3 issues, 4 different editors."[20]

Serialized comic books may not be the best product for Christian bookstores, given how the format relies on readers buying ongoing installments of a title to read the latest adventures of a character. All of Spire's titles and most issues of Chick's Crusader series were self-contained narratives. The Crusader titles had recurring characters, and the later Alberto issues were connected, but each issue had its own distinct title, which meant that they could be read on their own without the need to have read earlier issues, as was also the case for Hartley's work.

Much like the *Francis*, *John Paul II*, and *Mother Teresa* books, *Illuminator*'s artwork was generally in keeping with that of other current books, although Marvel did not use top talent such as John Buscema and Marie Severin this time around. The artwork by penciller Brasfield and inker Frank Turner was in line with the style of Marvel artists such as Ron Lim and Rob Liefeld (whose work in such series as *Silver Surfer*, *The Infinity Gauntlet*, and *The New Mutants* was popular in the early 1990s). Brasfield and Turner worked together on a few issues of Marvel's *Alpha Flight*, *Marvel Super Heroes*, and *What If . . . ?* in 1992 and 1993, so they were well suited to match the general art style of Marvel's superhero books at the time in the pages of *Illuminator*. Comics fans browsing the shelves of Christian bookstores could tell at a glance from the artwork that the Nelson books were similar to the Marvel titles they were used to seeing in other retail venues.

Along with the three issues of *Illuminator*, Nelson also co-published several stand-alone issues with Marvel in 1992 to 1994. The first was an adaptation of John Bunyan's 1678 novel *The Pilgrim's Progress*, an allegorical tale about the quest of a young man named Christian to bring salvation to his city. Hailed as "the first novel ever written in English," *Pilgrim's Progress* is a foundational text in Western literature.[21] It is also what literary scholar Kathleen M. Swaim describes as "a mirror of late seventeenth-century Puritan culture."[22] Nelson and Marvel saw a clear need to update the tale for modern audiences, much like Spire had done with many of their adaptations in the 1970s as a way to make the story more relevant and palatable (i.e., sellable) to readers. Much like Buscema's cover for *Francis*, artist Seppo Makinen's cover for *Pilgrim* emphasizes marketable genre elements with its image of the armor-clad protagonist fighting off a giant, winged demon with giant fangs while wielding a golden-hilted sword and a shield.

As the story begins, writer Martin Powell sticks relatively close to Bunyan's opening while making strategic edits to allow for a modern setting. The original story begins, "As I walk'd through the wilderness of this world, I lighted on a certain place where there was a Den, and I laid me down in that place to sleep; and as I slept, I dreamed a Dream."[23] Powell's version instead opens: "As I walked through the wilderness of this world, I stopped in a certain place . . . and having fallen asleep, I dreamed a dream."[24]

While the basic details remain the same in the adaptation, Powell's elimination of a specific setting in the Marvel version allows Makinen's opening artwork to reference modern-day cityscapes, creating an updated allegory for 1990s readers. Christian's wilderness now consists of garbage-strewn streets lined with bars and casinos. A police car's sirens flash in the distance, and addicts line the streets. A newspaper vendor proclaims that doomsday is approaching, citing pollution and global warming as factors. As he leaves his family to begin his quest, Christian is guided by a mysterious figure named the Evangelist (drawn to resemble a cross between The Phantom Stranger and Gandalf from *The Lord of the Rings*). Powell and Makinen create an appropriately exciting epic in their adaptation, one that could potentially appeal to a wide range of readers.

In 1994, Marvel and Nelson adapted another famous Christian work—Charles Monroe Sheldon's 1896 novel *In His Steps*. The book's subtitle—*What Would Jesus Do?*—is used to frame the story's message about morality and brotherly love as a minister in Topeka, Kansas, asks his congregation to follow Jesus's example in their own encounters with others. Al Hartley had already adapted the novel for Spire in 1977. In that version Hartley offered a modern setting and adolescent or college-age characters wearing modern fashions in the hope that they would appear more relevant to Spire's younger target audience. Marvel's version, written by Powell and drawn by Fred Carrillo, retains the nineteenth-century setting of Sheldon's novel, making it feel like a period piece to 1990s readers. While Hartley's Spire output was often

FIGURE 46 The opening page of Marvel/Nelson's 1993 adaptation of John Bunyan's *The Pilgrim's Progress* updates the story's setting to a modern, urban (but unnamed) city in the book's opening.

extremely heavy-handed in its evangelical approach, his updating of the story's setting in his 1977 adaptation did make room for several Black characters to play meaningful (albeit brief) roles. The Marvel adaptation contains only a few characters of color in minor background roles—as laborers or as part of a crowd, but never in a way that gives them a voice.

As outdated as Hartley's views were about gender roles and the social value of science, he did occasionally introduce racial diversity in his Spire books. While his Christian comics might have seemed dogmatic at times to all but his most devout readers, many of the titles that set Bible tales in modern or future eras are undeniably engaging in their outlandishness; examples include *Adam and Eve* and *Alpha and Omega*. Hartley took admirable creative risks in adaptations such as *In His Steps*, whereas Marvel's version of the same novel is a relatively dry affair. Carrillo's artwork appropriately captures the story's Victorian era and moral tone, but for 1990s readers it likely felt akin to an installment of *Classics Illustrated* published many decades earlier.

But in 1994, Nelson and Marvel teamed up to produce a far more visually interesting book in their version of C. S. Lewis's *The Screwtape Letters*. Given the solemnity of *In His Steps* and the epic gravitas of *Pilgrim's Progress*, Nelson's choice of the sardonic *Screwtape Letters* as a follow-up effort was an odd choice. Adapted and drawn by Charles E. Hall, the book is irreverent and humorous and features artwork that is more like that of *Zap Comix* artists S. Clay Wilson and Rick Griffin or alternative cartoonists such as Basil Wolverton and Gary Panter than anything else Marvel published in the 1990s. Hall's artistic career was not a long one; the bulk of his work was done for editor Mort Todd on the magazines *Cracked* (a rival take on *Mad Magazine*) and *Monsters Attack!* (an homage to famous movie monsters).

Written in an epistolary format, *The Screwtape Letters* offered readers numerous letters from an aging demon named Screwtape to his young nephew/apprentice Wormwood. Hall's version left Lewis's text mostly unaltered. He presented the tale in the form of scroll-like letters surrounded by various images. Hall didn't quite use panels in most cases, preferring instead to surround each of Screwtape's letters with mosaic-like artwork. We watch various scenes of temptation and torment unfold around each letter, with Hall's scenes thematically reinforcing Lewis's words (on one page, a man is boiled alive in a cauldron by one devil while another detonates train tracks beneath it to represent the demise of his "train of thought").[25]

The end result, with its cartoonish artwork of ugly demons, feels similar to S. Clay Wilson's depictions of stylistically grotesque devils in his *Zap* stories, albeit without the extreme sexuality. Hall's satirical work for *Cracked* was clearly an influence on his approach to adaptation in *The Screwtape Letters*, and the book is one of the most unique Christian comics ever to see print.

The range of genres in Nelson's line of Marvel titles was broad, including superhero stories, epic fantasy, Victorian-era melodrama, and satirical epistolary. In hindsight it appears disjointed; each new title seemed aimed at a new audience entirely. Superhero fans might have enjoyed *Illuminator* while being confused by the irreverence of *The Screwtape Letters*. Fans of the exciting events in *Pilgrim's Progress* might have found *In His Steps* a dull affair, just as fans of the latter might have been put off by the violence in *Pilgrim's Progress*. The entire line of titles was clearly an experiment designed to test the market for Christian graphic novels as Nelson tried to grow its product line.

But Christian comics are not a genre unto themselves in the same way that superhero or fantasy titles are, in which common tropes and images ground readers' expectations about the type of stories found in a book's pages. All that unites this category of comics is the fact that they are designed for Christian readers. Their content might adapt the Bible or not. Their stories could be overtly allegorical (*Pilgrim's Progress*) or feature only loose connections to Christian faith (*Illuminator*). The differences between Nelson's various comics would have been particularly evident when they were shelved together at Christian bookstores. Hartley and Chick's lasting success was due in no small part to how their titles were so visually and tonally similar year after year, much as output of early publishers such as the Catechetical Guild and George A. Pflaum was.

The two remaining comics that Marvel and Nelson published together were more traditional than the underground-inspired work of Hall and the faith-based superheroes of *Illuminator*. In 1993, they released two separate books about the life of Christ—*The Christmas Story* and *The Easter Story*. Much like *Picture Stories from the Bible*, each book was drawn in a style similar to many of Marvel's other series. Scott McDaniel, a popular artist on books such as *Daredevil* and *Nightwing* in the 1990s, drew the cover for *The Easter Story*, and Mary Wilshire did the interior artwork for *The Easter Story* and *The Christmas Story*. Wilshire was an experienced hand at adapting well-known figures to comics. She had drawn such series as *Barbie*, *Barbie Fashion*, and *Disney's The Little Mermaid* for Marvel, further evidence of the overlaps in the publisher's try-everything approach to licensing in this era.

Each of the *Story* titles attempt fidelity in presenting events from the New Testament, but unlike the sparse use of text in earlier comics such as *The Life of Christ Visualized* (which stuck closely to the actual words of the Bible), writer Louise Simonson expanded much further on details from the books of Matthew, Mark, Luke, and John. She often added new dialogue and thought balloons as a way of offering readers new insights into the personalities of these well-known figures.

When Mary tells Joseph about her encounter with the angel Gabriel, we soon learn what her husband thinks about her pregnancy in ways that the Bible never tells us. "I want to believe her . . . but how *can* I?" Joseph thinks to himself. "Angels appear and miracles happen . . . in stories and in history. But not to ordinary people like us. I can't marry her now . . . and yet I don't want to shame her publicly. I just . . . don't know what to do." Before an angel visits him in a dream, he thinks, "I'll have to call off our wedding quietly. It is the only thing to do."[26] While *Picture Stories from the Bible* offered brief insights into Joseph's personality that the Bible doesn't, *The Christmas Story* takes this approach even further by showing his inner conflict by way of thought balloons. Marvel readers in the 1990s would have been familiar with this narrative strategy after three decades of superhero angst in the pages of *Amazing Spider-Man*, *Uncanny X-Men*, and other series containing subplots about their heroes' personal lives.

Similarly, we learn of Judas Iscariot's inner torment in *The Easter Story* as he tries to accept his fate, adding pathos to someone known primarily for his act of betrayal. "Jesus said, 'Before a rooster crows, you will say three times that you don't know me.' I love him . . . but I betrayed him. If he knows the truth of my betrayal . . . might he also know the truth of his own death?" thinks Judas.[27] These writerly flourishes add a layer of melodrama to the events in a way that had become common narrative elements of comic-book storytelling (especially at Marvel) in more recent decades.

Nelson and Marvel parted ways in 1994 after publishing only eight issues together over the course of a year and a half—three installments of *Illuminator*, the three literary adaptations, and two installments about the birth and death of Jesus. While the Nelson line was an interesting experiment, it wasn't given enough time to establish any kind of consistency.

Some commentators have criticized these Marvel books as a turn in the wrong direction for Christian publishing. Shortly after their deal ended, D. Aviva Rothchild wrote about the line in her 1995 guidebook *Graphic Novels: A Bibliographic Guide to Book-Length Comics*. She described *Pilgrim's Progress* as a "radically altered" version of the original and seemed to critique *Illuminator* as being too violent for a Christian title. Rothchild felt that the earlier series of *Tullus* comics found in weekly issues of *Sunday Pix* were a worthier alternative to Marvel's work with Nelson. Despite artwork in *Tullus* comics that Rothchild described as "generic and unimaginative" and stories that "seem only minimally believable," she praised the fact "their message is gentler and the vehicles far less violent" than in Marvel and Nelson titles such as *Illuminator*.[28]

But any violence seen in the pages of *Illuminator* is well in keeping with the type and amount found in long-standing Marvel superhero titles such as *Fantastic Four* and *Iron Man*, which is exactly the point of the series. It was clearly intended to look and feel like other superhero comics but with the addition of a Christian hero whose powers are tied to his growing faith. *Illuminator* is an enjoyable enough series, and Herdling's scripts match the tone and scope of other young heroes in training who were mastering their new powers in other Marvel series of the 1990s, such as *Darkhawk*, *Spider-Man 2099*, and *The New Warriors*. Compared to the graphic violence found in many issues of Chick's Crusader titles in previous decades (such as the first issue's cannibalistic, finger-eating satanist), Nelson's Marvel titles are relatively tame. And with *Illuminator*'s more inclusive approach to Christian outreach, preaching love and leading by example, the Nelson comics contain none of the overt hatred and demonization of marginalized groups found throughout Chick's output. They also do not stress the need to trust in faith over science or to reject modern advances in gender equality as Hartley's work for Spire did.

Illuminator makes room for nuance in its spiritual message, a rarity among comics created for Christian bookstores. Hall's work in *The Screwtape Letters* is the opposite of unimaginative in its visual reimagining of Lewis's satirical novel. And while *In His Steps* might have been safe and generic in its approach to adaptation, the updating of the central allegory of *Pilgrim's Progress* for modern times might have seemed radical compared the traditional approach to adaptation in Christian comics of earlier decades.

But the comic-book marketplace had changed—radically—by the 1990s. Most of the industry's American publishers of the 1940s through 1970s had vanished; the only major ones left from that era were Marvel and DC along with Archie Comic Publications. The rise of the direct market allowed for a wider range of titles to be sold to an increasingly older audience. In addition, new publishers began creating comics in the 1980s and 1990s, often with a decidedly different intent for the use of Christianity in their stories.

Dark Horse: *Grendel* and *Hellboy*

As comics fans increasingly bought their favorite titles at specialty stories instead of newsstands in the 1980s, a number of new independent publishers emerged. Pacific Comics debuted in 1981 with Jack Kirby's *Captain Victory and the Galactic Rangers*. Comico began publishing in 1982, finding success with original series such as Matt Wagner's *Mage* and Bill Willingham's *Elementals* as well as licensed titles based on animated series such as *Robotech*. First Comics launched in 1983, publishing acclaimed series such as *American Flagg!* by Howard Chaykin, *Dreadstar* by Jim Starlin, and *Nexus* by Mike Baron and Steve Rude.

They were joined in 1986 by Dark Horse Comics, which Mike Richardson founded as a way to offer readers a wider range of genres and to let creators own the rights to what they produced. Richardson "thought the comic book marketplace was one-dimensional—nothing but superheroes" by the 1980s. "I also wanted to produce the kind of comics I wanted to read ... and whether it was super-heroes or undergrounds, I wanted there to be content. I also wanted to let creators own and create their own work," he says.[29] Because Dark Horse and other independent publishers were primarily sold through the direct market, they didn't need approval from the Comics Code Authority to ensure distribution to traditional retail venues and thus could offer stories and images that the CCA deemed morally questionable.

While the code was updated in 1971 after its earlier 1954 iteration, the emphasis was still on moral rectitude: "To make a positive contribution to contemporary life, the industry must seek new areas for developing sound, wholesome entertainment," the Comics Magazine Association of America wrote in the preamble to the 1971 update. The code's rhetoric still placed limits on how criminals could be represented and made it clear that the expectation was that "good shall triumph over evil and the criminal [shall be] punished for his misdeeds."[30] Accordingly, the code dictated that "scenes of horror, excessive bloodshed, gory or gruesome crimes, depravity, lust, sadism, masochism shall not be permitted." There were also limits on how race and religion were to be portrayed; the code stated that "ridicule or attack on any religious or racial group is never permissible."[31] What constituted an attack, however, was not specifically defined, which meant that the boundary between commentary and critique was blurry.

But as creators regularly circumvented these requirements via independent publishers such as Dark Horse in the 1980s, the CCA updated its code again in 1989. Many of the particulars related to what kinds of specific plot points and images weren't allowed became replaced by more general guidelines such as "socially responsible attitudes will be favorably depicted and reinforced"—a criterion so vague that it was largely meaningless. The 1989 update also took strides in its efforts to discourage the use of stereotypical representations, stressing that "character portrayals will be carefully crafted and show sensitivity to national, ethnic, religious, sexual, political and socioeconomic orientations."[32] But the boundaries between sensitivity and insensitivity were largely malleable according to who was defining them, and the code's guidelines proved less and less relevant as the twentieth century wound down. By 2001, Marvel had stopped submitting their books for CCA approval. Given just how much the direct market had replaced newsstand sales, publishers recognized that the CCA had grown irrelevant.[33]

Without the reins of the CCA to guide creators, many of Dark Horse's titles combined violence and religion in bold ways that had previously been forbidden in mainstream comics. When Comico filed for bankruptcy in the 1990s, Dark Horse took over the publication of writer-artist Matt Wagner's *Grendel* about a masked assassin. Dark Horse also reprinted Wagner's "God and the Devil" storyline from 1988 and 1989 in 2003, offering readers a second look at the futuristic tale of a dystopian society ruled by a tyrannical Catholic church. "And this is how the world stands," the narrator tells us early on, describing how the world now faces "the aftermath of explosive culture shock and physical hardship. Not surprisingly, religion is paramount, indulgent and corrupt."[34]

Church attendance began to decline in America throughout the 1960s and 1970s after peaking in the 1950s, especially among younger congregants. By the late 1990s, attendance had fallen even further. Churchgoing rates had declined by almost one-third among those under the age of thirty compared to that age group's attendance in the early 1970s. General participation in church activities (in both Sunday services and in other activities) also fell by one-third, from a weekly average of ninety-seven minutes of church-related activities in 1965 to only sixty-seven minutes per week by 1995.[35]

Many in the religious community turned to politics in aid of maintaining their influence over social and cultural norms. Frances Fitzgerald describes in *The Evangelicals: The Struggle to Shape America* how the rise of right-wing Christian fundamentalism was a "forceful reaction, not against liberal theology, but rather against the social revolution of the 1960s. Its dominant theme was nostalgia for some previous time in history—some quasi-mythological past—in which America was a (white) Christian nation."[36] Stories such as *God and the Devil* became a reaction to the ways religious groups sought to maintain control of cultural politics in the wake of social changes in the late twentieth century ("God's had his chance! He blew it! So give the devil his due!" cries Grendel as he attacks an agent of the church).[37]

As Dark Horse's success as an independent publisher grew, Richardson worked with Frank Miller to create an imprint called Legend to recruit more talent. Along with Miller's *Sin City* and Mike Allred's *Madman*, one of the most prominent Legend titles was Mike Mignola's *Hellboy*, which began with the 1994 miniseries *Hellboy: Seed of Destruction*. Although writer-artist John Byrne penned the first story, later *Hellboy* miniseries were written and drawn by Mignola, the character's creator and the eventual architect of a larger line of *Hellboy*-related titles including *B.P.R.D.*, *Abe Sapien*, *Lobster Johnson*, and *Sir Edward Grey: Witchfinder* (collectively called the Mignolaverse by fans).

Christianity was central to *Hellboy*—not for the purposes of social commentary as in *Grendel*, but for narrative world building. Mignola used Hellboy's origins as the son of Satan to introduce religious iconography to the series in conjunction with various mythological tropes and figures. Comics scholar Scott Bukatman notes in *Hellboy's World: Comics and Monsters on the Margins* that Mignola "has succeeded in building a world (or cosmos) for Hellboy and his associates and nemeses."[38] Catholicism played a key part in this construction of a larger, layered narrative.

In *The Chained Coffin*, we learn that Hellboy's human mother had two other children who became a priest and a nun in centuries past and can now appear before him as ghosts. Supernatural threats in and around centuries-old churches abound in *Hellboy* tales such as *The Corpse*, *A Christmas Underground*, *Almost Colossus*, and *The Right Hand of Doom*. In various stories, Hellboy consults with numerous religious leaders such as Father Adrian Frost, who helps him understand the origins of his giant stone hand as the key to his hell-born power. Frost quotes the words of Pope Sylvester II from AD 999 to Hellboy: "And I looked down into the end of the world and saw the beast, and in his right hand was the key to a bottomless pit."[39]

In the later series *Hellboy in Hell*, his right hand is revealed to be the key "that can break down those walls that separate hell from heaven and Earth." It also has the power to "breathe life" into a hell-spawned army that can conquer the world.[40] Mad monks, demons, and satanic rituals abound in stories such as *Almost Colossus* and *Box Full of Evil*. Pentagrams and inverted crucifixes become common images in such stories, a way of tying the horrific elements of each narrative to older spiritual traditions.

But Mignola's approach to the supernatural is not pointedly evangelical in its intent. Instead, he uses certain facets of Christianity in connection with

FIGURE 47 Page 15 of Mike Mignola's *Hellboy in Hell* issue 2 reveals that Hellboy's stone hand can separate the walls between Heaven and Hell.

other elements of the horror genre, specifically the work of H. P. Lovecraft, to craft a unique version of the afterlife. Biblical forces are intertwined with those inspired by Lovecraft's fictional *Necronomicon* (also known as the *Book of the Dead*). For example, *Seed of Destruction* introduces the Ogdru-Jahad, serpentlike gods. "Chained in heaven are they. Seven is their number. Bred in the depth of the ocean," says the villainous Grigori Rasputin, who compares them to "enormous serpents" and "tempest monsters" as he sets the stakes for their world-ending power. Seemingly inspired by Lovecraft's ancient deities called the Great Old Ones and the biblical serpent in Revelation, the Ogdru-Jahad serve as one of many examples of how Mignola entwines biblical, literary, and mythical elements in a new vision of the supernatural in *Hellboy* as its titular hero and his team investigate occult phenomenon.

"The cosmology that underlines Hellboy derives from the fiction associated with the pulp magazine *Weird Tales*, specifically the writings of Lovecraft and the authors who follows him during the magazine's glory years in the 1920s and '30s," explains Bukatman.[41] Mignola combines these literary influences with Christian symbolism, for example the images and objects commonly found in the centuries-old European monasteries that Hellboy visits during his investigations, as a way of grounding his tales about an occult detective in real-word spiritual traditions.

Much like *Hot Stuff* used the trappings of hell for comedic purposes, *Hellboy* uses the demonic as a starting point for its tales that blend fantasy, adventure, horror, and science fiction. *Hellboy* uses Christianity not for the purposes of evangelism, like *Illuminator*, or allegory, like *Batman: Arkham Asylum*, or even for the social commentary of *Grendel*. As a character, Hellboy does not struggle to accept his demonic lineage in the same melodramatic way that Damien Hellstrom does. Mignola does not build off current trends in popular culture, as *Ghost Rider* and *Son of Satan* did with the satanic panic trend. He neither critiques nor celebrates the Church. Instead, Mignola uses *Hellboy* to tell stories about hell, the devil, and the Church in a way that is driven by a desire to astound and astonish rather than proselytize or scrutinize.

Vertigo: *The Sandman*, *The Mystery Play*, and *Hellblazer*

While Mignola had been an artist for Marvel and DC throughout the 1980s on such series as *Rocket Raccoon*, *Alpha Flight*, and *Cosmic Odyssey*, his move to a creator-owned book such as *Hellboy* was part of a larger shift in the industry in the 1990s. As the decade began, the success of writers such as Grant Morrison on *Batman: Arkham Asylum* and *Animal Man* and Neil Gaiman on *The Sandman* led DC to reconsider its audience in a way that few publishers had done before. By 1989, Morrison had taken over writing *Doom Patrol*, adding new depth to the book's central trope of outsider superheroes by using postmodern storytelling devices and exploring themes of mental illness, disability, and gender identity.

That same year, the first story arc of Gaiman's *Sandman* was published. The series was an update of two earlier characters with the same name—Wesley Dodds, who debuted in *Adventure Comics* issue 40 (1939) and used a gun full of sleeping gas to subdue his opponents, and Garret Sanford, who had the power to access people's dreams in *The Sandman*, published in 1974. Jack Kirby co-created both earlier versions. He presented Dodds as a crime-fighting adventurer and Sanford as a costumed superhero who was given honorary membership in the Justice League of America.

While Gaiman was also interested in tales about the dream realm, his 1989 updating was less tied to a specific genre and more interested in grounding its stories in larger myths and spiritual traditions. The series centers on Morpheus, the lord of dreams, and his family (Destiny, Death, Delirium, Desire, Despair, and Destruction, collectively known as the Endless, a group of eternal beings). Christianity is referenced often, but not exclusively. Issue 50 of *The Sandman* tells a story entitled "Ramadan," in which Morpheus encounters King Haroun al-Raschid in eighth-century Baghdad. When al-Raschid summons Morpheus (describing him as "the lord of sleep, the prince of stories, he to whom Allah has given dominion over that which is not, and was not, and shall never be"), he asks whether the dream lord is of the Muslim faith. "I am of all faiths, in my fashion," Morpheus replies.[42]

Other tales focus on specific mythological traditions, such as "The Song of Orpheus" in *The Sandman Special* issue 1, which draws on the Greek myth of Orpheus and Eurydice and reveals that Orpheus is Morpheus's son. The issue chronicles the pair's wedding, Eurydice's death, and Orpheus's descent into the underworld to recover her from King Hades. Gaiman adapts the myth relatively faithfully while also using it for the purposes of world building. He creates a further backstory for the members of the Endless by having them all attend Orpheus and Eurydice's wedding. Each is referred to by their Greek names of the era: Death as Teleute, Despair as Aponia, and so forth.[43]

Along with Greek mythology and Islam, Gaiman also regularly drew on the Bible as a part of *The Sandman*'s larger narrative world. But Christianity was just one of many spiritual traditions Gaiman used to create the overarching vision of the metaphysical in the series. As the "prince of stories," Morpheus is a connecting thread between all of the various beliefs used throughout eternity to explain the universe and everything in it. Different religions throughout the ages do not contradict one another in Gaiman's hands, they coexist as part of a larger, longer tradition of storytelling. Each spiritual tradition becomes another story that Gaiman uses to explain the connections between human beings and larger forces, be they natural, celestial, and/or supernatural. And despite any apparent differences, each story is united by the constant presence of universal aspects of human life, such as death, desire, despair, and dreams—that is, the figures who make up the Endless.

Gaiman easily wove biblical figures such as Cain and Abel and Adam and Eve into *The Sandman*'s narrative in a way that presents the Bible as just one story among many that has been used to explain the world throughout human history. The book of Genesis figures prominently in several issues, in keeping with its focus on the origins of the universe and human development. But Gaiman makes clear that there are numerous ways to read the Bible and that while some people might take aspects of it literally, others see the same events and concepts as metaphorical. In issue 40, for example, Eve recounts how she and Adam "lived together until death parted them. Some there are that say this is true history, and that there really was an earthly paradise. Others claim the tale is merely a metaphor for the rise of consciousness; the bittersweet fruit of wisdom."[44]

Eve also tells how she was Adam's third wife, not his first. His first mate, Lilith, was "expelled from Eden," possibly because "she insisted on climbing on top" of Adam during sexual intercourse. "A position of equality. Superiority, perhaps," Eve notes. Lilith subsequently "planted her own garden. They say she copulated with demons, or with the sons of God. She had many children." God then created Adam's second, nameless wife "out of nothingness," but she was "destroyed" when Adam refused to touch her.[45] While the Bible explicitly names only Eve as Adam's wife, in Judaism the tradition of Midrash (interpretive rabbinic commentary on scripture from the Talmud) explored Lilith's origins in detail. Modern feminism has claimed Lilith as a foundational figure of female empowerment.[46]

Lilith's creation is explained in *The Sandman* as stemming from Adam's inherent gender fluidity: God created Adam, in other words, as both man and woman. The opening chapter of the Bible clearly offers language that contradicts the ideas of those who see gender as a strictly binary concept. Taken at its literal word, Genesis 1:27 describes the first man created by God as both

FIGURE 48 Page 13 of *The Sandman* issue 40 explores the roles of Adam and Lilith in the book of Genesis.

"him" and "them." Gaiman has Eve explain, "They say he was hermaphrodite, an androgyne giant, back in the beginning, in the dawn. 'Male and female created He them, and he called their name Adam.' Four arms, four legs, two heads, two sets of sexual organs, two bodies joined back to back. And God divided Adam into two beings. One male, one female. Adam and Lilith."[47]

These notions of Lilith's origins and Adam's gender fluidity stem directly from biblical scripture in the opening pages of Genesis: in 1:26–27, well before Eve's introduction in 2:22, it says, "Then God said, 'Let us make man in our image, in our likeness, and let them rule over the fish of the sea and the birds of the air, over the livestock, over all the earth, and over all the creatures that move along the ground.' So God created man in his own image, in the image of God he created him; male and female he created them. God blessed them and said to them, 'Be fruitful and increase in number; fill the earth and subdue it.'"

Here, the world's first man is referred to as both "him" and "them," and as being "created" as both "male and female," signaling the androgyny that Gaiman alludes to. Gaiman's work offers a prescient look at gender identity, transgender rights, and women's rights, issues that have become central to modern culture wars in America, via the figures of Adam and Lilith. But whereas Mignola uses Christianity in more general ways as a backdrop for *Hellboy*'s stories about its characters' place in the universe, Gaiman specifically grounds his story in biblical texts as a way to provide evidence of and not just interpretation about the origins of humanity.

Adam's sons, Cain and Abel, are also prominent characters in *The Sandman*, beginning with the second issue of the series. Gaiman uses the incarnations from *House of Mystery* and *House of Secrets*, declaring that they are the same figures from Genesis in a way that those earlier series did not.[48] The pair's sibling rivalry is established early on; Abel describes his brother as "the kind who kills me whenever he's uh . . . mad at me, or bored, or just in a lousy m-mood."[49] During the pivotal storyline "Seasons of Mists," in which Morpheus travels to hell, Cain serves as the dream lord's messenger to tell of his coming.

The two brothers proved to be such important supporting characters that they were given the lead roles in the 1996 spin-off series *The Dreaming*, a book for which Gaiman served as a consultant but not a direct creator following the end of *The Sandman* that same year. *The Dreaming* offered readers further explorations of Cain and Abel's troubled relationship, the return of Eve, and additional background about Adam and Eve's time in Eden. While the narrative world of *The Sandman* and its related series regularly used myths from a wide range of eras and nations as the basis for its stories, Christianity (and especially the book of Genesis) was a recurring influence on the supporting characters Gaiman used in his tales about the Endless and their role in a veritable eternity of human history.

But while Cain, Abel, and Eve all play important roles in the series, the most significant biblical figure in *The Sandman* (and in the later series stemming from it) has to be Lucifer. The series frequently depicts hell as one of several metaphysical realms of existence, and Lucifer is its ruler as the series begins. Gaiman positions hell as an ethereal realm of existence that has served many roles and has been known by many names in various spiritual traditions. "Once upon a time, there was a place that wasn't a place," the narrator tells us. "It had many names: Avernus, Gehenna, Tartarus, Hades, Abaddon, Sheol. . . . It was an inferno of pain and flame and ice, where every nightmare had come true long since. We'll call it Hell," writes Gaiman, drawing on Judaism and Greek myth.[50] Hell is also established in *The Sandman* as part of an inherent dualism with heaven—a connection that earlier DC and Marvel series such as *Blue Devil* and *Ghost Rider* did not make explicit: "Tell yourself, Lucifer Morningstar . . . ask yourselves, all of you. . . . What power would Hell have if those imprisoned were not able to dream of Heaven?" asks Morpheus.[51]

Gaiman equates Lucifer with the archangel Samael, a connection that stems from the Talmud.[52] "He was the Creator's finest creation: the angel Samael, called Lucifer. It means 'the bringer of light.' Of all the angels he was the wisest, the most beautiful, the most powerful. Saving only his Creator, he is, perhaps, the most powerful being there is," Morpheus tells us.[53] But as the series progresses, we gain new insights into Lucifer's characterization, such as the fact that he tires of ruling in hell: "Ten billion years I've spent in this place. That's a long time . . . and we've all changed, since the beginning," he tells Morpheus. "Rank never mattered to me, not really. But the demons expected it . . . which is one reason I've quit. There are others . . . I'm tired, Morpheus. So tired."[54]

In *The Sandman* issue 69, Lucifer describes his feud with God and his changing attitude toward the universe: "I had the hubris originally to regard myself as a collaborator, as a co-author. . . . Very rapidly I found myself reduced to the status of a character, following something of a disagreement in the fundamental direction of the creation. Now I sometimes feel I'm simply waiting around to see which of us was right, which was wrong. But even if it turns out that I *was* right, what good does it do me?"[55] Much as John Milton was

FIGURE 49 Morpheus confronts Lucifer about his decision to vacate Hell in *The Sandman* 23, (February 1991), page 14.

interested in exploring Lucifer as a tragic character in *Paradise Lost*, Gaiman constructs him as a complex figure worthy of exploration.

While Gaiman set Lucifer up as a supporting character in *The Sandman*, he admits that he always envisioned Lucifer as "a star" who deserved his own ongoing series. This eventually happened in 2000 with the Vertigo series *Lucifer* from writer Mike Carey. In a foreword to the collected edition of the series, Gaiman notes that while writing the character in the pages of *The Sandman*, Lucifer "above all, had his own agenda from the moment he first came on stage.... Lucifer needed his own comic. It seemed obvious, at least to me. He was arrogant, funny, manipulative, cold, brilliant, powerful." The solo series lasted for seventy-five issues—the same number as *The Sandman*—and spawned several rebooted series in 2013, 2016, and 2019. Gaiman recalls pitching the idea for such a series as early as 1991 but says that he was often met with hesitancy: "I think they were mostly worried that a comic starring the devil (even a devil who had got bored, and tired, and resigned) might lead some to burn down the DC offices. This was particularly true when they were located at 666 Fifth Avenue."[56]

As comics such as *The Sandman* grew more popular by the 1990s, it became clear to the executives at DC Comics that many of their titles were a success in large part *because* they were decidedly not for kids. In 1993, the publisher united *The Sandman*, *Shade the Changing Man*, *Doom Patrol*, and *Animal Man* under the banner of their new imprint—Vertigo Comics. The move was a way to recognize—and institutionalize—the fact that many of the publisher's titles were adult oriented and should be avoid by younger readers because they were often sexually explicit and graphically violent and used profanity.

In prior years, DC had added a tagline in tiny print to the covers of series they thought younger readers (or their parents) should avoid purchasing: "Suggested for Mature Readers." The phrase appeared on issues of *Green Arrow*, *The Question*, *The Shadow*, *Vigilante*, *V for Vendetta*, and other such series about violent protagonists who blurred the line between hero and antihero. *V for Vendetta* was written by Alan Moore, who first found success in America writing *Saga of the Swamp Thing* in 1984 to 1987. That series also featured the "mature readers' tag, using it as a way to get around the need for approval from the Comics Code Authority by flagging it as explicitly oriented to adults. DC could either submit issues of a series for approval by the code so they could display the CCA's seal of approval on the cover or they could defer to the 'mature readers" tag if they knew the issue was unlikely to be approved.[57] But with comics fans increasingly turning to the direct market to find their favorite books, the CCA's influence was clearly waning as the twenty-first century approached.

Sage of the Swamp Thing also introduced a character who became a stalwart of Vertigo and an example of all things blasphemous: John Constantine, aka Hellblazer. Constantine, skilled in the art of black magic, made his first appearance in *Saga of the Swamp Thing* issue 37 (1985) as a vessel for Moore to tell more occult-based tales. By 1988, he had gained his own series, *Hellblazer*. The series was initially written by Jamie Delano and illustrated by artist John Ridgeway but eventually a series of high-profile writers and artists contributed throughout the 1990s including Neil Gaiman, Grant Morrison, Garth Ennis Paul Jenkins, Warren Ellis, Mark Buckingham, Rick Veitch, Sean Phillips, and Steve Dillon. *Hellblazer* became Vertigo's longest-running series, finally ending in 2013 with its 300th issue.

While other DC series used their "Suggested for Mature Readers" tagline as a way of increasing the amount of violent and/or sexually suggestive content, *Hellblazer* leaned on the label to handle religion in ways that had not been permitted in mainstream comics in previous decades. Much like Johnny Blaze in *Ghost Rider*, Constantine makes a deal with the devil and confronts various hell-spawned forces along the way. Early issues of *Hellblazer* featured a range of Christian tropes, figures, and symbols, such as crucifixes, baptism, the gates of heaven, a televangelist, and Constantine's haunting by the ghost of a nun named Sister Anne Marie.

But unlike Marvel's antiheroes of the satanic-panic era, *Hellblazer* often used its religious themes for the purposes of social commentary and not just lurid entertainment. In the third issue of the series, writer Jamie Delano drew a parallel between capitalism and politics by establishing the notion that hell has a "financial district" in which demons serve as "commodity dealers" who literally profit from their trade in human souls. The story opens with a man who dies of a heart attack while jogging. We learn that he has fallen into debt after his risky stock-market picks go wrong. His soul is claimed by the demonic dealers, who laud the current political climate as being good for business. "On the ground we can buy cheap strip assets, swell our reserves—and boost the infernal dollar" says one junior dealer. "Politically, the time is right. The haves are so terrified of becoming have-nots that it's dog eat dog up there," says another.[58]

Set in London on June 11, 1987, election day, the story shifts between the reelection of Prime Minister Margaret Thatcher and her Conservative Party and Constantine's efforts to trick the profiteering demons. Delano contrasts the greed of the demons (and those who sell their souls to them in the name of commerce) with the "despair" and "poverty" of those struggling to feed their families. "All part of the great British 'return to Victorian values,' I guess," Constantine muses, adding, "I'm not here to write social comment documentaries. I'm here to investigate dead yuppies."

Delano, however, is clearly using the story for the purpose of social commentary. For example, Constantine learns that the rising trendline in dead yuppies is tied to gentrification efforts: "OK, so yuppies are moving into the old, run-down areas and making them fashionable. But only where they can make a profit. The property's got to be worth developing."[59] Thatcher's rule has been good for the business of soul selling, we learn, as upwardly mobile entrepreneurs profit from the misery of the less well off.

Hell, we learn, is very invested in earthly politics and in maintaining pro-capitalist governments such as Thatcher's. If a "left wing" government wins an election, the "soul market is going to crash" one demon posits, making a distinction between the spiritual well-being of a society and the ways its political leaders do more to support either their nation's citizens or corporate interests. There's even an "election party" in hell where Thatcher's win is celebrated as denizens watch the results on television and toast her success (blood being the cocktail of choice). "Hooray. Mag-gie, Mag-gie, Maggie Maggie Thatch-er," shouts one demon. As we see Thatcher's face on television and listen to her proclamation of how "Britain will be great again, a nation of growth and opportunity—a symbol of strength," Constantine hangs upside down in the pits of hell.[60] From the story's opening, the stark visual contrast between Constantine's torment and Thatcher's exultant message of prosperity reinforces the growing social divide between wealth and poverty.

Although Constantine eventually triumphs in his efforts to thwart hell's greedy ghouls, his victory is soon tempered by the realization that his country is about to enter a third term of Thatcher's rule: "Then I remember, I'm hanging upside-down in front of a TV screen that's going to be broadcasting election news 'til dawn. Like I said, there's more than one road to Hell," he thinks.[61] The use of the afterlife as a metaphor for politics is just one way that Delano regularly subverts the reader's traditional expectations about the role of Christianity in comic-book storytelling. The series was not shy about including content that could be decried as blasphemous, from Constantine's cheeky approach to angels and demons alike to his sacrilegious rhetoric ("I owe him a monstrous debt, and I swear—between the despair of Heaven and the hope of Hell—that debt will be paid in full," he vows, for instance, while also using Christ's name as a curse word on other occasions).[62]

Historian David Nash defines blasphemy as "the attacking, wounding or damaging of religious belief" and surmises that changes in the legal implications of blasphemous behavior are indicative of "changing views of the sacred and how far these have regulated societies and behavior in them."[63] Between the 1940s and 1980s, the shift in how permissible blasphemous words and images were in comic books from mainstream publishers is an indication that American society's views on religion (and how popular culture can represent religion) were changing as the twentieth century progressed. Even if the CCA hadn't emerged in the 1950s to set guidelines about what comic books couldn't include, the most outlandish tales from EC Comics of that era would never dared to have its characters mutter more than an exasperated "Good Lord," let alone offer up ghost nuns, politically motivated demons, or an angel who impregnates a succubus, as *Hellblazer* issue 60 (1992) did. The latter pair arrive at Constantine's door seeking shelter just before Christmas in a moment meant to emulate the Nativity story. ("You can park your donkey round the back," John jokes.)[64]

But if *Hellblazer* can be considered blasphemous because of its subversive use of religion, the series also clearly mocks the Satanists that Chick and others were so worried about in this era. In issue 18, Constantine complains during an investigation that "the only people who will talk to me are the bloody hard-line Satanists. You know the sort. Those sweaty little perverts with horrible skin diseases who can only get it up if it's been dipped in goat's blood first. And they think that bollocks is *magic*."[65] DC's Vertigo line may have given creators a platform to be more iconoclastic in how they handled divisive subjects such as religion, but that doesn't mean they had any love for the more extreme spiritual factions such as Satanists.

Instead, Vertigo gave a new generation of comics creators a space for using popular genres such as horror, fantasy, mystery, and superhero tales to introduce deeper metaphysical overtones and address larger cultural issues, often while using Christianity as an entry point. Grant Morrison and Jon J Muth's graphic novel *The Mystery Play* (1994), for instance, uses its central plot device of a murder mystery as a way of updating a centuries-old form of storytelling. Mystery plays in which actors traveled between towns to put on shows based on biblical events were popular in medieval Europe.[66] Theater scholar Elizabeth Shafer describes how the format was used during the medieval era as a way of "blurring the boundaries between aesthetic, theatrical and spiritual impact" in order to satisfy both audiences seeking to be entertained and authority figures seeking to edify an illiterate populace."[67] Morrison and Muth's updating finds the actor who plays God in a modern-day mystery play lying murdered offstage during a performance.

The writer-artist team uses the religious overtones of the murder to explore larger questions about God's existence and the role of faith in modern times. "It's not every day one has God on the slab, eh?" says the coroner during the actor's autopsy,[68] invoking the notion that modern philosophy has disproven God's existence. As Friedrich Nietzsche said, "God is dead."[69] The tale reinforces this idea when a detective interviews a local minister. We soon learn that the faith of the man of God has been shaken by his wife's recent death from cancer. "I've served God all my life. I thought that counted for something, but I prayed and prayed for my wife's recovery and she still died," he says. "We're dumb, frightened animals, petitioning the empty sky, and if I can help ease the fear of my fellow creatures by lying to them about heaven, then I shall ... but why should I feel the need to kill God when he is so clearly already dead?" he tells the detective when he is confronted as a suspect in the murder.[70]

The Mystery Play, along with *Hellblazer* and new series such as *Kid Eternity* and *Transmetropolitan*, were part of a larger pattern among Vertigo creators of overtly using Christianity to assess changing social attitudes toward religion in the 1990s. Such comics weren't necessarily opposed to faith, but they frequently explored the uses and abuses of religion among various institutions as well as the very question of God's existence.[71] In the early 1990s, a major shift began in the number of Americans who declared no religious affiliation, a trend that culminated in 2019, when "no religion" statistically outweighed the number of reported Catholics for the first time in one survey.[72] Analyzing the rise in secularism in connection with political and religious affiliation, David E. Campbell, Geoffrey C. Layman, and John C. Green surmised in *Secular Surge: A New Fault Line in American Politics* that the increase in how the religious right has used Christianity for political gain in recent decades has created a "backlash to politicized religion" in which many congregants stopped attending church and have come to describe themselves as nonreligious.[73]

Along with this "secular divide" comes what Campbell, Layman and Green describe as a rise in "affective polarization" in which politics and religion collide: "The fact that political orientations influence change in nonreligiosity and secularism ultimately may be related to greater social polarization, as people in the Democratic and liberal political camps grow more secular and less religious, while members of the Republican and conservative political teams grow more religious and less secular."[74] Because this larger change began in the 1990s, many Vertigo books can be read as a reflection of a growing social shift in which many Americans turned away from Christianity while those who remained with their church increasingly tied their faith to their political identity.

Preacher

Perhaps no comic book is a greater reflection of the ways millions of people were reassessing the role of the church in society in the 1990s than *Preacher*. Adapted into a television series for AMC in 2016, *Preacher* was written by Garth Ennis and drawn by Steve Dillon (who had previously worked together on *Hellblazer*). The comic-book series ran from 1995 to 2000. It ended not because its popularity had faded but because its story had reached its intended ending. While a publisher's goal for most comic books is to continue it indefinitely, Vertigo books regularly ended when their creators decided it was time for their tale to conclude. Many comic books use serialization to tell their stories in ways akin to the story arcs of television soap operas: they simply never end, instead relying on subplots and continuity revisions to keep the story going and tie any loose narrative ends together.

However, Ennis and Dillon designed their story to work toward a predetermined finale even though the celestial scope of the tale could have sustained many more years of subplots. *Preacher* centers on a small-town minister named Jesse Custer who seeks to track down the Lord after gaining Godlike power himself. Possessed by an entity known as Genesis—the offspring of an angel and a demon (a plot point inspired by Ennis's aforementioned story for *Hellblazer* about a similar romantic pairing)—Custer gains the power of "the word of God." He is able to command anyone to do anything. "This thing I got: I think it's as strong as God almighty," Custer says.[75]

God, we learn, has abandoned heaven in the wake of Genesis's birth. "He quit," an angel named DeBlanc tells Custer. "He's gone. He came to us one day, all of His angels, and said He had to go on a journey to Earth. He left straight away, and He hasn't been heard from since." DeBlanc adds, "He's gone and nothing's changed. No apocalypse, no lion lying down with the lamb, four horsemen still in the stable," describing how the events of Revelation have not come to pass in the wake of God's absence.[76]

Preacher serves as a larger thematic exploration of Nietzsche's notion that God is dead and of the growing disillusionment with Christian religion in the 1990s. In the first issue of the series, Custer reveals his own lack of faith as the reader first encounters him. When his girlfriend Tulip says, "The way

I hear it, there's two good places you can look for God: in church, or at the bottom of a bottle," Custer replies, "Maybe I'll go find a liquor store then . . .'cause lemme tell you: it sure as hell ain't the church."[77]

Ennis built his comics career by regularly challenging and subverting Christian tropes and institutions. In the early 1990s, religion was at the heart of his work on *Troubled Souls* (about the violent conflict between Catholics and Protestants in Ireland) and *True Faith* (about a terrorist plot to confront God) for the British publisher Fleetway Publications and for his work on the DC series *The Demon* in 1993 to 1995. By the time *Preacher* debuted in 1995, Ennis had already written numerous stories that wielded satire as its primary method of critiquing organized religion and its dogma.

While not raised as churchgoer, Ennis became interested at a young age in the social effects of religion: "When I went to school I ran into organized religion for the first time, and I suppose I became aware of its influence a lot more. So while religion is not something that had any direct relevance on my life, it's something that always fascinated me; the Church, faith, the idea of the keepers of the faith and the abuses of it. Faith, I suppose, is a fairly harmless thing. It's when people see ways to manipulate other people's faith that the trouble starts."[78]

In *Preacher*, in addition to Ennis's subversive take on God and heaven, he also lampooned the Catholic Church by showing how it has supposedly shielded a centuries-old secret—that Jesus had a child whose lineage has been protected by a secret order called the Grail. But we learn that after two centuries of inbreeding, the most recent descendants have extreme mental and physical impairments. One character confesses that the newest messiah (known as Humperdoo) "looks like some kind of spastic antichrist, and you know it."[79] The series is blasphemous by design, so it should not be surprising that it drew the ire of many Christians when it was adapted for television. One Christian organization, One Million Moms, described the TV version of *Preacher* as "disgusting" and "sacrilegious" (although this group even labeled *The Muppets* as perverted, which says more about the Moms than it does about Kermit the Frog).[80]

Media representations of religion that some might deem blasphemous are regularly protected as free speech when done in the aid of satire. As legal scholars András Koltay and Jeroen Temperman note in *Blasphemy and Freedom of Expression*, while the line between hatred and freedom of speech can be blurry when it comes to expressions about religion, this should not preclude mocking and critiquing religions. The conclusion of a United Nations Special Rapporteur that "individual human rights law protects individuals and not abstract concepts such as religions, belief systems or institutions.... Moreover, the right to freedom of religion or belief, as enshrined in relevant international legal standards, does not include the right to have a religion that is free from criticism or ridicule."[81]

Preacher clearly sets out to ridicule various facets of Christianity, all the way from the heavenly hosts to the Catholic Church to small-town America. Ennis's approach to religion is personal, stemming from his experiences at a young age:

> I remember the first time I ran across religion. I have this memory of the teacher sitting us all down and telling us about God, who was a special friend who lived in our heart and who knew what we were doing always. He loved us and watched us, and if we loved him back—this was put in terms that a five or six year-old could understand—and did right by him, then he would reward us. Exactly what would happen to us if you didn't was glossed over at that point. Outside in the playground afterwards all the other kids were going, "Do you love God?", "Yeah I love God". And I remember when they came to me, I said "No, I think I hate him", simply because I was so freaked out at the idea of him being in in your heart and seeing everything you do. I didn't like that at all. I went home from school and told my mum, and I have this sense that it didn't trouble her much, because she just said to me, "What do you think of that then?" I replied, "Well, it all seems a bit stupid", and she said "There you are", and that was it. That was my first exposure to the idea of religion and I suppose it's never made more sense than that.[82]

Ennis used this childhood experience as a way of building a key character moment for Jesse early on in *Preacher*. Recalling a moment from his youth, Custer describes a foundational conversation with his grandmother. The grandmother says, "Today, Jesse, Gran'ma's going to tell you all about your special friend: *God*. God's special because he's always with you, Jesse. He lives inside you, in your heart, and he sees everything you do, and he knows what you're thinking, *always*. God loves you very much because He made you. And God wants you to love him, because if you love him and do good things all your life, He'll take you away to live with Him when you die. Now: isn't it nice to have a friend like God?" Jesse replies, "No, Gran'ma. It's kind of scary," prompting the woman to slap him across the face, drawing blood.[83]

Much like Al Hartley and evangelist creators had done in years past, Ennis uses his own experiences with Christianity as a driving force for stories motivated by spirituality. But unlike Hartley's Spire titles, *Preacher*'s exploration of the personal and social impacts of religion is intended to make readers question Christianity, not embrace it. "I would say we created God because we needed to," Ennis said in a 1998 interview, "when we were huddling round our caves and scared of the dark, and scared of what was waiting beyond." While he admits that he can "understand faith" as playing a major role in people's lives, he is critical of the role organized religion plays: "I think it's generally a bad thing. I think it's caused more trouble than it's done good over the years. I think that any kind of structured religion is going to have some kind of hierarchy of power, which means people being in charge of other people, telling them what to believe. Because of that hierarchy, I tend to dislike it."[84]

Ennis ended the series with the revelation that God needs his creations to love him, much as a young Garth Ennis was told in school that he had to love God back. Custer tells Tulip, "The Lord is not the loving God He swore to us He was. Instead, He's just a God who feeds on love. The creation of mankind was the act of an egomaniac, plain and simple—to choose to follow God would be a conscious act, and therefore all the more pleasing to him. The result was a world that can never know peace, but I guess that never bothered Him." Custer adds: "These are not the actions of a loving God. They are f-cked-up, twisted machinations of a being dangerously set on being adored, and I believe humanity must be free of Him, if we're to have any chance of making it at all."[85]

Ennis used the last few pages of *Preacher*'s final issue to depict the death of God, but only after God admits what Custer and Ennis had suspected all along. "You cannot understand. You cannot know what it was like to be the creator in the time before creation. There had to be a world. It had to be the way it was. Men had to choose to love me. I was alone. I wanted to loved," God confesses.[86] The bigger question *Preacher* poses, Ennis said when interviewed, "is whether we created God or he created us."[87]

From the first issue to the last, Ennis's work on *Preacher* was as much driven by the need to explore how Christianity affected his personal world view, as was the work Hartley did for Spire or Crumb did in *Zap Comix* or Justin Green did in *Binky Brown Meets the Holy Virgin Mary*. Each creator used comics as a way of exploring what faith meant to them, whether critically or lovingly. The fact that comics have been able to regularly encompass both approaches to religion over the past several decades is a testament to the depth and diversity of the medium's output.

Throughout the 1990s, creators such as Grant Morrison, Jamie Delano, Neil Gaiman, and Garth Ennis used Christian tropes as a way to tell more

FIGURE 50 In the final moments of the series finale, God reveals why he created the world in *Preacher* 66 (2000), page 19.

thematically complex stories than the relatively simplistic heaven-versus-hell battles found in 1970s titles such as *Ghost Rider* and *Son of Satan*. Comics became a forum not just for using spiritual figures to wage war but also for exploring, questioning, and/or rejecting faith. At the same time, Mike Mignola used Christianity to build a bigger narrative world for his paranormal investigators to explore, while Marvel and Nelson used the superhero genre as a forum for telling thoughtful stories about a young hero finding his faith and a new set of powers in *Illuminator*.

This diverse approaches to Christianity in order to offer more complex narratives than in decades past was symptomatic of how comics publishers expanded the types of stories their creators could tell in the 1990s. The superhero genre has long dominated the history of comic books, but series such as *Hellblazer*, *The Sandman*, *Hellboy*, and *Preacher* brought in new readers by using genres such as horror, fantasy, and westerns as platforms for stories that offered new takes on familiar Christian themes and images. As the twenty-first century loomed, comics moved beyond faithful adaptation and the allegorical and into the realm of satire and social commentary with the rise of various Vertigo titles. Thanks to Ennis, Gaiman, and others, in the decades that followed, a new generation of creators pushed the limits of how comics could tell stories about Christianity even further.

6

The 2000s

• • • • • • • • • • • • •

Genres and Auteurs

By the beginning of the twenty-first century, the comic-book industry had reached a turning point. Comics had gained mainstream exposure due to increasing number of film and television adaptations. In the first decade of the century, superheroes gained new weight in popular culture as the *Spider-Man* and *X-Men* movie franchises were joined by the Marvel Cinematic Universe and Christopher Nolan's Oscar-worthy *Dark Knight* trilogy. At the same time, with the award-winning success of books such as Art Spiegelman's *Maus*, Harvey Pekar and Joyce Brabner's *Our Cancer Year*, and Marjane Satrapi's *Persepolis*, graphic novels became an increasingly respected publishing format among critics and educators, and graphic novel sales from traditional booksellers grew. Along with Vertigo series such as *The Sandman*, books such as *Maus* awakened many to the fact that not all comics centered on the adventures of intrepid costumed heroes. In turn, comics creators found new opportunities for personal expression and innovation in genre-based tales from Marvel and DC and in more unorthodox stories for independent publishers.

As the market for graphic novels grew, religion became a frequent focus for creators new and old. Some Christian publishers used the tested strategy of adapting the books of the Bible, such as Kingstone Comics' *The Kingstone Bible* and David C. Cook's *Action Bible*. Others created new titles for Christian bookstores such as the superhero series *Power Mark* from PowerMark Productions. Many creators used humor as a way to reach readers, such as David Wilkie's *Coffee with Jesus*, Liana Finck's *Let There Be Light*, and John Hendrix's *The Holy Ghost*. Each takes a lighter tone regarding questions of faith while still being serious about scriptural subjects. Wilkie says that his intent was to show Christ as "a practical savior, one who used humor, sarcasm and gentle ribbing to address their concerns," for instance.[1]

Independent creators such as Chester Brown used the longer form of the graphic novel to explore Christian history in more provocative works such as *Mary Wept over the Feet of Jesus*, while Ho Che Anderson and Kyle Baker used the format to show the impact of Christianity on the lives of major Black historical figures in *King* and *Nat Turner*, respectively. Newer creators such as Ebony Flowers (*Hot Comb*), Gene Luen Yang (*Saints*), and Craig Thompson (*Blankets*) also offered both historical and personal accounts involving Christianity. In the wake of Vertigo's success, Marvel, DC, and newer publishers such as Image, Avatar, and IDW used new strategies to offer readers more adult-oriented storylines, often incorporating spiritual themes in ways that were more sophisticated than the sensationalist styles of older series such as *X-Factor* and *Mephisto Vs*. In early 2000s, creators had more opportunities to explore, question, challenge, and celebrate faith than ever before thanks to the medium's rising popularity. In turn, the number of comics featuring Christian elements multiplied at a pace never seen before.

Auteurs and the Graphic Novel

Most historians typically credit the rise of the graphic novel to Will Eisner's 1978 hardcover book *A Contract with God and Other Tenement Stories*, published by Baronet Books, which featured four tales of New York tenement life. At over 175 pages, Eisner's was not the first work of long-form comics. There had been predecessors, such as Harvey Kurtzman's *Jungle Book* in 1959 from Ballantine Books and *It Rhymes with Lust* from St. John Publications, a squarebound crime comic with a cover billing itself as a "Picture Novel."[2] Even earlier, there had been extended works such as Henry Kiyama's *The Four Immigrants Manga* in 1931, and nineteenth-century artists such as Rudolphe Töpffer had also experimented with novel-length works, such as *Histoire de M. Vieux Bois* in 1837.[3] Even M. C. Gaines's collected paperback editions of

Picture Stories from the Bible in the 1940s could be considered graphic novels by most modern standards. And today, most people would label the collected editions of series that were initially serialized such as *Watchmen* and *The Dark Knight Returns* graphic novels.

But Eisner's interest in using comics to tell longer-form stories starting with *A Contract with God* in 1978 (and followed by such books as *Life on Another Planet* [1983], *The Dreamer* [1986], *A Life Force* [1988], and *To the Heart of the Storm* [1991]) was the start of the modern movement of graphic novelists using the medium of comics in new ways and to reach new readers. Eisner had initially considered "using the subtitle 'An Experiment in Comics'" for the paperback release of *A Contract with God*, an indication of just how uncommon the format was in the late 1970s.[4]

While the religious focus of *A Contract with God* is not specifically Christian, given that the story centers around the life of Jewish man named Frimme Hersch and his relationship with God, Eisner explained in a preface to a new edition of the book in 2004 that its central premise is meant to be universal, regardless of one's faith. A personal relationship with God, Eisner says, "is a very human preoccupation," emphasizing that it is a universal phenomenon and not a denominational one. Such a relationship, he argues, "stems from the primal concern for survival. We are told early on that God will either punish or reward us, depending on our behavior, in accordance with a compact. The clergy provides the terms, edicts and conditions, and our parents enforce this contract."[5] But the title story of *A Contract with God* explores what happens when we feel that this contract has been broken. Eisner used his own experience of questioning his Jewish faith after the death of his sixteen-year-old daughter as the basis for the story about Hersch's similar loss. Later graphic novels such as *Maus*, *Persepolis*, and *Fun Home* solidified the graphic novel's potential for exploring trauma, grief, and death and its ability to encompass an author's personal experience, often in the form of memoir.

By the time Top Shelf Productions published Craig Thompson's autobiographical graphic novel *Blankets* in 2003, graphic novels had become a much more widely accepted format thanks to the international success of award-winning creators such as Spiegelman and Satrapi. Eisner marveled at the format's growth over the previous two decades, noting in 2004 that "I couldn't find a major publisher to take *A Contract with God* only a quarter century ago, and now graphic novels represent the book industry's fastest growing genre."[6]

Thompson won numerous awards for *Blankets*, a memoir of his adolescence in Midwest America, where he struggled with faith, adolescence, and a domineering father. Early in the book, a young Craig is told by his Sunday school teacher that "if you don't ask Jesus in your heart, you'll spend an eternity in Hell. And Hell is the opposite of Heaven. It's the worst place you could ever imagine—where you are on fire being burned & in constant pain . . . a pain that hurts so much that the Bible says you will never stop screaming or grinding your teeth. It's completely dark . . . and all around you are the souls of other people screaming and moaning."[7] This terrifying vision of the afterlife prompts Craig to regularly pray for forgiveness for what he believes to be his childhood sins. "I'm sorry, God, for the sneaking out of the cabin and lying and not reading the Bible and not witnessing to people and picking on my little brother and calling someone 'Ass' and drawing a lady without any clothes on that one time and disappointing my parents and everything else. Please forgive me," he prays through his tears at church camp.[8]

As a teenager, Thompson eventually experiences religious doubt, which he attributes to his time at camp. He describes how "church camp awakened a new skepticism in my faith" because "it was nearly impossible for [him] to accept that a group of people could adhere to the same belief, to be one in heart and mind, much less to join together in a constructive goal." As Ennis had done before him in *Preacher*, Thomson begins to distinguish between organized religion and personal faith: "The personal savior concept of Christianity is what appealed to me, the good shepherd neglecting the herd to search for the lonely, lost lamb . . . not this mass mentality."[9]

As a young man, Thomas connects sex and religion in the moments after sleeping with his girlfriend, Raina. "I studied her," he says as she falls asleep. "Aware that she'd been created by a divine artist. Sacred, perfect, and unknowable. And with reverence, I covered her body with the quilted blanket she had made me," he says before turning to a picture of Christ on his wall.[10] The image begins to move within the picture frame as Jesus turns his head to meet Thompson's gaze, a slight smile on his face.

Much as Justin Green had done over forty years earlier in *Binky Brown Meets the Holy Virgin Mary*, Thompson used *Blankets* as a forum for exploring how religion shaped his upbringing and his sexual development. Ebony Flowers similarly uses Christianity as a way of exploring the intersections of childhood and adulthood in *Hot Comb* in the story "Big Ma," about a woman named Cora and her grandmother's funeral. The story opens with the mourners lining up at Big Ma's casket, with Cora touching her grandmother's hair. Cora flashes back to childhood memories of Big Ma getting her hair done during the funeral service. An auntie thanks Jesus for her sobriety, while the pastor describes how "God called our beloved Eden Dorella Johnson home."[11]

FIGURE 51 Craig Thompson recounts his childhood memories of Bible camp in *Blankets* (2003). This is page 61.

FIGURE 52 Ebony Flowers uses religion to explore the connections between hair, memory, gender, and racial identity in *Hot Comb* (2019).

The story ends with the singing of a hymn called "His Sweet Mercy," using a religious ceremony as a framing device for *Hot Comb*'s recurring focus on the connections between Black women's hair and identity. This connection is also seen in the book's earlier story, "The Lady on the Train," in which a passenger asks a woman whose hair is wrapped if she is from Africa and then if she is Muslim. When the woman replies no, the nosy passenger asks, "Then why is your hair covered?" The woman patiently replies, "Because I want to cover my hair today."[12] Flowers regularly uses religion as an entry point for her readers to consider how Black hair is what comics scholar Hillary Chute calls "a source of intimacy, community and tension."[13]

Other creators used the graphic novel as a way to tell religious stories that were more journalistic, such as Guy Delisle's *Jerusalem: Chronicles from the Holy City*. Delisle, who describes himself as "not religious in any way," chronicles his experiences in the city of Jerusalem, including his encounters with its Christian, Muslim, and Jewish residents, and the city's history and cultural practices.[14] He visits the Church of the Holy Sepulchre, for instance, which he describes as "the holiest site in Christendom" for the role it played in Christ's crucifixion. "In the entrance is the stone on which Jesus's body was washed after his death on the cross," he notes. "To the right is Golgotha, where he was crucified with two thieves," while "below is the crypt in which Jesus was laid before resurrection." He tells readers that "the walls leading to the crypt" contain "countless little crosses, carved by pilgrims during the crusades."[15]

While Thompson offers readers a memoir about the trajectory of his personal faith, Delisle shows us how comics can also be used as an objective form of reporting, much like how other visual media are used for journalistic purposes. In *Disaster Drawn: Visual Witnessing, Comics and Documentary Form*, Chute describes how the medium of comics can be used "as nonfiction—as a form of documentary, as a form of witnessing" as well as for creating fictional stories. Comics, she points out, can be used "to express history," to "visualize testimony," and to "engage spectacle, memory, and lived lives," among other things.[16] Creators such as Delisle and Joe Sacco have used comics to document the present and the past in the same ways documentarians and news reporters do, often exploring how different religions navigate territory considered holy, for example in *Jerusalem* and Sacco's *Palestine*.

Nonfiction comics were a part of the medium long before the rise of the graphic novel, of course, as with titles such as *Marvels of Science, Heroes All*, and *Martin Luther King and the Montgomery Story*. While the fact that the latter was only sixteen pages long meant that its account of Martin Luther King Jr.'s work in the civil rights movement was relatively limited in scope, Ho Che Anderson offered readers a more in-depth account of King's life in *King*. Anderson's graphic novel was published by Fantagraphics in three installments from 1993 to 2003 before being collected into one volume.

Anderson used King's faith as a framing device for the reader, much as the 1957 book did. *King* begins with Martin as a boy in his father's church, where his father asks his son, "Why you standing in the shadows?" before calling the boy a "troublemaker" for not joining his siblings in the pews. The parallels between faith, activism, and morality are combined in this brief moment between father and son, foreshadowing the role of King's faith in the advances of the civil rights movement that lay ahead.

A few pages later, we meet King as a young man, getting dressed as Nat King Cole's "Sweet Loraine" plays on the radio. Across three panels, we see

FIGURE 53   Martin Luther King Jr.'s life is chronicled in Ho Che Anderson's *King* (2010).

him pick up a scapular medal necklace hanging from a large crucifix. It is seen first in silhouette, then in light before King grasps it. These same three panels are then reversed on the book's final page, concluding the graphic novel with the silhouetted image of King's head before the crucifix. This repetition frames King's faith as a defining characteristic, a theme Anderson reiterates throughout the book. King calls for people to "protest courageously, and yet with dignity and Christian love." He equates "love" with courage" while preaching to his congregation about civil rights and calls himself "an instrument of God's will" when he is asked in a television interview about his plans for community activism.[17]

This use of Christian rhetoric for the purpose of character development is also central to how Representative John Lewis presents himself in his memoir, *March: Book One*. He describes learning to read the Bible at age five and being struck by the passage from John 1:29 that says "Behold the lamb of God which taketh away the sin of the world." Artist Nate Powell embeds these words in a silhouetted image of the young Lewis, evoking the shadows that King's father asked him to step out from both literally and symbolically.

We watch as Lewis preaches to his chickens in the henhouse that "would never quite say Amen." Lewis says that he "imagined that they were my congregation, and me—I was a preacher."[18] Lewis later recounts his work with Jim Lawson of the Fellowship of Reconciliation, and tells how the Fellowship's 1957 comic book about King's life proved inspirational because it "explained the basics of passive resistance and non-violent action as tools for desegregation."[19] Much as the 1957 comic book inspired Lewis, his own life has inspired a new generation to heed his advice to "never, ever be afraid to make some noise and get in good trouble, necessary trouble."[20] The way Martin's father calls him a "troublemaker" in *King* and Lewis uses his Christian faith to frame his efforts to get into "good trouble" in *March* are equally inspiring.

While many comics auteurs have used the medium for the purposes of both journalism and personal memoir, other creators have merged history with both nonfiction and fictional storytelling as to way to explore religious identity in new ways. In *Nat Turner*, Kyle Baker chronicles the life of an enslaved preacher who died in 1831 leading a revolt on a Virginian plantation. Quoting directly from Thomas R. Gray's 1831 book *The Confessions of Nat Turner*, which contains interviews with Turner prior to his execution. Baker uses passages in which Turner says that his parents told him he "was intended for some great purpose" and how he was struck by the passage from Matthew 6:33 that commands, "Seek ye the kingdom of Heaven and all things be added to you."[21] We watch as Turner ages from boy to man while reading the Bible across three subsequent panels. He explains how his role in leading the rebellion stemmed from the "influence I had obtained over the minds of my fellow servants" as a preacher of the gospel, "by the communion of the Spirit whose revelations I often communicated to them, and they believed and said my wisdom came from God."[22]

Baker ends the book's second section with a full-page panel of Turner holding his Bible while preaching to his fellow slaves, visually reinforcing Turner's words about how he believed that God wanted him to lead the revolt. Turner describes how he heard "a loud noise from the heavens, and

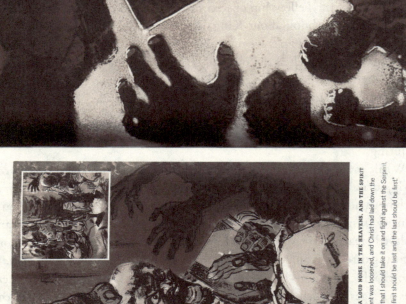

FIGURE 54 The Bible plays a key role in Kyle Baker's *Nat Turner* (2008).

the Spirit instantly appeared to me" and told him to take action. God, Turner says, told him he should "fight against the serpent, for the time was fast approaching when the first should be last and the last should be first."[23] With Baker's image of a backlit Turner holding the Bible aloft among a crowd of raised fists, the graphic novel uses this juxtaposition of text and image as another way of commenting on the connections between spiritual faith and resistance (albeit here through violence rather than the nonviolent protests of King and Lewis).

Another graphic novelist who took a spiritual approach to historical events is Gene Luen Yang, whose two 2013 graphic novels, *Boxers* and *Saints*, are meant to be read together as a way of offering readers complementary takes on the Boxer Rebellion in late eighteenth-century China. Each offers a different take on China's response to Christian missionaries. *Boxers* chronicles the efforts of a young man named Lee Bao to recruit warriors and repel the missionaries and *Saints* focuses on a girl known as Four-Girl who embraces Christianity. After learning of Christ's resurrection in the New Testament from a local acupuncturist named Dr. Won, Four-Girl seeks a way to bring back her recently deceased grandfather. "In one of Dr. Won's stories, the foreign devils raised their dead! There must be a way!" she shouts, before encountering what appears to be an apparition of Joan of Arc.[24]

Described by Dr. Won as "a young woman of extraordinary spiritual sensitivity,"[25] Four-Girl has continuing visions of Joan of Arc that lead her to convert to Christianity and take the new name Vibiana before proclaiming that God wants her to be trained "into a maiden warrior!"[26] She takes up arms against Lee Boa's army as they attack the missionaries, connecting her personal journey to the narrative in *Boxers*. Captured and bound by Bao, she has a vision of Joan being burned alive and then a vision of Christ, who tells her the story of the good Samaritan before saying: "So please, Vibiana. Be mindful of others as I am mindful of you."[27] Vibiana then teaches Bao to pray using Christ's lesson before he strikes her down with his sword.

Yang, who describes himself as a "practicing Christian—a Roman Catholic to be specific," uses the two books as a way to explore issues about the intersection of personal identity and spirituality: "The central tension in Boxers & Saints is very personal," he says, given how the overlap between Chinese identity and his Christian faith raised questions about "cultural preservation." During the era depicted in the books, "being a Chinese Christian was seen as a contradiction," says Yang. *Boxers* and *Saints* were his way of personally "wrestling with" that cultural tension.[28]

FIGURE 55 Four-Girl has a vision of Joan of Arc in Gene Luen Yang's *Saints* (2013), page 55.

Yang's use of the medium of comics to grapple with how his spirituality impacts his identity is a phenomenon that now spans several eras of comics history, following the path set decades earlier by Justin Green, Robert Crumb, and other underground comix creators. Many of the most acclaimed graphic novels and comic books of recent years use religion in prominent ways (whether Christianity in *Blankets*, *Boxers*, and *Saints*; Judaism in *A Contract with God* and James Sturm's *The Golem's Mighty Swing*; or Islam in *Persepolis* and *Ms. Marvel* by G. Willow Wilson and Adrian Alphona), and issues of spirituality and faith seem to be ones that the medium of comics handles especially well. Many creators returned to explorations of religion throughout their career, be it Justin Green following up *Binky Brown* with *Sacred and Profane*; Mike Mignola's regular use of Christian iconography in *Hellboy* and its spin-off series; Garth Ennis's steady emphasis on Christianity throughout the 1990s in *True Faith*, *John Constantine*, *Hellblazer*, and *Preacher*; Robert Kirkman following up the satirical *Battle Pope* with a more serious focus on religion in *Outcast*; or Grant Morrison's work on *The Mystery Play* and *Kid Eternity* in the 1990s and *The Savage Sword of Jesus Christ* (in *Heavy Metal* magazine) decades later.

Chester Brown, the creator of such titles as *Ed the Happy Clown*, *Louis Riel*, and *I Never Liked You*, has adapted numerous stories from the Bible in his work, such as *Mary Wept over the Feet of Jesus* (2016). Subtitled *Prostitution and Religious Obedience in the Bible*, the book is an exploration of how the Bible depicts prostitutes and their clients. The intersections between morality and sexuality have long held interest for Brown, whose 2011 graphic novel *Paying for It* is about his experiences paying for sex as a john. While Brown is interested in historical accuracy in his approach to adapting the Bible, he also approaches the task with an awareness of the artist's need for interpretation. His exploration of stories from the book of Ruth and the gospel of Matthew in *Mary Wept over the Feet of Jesus* contain extensive dialogue and thought balloons to give the reader new insights into the inner life of these key biblical figures, especially regarding the issue of prostitution. Brown even explores the question of whether Mary was a prostitute as Matthew thinks to himself while writing his gospel, "All the evidence indicates that Jesus's mother was a whore. Jesus himself said so. But many of my fellow Christians are against prostitution, and they don't want to hear the truth. Even if wrote it, it would just be censored when the scribes copy out the book. But I want to acknowledge the truth in some manner. Is there a way of hinting at it without being censored?"[29]

FIGURE 56   Chester Brown's *Mary Wept over the Feet of Jesus* (2016), page 146.

Brown's combination of historical revisionism and personal interpretation in *Mary Wept over the Feet of Jesus* exemplifies the ways many creators have approached the Bible and Christianity in their work since the start of the 2000s. In recent decades, there has been a receptive audience for comics—especially in the form of graphic novels—that challenge dominant assumptions about the Bible, from the ways Vertigo creators such as Neil Gaiman and Garth Ennis handle characterizations of biblical figures to showing how Christian faith affects personal development in *Blankets*.

This shift in the role of religion in comics began decades earlier in works such as *Binky Brown* and *A Contract with God*, but the rapid rise of comics that examine Christianity in increasingly complex ways parallels the steady increase in the popularity of the graphic novel format over the past two decades. Simply put, graphic novels have allowed comics creators to reach a wider readership with longer, often more nuanced forms of stories, and those stories have increasingly been about reenvisioning the Bible and about the connections between Christian faith and personal identity.

Marvel and DC

Much as Brown and others were interested in interpreting the Bible in new historiographic and visual ways, publishers such as Marvel and DC were increasingly interested in exploring how Christian elements could be used in more thoughtful ways by the early 2000s. At DC Comics, many superhero stories used Christianity to achieve new levels of character development while also tying into larger crossover events that spanned numerous titles, much like *X-Factor* had done in the 1980s with events such as "The Fall of the Mutants" and "Inferno." But while *X-Factor* spent relatively little time exploring how its use of biblical tropes affected characters such as Angel or Apocalypse in favor of supernatural-themed spectacle, DC often used Christianity in a way that added new layers to its characters.

In 1999, The Spectre—the wrath of God incarnate—gained a new human host. Hal Jordan (who had been the hero Green Lantern until that character's death a few years earlier) took over the role from former host Jim Corrigan. In the miniseries *Day of Judgment*, magical heroes such as Zatanna, Deadman, and Zauriel (an angel) travel to the gates of heaven to convince Corrigan that he is still needed as The Spectre. When Corrigan declines, the archangel Michael tells the group to search the realm of limbo for a new soul: "But just because Heaven cannot provide a disembodied soul, it doesn't mean your quest is over . . . here to one side of the pearly gates is the portal to a lesser realm. Purgatory—the hall of those unjudged."[30] The DC universe, it seems, adheres to the Roman Catholic Church's conception of the afterlife, including purgatory as a transitionary realm between heaven and earth.[31]

Jordan's new role as The Spectre allowed him to become a character study in redemption. Prior his death, Jordan had grown distraught with grief and transformed himself into a murderous supervillain called Parallax. As Jordan merges his soul with The Spectre's body, he confesses to his peers, "This is what I've been waiting—praying for. A chance to make it up to you—all of you. . . . I can answer for my sins."[32]

When Jordan gained a new solo series, *The Spectre*, in 2001, he was regularly positioned against a wide range of heavenly figures and settings. The first issue finds him experiencing a glimpse of heaven, which he describes as "not a place—but a state of consciousness. Every particle in my being vibrates with power and bliss . . . knowledge and . . . love! No . . . beyond love! So scared . . . so pure . . . that it's inexpressible."[33] Much as some theologians have updated the conception of hell from the older fire-and-brimstone model to one centered on the absence of God rather than endless physical torment,[34] notions about heaven as a specific location were also evolving by the beginning of the twenty-first century (for example, ministry leader Randy C. Alcorn's idea that we might conceive of heaven "as not in another universe but simply as a part of ours that we are unable to see, due to our spiritual blindness").[35]

The Spectre's adventures have regularly centered on Christianity since his debut in the 1940s, from the implied presence of the Lord's disembodied voice in *More Fun Comics* to the increasingly direct ways the character serves as God's wrath in modern incarnations. But with the former Green Lantern taking over as host, DC added new layers to the character—using faith and redemption as a way to explore Jordan's personal spiritual journey and his road to absolution for his past sins. Whereas earlier versions of The Spectre saw the supernatural hero punish sinners directly, Jordan challenges the notion that sinners need to be actively punished before they can achieve redemption. Weighing his role as a supposedly wrathful servant, he exclaims: "I can't . . . I won't . . . redeem myself by bringing suffering to others! I've caused enough suffering in my life!" When asked why he would attempt to "arrogantly" alter his mission and "challenge" God's will, Jordan replies, "Because I've been given a chance to make amends! To atone for the hurt and pain I've caused! . . . Is it arrogance to believe that it doesn't have to be that way anymore? That we've outgrown the need for a vengeful God who sits on high—judging us all? The God who offered me redemption . . . after all I'd done . . . wasn't vengeful! So why shouldn't he make the same offer . . . to all mankind?"[36]

Another DC character who was grappling with his own demons in the early 2000s was Blue Devil (aka Daniel Cassidy), who shifted from the happy-go-lucky hell-spawned hero of his 1980s title to a conflicted Catholic in more recent years. Unable to enter a church due his demonic nature, he meets with two priests in a church courtyard to discuss "a massive act of atonement" in *Shadowpact* issue 16 in the hope of saving his soul. When one of them expresses disgust over how Cassidy sold his soul for fame to become Blue Devil, Daniel admits his "many other sins," but he also tells the priest to "rein in the venom a bit, huh? You can't possibly make me feel worse than I already do."[37] While the adventures of both Blue Devil and The Spectre were tinged with Christian tropes in earlier decades, by the 2000s their characterization had become tied more closely to their personal faith and their need to atone for their sins.

Even Superman embraced the church in the 2004–2005 storyline "For Tomorrow," in which he confesses what he believes are his sins to a priest dying of cancer. Their bond allows writer Brian Azzarello to use human spirituality as a vessel for the alien hero's doubts about his efficacy as the world's protector. While Vertigo series such as *The Sandman* and *Preacher* opened up space for comics to analyze and critique religion in new ways by the end of the twentieth century, this shift also saw many creators use Christianity in aid of combining the fantastic with the spiritual in traditional superhero storytelling.

As religious studies scholar John G. Stackhouse Jr. notes in his 2020 book *Can I Believe? An Invitation to the Hesitant*, in recent decades, skepticism toward (and disaffection from) Christianity has increased in an era of rapidly advancing scientific and technological progress. But, he argues, weighing the merits of Christianity should involve an acknowledgement that "Christian faith remains very strange" and often involves a degree of "mystical experience."[38] In turn, the adventures of many DC heroes have increasingly encompassed this spiritual "strangeness" as a vehicle for character development.

At Marvel, the impact of Vertigo's success was seen by the late 1990s with the debut of their new Marvel Knights imprint, which brought new talent and new approaches. Filmmaker Kevin Smith revamped lawyer-turned-superhero Daredevil (aka Matt Murdock) in 1998, and Garth Ennis offered a new take on the violent vigilante The Punisher after *Preacher* concluded.

FIGURE 57 Blue Devil meets with two priests to discuss faith and atonement in DC's *Shadowpact* 16 (2007), page 19.

Smith used faith as a central framework for his story "Guardian Devil," building further on the Catholicism depicted in Frank Miller's "Born Again" storyline by portraying Murdock as a committed Catholic to an extent that previous writers had not.

Smith opens his story with captions from a letter written to Murdock by his former girlfriend Karen Page: "Dear Matthew... I'm not a woman of faith... it's something you've always teased me about. 'When you go to Hell, Karen Page,' you'd joke, when I'd snore through your weekly request to join you at Sunday Mass, [you'd say] 'I won't be able to rescue you. Don't think I have any pull down there... just because of the outfit.'"[39]

These captions are layered over top of the first panel of Joe Quesada's artwork, which depicts a church rooftop with a giant crucifix. Legal scholar Timothy D. Peters argues that Smith and Quesada position Daredevil "in an explicitly theological context—with virgin births, Christian redeemers, antichrists and demons—encouraging him to exercise a theological seeing by faith."[40] While these Christian elements are eventually revealed to be illusions created by the villainous Mysterio, Peters notes that such deceptions "play explicitly on Daredevil's faith—invoking his supposed ability to spiritually 'see' without his eyes."[41]

Compared to Miller's relatively sparse but strategic use of Catholic iconography in "Born Again," Smith's approach is far more extensive and more entrenched. Miller used Catholic imagery as a vehicle for character development, mostly in the latter part of his story. Smith's use of Catholicism, on the other hand, underlies his tale's structure from the outset, moving from church scenes to the confession booth to discussions about Murdock's years in Catholic school and his own personal faith (and his lapses from that faith) across the eight-issue story arc. The concluding moments find Daredevil returning to the confession booth, bringing the story back to Murdock's faith as a structural frame that opens and closes "Guardian Devil."

Marvel followed their Marvel Knights line with a new imprint called Marvel MAX in 2001, which was geared explicitly to adults. Covers bore such warning labels as "Explicit Content" and "Parental Advisory: Explicit Content" in the hope of keeping the comics out of children's hands. Most MAX series took Marvel's most violent characters, such as Deadpool and The Punisher, and added new levels of gore and violence. Others offered updated takes on older characters such as Howard the Duck, Rawhide Kid, and Damien Hellstrom.

In *Hellstorm: Son of Satan*, writer Alexander Irvine explores religion in ways that the character's earlier series never could have done in the 1970s because of the Comics Code Authority and because of Marvel's fears about offending religious readers. The adults-only MAX label allowed the new series to question Christianity in ways that some might find blasphemous. As Hellstrom enters a church, he narrates the moment in first-person captions. Standing before a stained-glass window depicting Jesus on the cross, Hellstrom tells us: "Because people know they're going to die, they want their Gods to die too. And because our Gods don't really die, killing them off makes people feel better. The God who dies is a Hallmark card. We mail it to ourselves, and fill in whatever return address we can think of."[42] Referred to many times in the series as "the God who dies," Christ is positioned as one of many religious archetypes throughout human history. For example, Hellstrom says that the underworld "looks different, depending on where you come in. Maybe you've got a three-headed dog. Maybe you've got a lake of fire. Maybe you've got a ferryman with his head on backwards." He adds: "I've heard there's a place where all the domains come together. That's where the archetypes walk. One of them is the God who dies."[43]

Christianity, according to Hellstrom, is but one story among many about why we exist and what happens when we die. In *Hellstorm: Son of Satan* the notion of a "God who dies" becomes an archetype that Irvine uses to explain the world and our place in it. Archetypes are what psychiatrist Carl Jung defined as "inherent patterns of experience and behaviour" that serve to organize "people's experience of the world" and to "shape the way people encounter their environments."[44] Irvine positions "the God who dies" as an easily understood concept, succinct enough to fit on a greeting card—so simple that even a child could grasp it.

Human beings have always used stories to help explain the world, whether through cave paintings, oral traditions, poems, plays, novels, or comic books. Irvine's story combines the spiritual traditions of Christianity with those of ancient Greece and Egypt, allowing deities such as Horus and Isis to coexist with the son of Satan, similar to Gaiman's multifaith approach in *The Sandman*. In positioning Christ as 'the God who dies,' *Hellstorm* uses Christianity in a way that was uncommon in comics until the turn of the new century—not as material to be adapted or primarily used for thematic and character-driven purposes but as a venue for exploring the role that religion plays in human consciousness.

Author Douglas Rushkoff uses a similar approach in *Testament*, a Vertigo series that reimagines stories from the Old Testament in a futuristic societal context. Rushkoff has said that even though he isn't religious, one doesn't "have to believe in God in order to believe in a just universe."[45] *Testament* was

FIGURE 58 Damien Hellstrom, the Son of Satan, theorizes about Christianity in *Hellstorm: Son of Satan* 2 (January 2007), page 8.

an opportunity for Rushkoff to reimagine the Bible's moral and ethical lessons as they apply to both modern and future societies. Abraham's attempted sacrifice of his son Isaac in Genesis chapter twenty-two, for instance, is reimagined as a father and son facing a government-mandated military draft in an era of digital surveillance technology, while Adam and Eve are envisioned as a pair who upload a new form of artificial intelligence instead of the figures who ate fruit from the tree of knowledge of good and evil.

Rushkoff, a media theorist at CUNY/Queens whose academic work examines the impact of new technologies, argues that when stories become "mythical narratives" they can be used a forum for "how populations are kept in control."[46] While Stackhouse feels that the focus on rationality in a modern technological era has fed increased religious skepticism, Rushkoff sees the present moment as one when we might reframe the very ways we conceive of religion's role in society. Whenever new media emerge, says Rushkoff, they allow societies to renegotiate the meanings and the stakes of these "mythical narratives," "providing the opportunity to again challenge unquestioned laws and beliefs and engage with our foundation myths as participatory narratives, as stories still in the making."[47] He sees the rise of the internet as one such moment, much as the invention of the alphabet and the printing press were in earlier centuries.

That trajectory can even be seen in the histories of specific media. As the medium of comics made room for the graphic novel as a regular publishing format by the end of the twentieth century, the more extensive storytelling that the longer format facilitated and the new audiences that it reached allowed for increasingly complex narratives and more nuanced approaches to theme, characterization, and symbolism. By the early 2000s, the growth in graphic novels (and the increasing number of single issues being reprinted as collected storylines in paperback editions) had led to new approaches to using religion as mythical narratives in order to explore complex social, cultural, and spiritual phenomena.

New Independent Voices

Many new series took a closer look at the purpose of faith in modern life. Some strove for a relatively neutral take on Christianity's role, others outright rejected or mocked the influence of organized religion. But even if you disagree with them, the stories that criticize or satirize the church, the Bible, and their followers are ultimately valuable for understanding the overarching role

Christianity plays in our modern lives. The influx of new titles using religion as the basis of their storytelling, whether they reinforce Christian beliefs or tear them down, are a sign of the continuing influence Christianity has on Western civilization. Culture, as anthropologist Clifford Geertz said, is "the ensemble of stories we tell ourselves about ourselves."[48] If something loses its cultural influence, we stop telling stories about it—and in turn, we stop negotiating its meaning. It would seem, then, that the renegotiation of Christianity's influence on Western culture is a key concern, because there have never been more comics telling stories about Christianity than in the past two decades. The following series are just some of many new titles that arose to tell new tales about Christian figures, themes, and events.

Some Vertigo series used biblical elements as an updated take on familiar themes, such as *Proposition Player*'s use of Las Vegas poker tournaments as a venue for waging a battle between the forces of heaven and hell for dozens of souls. But other Vertigo series took Rushkoff's notion of challenging the foundational narratives of Christianity in new directions. *Four Horsemen* used the turn of the millennium (and Y2K-era fears of civilization's potential collapse) to reimagine the Apocalypse and its four harbingers. The story's central irony is that modern society does not recognize the severity of the horsemen's threats because war, famine, and disease have already become entrenched across the globe. Other series were more experimental and/or personal, such as Ted McKeever's *Miniature Jesus*, in which an alcoholic ponders the future of his addiction, his faith, and his soul after encountering a tiny version of Jesus Christ who steps down from his crucifix on the wall of a local church.

Another profound take on the Son of God came with Vertigo's *Punk Rock Jesus* by Sean Murphy. Here, a clone of Jesus Christ named Chris is positioned as the earth's salvation but eventually rejects organized religion entirely. "Religion is dangerous—it impedes human progress like a virus. It's a global opiate for the masses. It numbs us with feel-good magical thinking and inflates our egos. Two billion people starve each day while America hoards global resources for obscene overconsumption. We're gorging on oil, fast food, and entertainment while we remain isolated from the true cost of our habits. And I'm the embodiment of it!" he tells his followers.[49] Whereas *Preacher* embedded its religious critique in the tropes and themes of the western genre as a way of exploring American identity and the potential fallibility of faith (with God's imperfections revealed only in the last moments of its conclusion), *Punk Rock Jesus* is more direct in its social criticism by making Jesus Christ (or an embodiment thereof) a central character who warns the audience directly of the dangers of putting all their faith in him.

FIGURE 59 A cloned version of Jesus Christ rejects organized religion in *Punk Rock Jesus* 4 (2012), page 17.

Vertigo's success with titles such as *Preacher* and *Punk Rock Jesus* led other publishers, such as Image Comics and Avatar, to try similar approaches. A reincarnated Jesus Christ is the central figure in Image's *American Jesus*, in which a twelve-year-old boy named Jodie discovers new powers and abilities after an accident. He soon learns that he is the second coming of Christ. Writer Mark Millar, best known for such exceedingly violent series as *Kick-Ass* and *Wanted*, says that he "wanted to write something about the church without taking the piss out of it, and [write] something about Jesus that wasn't judgmental or mocking."[50]

Similarly, Joe Casey and Benjamin Marra's graphic novel *Jesusfreak* from Image Comics tells the story of a young carpenter from Nazareth and an eventually beheaded preacher named John in the year 26 of the Gregorian calendar. The book is explicitly positioned as nonreligious despite the fact that its setting, figures, and events are drawn from biblical history. Casey notes in his introduction, "We're not adapting the gospels. We're not espousing any particular point of view. We know the world is full of various religious persuasions and denominations. Your mileage may vary when it comes to their validity, but they're all out there and they're all a part of the vast mosaic that is the human race."

Casey further notes that *Jesusfreak* should be read as a story that draws on religion for its narrative but not as a religious story: "There are plenty of existing stories that deal with religion head-on. This is not one of them. Whatever you believe in your life, more power to you. But this book is not meant to provide any deep, spiritual insight into anything of a religious nature. You want spiritual insight? Read the Bible. Read the Torah. Read the Quran or the Vedas or the Buddhist Sutras. Go to church. Go to temple. Meditate. Do whatever you need to do. But you're probably not going to find any answers here."[51]

Jesusfreak and *American Jesus*, then, like so many other series from Image, Vertigo, and other publishers in recent decades, are stories *about* Christianity, not stories told with the primary goal of witnessing for Christ and converting readers into new believers, as earlier titles by Al Hartley and others were. The fact that Jesus knows martial arts and battles reptile men in *Jesusfreak* further underscores Casey's point that he is writing a story about Jesus without making it a book that serves the needs of a Christian ministry. It's a story about Jesus, much as *Abraham Lincoln, Vampire Hunter* is a story about America's sixteenth president.

The way Casey positions his book as a nonreligious story about religious figures reminds us that the comic-book market was very different by the 2000s than it had been just a few decades earlier. Series such as *Ghost Rider* and

House of Mystery were genre-based efforts at building narratives around biblical figures such as Cain, Abel, and Satan in the 1970s, much like *Jesusfreak* uses martial arts for much of its conflict. But when writer Tony Isabella introduced The Friend as a thinly veiled version of Jesus in *Ghost Rider*, the character was quickly abandoned because of editor Jim Shooter's hesitations. It seemed there wasn't room for Christ to become a recurring figure in Marvel comics of that era, let alone establish a meaningful friendship with a Satan-serving motorcyclist. Instead, Satan merely served as a supervillain in *Ghost Rider*, much like how publishers had been presenting him since the early 1940s.

But by the 2000s, biblical figures frequently became the stars of their own titles. Some were ongoing series, others were graphic novels. But in each case, they were published by some of the largest comic-book publishers of the modern era. In earlier decades, most comics about biblical figures had been created by exclusively Christian publishers such as the Catechetical Guild and Spire Christian Comics and were not sold in the mainstream retail outlets of their day such as newsstands and drugstores. But modern series such as *Lucifer* can be found in a range of bookstores, comic shops, and public libraries, attracting a wider readership with diverse spiritual backgrounds.

What's more, modern publishers regularly release Christian-themed titles alongside series in an array of genres. This means that a comic book about a biblical figure might be shelved next to a horror or superhero title and not just next to other religious titles. In the modern marketplace, comics about Christianity have moved from a niche product created for a targeted readership that is distributed primarily in Christian bookstores and schools to a product created by some of the most popular authors in the business and consumed by dedicated comics fans and casual readers alike.

At DC, Lucifer's initial Vertigo series in 2000 was followed by two more in 2016 and 2018 and was adapted as a television series that lasted six seasons. At IDW, artist Scott Hampton (whose 1999 miniseries *The Sandman Presents: Lucifer* was a precursor to the character's solo series) and writer Keith Giffen created the graphic novel *The Bible: Eden*, which chronicles the lives of Adam and Eve in a style intended for adult readers with its explicit images of nudity, sex, and vaginal birth. Boom Comics published the four-issue miniseries *Judas* in 2018, giving readers an in-depth character study of Judas Iscariot and his reasons for betraying Christ.

At Image Comics, with artist Ari Handel, Darren Aronofsky, an Academy Award–nominated director of such films as *Requiem for a Dream*, *Black Swan*, *The Wrestler*, and *The Whale*, adapted his screenplay for the 2014 film

Noah into a graphic novel based on the events of chapters five through nine of the Book of Genesis. Aronofsky, Aronofsky's adaptation shows how the same take on a biblical story can be used for both adult-oriented comics storytelling and a Hollywood film starring popular actors such as Russell Crowe, Jennifer Connelly, Emma Watson, and Anthony Hopkins. The scope of such a star-powered cross-media collaboration was far beyond the reach of earlier Christian publishers such as the Catechetical Guild, George Pflaum, and even Spire (which could only create tenuous connections to Hollywood blockbusters with titles such as *Paul: Close Encounters of the Real Kind*).

Also at Image, writer Jason Aaron and artist R. M. Guéra debuted a series in 2015 exploring several books of the Old Testament called *The Goddamned*. A revisionary tale of life "1600 years after Eden," Aaron and Guéra depict the world as a savage, violent realm in which "ravagers and pillagers and defilers" rob, murder, and terrorize.[52] *The Goddamned* offers a serious take on events from the Book of Genesis. Aaron opens the first issue with a quote from Genesis 6:5–6 about the "wickedness" of human beings and their preponderance to do "evil."[53] An ageless, nomadic Cain—cursed with eternal life after killing his brother—wanders the land, seeking death that never arrives.

Cain reflects on his family's legacy and the state of humanity since Adam and Eve's exile from Eden. "I had a family once. It didn't work out," he says, adding:

> My parents were born into paradise. A place without death. A perfect garden they could live in for all eternity. It took them a couple weeks to get themselves kicked out. That's about when my brother and I came along. Life was hard in those days, but the world was still a tranquil place. Bountiful. Immaculate. And we were a family. We had each other. We had all we needed. If only I could have been content with that. If only I hadn't gotten so goddamn angry. My brother was always an asshole. The first two children born into the world, and we couldn't f-cking stand each other. That alone ought to tell you how f-cked we all are. One day the bastard went and made me so angry, I did something no one had ever done before. I killed him. Since then, well . . . things around here have kind of gone to hell.[54]

Cain's starring role in *The Goddamned* arrived the same year as the Image series *Lake of Fire*, in which thirteenth-century crusaders challenge their mission and the Church itself as they face off against unearthly creatures. The historical setting and sci-fi elements of the series are used to confront the difference between spirituality and organized religion, a divide that has grown

FIGURE 60   Cain discusses his parents' exile from the Garden of Eden in *The Goddamned* 1 (November 2015), page 18.

in recent decades as more people give up regular church attendance. (The Pew Research Center projects that by 2070, Christians will no longer be a majority of America's population.)[55] "The church?! You would speak of the church?! Their only interest has ever been power and wealth! Your foul Pope sits on his throne of gold" a young woman named Bernadette cries after she escapes from being burned alive for heresy.[56] Even after this harrowing experience, Bernadette still espouses a belief in the Gnostic movement of Catharism.[57]

Earlier publishers used comic books as platform to spread the gospel in 1940s titles such as *Picture Stories from the Bible* and *Life of Christ Visualized* to recruit new students to the seminary/nunnery in 1950s comics such as *Call from Christ* and *In Love with Jesus*, or to take advantage of social concerns about satanism in 1970s series such as *Ghost Rider* and *Son of Satan*. But by the 2000s, publishers regularly allowed their creators to use comics as a medium for challenging and reinterpreting aspects of Christianity and the church in ways they never could have done before.

Such approaches did not necessarily simply tear down and chastise. *Lake of Fire* concludes with a reaffirmation of faith from several characters (including Bernadette) as they defeat the monstrous alien horde. *The Goddamned* serves to make the "wickedness" described in the Bible more concrete and more explicit for readers by emphasizing the brutality of life in the age of Cain and Noah. Aaron and Guéra don't critique the details they draw on from early chapters of the book of Genesis but rather add nuance and complexity to them. Editors now regularly encourage their creators' plans to use explicitly biblical figures in their works instead of interfering with them as Shooter did with *Ghost Rider*, allowing for more than just the general use of Satan as a supervillain and the Four Horsemen of the Apocalypse as mutant-battling villains.

The larger pattern of storytelling seen in late twentieth-century Marvel and DC titles frequently used angels and demons in horror, fantasy, and superhero tales (in such series as *House of Mystery, House of Secrets, Ghost Rider, The Phantom Stranger, Mephisto Vs.,* and *Blue Devil*) as a way of adding religious credence to stories about the supernatural in a way that didn't offend Christian readers. But the shifting strategies that arrived first with Vertigo series such as *John Constantine, Hellblazer,* and *Preacher* by the 1990s and then with twenty-first-century series such as *Testament* and *The Goddamned* tells us that the larger narrative about the role of religion in society is one we have not yet finished writing.

Testament and *The Goddamned* retell various parts of the Bible through futurist or revisionist lenses and can be read as self-contained stories if readers so choose. But comics like these are also symptomatic of a desire by many readers to see religion approached from the perspective of storytelling in a much larger sense—to have Christianity and its role in human history explored via such frameworks as myth, allegory, and symbolism with the same level of care that these elements are presented in their favorite novels and films. Christian readers might see *Testament* as a valuable pedagogic tool for building connections with non-Christians in much the same way as M. C. Gaines envisioned the instructive potential of *Picture Stories from the Bible*. Similarly, nonreligious readers might find *The Goddamned* a valuable exploration of how early societies from the Old Testament developed. In each case, the larger story of Christianity in the comics of the past few decades is exploratory in scope, often critical and/or analytic in execution, but mostly earnest in intent.

That story has also taken a decidedly silly turn at times, of course. Image's 2006 series *Loaded Bible* is a horror comedy that uses the second coming of Christ as its starting premise—chronicling what would happen if Jesus were a vampire slayer. "Your followers can relate to you . . . see their problems through your eyes. Ask themselves what *you* would do," a bishop tells Christ as an alarm sounds that warns of a vampire attack. "Right now, what Jesus would do is go *kill* some suckers," the Son of God replies.[58] Wielding a flaming sword, Jesus is depicted as a man of action and bloodshed—one who decidedly does *not* turn the other cheek when it comes to the undead. "Come get your communion, suckers" he tells a group of vampires after cutting off the head of one of them.[59]

Jesus soon discovers that he is a clone in *Loaded Bible*, a fact that he struggles to accept: "No . . . that's bullshit! I was born to a woman! I remember my first life, I remember Heaven," he says. A vampire tells him in response that this is the result of "implanted memories . . . fabrications created by the most powerful technology money can buy. Why, I'm surprised they didn't make you look just like those awful paintings people made for centuries."[60] The differing genres for tales about a cloned Christ in *Punk Rock Jesus* and *Loaded Bible* are one illustration of how comics have regularly explored the intersections of technology and religion in the twenty-first century, much as how Rushkoff tells us that new media allow us to challenge and renegotiate the stories that have long served as our foundation myths.

Conclusion: Satire, Censorship, and Beyond

As the success of comics such as *Preacher* and *Lucifer* opened up new lanes in the early 2000s for creators to use Christianity to tell violent and sardonic stories such as *The Goddamned* and *Loaded Bible*, publishers grew increasingly confident about allowing premises that some might call audacious and others might call blasphemous. One came from writer Grant Morrison in *Savage Sword of Jesus Christ*, featuring a reinterpretation of Jesus as a Conanesque warrior. Another was the Image series *Battle Pope*, created by writer Robert Kirkman and artist Tony Moore. Kirkman and Moore self-published the series in 2000 before continuing it with Image in 2005 after the massive success of their 2003 series *The Walking Dead*.

Battle Pope depicts the gleefully blasphemous adventures of Pope Oswald Leopold II, who drinks a lot, sleeps around (with fans, demons, and the Virgin Mary), and settles scores with his fists. Early ads for the action comedy series declared it to be "Blasphemy With a Spine!" and sold the premise with taglines such as "When he's not leading mass . . . he's out kicking ass!" and "Cleansing the world of sin . . . one beating at a time."[61] In the series finale, God arrives to settle a score with the pope for sleeping with Mary, an act that draws her ire as she confronts God about his role in her son's birth. "You love me and leave me! I have your child and then I can't even see you! You don't call, you don't visit, I don't even get a letter!" says Mary.[62] God and Mary soon reconcile and get married in a church service officiated by Pope Oswald and attended by Jesus and Santa Claus.

Other comedic titles include *The Bible 2* from Source Point Press, a 2012 sequel to the Bible in which Jesus can fly thanks to his trusty rocket-sandals. Its cover features a machine-gun-toting Christ riding a pink unicorn and shooting laser beams from his eyes. And in the 2016 Webtoons comic *Adventures of God*, the Lord is depicted as an alcoholic who sends gay people to hell in the hope that Satan (aka God's son Lucy) will want to date one of them.

While there has been steady growth in the number of comics that are deliberately and often playfully sacrilegious in the last two decades, there are signs that some publishers are beginning to question whether there are limits. After DC announced in 2018 that it would publish the series *Second Coming* as a Vertigo title, it canceled its plans after facing significant protest and a petition from a far-right conservative group called CitizenGo (which called the series "outrageous and blasphemous").[63] *Second Coming* is a superhero comedy/sitcom from writer Mark Russell and artist Richard Pace about Christ returning to Earth to be the roommate of a Supermanesque hero named Sunstar. Disappointed in his son for only lasting thirty-three years on earth the first time around before being killed, God sends Jesus back to learn some new life lessons from Sunstar: "I mean, he's a good kid and all, he's just so sheltered. He has like zero survival skills. It's my fault really. I was just gone so much when he was young," God tells the hero. "So what do you say? One omnipotent being to another—will you help me out? You know, take Jesus under your wing... show him how a real hero handles his chili?" asks God.[64]

Russell is a satirist by trade, best known for the humor series *The Flintstones*, *Wonder Twins*, and *Not All Robots*; the latter won the Eisner Award for Best Humor Publication in 2022. After DC requested changes in the wake of the controversy, Russell and Pace took the book to the independent publisher Ahoy Comics. There, its initial six-issue run was followed in 2020 with the miniseries *Second Coming: Only Begotten Son* and *Second Coming: Trinity* (2023).

Much as *The Goddamned* and *Mary Wept over the Feet of Jesus* are about how revisionism is central to the ability to approach religion through a critical, speculative, and/or analytic lens in many modern societies, books such as *Second Coming*, *Battle Pope*, and *Loaded Bible* show us how satire is a key part of that process as well. In his introduction to the collected edition of *Second Coming: Only Begotten Son*, political cartoonist Matt Bors notes that "the superhero genre, much like religion, serves up allegories about how to act morally," with Russell and Pace "carrying on the long tradition" of storytelling practices that "riff on eons-old archetypes and constantly reinterpret them for new generations of readers."[65] With superheroes currently dominating popular culture in franchises such as the Marvel Cinematic Universe, it's only natural that titles such as *Second Coming* would arise to use such stories as forums for satirical examinations of the impact of Christianity on our lives.

Religion's current role in Western society allows us to critique it and laugh at it and be playful with it without fear of reprisal—at least for now. North Americans now live in an era of religious freedom when we can mock, critique, or question Christianity in films such as *Dogma* (1999) and *Doubt* (2008), television shows such as *South Park* (1997–present) and *Black Jesus* (2014–2019), novels such as Dan Brown's *The Da Vinci Code* (2003), and nonfiction works such as Richard Dawkins's *The God Delusion* (2006).

But the rise of Christian nationalism and its role in influencing modern American politics has led to increased calls to ban a growing number of books (both comics and otherwise) from schools and libraries.[66] In Tennessee, Republican representative Jerry Sexton suggested in 2022 that books banned from his state's libraries should be burned. When asked what would happen to the books pulled from Tennessee libraries, Sexton replied, "I don't have a clue, but I would burn them."[67] A year earlier, two Virginia school board members had advocated that books be pulled from school libraries and burned, echoing the midcentury examples in chapter 2 in which communities rallied around schoolyard bonfires. Representative Rabih Abuismail said that "we should throw these books in a fire," while Representative Kirk Twigg said that book burnings were a way of "eradicating this bad stuff."[68]

But as Russell says of those who seek to censor, ban, and burn books, "Some enemies are worth having." Describing the power that is inherent in the ability to control how stories are told, Russell adds: "I think the religious fundamentalists and critics who are trying to stop *Second Coming* aren't interested in protecting Christ so much as their ability to control his narrative.... They probably (correctly) suspect that it's not Christ who's being parodied, but themselves and how they've twisted his teachings of mercy for the powerless into a self-serving tool of the powerful."[69]

Comics have evolved past the juvenile narrative and thematic approaches taken in the 1940s, which presented Satan as a supervillain and Samson as a superhero. As cultural values evolve and distinctions between what is moral and immoral shift over time, representations of villainy and heroism become more complex in the stories we tell. Comics have also been taken more seriously as a literary format since the 1940. Gene Yuen Lang and Alison Bechdel won prestigious "genius grants" from the MacArthur Foundation and Art Spiegelman won a Pulitzer Prize for *Maus: A Survivor's Tale*. But even *Maus* was banned from some schools in 2022, again in Tennessee and in Missouri, while school districts in some St. Louis suburbs have banned popular comics such as *Watchmen* and *The Walking Dead*.[70]

As of 2022, it has been eighty years since M. C. Gaines published his first installment of *Picture Stories from the Bible*. Gaines hoped that comics could achieve educational goals as well as offer entertainment, but those two forces have increasingly been at odds with one another in the past few years. Culture is a constantly evolving force that is always being renegotiated. While many would like to think that we've moved beyond the book burnings of past decades, modern calls from many conservative politicians, pundits, and parents to ban an increasing number of graphic novels from schools and libraries may mean that books such as *The Sandman, Preacher, The Goddamned, Nat Turner, The Book of Genesis Illustrated, Jesusfreak, Mary Wept over the Feet of Jesus*, and *Miniature Jesus* could face future scrutiny and censorship for how they tell stories about Christianity.

Gaines sought to elevate the medium of comics by pointing out its connection to much older traditions of storytelling. His 1942 article "Narrative Illustration: The Story of the Comics" describes how humanity has "continued to use the picture-story as one of the most eloquent mediums of expression," given how a human being "thinks in images" beginning at infancy.[71] The importance of "graphic representation" has been seen since "before the beginnings of recorded history" in literary forms—first with cave paintings, then with hieroglyphics and other systematic forms of sequential images.[72] Comics, Gaines argued, were quickly becoming a vital visual form by the 1940s, not only for their creative "ingenuity" and "imagination" but also for their potential to instruct and their social role in shaping how readers engage with cultural and historical forces.[73]

Whether adapting the Bible in series such as *Life of Christ Visualized* or later titles from Marvel/Nelson, demonstrating the natural connections between faith and science in *Catholic Comics*, or teaching allegorical lessons in series such as *Treasure Chest of Fun and Fact*, many publishers have used comics as a medium that combines the scriptural and the pedagogical. At the same time, other creators have increasingly used comics for religious self-expression and an exploration of their personal experiences with Christianity, such as Al Hartley's work for Spire, Jack Chick's Crusader Comics, the underground comics of Justin Green and Robert Crumb, Vertigo and Image books such as *Preacher* and *Miniature Jesus*, and graphic novels such as *Boxers*, *Saints*, and *Blankets*.

The story of how comics has evolved as a medium since the 1940s is closely tied to its ability to present religious subjects, themes, and images—at first primarily as devout-minded adaptations and relatively innocuous genre tales and later by auteurist-driven explorations of the personal and social impacts of religious faith. By the end of the twentieth century, creators and publishers felt increasingly liberated to give readers stories that challenged dominant cultural norms about and representations of Christianity. As such, comics became a vehicle for revisionist, speculative, and investigatory work to do with the Bible and its legacy.

Whether comics will remain a viable format for such goals in the decades ahead will likely be tied to the dominant ways religion is embedded in the cultural, political, and ideological forces of a nation or an era. Stories about Christianity will surely still be told in comics for as long they remain published, but *how* and *why* those stories about heaven and hell are told is ultimately up to all of us.

Acknowledgments

My thanks, as always, to Erin, Audrey and Ewan for everything, every day.

At Rutgers University Press, thank you to editor Nicole Solano, as well as Bianca Battaglia, Kara Krivanos, Sonia Tam, and everyone else who has helped me along the way. At Westchester Publishing Services, my thanks go to production editor Mary C. Ribesky and copy editor Kate Babbitt.

At DePaul University, I appreciate the financial support of this project from the Division of Mission and Ministry's Vincentian Endowment Fund, Academic Affairs' University Research Council, and the College of Communication's Summer Research Grant program. I'm also grateful to the DePaul Library's Special Collections and Archives for housing my donation of many of the titles from the 1940s through 2000s that I analyze in this book and for creating the Blair Davis Christian Comic Book Collection so that others can do research with these materials. Many thanks for their support of this project along the way go to Provost Salma Ghanem, Dean Alexandra Murphy, and my colleagues in the Media and Cinema Studies program, Michael DeAngelis, Luisela Alvaray, Paul Booth, Samantha Close, and Kelly Kessler.

Notes

Introduction

1. Religious scholar Terry Ray Clark describes how in addition to offering answers about bigger questions to do with the universe and the place of human beings within it, "religion provides its practitioners with what are believed to be very rational and practical strategies for coping with the challenges of everyday life"; "Introduction," in *Understanding Religion and Popular Culture*, ed. Terry Ray Clark and Dan W. Clanton Jr. (London: Routledge, 2012), 5.
2. Claude Lévi-Strauss, *Myth and Meaning* (Toronto: University of Toronto Press, 1978), 35.
3. *Testament*, no. 6 (New York: DC Comics, July 2006), 1–2.
4. *The Department of Truth*, no. 6 (Portland, OR: Image Comics, February 2021), 16.
5. *God Is Dead*, no. 2 (Rantoul, IL: Avatar Press, September 2013), 13.
6. Joshua Meyrowitz, "Medium Theory," in *Marshall McLuhan: Critical Evaluations in Cultural Theory*, vol. 2, ed. Gary Genosko (London: Routledge, 2005), 122.
7. See, for instance, Joakim Jahlmar, "'Give the devil his due': Freedom, Damnation, and Milton's *Paradise Lost* in Neil Gaiman's *The Sandman: Season of Mists*," *Partial Answers: Journal of Literature and the History of Ideas* 13, no. 2 (2015): 267–286; Adam Porter, "Neil Gaiman's Lucifer: Reconsidering Milton's Satan," *Journal of Religion and Popular Culture* 25, no. 2 (2013): 175–185; and Mike Grimshaw, "On Preacher (Or, the Death of God in Pictures)," in *Graven Images: Religion in Comic Books and Graphic Novels*, ed. A. Davis Lewis and Christine Hoff Kramer (New York: Continuum, 2010), 149–165.
8. Ben Saunders, *Do the Gods Wear Capes? Spirituality, Fantasy, and Superheroes* (New York: Continuum, 2011).
9. Danny Fingeroth, *Disguised as Clark Kent: Jews, Comics, and the Creation of the Superhero* (New York: Continuum, 2007).
10. John T. Galloway Jr., *The Gospel According to Superman* (Philadelphia, PA: A. J. Holman Co., 1973).

11 Daniel G. Reid, Robert D. Linder, Bruce L. Shelley, Harry S. Stout, and Craig A. Noll, eds., *The Concise Dictionary of Christianity in America* (Eugene, OR: Wipf and Stock Publishers, 1995), 74.
12 Wilfred Cantwell Smith, *The Meaning and End of Religion* (Minneapolis, MN: Fortress Press, 1991), 49.
13 Roger E. Olson, Frank S. Mead, Samuel S. Hill, and Craig D. Atwood, *Handbook of Denominations in the United States*, 14th ed. (Nashville, TN: Abingdon Press, 2018).
14 A. Davis Lewis and Christine Hoff Kramer, eds., *Graven Images: Religion in Comic Books and Graphic Novels* (New York: Continuum, 2010); Assaf Gamzou and Ken Koltun-Fromm, eds., *Comics and Sacred Texts: Reimagining Religion and Graphic Narratives* (Jackson: University of Mississippi Press, 2018).

Chapter 1   The 1940s

1 Before the debut of *Famous Funnies* in 1934, Eastern Color Printing tested the market for comic books with *Famous Funnies: A Carnival of Comics* in late 1933. The publisher printed a few dozen copies of the book and "talked a couple of newsstands in to participating in this experiment. The copies sold out over the weekend and the newsies asked for more." Robert Lee Beerbohm and Richard, D. Olson, "The American Comic Book: 1929–Present, A Concise History of the Field as of 2008," in *The Overstreet Comic Book Price Guide*, 38th ed. (New York: House of Collectibles, 2008), 396.
2 *New Fun* no. 1 also featured Oswald the Rabbit, a promotional effort for Ralston Purina dog food starring movie cowboy Tom Mix, and an adaptation of the Walter Scott novel *Ivanhoe*, symptomatic of the everything-and-anything approach taken by early comic-book publishers.
3 Gerard Jones, *Men of Tomorrow: Geeks, Gangsters and the Birth of the Comic Book* (New York: Basic Books, 2004), 95–96; Jim Amash, "I Graduated from Plato and Aristotle to Superman and Batman," *Alter Ego* 3, no. 93 (May 2010): 53–54.
4 See Jones, *Men of Tomorrow*, 121–125; Jim Amash, "His Goal Was the Graphic Novel," *Alter Ego* no. 88 (August 2009): 27–32.
5 Jones, *Men of Tomorrow*, 95–97, 163.
6 John T. Galloway Jr., *The Gospel According to Superman* (Philadelphia, PA: A. J. Holman Co., 1973), 23.
7 Both films feature dialogue from Marlon Brando invoking the connection in the Holy Trinity between son and father, while both *Superman Returns* (2006) and *Man of Steel* (2013) present the hero in a crucified pose.
8 Marshall McLuhan, *The Mechanical Bride: Folklore of Industrial Man* (Boston: Beacon Press, 1951), 103.
9 *The Golden Age Spectre Archives*, vol. 1 (New York: DC Comics, 2003), 12.
10 *The Golden Age Spectre Archives*, vol. 1, 19.
11 *The Golden Age Spectre Archives*, vol. 1, 56.
12 Vivian Jacobs, and Wilhelmina Jacobs, "The Color Blue: Its Use as Metaphor and Symbol," *American Speech* 33, no. 1 (1958): 29–46.
13 *The Golden Age Spectre Archives*, vol. 1, 173.
14 *The Golden Age Spectre Archives*, vol. 1, 91.
15 Stewart Goetz and Charles Taliaferro, *A Brief History of the Soul* (West Sussex: Wiley-Blackwell, 2011), 1.

16 Eliezer Gonzalez, "Anthropologies of Continuity: The Body and Soul in Tertullian, Perpetua, and Early Christianity," *Journal of Early Christian Studies* 21, no. 4 (Winter 2013): 482.
17 Desmond M. Clarke, *Descartes's Theory of Mind* (New York: Oxford University Press, 2005), 17, 37.
18 *The Golden Age Spectre Archives*, vol. 1, 153.
19 *The Golden Age Spectre Archives*, vol. 1, 173.
20 *Sampson* no. 1 (New York: Fox Feature Syndicate, Fall 1940), 2.
21 Quoted in Edward Said, *Orientalism*, 25th Anniversary Edition (New York: Knopf Doubleday, 2014), 97.
22 *Sampson* no. 1, 3.
23 See Luigi Andrea Berto, *Christians under the Crescent and Muslims under the Cross c. 630–1923* (New York: Routledge, 2021).
24 Wilfred Cantwell Smith, *The Meaning and End of Religion* (Minneapolis: Fortress Press, 1963), 2–3.
25 *Sampson* no. 1, 3.
26 Richard King, *Orientalism and Religion: Postcolonial Theory, India and "The Mystic East"* (London: Routledge, 2013), 96.
27 Will Eisner, "The Origin of the Spirit," June 2, 1940. Reprinted in *Will Eisner's The Spirit: A Celebration of 75 Years* (Burbank, CA: DC Comics, 2015).
28 Bob Andelman, *Will Eisner: A Spirited Life* (Milwaukie, OR: M Press Books, 2005), 57; Danny Fingeroth, *Disguised as Clark Kent: Jews, Comics, and the Creation of the Superhero* (New York: Continuum, 2007), 62.
29 Sharon Packer states that "American superheroes are self-consciously secular" in *Superheroes and Superegos: Analyzing the Minds behind the Masks* (Santa Barbara: ABC Clio, 2009), 76, while Paul Simpson, Helen Rodiss, and Michaela Bushell describe "superheroes as a secular, slightly tongue-in-cheek answer to a longing which is as old as [humanity]" in *The Rough Guide to Superheroes* (London: Penguin Books, 2004), 9.
30 Harold Bloom, "Introduction," in *Satan* (Philadelphia: Chelsea House Publishers, 2005), 8.
31 *Pep Comics* no. 17 (St. Louis: MLJ Magazines, Inc., July 1941), 47.
32 *Pep Comics* no. 16 (St. Louis: MLJ Magazines, Inc., June 1941), 46.
33 See, for instance, Luther Link, *The Devil: The Archfiend in Art from the Sixth to the Sixteenth Century* (New York: Harry N. Abrams, 1996).
34 *Pep Comics* no. 18 (St. Louis: MLJ Magazines, Inc., August 1941), 47.
35 *Pep Comics* no. 17 (St. Louis: MLJ Magazines, Inc., July 1941), 51.
36 *Pep Comics* no. 19 (St. Louis: MLJ Magazines, Inc., September 1941), 50.
37 *Pep Comics* no. 20 (St. Louis: MLJ Magazines, Inc., October 1941), 46, 48.
38 For a history of how teenage titles, horror, and superhero comics evolved throughout the 1940s, see Peyton Brunet and Blair Davis, *Comic Book Women: Characters, Creators and Culture in the Golden Age* (Austin: University of Texas Press, 2022).
39 *Kid Eternity* no. 15 (Buffalo: Comic Magazines, May 1949), 3.
40 Bart D. Ehrman, *Heaven and Hell: A History of the Afterlife* (New York: Simon & Schuster, 2020), 262–263.
41 William C. Creasy, "The Shifting Landscape of Hell," *Comitatus: A Journal of Medieval and Renaissance Studies* 11, no. 1 (1980): 40.
42 *Pocket Comics* no. 1 (New York: Harvey Comics, August 1941), 1.
43 *Pocket Comics* no. 1, 4.

44 *Pocket Comics* no. 3 (New York: Harvey Comics, November 1941), 62.
45 *Pocket Comics* no. 3, 66.
46 See, for instance, Irving Richter, *Labor's Struggles, 1945–1950: A Participant's View* (New York: Cambridge University Press, 1994).
47 *Pocket Comics* no. 3, 67.
48 *Pocket Comics* no. 4 (New York: Harvey Comics, January 1942), 31.
49 *Suspense Comics* no. 5 (New York: Continental Magazines, August 1944), 9.
50 *Suspense Comics* no. 8 (New York: Continental Magazines, June 1945), 22.
51 *Suspense Comics* no. 9 (New York: Continental Magazines, August 1945), 20; *Suspense Comics* no. 10 (New York: Continental Magazines, Winter 1945), 20.
52 *Suspense Comics* no. 5, 9.
53 *Suspense Comics* no. 5, 11.
54 *Suspense Comics* no. 5, 14.
55 *Suspense Comics* no. 9, 16.
56 *Suspense Comics* no. 9, 19–20.
57 *Suspense Comics* no. 10, 15; *Suspense Comics* no. 12 (New York: Continental Magazines, September 1946), 36.
58 *Suspense Comics* no. 12, 40.
59 Elizabeth Eisenstein notes that the printing press "revolutionized all forms of learning" starting in the late fifteenth century. *The Printing Press as an Agent of Change* (New York: Cambridge University Press, 1979), 3. The ability to reproduce Christian images quickly and cheaply in later centuries in formats such as the comic book offered new possibilities for how readers engaged with the Bible and its teachings.
60 Frank Jacobs, *The Mad World of William M. Gaines* (Secaucus, NJ: Lyle Stuart, Inc., 1972), 58. Gaines had also tried to get *Superman* published as early as 1936, when he worked as a comic-book packager for publisher George Delacorte; Jones, *Men of Tomorrow*, 119.
61 See chapter two of Blair Davis, *Movie Comics: Page to Screen/Screen to Page* (New Brunswick, NJ: Rutgers University Press, 2017) for a detailed analysis of Gaines's *Movie Comics* series.
62 Qiana Whitted, *EC Comics: Race, Shock & Social Protest* (New Brunswick, NJ: Rutgers University Press, 2019), 10.
63 M. C. Gaines, "Narrative Illustration: The Story of the Comics," *Print* 3, no. 2 (Summer 1942): 29.
64 *Picture Stories from the Bible* no. 1, Old Testament Edition (Fall 1943): inside front cover.
65 Barbara Postema, *Narrative Structure in Comics* (Rochester, NY: RIT Press, 2013), 82.
66 *Picture Stories from the Bible* no. 1, New Testament Edition (Fall 1943): 6.
67 *Picture Stories from the Bible* no. 1, New Testament Edition (Fall 1943): inside front cover.
68 Both the red-letter format of the Bible and the colored hue added to the word balloons in *Picture Stories* were dependent on the production quality of the printing process. Ron Rhodes notes how the consistency with which red ink was applied varied from copy to copy, even from page to page: "You will notice some pages printed in a darker red, some pages printed in a medium red, and some pages printed in what looks like pink, sometimes even light pink"; *The Complete Guide to Bible Translations* (Irvine: Harvest House Publishers, 2009), 220. The outer edges of Jesus's word balloons are printed with lighter and darker shades of pink depending on the consistency of the

Notes to Pages 45–52 • 269

color reproduction. Some balloons are missing their color altogether in some editions; my 1945 printing of the New Testament Edition no. 2 is missing the pink tinge in Jesus's first word balloon on page one, for instance.

69 George Bluestone, *Novels into Film* (Berkeley: University of California Press, 1957), 5.
70 David Roche, Isabelle Schmitt-Pitiot and Benoît Mitaine, *Comics and Adaptation*, trans. Aarnoud Rommens and David Roche (Jackson: University of Mississippi Press, 2018), 14, 19.
71 *Picture Stories from the Bible* no. 2, Old Testament Edition (Winter 1942): inside back cover.
72 *Picture Stories from the Bible* no. 2, New Testament Edition (1945): inside back cover; *Picture Stories from the Bible*, no. 3, New Testament Edition (1946): inside back cover.
73 "The Church Department," *Educational Screen*, April 1948, 184.
74 Dale Jacobs, *Graphic Encounters: Comics and the Sponsorship of Multimodal Literacy* (New York: Bloomsbury, 2013), 130.
75 "The Church Department," 184.
76 For a detailed account of Max Gaines's death and his son William's inheritance of EC Comics, see Dwight R. Decker and Gary Groth, "An Interview with William M. Gaines," *Comics Journal* 81 (May 1983): 53–99.
77 Ted White, "Introduction to EC Comics," in *The EC Artists*, The Comics Journal Library, vol. 8 (Seattle: Fantagraphics Books, 2013), 7.
78 White, "Introduction to EC Comics," 8.
79 Jean Paul Gabilliet, *Of Comics and Men: A Cultural History of American Comic Books* (Jackson: University Press of Mississippi, 2010), 28.
80 *Picture Stories from the Bible*, no. 3, New Testament Edition (1946): inside front cover.
81 S. C. Ringgenberg, "Interview: William M. Gaines," in *The EC Artists*, The Comics Journal Library, vol. 8 (Seattle: Fantagraphics Books, 2013), 63.
82 Jones, *Men of Tomorrow*, 254.
83 Dwight Decker and Gary Groth, "Interview: William M. Gaines," in *The EC Artists Part 2*, The Comics Journal Library, vol. 10 (Seattle: Fantagraphics Books, 2016), 13.
84 *Tales from the Crypt* no. 20 (New York: EC Comics, October–November 1950), n.p.
85 Whitted, *EC Comics*, 22.
86 *The Living Bible* no. 3, St. Louis, MO: Living Bible Corporation, Spring 1946.
87 *Catholic Comics* 1, no. 5 (Holyoke, MA: Catholic Publications, Inc., October 1946), 14.
88 Ronald B. Flowers, *Religion in Strange Times: The 1960s and 1970s* (Macon: Mercer University Press, 1984), 37.
89 For a detailed history of the origins of *Catholic Comics*, see "Catholic Comics: An Essay," Digital Comics Museum, January 3, 2013, https://digitalcomicmuseum.com/forum/index.php?topic=4108.0. The author suggests that the new publishing entity of the series, Catholic Publications, Inc., formed by "a group of businessmen and public figures from the south-central Connecticut area," must have had a close connection with Charlton to allow both the continued numbering and reprinted material.
90 Jacqueline Howard and Veronica Stracqualursi, "Fauci Warns of 'Anti-Science Bias' Being a Problem in the US," *CNN*, June 18, 2020, https://www.cnn.com/2020/06/18/politics/anthony-fauci-coronavirus-anti-science-bias/index.html.

91 *Catholic Comics* 1, no. 5, 7.
92 "West Coast Merger Brings New Accounts," *Broadcasting*, April; 4, 1960, 72.
93 *Lots "O" Fun Comics* (Riverside, IL: Robert Allen Co., 1949) n.d.), inside front cover, inside back cover.

Chapter 2   The 1950s and 1960s

1 David Hadju, *The Ten-Cent Plague: The Great Comic Book Scare and How It Changed America* (New York: Picador, 2008), 117.
2 "Manners and Morals: Americana," *Time*, December 20, 1948, http://content.time.com/time/subscriber/article/0,33009,799525,00.html.
3 "Catholic School Pupils to Burn 'Undesirable' Comics," *Wisconsin Rapids Daily Tribune*, November 6, 1945, 1.
4 "600 Pupils Prepare Petitions Asking Ban on 'Indecent' Comics," *Chicago Daily Tribune*, December 7, 1947, 50.
5 Fredric Wertham, *Seduction of the Innocent* (New York: Rinehart, 1954), 333.
6 Wertham, *Seduction of the Innocent*, 265.
7 Wertham, *Seduction of the Innocent*, 337.
8 Margaret Frakes, "Comics Are No Longer Comic," *Christian Century*, November 4, 1942, 1349.
9 Reverend Frank E. Gartland, ed., *Our Sunday Visitor*, June 20, 1943, n.p.
10 Sister Mary Clare, SND, *The Comics* (Huntington, IN: Our Sunday Visitor Press, 1943), 8.
11 Sister Mary Clare, *The Comics*.
12 Garth S. Jowett, Ian C. Jarvie, and Kathryn H. Fuller, *Children and the Movies: Media Influence and the Payne Fund Controversy* (New York: Cambridge University Press, 1996).
13 Gabriel Lynn, *The Case against the Comics* (St. Paul, MN: Catechetical Guild, 1944), 12.
14 Lynn, *The Case against the Comics*, 19.
15 Lynn, *The Case against the Comics*, 29.
16 Gabriel Lynn, *The Teacher and the Comics* (St. Paul, MN: Catechetical Guild, 1946), 10–11.
17 Lynn, *The Teacher and the Comics*, 18–19.
18 Lynn, *The Teacher and the Comics*, 19–20.
19 Lynn, *The Teacher and the Comics*, 26.
20 Lynn, *The Teacher and the Comics*, 6.
21 Lynn, *The Teacher and the Comics*, 7.
22 *Timeless Topix* 1, no. 2 (St. Paul, MN: Catechetical Guild, (December 1942): 1.
23 *Topix* 5, no. 3 ([St. Paul, MN]: Catechetical Guild, November 1946), inside back cover.
24 Dale Jacobs, *Graphic Encounters: Comics and the Sponsorship of Multimodal Literacy* (New York: Bloomsbury, 2013), 133.
25 *Topix* 5, no. 4 ([St. Paul, MN]: Catechetical Guild, December 1946); *Topix* 5, no. 9 ([St. Paul, MN]: Catechetical Guild, June 1947).
26 Cynthia Gorney, "The Peanuts Progenitor," *Washington Post*, October 2, 1985, D1–D2.
27 Kenneth L. Wilson, "A Visit with Charles Schulz," in *Charles M. Schulz: Conversations*, ed. M. Thomas Inge (Jackson: University of Mississippi Press, 2000), 33.

28 Robyn Dean McHattie, "'My Comic Mom!!'—Part II: Continuing a Daughter's Memoir of Her Artist Mother Vee Quintal Pearson," *Alter Ego* 3, no. 127 (August 2014): 32.
29 *Treasure Chest of Fun and Fact*, no. 2 ([Dayton, OH]: George A. Pflaum Publisher, Inc., March 26, 1946), back cover.
30 Tom DeFalco, *Comics Creators on Fantastic Four* (London: Titan Books, 2005), 27.
31 Anne Blankenship, "Catholic American Citizenship: Prescriptions for Children from Treasure Chest of Fun and Fact: 1946–63," in *Graven Images: Religion in Comic Books and Graphic Novels*, ed. A. David Lewis and Christine Hoff Kraemer (New York: Continuum, 2010), 63–64.
32 *The World Is His Parish: The Story of Pope Pius XII* ([Dayton, OH]: George A. Pflaum Publisher, Inc., 1954), 33.
33 Hosffman Ospino and Patricia Weitzel-O'Neill, "Catholic Schools Serving Hispanic Families: Insights from the 2014 National Survey," *Journal of Catholic Education* 19, no. 2 (January 2016): 54–55.
34 For an overview of how western and jungle comics reinforced racist stereotypes, see Peyton Brunet and Blair Davis, *Comic Book Women: Characters, Creators and Culture in the Golden Age* (Austin: University of Texas Press, 2022). For details about how institutionalized racism prevented the success of *All-Negro Comics*, see Blair Davis, "All-Negro Comics and the Birth of Lion Man, the First African American Superhero," *Inks: The Journal of the Comics Studies Society* 3, no. 3 (Fall 2019): 273–297.
35 J. Michael Lyons, "From Alabama to Tahrir Square: 'Martin Luther King and the Montgomery Story' Comic as a Civil Rights Narrative," *Journalism History* 41, no. 2 (Summer 2015): 103.
36 Joanna C. Davis-McElligatt, "'Walk Together, Children': The Function and Interplay of Comics, History and Memory in Martin Luther King and the Montgomery Story and John Lewis's March: Book One," in *Graphic Novels for Children and Young Adults: A Collection of Critical Essays*, ed. Michelle Ann Abate and Gwen Athene Tarbox (Jackson: University Press of Mississippi, 2017), 306.
37 *Martin Luther King and the Montgomery Story* (Nyack, NY: Fellowship of Reconciliation, 1957), 15.
38 *Martin Luther King and the Montgomery Story*, 13.
39 *Martin Luther King and the Montgomery Story*, 1.
40 *Martin Luther King and the Montgomery Story*, 6.
41 *Martin Luther King and the Montgomery Story*, 15.
42 Lyons, "From Alabama to Tahrir Square," 109–110.
43 Jorge J. Santos Jr., *Graphic Memories of the Civil Rights Movement: Reframing History in Comics* (Austin: University of Texas Press, 2019), 55.
44 Quoted in Santos, *Graphic Memories of the Civil Rights Movement*, 52.
45 Qiana Whitted, ed., *Desegregating Comics: Debating Blackness in the Golden Age of American Comics* (New Brunswick, NJ: Rutgers University Press, 2023), 3.
46 McHattie, "'My Comic Mom!!'" 37.
47 *God's Heroes in America* ([St. Paul, MN]: Catechetical Guild Educational Society, 1956), 36.
48 *God's Heroes in America*, 45.
49 Abbe Gaston Courtois, *Saint Vincent de Paul* (St. Paul, MN: Catechetical Guild Educational Society, 1960), 1.

50 This tagline appeared in the editorial material of each issue of *Sunday Pix* for much of its run, as in vol. 16, no. 31 (August 2, 1964): 2.
51 *Sunday Pix*, September 27, 1964, 3.
52 Eastern ceased publication of its own titles in 1955 in the wake of the changing market conditions that ended many other comics publishers. The January 1956 issue of its quarterly *Tales from the Great Book* was among their final releases.
53 M. C. Gaines, "Narrative Illustration: The Comics," *Print: A Quarterly Journal of the Graphic Arts* 3, no. 2 (Summer 1942): 38.
54 Gaines, "Narrative Illustration," 29–30.
55 William Moulton Marston, "Why 100,000,000 Americans Read Comics," *American Scholar* 13, no. 1 (Winter 1943–1944), 37.
56 *Billy Graham with Cliff Barrows Presents The Story of Naaman the Leper* 1, no. 1 ([Minneapolis, MN]: Billy Graham Evangelistic Association, 1951), inside front cover.
57 *Oral Roberts' True Stories* 1, no. 1 ([Tulsa, OK]: Healing Waters Inc., 1956): 20.
58 *Oral Roberts' True Stories* 1, no. 1, 27–28.
59 Jacobs, *Graphic Encounters*, 136.
60 *Oral Roberts' True Stories* 1, no. 1, 32.
61 *Oral Roberts' True Stories* no. 107 ([Tulsa, OK]: Healing Waters Inc., 1958): 19–21.
62 *Oral Roberts' True Stories* no. 107, 28.
63 Wertham, *Seduction of the Innocent*, 36.
64 Wertham, *Seduction of the Innocent*, 253.
65 Wertham, *Seduction of the Innocent*, 222.
66 Richard J. Arndt, "Tales From the Code: The Sequel," *Alter Ego* 3, no. 113 (October 2012): 46.
67 "Comics Magazine Association of America Comics Code, 1954," quoted in Amy Kyste Nyberg, *Seal of Approval: The History of the Comics Code* (Jackson: University of Mississippi Press, 1998), 167.
68 *Weird Science* no. 13 [New York] (EC Comics, May–June 1952), 19, 21.
69 *Tales from the Crypt* no. 23 [New York] (EC Comics, April–May 1951), 14.
70 Robert S. Nelson and Kristen M. Collins, eds., *Holy Image, Hallowed Ground: Images from Sinai* (Los Angeles, CA: J. Paul Getty Museum, 2006), 141.
71 Wyn Craig Wade, *The Fiery Cross: The Ku Klux Klan in America* (New York: Oxford University Press, 1987), 146.
72 Juan O. Sánchez, *Religion and the Ku Klux Klan: Biblical Appropriation in Their Literature and Songs* (Jefferson, NC: McFarland, 2016), 151.
73 Qiana Whitted, *EC Comics: Race, Shock & Social Protest* (New Brunswick, NJ: Rutgers University Press, 2020), 87.
74 *Voodoo* no. 11 [New York] (Four Star Publications: September 1953), 17, 23.
75 "The Devil's Puzzle," *The Unseen* no. 14 [New York] (Standard, April 1954), n.p.
76 *If the Devil Would Talk* ([St. Paul, MN]: Catechetical Guild, 1950), inside front cover.
77 *If the Devil Would Talk*, 14.
78 George Jacob Holyoake, *The Principles of Secularism*, 3rd ed. (London: Austin & Co., 1871), 14–15.
79 *If the Devil Would Talk*, inside front cover.
80 *Christianity and Secularism: Report of a Public Discussion between the Rev. Brewin Grant and George Jacob Holyoake, Esq. Held in the Royal British Institution, London, Commencing Jan. 20 and Ending Feb. 24, 1853* (London: Ward and Co., 1853), v.

81 *If the Devil Would Talk*, 1.
82 *If the Devil Would Talk*, 3–4.
83 *If the Devil Would Talk*, 7.
84 *If the Devil Would Talk*, 7–8.
85 *If the Devil Would Talk*, 10, 12.
86 *If the Devil Would Talk*, 16.
87 *If the Devil Would Talk*, 21–22.
88 *If the Devil Would Talk*, 28–29.
89 *The Official Overstreet Comic Book Price Guide*, a generally reliable source for information about comics history, says of *If the Devil Would Talk*: "The original edition of this book was printed and killed by the Guild's board of directors. It is believed that a very limited number of copies were distributed. The 1958 version was a complete bomb with very limited, if any, circulation. In 1979, 11 original, 4 1958 reprints, and 4 B&W's surfaced from the Guild's old files in St. Paul, Minnesota." *The Official Overstreet Comic Book Price Guide*, 38th ed. (New York: House of Collectibles, 2008), 303. A copy of the 1950 issue was donated by the author to the DePaul Library for public viewing in the Special Collections department.
90 *If the Devil Would Talk* (St. Paul, MN: Impact Press, 1958), back cover.
91 *Blood Is the Harvest* (St. Paul, MN: Catechetical Guild, 1950), inside back cover.
92 *Is This Tomorrow: American under Communism* (St. Paul, MN: Catechetical Guild, 1947), inside front cover.
93 *Is This Tomorrow*, 5.
94 *Is This Tomorrow*, 30.
95 Jim Amash, "Come Back When You Learn How to Draw: Artist Ken Selig Talks about Harvey's Early Comics Code Days," *Alter Ego* 3, no. 89 (October 2009): 60.
96 Amash, "Come Back When You Learn How to Draw," 64.
97 *Hot Stuff* no. 23 [New York](Harvey Comics, May 1960), n.p.
98 *Hot Stuff* no. 78 [New York: NY] (Harvey Comics, June 1967), n.p.
99 *Stumbo Tinytown* no. 2 [New York: NY] (Harvey Comics, October 1963), n.p.
100 *Mad* no. 1 [New York] (EC Comics, October–November 1952), n.p.
101 *Tales from the Crypt* no. 20 [New York](EC Comics, October–November 1950), n.p.
102 Charles Hatfield, *Alternative Comics* (Jackson: University Press of Mississippi, 2005), 11.
103 Nicholas Sammond, "Comix," in *Keywords for Comics Studies*, ed. Ramzi Fawaz, Shelley Streeby, and Deborah Elizabeth Whaley (New York: New York University Press, 2021), 59.
104 Sammond, "Comix," 61; Hatfield, *Alternative Comics*, 11.
105 *The Complete Zap Comix: The Zap Story* (Seattle, WA: Fantagraphics Books, 2014), 904.
106 Sammond, "Comix," 58.
107 For analysis of Crumb and race, see, for instance, Corey Creekmur, "Multiculturalism Meets the Counterculture: Representing Racial Difference in Robert Crumb's Underground Comix," in *Representing Multiculturalism in Comics and Graphic Novels*, ed. Carolene Ayaka and Ian Hague (New York: Routledge, 2014), 19–33.
108 Rebecca Wanzo, *The Content of Our Caricature: African American Comic Art and Political Belonging* (New York: New York University Press, 2020), 5–6.
109 Wanzo, *The Content of Our Caricature*, 180, 184.
110 Michael Macrone, "Two Generations of Weirdos: An Interview with R. Crumb and Peter Bagge," *Comics Journal* no. 106 (March 1986): 65.

111 Patrick Rosencrantz, *Rebel Visions: The Underground Comix Revolution, 1963–1975* (Seattle: Fantagraphics Books, 2008) 30–31.
112 *Zap Comics* no. 0, 1968, reprinted in *The Complete Zap Comix*, vol. 1 (Seattle, WA: Fantagraphics Books, 2014), 23.
113 Susan Goodrick, "Apex Interview: R. Crumb" (1974), in *R. Crumb: Conversations*, ed. D. K. Holm (Jackson: University of Mississippi Press, 2004), 87–88.
114 *Zap Comics* no. 1, 1968, reprinted in *The Complete Zap Comix*, vol. 1 (Seattle: Fantagraphics Books, 2014), 54.
115 Jean-Pierre Mercier, "Who's Afraid of R. Crumb?" (1999), in *R. Crumb: Conversations*, ed. D. K. Holm (Jackson: University of Mississippi Press, 2004), 195.
116 Mercier, "Who's Afraid of R. Crumb?" 196–197.
117 David Stephen Calonne, *R. Crumb: Literature, Autobiography, and the Quest for Self* (Jackson: University of Mississippi Press, 2021), 4.
118 Robert Crumb, *The Book of Genesis Illustrated* (New York: W. W. Norton & Co., 2009), front cover.
119 *Zap: The Interviews*, The Comics Journal Library, vol. 9 (Seattle: Fantagraphics Books, 2010), 31.
120 Crumb, *The Book of Genesis Illustrated*, n.p.
121 B. N. Duncan, "A Joint Interview with R. Crumb and Aline Kominsky-Crumb," in *R. Crumb: Conversations*, ed. D. K. Holm (Jackson: University of Mississippi Press, 2004), 124.
122 Crumb, *The Book of Genesis Illustrated*, n.p.
123 Calonne, *R. Crumb*, 184.
124 Calonne, *R. Crumb*, 202.
125 R. Crumb, *Bible of Filth* (New York: David Zwirner Books, 2017).

Chapter 3 The 1970s

1 Ronald B. Flowers, *Religion in Strange Times: The 1960s and 1970s* (Macon, GA: Mercer University Press, 1984), 37–39.
2 *The Complete Wimmen's Comix* (Seattle: Fantagraphics Books, 2016), 337.
3 *The Complete Wimmen's Comix*, 497.
4 *The Complete Wimmen's Comix*, 562–563.
5 B. N. Duncan, "A Joint Conversation with R. Crumb and Aline Kominsky-Crumb," in *R. Crumb: Conversations*, ed. D. K. Holm (Jackson: University of Mississippi Press, 2004), 118.
6 Michael Macrone, "Two Generations of Weirdos: An Interview with R. Crumb and Peter Bagge," *Comics Journal* no. 106 (March 1986): 62.
7 Justin Green, *Binky Brown Meets the Holy Virgin Mary* (Berkeley: Last Gasp Ego-Funnies, 1972), front cover.
8 Green, *Binky Brown Meets the Holy Virgin Mary*, inside front cover.
9 Green, *Binky Brown Meets the Holy Virgin Mary*, 8.
10 Green, *Binky Brown Meets the Holy Virgin Mary*, 13.
11 Green, *Binky Brown Meets the Holy Virgin Mary*, 18, 24.
12 Green, *Binky Brown Meets the Holy Virgin Mary*, 40.
13 Justin Green, *Sacred and Profane* (Berkeley: Last Gasp Ego-Funnies, 1976), 2, 7.
14 Green, *Sacred and Profane*, 30, 33.
15 Green, *Sacred and Profane*, 35.

16 Hillary L. Chute, *Disaster Drawn: Visual Witness, Comics, and Documentary Form* (Cambridge, MA: Harvard University Press, 2016), 102, 153.
17 See Blair Davis, "Cartoonist, Draw Thyself," *Image of the Journalist in Popular Culture* 9, no. 1 (2021): 44–73.
18 Chute, *Disaster Drawn*, 153–154.
19 Duncan, "A Joint Conversation with R. Crumb and Aline Kominsky-Crumb," 117–118.
20 Chute, *Disaster Drawn*, 161.
21 Charles Hatfield, *Alternative Comics* (Jackson: University Press of Mississippi, 2005), 11.
22 Jim Phillips, *Eternal Truth* no. 1, [Akron, OH: Sonday Funnies Comic Corp.]1974, 24.
23 Craig Yoe, *Sammy Saved and Al Most*, no.1 (Akron: OH, Sonday Funnies Comic Corp., 1974), n.p.
24 Steve Gregg, *Holy Ghost Zapped Comix*, no.1 (Plainfield, NJ: Logos, 1973), n.p.
25 See, for instance, Samuel G. Green, *The Story of the Religious Tract Society* (London: The Religious Tract Society, 1899).
26 Robert B. Fowler, *The World of Jack T. Chick* (San Francisco: Last Gasp, 2001), n.p. Fowler notes that *This Was Your Life* was "most likely" created in 1961 but the initial work on the tract could date back to 1958. The tract was not published until 1964. In David W. Daniels's biography of Chick, he lists the years of publication for *Why No Revival?*, *A Demon's Nightmare*, and *Last Call* as 1961, 1962, and 1963, respectively. Daniels, *You Don't Know Jack: The Authorized Biography of Christian Cartoonist Jack T. Chick* (Ontario, CA: Chick Publications, 2017), 127.
27 Leonard Paul Kurtz, *The Dance of Death and the Macabre Spirit in European Literature* (New York: Columbia University Press, 1934), 209.
28 Jack Chick, *This Was Your Life* (Ontario, CA: Chick Publications, 1964), 15.
29 Chick, *This Was Your Life*, 18.
30 Because Chick's comics do not provide creator details, I am crediting the work done in all tracts and comic books published after Fred Carter was hired in 1972 to both Jack Chick and Fred Carter, given how the majority of the work appears to have been done with Chick as writer and Carter as artist. Chick's art was generally less detailed than Carter's, favoring rounder edges and less concern for realistic anatomy. Chick told author Jimmy Akin that he and Carter were the only two artists at Chick Publications and that his primary role in more recent years was that of writer instead of artist, although their work never formally listed who did what; Jimmy Akin, *The Nightmare World of Jack Chick* (San Diego: Catholic Answers, 2008), 85.
31 Danny Trejo with Donal Logue, *Trejo: My Life of Crime, Redemption and Hollywood* (New York: Atria, 2021), 54.
32 Trejo with Logue, *Trejo*, 58.
33 Chick Publications, *2019 Catalogue* (Ontario, CA: Chick Publications, 2019), 13–15.
34 James R. Lewis, *Satanism Today: An Encyclopedia of Religion, Folklore, and Popular Culture* (Santa Barbara, CA: ABC Clio, 2001), 46.
35 Sam Theilman, "Remembering Jack Chick: The Christian Cartoonist Who Tried to Save Us from Hell," *Guardian*, October 25, 2016, https://www.theguardian.com/books/2016/oct/25/jack-chick-christian-comic-cartoonist-death.
36 Quoted in Kurt Kuersteiner, *The Art of Jack T. Chick: Chick Tracts, Crusader Comics, and Battle Cry Newspapers* (Atglen, PA: Schiffer Publishing Ltd., 2004), 160.

37 Kuersteiner, *The Art of Jack T. Chick*.
38 Jack Chick and Fred Carter, *The Gay Blade* (Ontario, CA: Chick Publications, 1972), 4–5, 8.
39 Chick and Fred Carter, *The Gay Blade*, 18, 21.
40 Jack Chick and Fred Carter, *Home Alone?* (Ontario, CA: Chick Publications, 2008), 3, 7.
41 Jack Chick and Fred Carter, *Sin City* (Ontario, CA: Chick Publications, 2001), 17.
42 See Ayesha S. Chaudry, *Domestic Violence and the Islamic Tradition: Ethics, Law, and the Muslim Discourse on Gender* (Oxford: Oxford University Press, 2013).
43 Nancy Nason-Clark, Barbara Fisher-Townsend, and Catherine Holtmann, *Religion and Intimate Partner Violence: Understanding the Challenges and Proposing Solutions* (Oxford: Oxford University Press, 2018), 40.
44 Jack G. Shaheen, "Hollywood's Muslim Arabs," *Muslim World* 90, no. 1 (Spring 2000): 29.
45 Jack Chick and Fred Carter, *Camel's in the Tent* (Ontario, CA: Chick Publications, 2012), 12.
46 Kuersteiner, *The Art of Jack T. Chick*, 68.
47 Lewis, *Satanism Today*, 46.
48 See, for instance, Steve Brouwer, Paul Gifford, and Susan D. Rose, *Exporting the American Gospel: Global Christian Fundamentalism* (New York: Routledge, 1996); and George M. Marsen, *Fundamentalism and American Culture*, 2nd ed. (New York: Oxford University Press, 2006).
49 Jack Chick and Fred Carter, *The Nervous Witch* (Ontario, CA: Chick Publications, 1998), 2–3, 15.
50 Chick and Carter, *The Nervous Witch*, 20.
51 Jack Chick and Fred Carter, *Boo!* (Ontario, CA: Chick Publications, 1991), 16–20.
52 Jack Chick and Fred Carter, *Titanic* (Ontario, CA: Chick Publications, 1983), 3.
53 Jack Chick and Fred Carter, *The Missing Day* (Ontario, CA: Chick Publications, 2005), 12.
54 Jack Chick and Fred Carter, *Lisa* (Ontario, CA: Chick Publications, 1984), 6, 9.
55 Chick and Carter, *Lisa*, 22.
56 Kuersteiner, *The Art of Jack T. Chick*, 2.
57 Fowler, *The World of Jack T. Chick*, n.p.
58 Fowler, *The World of Jack T. Chick*, n.p.
59 *Eightball* no. 1 (Seattle, WA: Fantagraphics Books, August 1989), 14–16.
60 Jim Woodring, *Jesus Delivers* (Seattle, WA: Starhead Comix, 1996), n.p.
61 Jason C. Bivens, *Religion of Fear: The Politics of Horror in Conservative Evangelism* (New York: Oxford University Press, 2008), 25, 27.
62 Jack Chick and Fred Carter, *He Never Told Us!* (Ontario, CA: Chick Publications, 1993), 19.
63 Ronald Yates, "Crusader Comics: A Bizarre Band of Christian Heroes," *Chicago Tribune*, June 8, 1981, B1.
64 Chick Publications, *2019 Catalogue*, 52.
65 Jack Chick and Fred Carter, *Operation Bucharest*, Crusader Comics, vol. 1 (Ontario, CA: Chick Publications, 1974), 6–7.
66 Chick and Carter, *Operation Bucharest*, 10–11.
67 Chick and Carter, *Operation Bucharest*, 6–8.
68 Chick and Carter, *Operation Bucharest*, 29.
69 Kuersteiner, *The Art of Jack T. Chick*, 9.

70 Chick Publications, *2019 Catalogue*, 24–25.
71 See Dan Johnson, "Becoming His Own: The Evolution of John Stewart, Green Lantern," *Back Issue* 1, no. 117 (December 2019): 4.
72 Jack Chick and Fred Carter, *The Broken Cross*, The Crusaders, vol. 2 (Ontario, CA: Chick Publications, 1974), 15.
73 Chris Mathew, *Modern Satanism: Anatomy of a Radical Subculture* (Westport, CT: Praeger, 2009), 131.
74 Claire Baez, "'I'm a Cannibal' : Victim's Neighbor Recalls Horrific 1970 Murder," *USA Today*, July 3, 2015, https://www.usatoday.com/story/news/nation/2015/07/03/cannibal-montana-great-falls/29658643/.
75 Chick and Carter, *The Broken Cross*, 32.
76 Chick and Carter, *The Broken Cross*, 31.
77 Jack Chick and Fred Carter, *The Gift*, The Crusaders, vol. 8 (Ontario, CA: Chick Publications, 1977), 7.
78 Chick and Carter, *The Gift*, 9.
79 Jack Chick and Fred Carter, *The Force*, The Crusaders, vol. 15 (Ontario, CA: Chick Publications, 1983), 21.
80 Jack Chick and Fred Carter, *Sabotage?* The Crusaders, vol. 11 (Ontario, CA: Chick Publications, 1979), 23.
81 Chick and Carter, *Sabotage?* 27.
82 Gary Metz, "Jack Chick's Anti-Catholic Alberto Comic Book Is Exposed as a Fraud, *Christianity Today*, March 13, 1981, https://www.christianitytoday.com/ct/1981/march-13/jack-chicks-anti-catholic-alberto-comic-book-is-exposed-as.html.
83 Jack Chick and Fred Carter, *Alberto*, The Crusaders, vol. 12 (Ontario, CA: Chick Publications, 1979), 15.
84 Jack Chick and Fred Carter, *The Godfathers*, The Crusaders, vol. 14 (Ontario, CA: Chick Publications, 1982), 9.
85 Chick and Carter, *Alberto*, 28.
86 Jack Chick and Fred Carter, *Double-Cross*, The Crusaders, vol. 12 (Ontario, CA: Chick Publications, 1981), 29.
87 Chick and Carter, *The Force*, 23.
88 Chick and Carter, *The Godfathers*, 10.
89 Chick and Carter, *The Godfathers*, 17.
90 Chick and Carter, *The Godfathers*, 19–20.
91 Chick and Carter, *The Godfathers*, 21.
92 Chick and Carter, *The Godfathers*, 23.
93 Chick and Carter, *Alberto*, 12.
94 Chick and Carter, *Double Cross*, 14.
95 Chick and Carter, *The Godfathers*, 31.
96 Jack Chick and Fred Carter, *The Prophet*, The Crusaders, vol. 18 (Ontario, CA: Chick Publications, 1988), 18.
97 Chick and Carter, *The Force*, 10.
98 Chick and Carter, *The Force*, 29–30.
99 Chick and Carter, *Double Cross*, 25.
100 Chick and Carter, *The Godfathers*, 31.
101 Chick and Carter, *The Godfathers*, 32.
102 Chick and Carter, *The Force*, inside back cover.
103 Yates, "Crusader Comics," B3.
104 Yates, "Crusader Comics," B3.

105 Chick and Carter, *The Force*, 17.
106 Jack Chick and Fred Carter, *Who's the Real Hater?* (Ontario, CA: Chick Publications, 2012), 13, 22.
107 Akin, *The Nightmare World of Jack Chick*, 3.
108 Al Hartley, *Come Meet My Friend!* (Old Tappan, NJ: New Life Ventures, 1977), 12.
109 Hartley, *Come Meet My Friend!* 48.
110 Al Hartley, *Crossfire* (Old Tappan, NJ: Fleming H. Revell Co., 1976), 29.
111 Al Hartley, *Adventures with the Brothers: Hang In There* (Old Tappan, NJ: Fleming H. Revell Co., 1972), 32.
112 Al Hartley, *Adam and Eve* (Old Tappan, NJ: Fleming H. Revell Co., 1975), 19, 30.
113 Al Hartley, *There's a New World Coming* (Old Tappan, NJ: Fleming H. Revell Co., 1974), 1.
114 Daniels, *You Don't Know Jack*, 45.
115 Hartley, *There's a New World Coming*, 21.
116 Hartley, *There's a New World Coming*, 31.
117 Gerald L. Stevens, ed., *Essays on Revelation: Appropriating Yesterday's Apocalypse in Today's World* (Eugene, OR: Pickwick Publications, 2010), xvii.
118 Bart D. Ehrman, *Armageddon: What the Bible Really Says about the End* (New York: Simon & Schuster, 2023), 16–17.
119 Al Hartley, *Alpha and Omega* (Old Tappan, NJ: Fleming H. Revell Co., 1978), 7.
120 Hartley, *Alpha and Omega*, 9.
121 Hartley, *Alpha and Omega*, 31–32.
122 Hartley, *Come Meet My Friend!* 38. For an analysis of how Hartley inserted Christian themes into his non-Spire Archie comics, see Dale Jacobs, *Graphic Encounters: Comics and the Sponsorship of Multimodal Literacy* (New York: Bloomsbury, 2013), 147–151.
123 Al Hartley, *Archie's One Way* (Old Tappan, NJ: Fleming H. Revell Co., 1973), 14, 19.
124 Al Hartley, *Archie's One Way*, 47.
125 Edward B. Fiske, "Jughead, Archie and Their Friends Get Religion and Help in Spreading the Word," *New York Times*, August 23, 1973, 39.
126 Hartley, *Come Meet My Friend!* 37.
127 Al Hartley, *God's Smuggler* (Old Tappan, NJ: Fleming H. Revell Co., 1972), inside back cover.
128 *Archie's Love Scene*, Old Tappan, NJ: Fleming H. Revell Co., 1973, 32.
129 Al Hartley, *Barney Bear Wakes Up* (Old Tappan, NJ: Fleming H. Revell Co., 1977), 32; Al Hartley, *Jesus* (Old Tappan, NJ: Fleming H. Revell Co., 1979), 32.
130 Jack Chick and Fred Carter, *Heart Trouble?* (Ontario, CA: Chick Publications, 2006), 4–5.
131 Chick and Fred Carter, *Heart Trouble?* 13–14.
132 Jack Chick and Fred Carter, *Bad Bob* (Ontario, CA: Chick Publications, 1983), 3.
133 Al Hartley, *Archie's Family Album* (Old Tappan, NJ: Fleming H. Revell Co., 1978), 26, 28–29.
134 Al Hartley, *Barney Bear: The Swamp Gang* (Old Tappan, NJ: Fleming H. Revell Co., 1980), 3.
135 Hartley, *Adam and Eve*, 5–6.
136 Al Hartley, *Archie Gets a Job* (Old Tappan, NJ: Fleming H. Revell Co., 1977), 17–18.
137 Jack Chick and Fred Carter, *There Go the Dinosaurs!* (Ontario, CA: Chick Publications 2007), 12.

138 Jack Chick and Fred Carter, *The Mad Machine* (Ontario, CA: Chick Publications 2007), 11.
139 Jack Chick and Fred Carter, *Global Warming* (Ontario, CA: Chick Publications, 2012), 3. This tract also uses the ill-informed belief that global warming can't be real if we are enduring extreme winter weather. The narration mentions that in 2011, "travelers by the thousands were stranded by snowstorms," adding "Global warming. Are you *sure*?" (11).
140 Chick and Carter, *Global Warming*, 8.
141 Chick and Carter, *Global Warming*, 12–13.
142 Ehrman, *Armageddon*, 14–15.
143 Chick and Carter, *Global Warming*, 20.
144 Ehrman, *Armageddon*, 107.

Chapter 4   The 1970s and 1980s

1 Sheldon Mayer and Joe Kubert, *The Bible*, Limited Collectors' Edition 4, no. C-36 (New York: DC Comics, 1975), 2–3.
2 Dennis O. Lamoureux, *Evolutionary Creation: A Christian Approach to Evolution* (Cambridge, UK: The Lutterworth Press, 2008).
3 Eddy Zeno, "DC Comics' The Bible," *Back Issue!* 61 (May 2018): 23.
4 Mayer and Kubert, *The Bible* 4, no. C-36, 61–62.
5 Zeno, "DC Comics' The Bible," 20.
6 Zeno, "DC Comics' The Bible," 23.
7 *House of Secrets*, no. 87 (New York: DC Comics, August–September 1970), 1.
8 *House of Secrets*, no. 89 (New York: DC Comics, December 1970–January 1971), 28.
9 *House of Mystery*, no. 175 (New York: DC Comics, July–August 1968), 1.
10 Brian Cronin, "Comic Book Legends: Which Comics Creators Were the Models for Cain and Abel?" Comic Book Resources, September 16, 2017, https://www.cbr.com/comic-creators-models-cain-and-abel-len-wein/.
11 *House of Secrets*, no. 81 (New York: DC Comics, August–September 1969), 15.
12 *House of Mystery*, no. 182 (New York: DC Comics, September–October 1969), 15.
13 *House of Mystery* 184 (New York: DC Comics, January–February 1970), 11.
14 *The Spectre* 1, no. 1 (New York: DC Comics, November–December 1967), 6.
15 *Adventure Comics* 4, no. 431 (New York: DC Comics, January–February 1974), 10.
16 *Adventure Comics* 4, no. 434 (New York: DC Comics, July–August 1974), 19.
17 *The Spectre* 3, no. 14 (New York: DC Comics, January 1994), 7.
18 R.V.G. Tasker, *The Biblical Doctrine of the Wrath of God* (London: Tyndale Press, 1951), 5.
19 The Phantom Stranger's backstory was revised in *Secret Origins* 10 (1986). For more on the legend of the wandering Jew, see, for instance, Moncure Daniel Conway, *The Wandering Jew* (London: Chatto and Windus, 1881); and Hyam Maccoby, "The Legend of the 'Wandering Jew,'" *Jewish Quarterly* 20, no. 1 (1972): 3–8.
20 *The Phantom Stranger* 4, no. 0 (New York: DC Comics, November 2012), 4–5.
21 *Blue Devil*, no. 20 (New York: DC Comics, January 1986).
22 Blair Davis, "The Lark/Light Returns: DC's Humorous Heroes of the 1980s," in *The Other 1980s: Reframing Comics' Crucial Decade*, ed. Brannon Costello and Brian Cremins (Baton Rouge: Louisiana State University, 2021).
23 *Blue Devil*, no. 30 (New York: DC Comics, December 1986), 5.

24. Bart D. Ehrman, *Heaven and Hell: A History of the Afterlife* (New York: Simon & Schuster, 2020).
25. Ehrman, *Heaven and Hell*, 24.
26. Jim Amash, "Mike Esposito: The DC & Marvel Years," *Alter Ego* 3, no. 54 (November 2005): 25.
27. *The Official Handbook of the Marvel Universe*, no. 7 (New York: Marvel Comics, July 1983), 13.
28. *The Fantastic Four*, no. 277 (New York: Marvel Comics, April 1985), 7, 11.
29. *Marvel Spotlight*, no. 5 (New York: Marvel Comics, August 1972), front cover.
30. *Marvel Spotlight* 5, 4–5.
31. *The Official Handbook of the Marvel Universe*, no. 13 (New York: Marvel Comics, February 1984), 20.
32. *Ghost Rider*, no. 2 (New York: Marvel Comics, October 1973), 3. While earlier issues depict Satan as the central force in Blaze's deal with the devil, later issues retroactively changed the narrative continuity to make Mephisto the dealmaker and to label the Ghost Rider persona as a demon named Zarathos.
33. See, for instance, Joshua Hanna, "For Unlawful Carnal Knowledge: The Satanic Panic in the United States, 1968–2000" (PhD diss., Oklahoma State University, 2021); and Kier-La Janise and Paul Corupe, eds., *Satanic Panic: Pop-Cultural Paranoia in the 1980s* (Godalming, Surrey: FAB Press, 2016).
34. Jason C. Bivens, *Religion of Fear: The Politics of Horror in Conservative Evangelicalism* (New York: Oxford University Press, 2008), 34.
35. Simon J. Bronner, ed., *Encyclopedia of American Folklife* (New York: Routledge, 2006), 253.
36. J. S. Victor, "Social Construction of Satanic Ritual Abuse and the Creation of False Memories," in *Believed-In Imaginings: The Narrative Construction of Reality*, ed. J. de Rivera and T. R. Sarbin (Washington, DC: American Psychological Association, 1998), 191–216.
37. See Nadja Schreiber, Lisa D. Bellah, Yolanda Martinez, Kristin A. McLaurin, Renata Strok, Sena Garven, and James M. Wood, "Suggestive Interviewing in the McMartin Preschool and Kelly Michaels Daycare Abuse Case: A Case Study," *Social Influence* 1, no. 1 (2006): 16–47; Paul Eberle, *The Abuse of Innocence: The McMartin Preschool Trial* (Buffalo, NY: Prometheus Books, 2010).
38. See Jennings Bryant and Mary Beth Oliver, eds., *Media Effects: Advances in Theory and Research* (New York: Routledge, 2009).
39. *Marvel Spotlight*, no. 6 (New York: Marvel Comics, October 1972), 7.
40. *Marvel Spotlight*, no. 7 (New York: Marvel Comics, October 1972), 9.
41. *Ghost Rider*, no. 2, 15.
42. *Ghost Rider*, no. 1 (New York: Marvel Comics, September 1973), 8.
43. *Marvel Spotlight*, no. 14 (New York: Marvel Comics, March 1974), 3–4.
44. *Marvel Spotlight*, no. 17 (New York: Marvel Comics, September 1974), 14, 16.
45. *Ghost Rider*, no. 9 (New York: Marvel Comics, December 1973), front cover.
46. *Ghost Rider*, no. 9, 16.
47. David Torsiello, "Ghost Rider's First Ride," *Back Issue* 1, no. 95 (April 2017): 15.
48. *Ghost Rider*, no. 12 (New York: Marvel Comics, June 1974), 11.
49. *Ghost Rider*, no. 15 (New York: Marvel Comics, December 1975), 17.
50. See, for instance, Matthew 8:15, Matthew 9:15, Mark 1:31, Mark 5:41, and Luke 8:54.
51. Torsiello, "Ghost Rider's First Ride," 16–17.

52 *Ghost Rider*, no. 19 (New York: Marvel Comics, August 1976), 3.
53 *The Mighty Thor*, no. 303 (New York: Marvel Comics, January 1981), 7.
54 *Cloak and Dagger* 1, no. 1 (New York: Marvel Comics, October 1983), 2.
55 Kurt Busiek, "The Marvel Age Interview: Bill Mantlo," *Marvel Age* 1, no. 25 (April 1985), 9.
56 *Cloak and Dagger* 1, no. 3 (New York: Marvel Comics, December 1983), 19.
57 *Cloak and Dagger* 1, no. 1, 21. New York: Marvel Comics, October, 1983.
58 *Cloak and Dagger* no. 4 (New York: Marvel Comics, January 1984), 23.
59 *Cloak and Dagger* 2, no. 1 (New York: Marvel Comics, May 1985), 13.
60 Paul Young notes that "as a devout Catholic, Miller's Murdock believes in the metaphysical thermodynamics of sin: the sinner is held to account by a higher power and must atone for each sin committed in turn by embracing Christ"; *Frank Miller's Daredevil and the Ends of Heroism* (New Brunswick, NJ: Rutgers University Press, 2016), 72.
61 *Daredevil* 1, no. 119 (New York: Marvel Comics, March 1975), 10.
62 *Daredevil* 1, no. 229 (New York: Marvel Comics, April 1986), 21.
63 *Daredevil*, 1, no. 230 (New York: Marvel Comics, May 1986), 1.
64 *Daredevil*, 1, no. 230, 20.
65 Christopher Knowles, *Our Gods Wear Spandex: The Secret History of Comic Book Heroes* (San Francisco, CA: Weiser Books, 2007), 152.
66 Young, *Frank Miller's Daredevil and the Ends of Heroism*, 78.
67 Revelation 6:8, New International Edition. See also Andrew Cunningham and Ole Peter Grell, *The Four Horsemen of the Apocalypse: Religion, War, Famine and Death in Reformation Europe* (New York: Cambridge University Press, 2000); and Ian Boxell and Richard M. Tresley, eds., *The Book of Revelation and Its Interpreters* (Lanham, MD: Rowman and Littlefield: 2016).
68 *X-Factor* 1, no. 17 (New York: Marvel Comics, June 1987), 6.
69 *X-Factor* 1, no. 19 (New York: Marvel Comics, September 1987), 11.
70 *X-Factor* 1, no. 24 (New York: Marvel Comics, January 1988), 20.
71 *X-Factor* 1, no. 24, 23.
72 Kenneth Baker, *Fundamentals of Catholicism: God, Trinity, Creation, Christ, Mary* (San Francisco: Ignatius Press, 1983), 173.
73 *Francis, Brother of the Universe* 1, no. 1 (New York: Marvel Comics, 1980), 1.
74 *Francis, Brother of the Universe* 1, no. 1, inside front cover.
75 *Francis, Brother of the Universe* 1, no. 1, 3.
76 Mark DiFruscio, "Saints and Superheroes: The Brief Union of Marvel Comics and the Catholic Church," *Back Issue* 1, no. 37 (February 2009): 63.
77 *The Life of Pope John Paul II* 1, no. 1 (New York: Marvel Comics, January 1983), inside back cover.
78 *The Life of Pope John Paul II* 1, no. 1, 1–2.
79 *The Life of Pope John Paul II* 1, no. 1, 55.
80 *The Life of Pope John Paul II* 1, no. 1, inside back cover.
81 Keith Dallas, *American Comic Book Chronicles: The 1980s* (Raleigh, NC: TwoMorrows Publishing, 2013), 97.
82 DiFruscio, "Saints and Superheroes," 66.
83 DiFruscio, "Saints and Superheroes," 66, 69.
84 DiFruscio, "Saints and Superheroes," 66.
85 *The Life of Pope John Paul II* 1, no. 1, 60.

86 DiFruscio, "Saints and Superheroes," 66.
87 DiFruscio, "Saints and Superheroes," 65. See also Tim Lasciuta, *Brush Strokes of Greatness: The Life and Art of Joe Sinnott* (Raleigh, NC: Two Morrows Publishing, 2007), 33.

Chapter 5   The 1990s

1   See, for instance: William Proctor, "The Dark Age: Superheroes in the 1980s," in *Handbook of Comics and Graphic Narratives*, ed. Sebastian Domsch, Dan Hassler-Forest, and Dirk Vanderbeke (Berlin: De Gruyter, 2021), 343–357; and Blair Davis, "The Lark/Light Returns: DC's Humorous Heroes of the 1980s," in *The Other 1980s: Reframing Comics' Crucial Decade*, ed. Brannon Costello and Brian Cremins (Baton Rouge: Louisiana State University Press, 2021), 206–221.
2   *Samson: The Kid Who Never Got a Haircut* (Wheaton, IL: Tyndale House Publishers, 1987), 3, 14.
3   Jochen Ecke, *The British Comic Book Invasion* (Jefferson, NC: McFarland & Company, Inc., 2019).
4   Grant Morrison and Dave McKean, *Batman: Arkham Asylum* (New York: DC Comics, 1989), n.p.
5   Grant Morrison, *Batman: Arkham Asylum*, 15th Anniversary Edition (New York: DC Comics, 2004), n.p.
6   Alan Brennert and Norm Breyfogle, *Batman: Holy Terror* (New York: DC Comics, 1991), n.p.
7   Brennert and Breyfogle, *Batman: Holy Terror*.
8   "Grim" and "gritty" are commonly used terms in reference to superhero comics of this era. Jeffrey Dauber notes, for instance, that Marvel and DC had created "adult, dark and gritty" worlds (*American Comics: A History* [New York: Norton, 2021], 128), while Randy Duncan and Matthew J. Smith's encyclopedic *Icons of the American Comic Book: From Captain America to Wonder Woman*, vol. 1 (Westport, CT: Greenwood Press, 2013) contains numerous entries using the phrase "grim and gritty."
9   "Newswatch," in *Marvel Age*, no. 91 (New York: Marvel Comics, 1990), 9.
10 "Moebius Graphic Novels," in *Marvel Age*, no. 94 (New York: Marvel Comics, November 1990), 22–23.
11 "Kid 'N Play," in *Marvel Age*, no. 115 (New York: Marvel Comics, August 1992), 3.
12 "Barbie," in *Marvel Age*, no. 94 (New York: Marvel Comics, November 1990), 20.
13 *Illuminator*, no. 1 (New York: Marvel Comics, 1992), n.p.
14 *Illuminator*, no. 1 (1992), n.p.
15 *Illuminator* no. 1 (1992), n.p.
16 *Illuminator*, no. 3 (New York: Marvel Comics, 1993), n.p.
17 Andy Stanley, *Not in It to Win It: Why Choosing Sides Sidelines the Church* (Grand Rapids, MI: Zondervan, 2022), n.p.
18 *Illuminator*, no. 1 (New York: Marvel Comics, 1993), back cover.
19 *Illuminator*, no. 2 (New York: Marvel Comics, 1993), back cover.
20 Tyler Huckabee, "Meet the 1990s Marvel Christian Superhero Disney Doesn't Want You to Know About," *Relevant*, June 15, 2021, https://relevantmagazine.com/culture/movies/meet-the-1990s-marvel-christian-superhero-disney-doesnt-want-you-to-know-about/.

21 Benjamine Toussaint-Thiriet, "'The Heart of John Middleton': A Pilgrim's Progress towards a New, Feminized Form of Christianity," *The Gaskell Society Journal* 18 (2004): 71.
22 Kathleen M. Swaim, *Pilgrim's Progress, Puritan Progress: Discourses and Contexts* (Urbana: University of Illinois Press, 1993), 2.
23 John Bunyan, *The Pilgrim's Progress* (1678; repr., Mineola, NY: Dover, 2003), 13.
24 *The Pilgrim's Progress* (New York: Marvel Comics, 1992), n.p.
25 Charles E. Hall, *The Screwtape Letters* (New York: Marvel Comics, 1994), n.p.
26 *The Life of Christ: The Christmas Story* (New York: Marvel Comics, 1993), 7.
27 *The Life of Christ: The Easter Story* (New York: Marvel Comics, 1993), 9.
28 D. Aviva Rothchild, *Graphic Novels: A Bibliographic Guide to Book-Length Comics* (Westport, CT: Libraries Unlimited, 1995), 103.
29 Steve Duin and Mike Richardson, *Comics between the Panels* (Milwaukie, OR: Dark Horse Comics, Inc., 1998), 115.
30 Quoted in Amy Kiste Nyberg, *Seal of Approval: The History of the Comics Code* (Jackson: University of Mississippi Press, 1998), 170–171.
31 Nyberg, *Seal of Approval*, 172–173.
32 Nyberg, *Seal of Approval*, 176–177.
33 Michael Dean, "Marvel Drops Comics Code, Changes Book Distributor," *Comics Journal* 234 (2001): 19.
34 Matt Wagner, *Grendel: God and the Devil* (Milwaukie, OR: Dark Horse, 2008), 31.
35 Robert D. Putnam, *Bowling Alone: The Collapse and Revival of American Community* (New York: Simon & Schuster, 2000), 72, 251.
36 Frances Fitzgerald, *The Evangelicals: The Struggle to Shape America* (New York: Simon & Schuster, 2017), 626.
37 Wagner, *Grendel*, 257.
38 Scott Bukatman, *Hellboy's World: Comics and Monsters on the Margins* (Berkeley: University of California Press, 2016), 25.
39 Mike Mignola, *Hellboy: The Chained Coffin and the Right Hand of Doom* (Milwaukie, OR: Dark Horse Comics, 2008), 225.
40 Mike Mignola, *Hellboy in Hell*, Library Edition (Milwaukie, OR: Dark Horse Comics, 2017), 49.
41 Bukatman, *Hellboy's World*, 57.
42 *The Sandman* 2, no. 50 (New York: DC Comics, June 1993), 19–20.
43 *The Sandman Special*, no. 1 (New York: DC Comics, November 1991), 5.
44 *The Sandman* 2, no. 40 (New York: DC Comics, August 1992), 16.
45 *The Sandman* 2, no. 40, 14.
46 See Ada Langworthy Collier, *Lilith: The Legend of the First Woman* (Boston: D. Lothrop and Co., 1885); Enid Dame, Lilly Rivlin, and Henny Wenkart, eds., *Which Lilith? Feminist Writers Re-Create the World's First Woman* (Lanham, MD: Roman & Littlefield, 1998); and Judith Plaskow, *The Coming of Lilith: Essays on Feminism, Judaism, and Sexual Ethics, 1972–2003* (Boston: Beacon Press, 2005).
47 *The Sandman* 2, no. 40, 13.
48 Issue 40 of *The Sandman* explicitly connects the versions of Cain and Able from *House of Mystery* and *House of Secrets* to those in Genesis. As Eve finishes her story about her creation and subsequent expulsion from Eden, Cain declares, "Wasn't that nice? A little piece of family history. Like flipping through the pages of the family album" (17).

49 *The Sandman* 2, no. 2 (New York: DC Comics, February 1989), 1.
50 *The Sandman* 2, no. 22 (New York: DC Comics, January 1991), 1.
51 *The Sandman* 2, no. 4 (New York: DC Comics, May 1989), 22.
52 See, for instance, Leo Jung, *Fallen Angels in Jewish, Christian, and Mohammedan Literature* (Eugene, OR: Wipf & Stock, 2007), 77–80.
53 *The Sandman* 2, no. 22, 8.
54 *The Sandman* 2, no. 23 (New York: DC Comics, February 1991), 14.
55 *The Sandman* 2, no. 69 (New York: DC Comics, July 1995), 16.
56 Neil Gaiman, "Foreword," in *Lucifer: Book One* (New York: DC Comics, 2013), 6.
57 Maaheen Ahmed notes that "Moore's Swamp Thing made a point of rejecting the conventions of the CCA and almost entirely stopped bearing its seal of approval after the thirtieth issue"; *Monstrous Imaginaries: The Legacy of Romanticism in Comics* (Jackson: University of Mississippi Press, 2020), 55.
58 *Hellblazer* 1, no. 3 (New York: DC Comics, March 1988), 7.
59 *Hellblazer* 1, no. 3, 5–6.
60 *Hellblazer* 1, no. 3, 17–19.
61 *Hellblazer* 1, no. 3, 22.
62 *Hellblazer* 1, no. 10 (New York: DC Comics, October 1988), 30.
63 David Nash, *Blasphemy in the Christian World* (New York: Oxford University Press, 2007), 1.
64 *Hellblazer* 1, no. 60 (New York: DC Comics, December 1992), 3.
65 *Hellblazer* 1, no. 18 (New York: DC Comics, May 1989), 3–4.
66 See, for instance, Margaret Rogerson, ed., *The York Mystery Plays: Performance in the City* (Woodbridge, Suffolk: York Medieval Press, 2011).
67 Elizabeth Shafer, *Theatre & Christianity* (London: Red Globe Press, 2019), n.p.
68 Grant Morrison, *The Mystery Play*, illustrated by Jon J Muth (New York: DC/Vertigo Comics, 1994), n.p.
69 Friedrich Nietzsche, *Thus Spake Zarathustra: A Book for All and None* (New York: Macmillan Co., 1896), 122. See also Robert R. Williams, *Tragedy, Recognition, and the Death of God: Studies in Hegel & Nietzsche* (Oxford: Oxford University Press, 2012).
70 Morrison, *The Mystery Play*, n.p.
71 For a particularly sharp critique of religion, see *Transmetropolitan* 6 (New York: DC Comics, 1998).
72 Neil Monahan and Saeed Ahmed, "There Are Now as Many Americans Who Claim No Religion as There Are Evangelicals and Catholics, a Survey Finds," *CNN*, April 26, 2019, https://www.cnn.com/2019/04/13/us/no-religion-largest-group-first-time-usa-trnd/index.html. The survey, conducted by political scientist Ryan Burge, found that 23.1 percent of respondents reported "no religion," compared to 23.0 percent who identified as Catholic and 22.5 percent who identified as evangelical Christian.
73 David E. Campbell, Geoffrey C. Layman, and John C. Green, *Secular Surge: A New Fault Line in American Politics* (Cambridge: Cambridge University Press, 2020), 104. The authors note, for instance, that one pastor said that the term "evangelical" has "become not a religious identification so much as a political one. These words perfectly reflect the trigger for the backlash to the Religious Right—the politicization of evangelicalism and, by extension, religion more broadly" (106).
74 Campbell, Layman, and Green, *Secular Surge*, 106.
75 *Preacher*, no. 3 (New York: DC Comics, June 1995), 22.

76 *Preacher*, no. 4 (New York: DC Comics, July 1995), 14–15.
77 *Preacher*, no. 1 (New York: DC Comics, April 1995), 1.
78 Mark Salisbury, *Writers on Comics Scriptwriting* (London: Titan Books, 1999), 76.
79 *Preacher Special: One Man's War*, no. 1 (New York: DC Comics, March 1998), 45.
80 Kevin Melrose, "Preacher: Christian Group Demands AMC Cancel 'Blasphemous' Series," Comic Book Resources, August 25, 2017, https://www.cbr.com/christian-group-cancel-preacher/.
81 Quoted in András Koltay and Jeroen Temperman, "Introduction," in *Blasphemy and Freedom of Expression: Comparative, Theoretical and Historical Reflections after the Charlie Hebdo Massacre*, ed. Jeroen Temperman and András Koltay (Cambridge: Cambridge University Press, 2017), 7–8.
82 Salisbury, *Writers on Comics Scriptwriting*, 77.
83 *Preacher*, no. 9 (New York: DC Comics, December 1995), 18.
84 Tom Spurgeon, "Garth Ennis," *Comics Journal* 207 (September 1998): 50–51.
85 *Preacher*, no. 66 (New York: DC Comics, October 2000), 2.
86 *Preacher*, no. 66, 19.
87 Spurgeon, "Garth Ennis," 50.

Chapter 6 The 2000s

1 David Wilkie, *Coffee with Jesus* (Downers Grove, IL: IVP Books, 2013), 13.
2 Paul Levitz, *Will Eisner: Champion of the Graphic Novel* (New York: Abrams Comicarts, 2015), 142.
3 See for instance, Stephen E. Tabachnick, ed., *The Cambridge Companion to the Graphic Novel* (New York: Cambridge University Press, 2017).
4 Levitz, *Will Eisner*, 150.
5 Will Eisner, "Preface," in *The Contract with God Trilogy: Life on Dropsie Avenue* (New York: W. W. Norton & Co., 2006), xvi.
6 Eisner, "Preface," xx.
7 Craig Thompson, *Blankets* (Marietta, GA: Top Shelf Productions, 2003), 61.
8 Thompson, *Blankets*, 87.
9 Thompson, *Blankets*, 105–107.
10 Thompson, *Blankets*, 429–430.
11 Ebony Flowers, *Hot Comb* (Montreal: Drawn and Quarterly, 2019), 79.
12 Flowers, *Hot Comb*, 54.
13 Hillary Chute, "Graphic Novels with Fresh Voices from the Margins," *New York Times*, August 29, 2019, https://www.nytimes.com/2019/08/29/books/review/hot-comb-ebony-flowers-dear-scarlet-teresa-wong.html.
14 Guy Delisle, *Jerusalem* (Montreal: Drawn & Quarterly, 2012), 114.
15 Delisle, *Jerusalem*, 110.
16 Chute, *Disaster Drawn: Visual Witnessing, Comics, and Documentary Form* (Cambridge, MA: Harvard University Press, 2016), 1–2.
17 Ho Che Anderson, *King: A Comics Biography* (Seattle, WA: Fantagraphics, 2010), 18, 46, 62.
18 John Lewis, Andrew Aydin, and Nate Powell, *March: Book One* (San Diego, CA: Top Shelf Productions, 2013), 27–28.
19 Lewis, Andrew Aydin, and Nate Powell, *March*, 76.
20 John Lewis, Twitter post, June 27, 2018, https://twitter.com/repjohnlewis/status/1011991303599607808?lang=en.

21 Kyle Baker, *Nat Turner* (New York: Harry N. Abrams, 2008), 70, 92.
22 Baker, *Nat Turner*, 93.
23 Baker, *Nat Turner*, 104–105.
24 Gene Luen Yang, *Saints* (New York: First Second, 2013), 48.
25 Yang, *Saints*, 52.
26 Yang, *Saints*, 103.
27 Yang, *Saints*, 158.
28 J. Caleb Mozzocco, "Interview: Gene Luen Yang on Boxers & Saints," *School Library Journal*, September 9, 2013, https://goodcomicsforkids.slj.com/2013/09/19/interview-gene-luen-yang-on-boxers-saints/.
29 Chester Brown, *Mary Wept over the Feet of Jesus* (Montreal: Drawn and Quarterly, 2016), 146. For a scholarly exploration of Mary's sexuality, see Emma Maggie Solberg, *Virgin Whore* (Ithaca, NY: Cornell University Press, 2018).
30 *Day of Judgment*, no. 2 (New York: DC Comics, November 1999), 13.
31 See Diana Walsh Pasulka, "Catholic Views of the Afterlife," in *The Routledge Companion to Death and Dying*, ed. Christopher M. Moreman (London: Routledge, 2018), 5–13.
32 *Day of Judgment*, no. 4 (New York: DC Comics, November 1999), 20.
33 *The Spectre* 4, no. 1 (New York: DC Comics, March 2001), 18.
34 See, for instance, Isabel Moreira and Margaret Toscano, eds., *Hell and Its Afterlife: Historical and Contemporary Perspectives* (Burlington, VT: Ashgate Publishing Co., 2010).
35 Randy C. Alcorn, *Heaven* (Wheaton, IL: Tyndale House Publishers, 2004), 178.
36 *The Spectre* 4, no. 4 (New York: DC Comics, June 2001), 12–13.
37 *Shadowpact*, no. 16 (New York: DC Comics, October 2007), 18.
38 John G. Stackhouse Jr., *Can I Believe? An Invitation to the Hesitant* (New York: Oxford University Press, 2020), 2.
39 *Daredevil* 2, no. 1 (New York: Marvel Comics, November 1998), 1.
40 Timothy D. Peters, "Theological 'Seeing' of Law: Daredevil, Christian Iconography, and Legal Aesthetics," in *Critical Directions in Comics Studies*, ed. Thomas Giddens (Jackson: University of Mississippi Press, 2020), 78.
41 Peters, "Theological 'Seeing' of Law," 90.
42 *Hellstorm: Son of Satan*, no. 2 (New York: Marvel Comics, January 2007), 8.
43 *Hellstorm: Son of Satan* 2, 12–13.
44 Christian Roesler, *C. G. Jung's Archetype Concept: Theory, Research and Applications* (London: Routledge, 2022), n.p.
45 Douglas Rushkoff, *Survival of the Richest* (New York: W. W. Norton & Co., 2022), 56.
46 Douglas Rushkoff, "Introduction," in *Testament: Akedah* (New York: DC Comics, 2006), n.p.
47 Rushkoff, "Introduction."
48 Clifford Geertz, *The Interpretation of Culture* (London: Hutchinson, 1975), 448.
49 *Punk Rock Jesus*, no. 4 (New York: DC Comics, December 2012), 17.
50 "The Gospel According to Millar and Gross," in Mark Millar and Peter Gross, *American Jesus, Book 1: Chosen* (Portland, OR: Image Comics, 2016), n.p.
51 Joe Casey, "Introduction," Joe Casey, *Jesusfreak* (Portland: Image Comics, 2019), 11.
52 *The Goddamned*, no. 1 (Portland, OR: Image Comics, November 2015), 3; *The Goddamned*, no. 2 (Portland, OR: Image Comics, December 2015), 4.
53 *The Goddamned*, no. 1, 1.
54 *The Goddamned*, no. 1, 21–24.

55. Kavya Beheraj, "America's Christian Majority Could End by 2070," Axios, September 21, 2022, https://www.axios.com/2022/09/21/pew-religion-christian-majority-2070.
56. *Lake of Fire*, no. 3 (Berkeley, CA: Image Comics, October 2016), 14.
57. See Andrew Phillip Smith, *The Lost Teachings of the Cathars: Their Beliefs and Practices* (London: Watkins Media Limited, 2015).
58. *Loaded Bible* 1, no. 1 (Portland, OR: Image Comics, April 2006), 23.
59. *Loaded Bible* 1, 25.
60. *Loaded Bible* 1, 37.
61. *Battle Pope*, vol. 1, *Genesis* (Portland, OR: Image Comics, 2009), n.p.
62. *Battle Pope*, no. 13 (Portland, OR: Image Comics, September 2006), n.p.
63. Alison Flood, "DC Cancels Comic Where Jesus Learns from Superhero After Outcry," *Guardian*, February 19, 2019, https://www.theguardian.com/books/2019/feb/19/dc-cancels-comic-where-jesus-learns-from-superhero-after-outcry.
64. *Second Coming*, no. 1 (Syracuse, NY: Ahoy Comics, 2019), 21.
65. Matt Bors, "Introduction," in Mark Russell, *Second Coming: Only Begotten Son* (Syracuse, NY: Ahoy Comics, 2021), 5.
66. See, for instance, Katherine Stewart, *The Power Worshippers: Inside the Dangerous Rise of Religious Nationalism* (New York: Bloomsbury, 2020); and Michelle Goldberg, *Kingdom Coming: The Rise of Christian Nationalism* (New York: W. W. Norton, 2007). For more about recent book bans, see, for a start, PEN America's 2022 report, "Banned in the USA: Rising School Book Bans Threaten Free Expression and Students' First Amendment Rights," PEN America: The Freedom to Write, April 2022, https://pen.org/banned-in-the-usa/.
67. Mariana Alfana and Amy B. Wang, "Tennessee Lawmaker Suggests Burning Banned Books," *Washington Post*, April 27, 2022, https://www.washingtonpost.com/politics/2022/04/27/tennessee-burning-banned-books/.
68. John Haltiwanger, "Virginia School Board Members Call for Books to Be Burned amid GOP's Campaign against Schools Teaching about Race and Sexuality," *Insider*, November 2021, www.businessinsider.com/virginia-school-board-members-call-for-books-to-be-burned-2021-11.
69. Flood, "DC Cancels Comic Where Jesus Learns from Superhero After Outcry."
70. Blythe Bernhard, "Suburban School Districts in St. Louis Area More Likely to Ban Books under New Law," *St. Louis Post-Dispatch*, September 25, 2022, https://www.stltoday.com/news/local/education/suburban-school-districts-in-st-louis-area-more-likely-to-ban-books-under-new-law/article_db89ae4d-f559-56e7-929a-8b1af4c374d5.html.
71. M. C. Gaines, "Narrative Illustration: The Story of the Comics," *Print* 3, no. 2 (Summer 1942): 26.
72. Gaines, "Narrative Illustration," 27.
73. Gaines, "Narrative Illustration," 38.

Selected Bibliography

Ahmed, Maaheen. *Monstrous Imaginaries: The Legacy of Romanticism in Comics.* Jackson: University of Mississippi Press, 2020.
Alcorn, Randy C. *Heaven.* Wheaton, IL: Tyndale House Publishers, 2004.
Amash, Jim. "Mike Esposito: The DC & Marvel Years," *Alter Ego* 3, no. 54 (November 2005): 3–40.
Andelman, Bob. *Will Eisner: A Spirited Life.* Milwaukie, OR: M Press Books, 2005.
Baker, Kenneth. *Fundamentals of Catholicism: God, Trinity, Creation, Christ, Mary.* San Francisco, CA: Ignatius Press, 1983.
Bivens, Jason C. *Religion of Fear: The Politics of Horror in Conservative Evangelism.* New York: Oxford University Press, 2008.
Blankenship, Anne. "Catholic American Citizenship: Prescriptions for Children from Treasure Chest of Fun and Fact: 1946–63." In *Graven Images: Religion in Comic Books and Graphic Novels,* edited by A. David Lewis and Christine Hoff Kraemer. New York: Continuum, 2010.
Bloom, Harold. "Introduction." In Bloom, *Satan.* Philadelphia, PA: Chelsea House Publishers, 2005.
Brunet, Peyton, and Blair Davis. *Comic Book Women: Characters, Creators and Culture in the Golden Age.* Austin: University of Texas Press, 2022.
Bukatman, Scott. *Hellboy's World: Comics and Monsters on the Margins.* Berkeley: University of California Press, 2016.
Bunyan, John. *The Pilgrim's Progress.* 1678. Repr., Mineola: Dover, 2003.
Busiek, Kurt. "The Marvel Age Interview: Bill Mantlo," *Marvel Age* 1, no. 25 (April 1985): 9–15.
Calonne, David Stephen. *R. Crumb: Literature, Autobiography, and the Quest for Self.* Jackson: University of Mississippi Press, 2021.
Campbell, David E., Geoffrey C. Layman, and John C. Green. *Secular Surge: A New Fault Line in American Politics.* Cambridge: Cambridge University Press, 2020.
"Catholic School Pupils to Burn 'Undesirable' Comics." *Wisconsin Rapids Daily Tribune,* November 6, 1945, 1.

Chute, Hillary L. *Disaster Drawn: Visual Witness, Comics, and Documentary Form.* Cambridge, MA: Harvard University Press, 2016.
Clare, Sister Mary, SND. *The Comics.* Huntington, IN: Our Sunday Visitor Press, 1943.
Creasy, William C. "The Shifting Landscape of Hell," *Comitatus: A Journal of Medieval and Renaissance Studies* 11, no. 1 (1980): 40–65.
Dallas, Keith. *American Comic Book Chronicles: The 1980s.* Raleigh, NC: TwoMorrows Publishing, 2013.
Davis, Blair. "All-Negro Comics and the Birth of Lion Man, the First African American Superhero," *Inks: The Journal of the Comics Studies Society* 3, no. 3 (Fall 2019): 273–297.
———. "Cartoonist, Draw Thyself." *Image of the Journalist in Popular Culture* 9, no. 1 (2021): 44–73.
———. "The Lark/Light Returns: DC's Humorous Heroes of the 1980s." In *The Other 1980s: Reframing Comics Crucial Decade*, edited by Brannon Costello and Brian Cremins. Baton Rouge: Louisiana State University Press, 2021.
———. *Movie Comics: Page to Screen/Screen to Page.* New Brunswick, NJ: Rutgers University Press, 2017.
Davis-McElligatt, Joanna C. "'Walk Together, Children': The Function and Interplay of Comics, History and Memory in Martin Luther King and the Montgomery Story and John Lewis's March: Book One." In *Graphic Novels for Children and Young Adults: A Collection of Critical Essays*, edited by Michelle Ann Abate and Gwen Athene Tarbox, 298–311. Jackson: University Press of Mississippi, 2017.
Decker, Dwight R., and Gary Groth. "An Interview with William M. Gaines." *The Comics Journal* 81 (May 1983): 53–99.
DiFruscio, Mark. "Saints and Superheroes: The Brief Union of Marvel Comics and the Catholic Church." *Back Issue* 1, no. 37 (February 2009): 61–69.
Duncan, B. N. "A Joint Conversation with R. Crumb and Aline Kominsky-Crumb." In *R. Crumb: Conversations*, edited by D. K. Holm. Jackson: University of Mississippi Press, 2004.
Ecke, Jochen. *The British Comic Book Invasion.* Jefferson, NC: McFarland & Company, Inc., 2019.
Ehrman, Bart D. *Armageddon: What the Bible Really Says about the End.* New York: Simon & Schuster, 2023.
———. *Heaven and Hell: A History of the Afterlife.* New York: Simon & Schuster, 2020.
Eisenstein, Elizabeth. *The Printing Press as an Agent of Change.* New York: Cambridge University Press, 1979.
Fingeroth, Danny. *Disguised as Clark Kent: Jews, Comics, and the Creation of the Superhero.* New York: Continuum, 2007.
Fiske, Edward B. "Jughead, Archie and Their Friends Get Religion and Help in Spreading the Word." *New York Times*, August 23, 1973, 39.
Fitzgerald, Frances. *The Evangelicals: The Struggle to Shape America.* New York: Simon & Schuster, 2017.
Flowers, Ronald B. *Religion in Strange Times: The 1960s and 1970s.* Macon, GA: Mercer University Press, 1984.
Fowler, Robert B. *The World of Jack T. Chick.* San Francisco, CA: Last Gasp, 2001.
Frakes, Margaret. "Comics Are No Longer Comic." *Christian Century*, November 4, 1942, 1349.
Gaiman, Neil. "Foreword." In *Lucifer: Book One*, 6. New York: DC Comics, 2013.

Gaines, M. C. "Narrative Illustration: The Story of the Comics." *Print* 3, no. 2 (Summer 1942): 25–38.

Galloway, John T., Jr. *The Gospel According to Superman*. Philadelphia, PA: A. J. Holman Co., 1973.

Gamzou, Assaf, and Ken Koltun-Fromm, eds. *Comics and Sacred Texts: Reimagining Religion and Graphic Narratives*. Jackson: University of Mississippi Press, 2018.

Geertz, Clifford. *The Interpretation of Culture*. London: Hutchinson, 1975.

Goetz, Stewart, and Charles Taliaferro. *A Brief History of the Soul*. West Sussex: Wiley-Blackwell, 2011.

Gonzalez, Eliezer. "Anthropologies of Continuity: The Body and Soul in Tertullian, Perpetua, and Early Christianity," *Journal of Early Christian Studies* 21, no. 4 (Winter 2014): 479–502.

Hartley, Al. *Come Meet My Friend!* Old Tappan, NJ: New Life Ventures, 1977.

Hatfield, Charles. *Alternative Comics*. Jackson: University Press of Mississippi, 2005.

Holyoake, George Jacob. *The Principles of Secularism*. 3rd ed. London: Austin & Co., 1871.

Jacobs, Dale. *Graphic Encounters: Comics and the Sponsorship of Multimodal Literacy*. New York: Bloomsbury, 2013.

Jacobs, Frank. *The Mad World of William M. Gaines*. Secaucus, NJ: Lyle Stuart, Inc., 1972.

King, Richard. *Orientalism and Religion: Postcolonial Theory, India and "The Mystic East."* London: Routledge, 2013.

Knowles, Christopher. *Our Gods Wear Spandex: The Secret History of Comic Book Heroes*. San Francisco, CA: Weiser Books, 2007.

Kuersteiner, Kurt. *The Art of Jack T. Chick: Chick Tracts, Crusader Comics, and Battle Cry Newspapers*. Atglen, PA: Schiffer Publishing Ltd., 2004.

Lamoureux, Dennis O. *Evolutionary Creation: A Christian Approach to Evolution*. Cambridge, UK: The Lutterworth Press, 2008.

Lévi-Strauss, Claude. *Myth and Meaning*. Toronto: University of Toronto Press, 1978.

Levitz, Paul. *Will Eisner: Champion of the Graphic Novel*. New York: Abrams Comicarts, 2015.

Lewis, A. David, and Christine Hoff Kramer, eds. *Graven Images: Religion in Comic Books and Graphic Novels*. New York: Continuum, 2010.

Lewis, James R. *Satanism Today: An Encyclopedia of Religion, Folklore, and Popular Culture* (Santa Barbara, CA: ABC Clio, 2001

Lynn, Gabriel. *The Case against the Comics*. St. Paul, MN: Catechetical Guild, 1944.

———. *The Teacher and the Comics*. St. Paul, MN: Catechetical Guild, 1946.

Lyons, J. Michael. "From Alabama to Tahrir Square: 'Martin Luther King and the Montgomery Story' Comic as a Civil Rights Narrative." *Journalism History* 41, no. 2 (Summer 2015): 103–111.

Macrone, Michael. "Two Generations of Weirdos: An Interview with R. Crumb and Peter Bagge." *The Comics Journal* 106 (March 1986): 50–71, 95.

Marston, William Moulton. "Why 100,000,000 Americans Read Comics." *American Scholar* 13, no. 1 (Winter 1943–1944): 35–44.

Mathew, Chris. *Modern Satanism: Anatomy of a Radical Subculture*. Westport, CT: Praeger, 2009.

McLuhan, Marshall. *The Mechanical Bride: Folklore of Industrial Man*. Boston: Beacon Press, 1951.

Nash, David. *Blasphemy in the Christian World*. New York: Oxford University Press, 2007.

Nelson, Robert S., and Kristen M. Collins, eds. *Holy Image, Hallowed Ground: Images from Sinai*. Los Angeles, CA: J. Paul Getty Museum, 2006.

Nyberg, Amy Kyste. *Seal of Approval: The History of the Comics Code*. Jackson: University of Mississippi Press, 1998.

Olson, Roger E., Frank S. Mead, Samuel S. Hill, and Craig D. Atwood. *Handbook of Denominations in the United States*. 14th ed. Nashville, TN: Abingdon Press, 2018.

Ospino, Hosffman, and Patricia Weitzel-O'Neill. "Catholic Schools Serving Hispanic Families: Insights from the 2014 National Survey." *Journal of Catholic Education* 19, no. 2 (January 2016): 54–80.

Peters, Timothy D. "Theological 'Seeing' of Law: Daredevil, Christian Iconography, and Legal Aesthetics. In *Critical Directions in Comics Studies*, edited by Thomas Giddens, 77–102. Jackson, MS: University of Mississippi Press, 2020.

Postema, Barbara. *Narrative Structure in Comics*. Rochester, NY: RIT Press, 2013.

Putnam, Robert D. *Bowling Alone: The Collapse and Revival of American Community*. New York: Simon & Schuster, 2000.

Reid, Daniel G., Robert D. Linder, Bruce L. Shelley, Harry S. Stout, and Craig A. Noll, eds. *The Concise Dictionary of Christianity in America*. Eugene, OR: Wipf and Stock Publishers, 1995.

Rhodes, Ron. *The Complete Guide to Bible Translations*. Irvine, CA: Harvest House Publishers, 2009.

Roche, David, Isabelle Schmitt-Pitiot, and Benoît Mitaine. *Comics and Adaptation*. Translated by Aarnoud Rommens and David Roche. Jackson: University of Mississippi Press, 2018.

Roesler, Christian. *C. G. Jung's Archetype Concept: Theory, Research and Applications*. London: Routledge, 2022.

Rushkoff, Douglas. *Survival of the Richest*. New York: W. W. Norton & Co., 2022.

Sánchez, Juan O. *Religion and the Ku Klux Klan: Biblical Appropriation in Their Literature and Songs*. Jefferson, NC: McFarland, 2016.

Salisbury, Mark. *Writers on Comics Scriptwriting*. London: Titan Books, 1999.

Sammond, Nicholas. "Comix." In *Keywords for Comics Studies*, edited by Ramzi Fawaz, Shelley Streeby, and Deborah Elizabeth Whaley. New York: New York University Press, 2021.

Santos, Jorge J., Jr. *Graphic Memories of the Civil Rights Movement: Reframing History in Comics*. Austin: University of Texas Press, 2019.

Saunders, Ben. *Do the Gods Wear Capes? Spirituality, Fantasy, and Superheroes*. New York: Continuum, 2011.

Shafer, Elizabeth. *Theatre & Christianity*. London: Red Globe Press, 2019.

"600 Pupils Prepare Petitions Asking Ban on 'Indecent' Comics." *Chicago Daily Tribune*, December 7, 1947, 50.

Smith, Wilfred Cantwell. *The Meaning and End of Religion*. Minneapolis, MN: Fortress Press, 1991.

Stanley, Andy. *Not in It to Win It: Why Choosing Sides Sidelines the Church*. Grand Rapids, MI: Zondervan, 2022.

Stevens, Gerald L. ed. *Essays on Revelation: Appropriating Yesterday's Apocalypse in Today's World*. Eugene, OR: Pickwick Publications, 2010.

Swaim, Kathleen M. *Pilgrim's Progress, Puritan Progress: Discourses and Contexts*. Urbana: University of Illinois Press, 1993.

Tasker, R. V. G. *The Biblical Doctrine of the Wrath of God*. London: Tyndale Press, 1951.

Torsiello, David. "Ghost Rider's First Ride." *Back Issue* 1, no. 95 (April 2017): 13–30.

Victor, J. S. "Social Construction of Satanic Ritual Abuse and the Creation of False Memories." In *Believed-In Imaginings: The Narrative Construction of Reality*, edited by J. de Rivera and T. R. Sarbin, 191–216. Washington, DC: American Psychological Association, 1998.

Wade, Wyn Craig. *The Fiery Cross: The Ku Klux Klan in America*. New York: Oxford University Press, 1987.

Wanzo, Rebecca. *The Content of Our Caricature: African American Comic Art and Political Belonging*. New York: New York University Press, 2020.

Wertham, Fredric. *Seduction of the Innocent*. New York: Rinehart, 1954.

Whitted, Qiana. *Desegregating Comics: Debating Blackness in the Golden Age of American Comics*. New Brunswick, NJ: Rutgers University Press, 2023.

———. *EC Comics: Race, Shock & Social Protest*. New Brunswick, NJ: Rutgers University Press, 2019.

Yates, Ronald. "Crusader Comics: A Bizarre Band of Christian Heroes." *Chicago Tribune*, June 8, 1981, B1.

Young, Paul. *Frank Miller's Daredevil and the Ends of Heroism*. New Brunswick, NJ: Rutgers University Press, 2016.

Index

Aaron, Jason, 255–257
Action Bible, 230
Action Comics, 12, 23, 39–40, 47
Adam (Biblical figure): Bamberg Bible and, 40; comics adaptations of, 41, 104, 146, 154, 162, 254; DC and, 154, 250; Marvel and, 168–169; *The Sandman* and, 212–214; Spire and, 139–141, 157, 202
Adam and Eve (Spire series), 139, 146, 157, 202
Adams, Neil, 105, 130
Adventures into the Unknown, 23
Adventures of God, 259
Adventures of Jesus, The, 100
Adventure with the Brothers, 139
Airtight Garage, The, 196
Alberto, 133
Alighieri, Dante, 20
All-American Publications, 39
All-Negro Comics, 72, 271n34
Alpha and Omega, 139, 141–142, 146, 202
Amazing Fantasy, 196
Amazing Spider-Man, 204
Ambush Bug, 189
American Jesus, 253
Anderson, Ho Che, 230, 235–236
Andru, Ross, 160
angels: Chick Publications and, 119, 123, 125; comix and, 108–109; DC and, 160, 191–193, 243, 257; *Hellblazer* and, 219–220; Marvel and, 162, 167, 174, 177–179, 204, 257; *Preacher* and, 22; *The Sandman* and, 215
Animal Man, 191, 211, 217
Archie (character), 22–23
Archie Comic Publications: book burnings and, 58; longevity of, 205; Spire and, 6, 138, 142–148, 185
Aronofsky, Darren, 254–255
Atlas Comics, 68, 76, 79, 137
Attack!, 138
Avatar Press, 230, 253
Avengers, The, 130, 182, 198

Baker, Kyle, 230, 237–239
Barbie, 196, 203
Batman: Arkham Asylum, 191–193, 210–211
Batman: Holy Terror, 193–194
Battle Pope, 241, 259–260
Bechdel, Alison, 261
Becker, Judy, 109
Behold the Handmaid, 70–71
Ben Israel, 118
Berger, Arthur Asa, 8
Bible: adaptations of, 31–38, 41–48, 152–154, 203–204; Bamberg version, 40; King James version, 45, 173; Red letter version, 45, 268n68
Bible: Eden, The, 254
Bible, The (DC Comics), 152–155

Bible 2, The, 259
Bible belt readers, 94, 96, 162
Bible in Life Pix, 76
Bible of Filth, 105
Bible Tales for Young Folk, 76–77
Binky Brown Meets the Holy Virgin Mary, 110–114, 149, 225, 232, 241
Black characters: Catechetical Guild and, 93; Chick Publications and, 129–130; DC and, 108, 152; EC Comics and, 84; golden age comics and, 72; graphic novels and, 230, 232, 234; historical figures as, 72–75, 235–239; Marvel and, 108, 152, 174, 202
Black readers, 72–73, 75, 107, 130
Blankenship, Anne, 70
Blankets, 230–233, 241, 243, 262
blasphemy: *Battle Pope* and, 259; *Hellblazer* and, 218–220, 223; legal implications of, 219–220, 223–224; Marvel and, 173, 248; *Second Coming* and, 259; Spire and, 144; *Zap Comix* and, 100
Blood Is the Harvest, 93
Blue Beetle, 40
Blue Devil, 159–161, 215, 245, 257
Bluestone, George, 45
book burnings, 57–58, 94, 260–261
Book of Genesis Illustrated, 104, 261
Boom Comics, 254
Boxers, 239, 241, 262
Brabner, Joyce, 239
Brennert, Alan, 193
Breyfogle, Norm, 193
Brodsky, Sol, 52
Brown, Chester, 230, 241–243
Buscema, John, 181–182, 199–200

Cain (Biblical figure): *Blue Devil* and, 159; *The Goddamned* and, 255–257; *House of Mystery* and, 155–158, 187, 254; Joe Kubert and, 154; Robert Crumb and, 104; *The Sandman* and, 212, 214–215
Call from Christ, 71, 257
Cameron, Don, 40, 47
Captain Marvel Adventures, 24
Carter, Fred: artwork depicting Black characters, 130; partnership with Jack Chick, 120, 130, 275n30
Case Against the Comics, The, 61–62
Casey, Joe, 253

Casper the Friendly Ghost, 27, 94
Catechetical Guild (publisher): Catholicism and, 70–71, 76, 105, 148, 180; Charles Schulz and, 67; communism and, 93–94, 98; concerns about non-religious comics, 61–64; Hispanic readers and, 71–72; *If the Devil Would Talk* and, 85–93, 118, 158; origins of, 61; parochial school distribution, 63, 254; titles for children, 6, 148
Catechism in Pictures, 71
Catholic Comics: artists of, 52–53; catholic readers and, 8, 51; origins of, 269n89; science and, 51–52, 148, 262; sports and, 52
Catholicism: Catechetical Guild and, 70–72, 94, 148; Chick Publications and, 133–136, 141, 148; comix and, 101–102, 109–112; DC Comics and, 159, 244; *Grendel* and, 207; *Hellboy* and, 208; *Lots "O" Fun Comics* and, 53–54; Marvel Comics and, 175–177, 179–187, 247; *Preacher* and, 223–224
Catholic Pictorial, 53
Catholic Publications Company, 63, 75
Catholic World, 32, 59
Charlton Comics, 51, 188, 269n89
Chick, Jack, 119, 137, 148–149
Chick Publications: Catholicism and, 133–136, 141, 148; Crusader Comics, 128–136, 199, 205; distribution strategies, 12, 136, 190; fundamentalism and, 124; as hate literature, 9, 122, 137, 205; publishing formats, 5, 119, 128; racism and, 123–124, 129–130, 132–133; retailers' rejection of, 136; science and, 146–147, 154; supporters of, 126–127
Chick Tracts: origins of, 119–120, 275n26; parodies of, 127–128; prisons and, 120–121; satanism and, 125, 131–132, 159, 166, 220
Christ, Jesus: *Ghost Rider* and, 170–171, 254; *Holy Ghost Zapped Comix* and, 116; Image Comics and, 253, 258–259; *Jerusalem* and, 235; Justin Green and, 113; *Second Coming* and, 259–261; Spire Comics and, 139, 144; Superman and, 13; Vertigo and, 251–252; *Zap Comix* and, 101, 108
Christian bookstores: bans on Chick titles, 133, 136; Marvel titles and, 182–183, 196, 199, 203–205; as retailer for Christian comics, 6, 119, 190, 254; serialized comic books and, 199; Spire titles and, 137, 143, 190; young readers and, 119, 190

Christmas Story, The (Marvel title), 38, 203–204
church attendance rates, 51, 107, 207, 221, 257
Chute, Hilary L., 113–114, 234–235
Clare, Sister Mary, 60
Classics Illustrated, 45, 202
Clowes, Dan, 127
Coffee with Jesus, 5, 230
Comico, 206–207
Comics Code Authority: comix and, 99–100; distribution and, 206, 217–218; horror comics and, 116; religion and, 81, 220, 248; *Treasure Chest of Fun and Fact* and, 80–81; updates to, 206–207
comix: gender and, 108–110; Marvel Comics and, 113; origins of, 99–100; readership of, 99, 114; religious versions of, 114–118
Comix Book, 113
communism, 93–94, 129, 134
Conan the Barbarian, 181–182
confession (Catholic practice); 112, 134–135, 171, 175, 247
Contract with God, A, 230–231, 241, 243
Cook, David C., 76
Crandall, Reed, 68, 70, 118, 182
creationism; 124, 132, 154
Creepy, 52, 68
Crimes by Women, 53
Crime Smasher, 68
Crime SuspenStories, 82
Crisis on Infinite Earths, 179
Crumb, Robert: artwork, 114–115; *Book of Genesis* and, 102, 104; Catholicism and, 101–102, 105, 109; Chick Publications and, 127; Justin Green and, 110; racism and, 100, 104, 273n107; *Zap Comix* and, 99–102, 105, 116
Crypt of Terror, The, 97

Dark Horse Comics, 195, 206–208
Dark Knight Returns, The, 189, 231
DC Comics: artwork of, 47, 68, 182; development of in late 20th century, 160, 179, 190, 195, 211; Max Gaines and, 39; origins of, 13–14; romance titles, 39; superhero genre and, 151–152, 243–245; Vertigo and, 217–220
Delano, Jamie, 193, 218–219, 225

Delisle, Guy, 234–235
Dell Publishing, 39, 49, 118
Dennis the Menace and the Bible Kids, 148
Department of Truth, The, 3
de Paul, Saint Vincent, 71, 76
Detective Comics, 12, 39–40, 53, 193
Devil Kids Starring Hot Stuff, 96
Dillon, Steve, 102, 125, 218, 222
Divine Comedy, 23
Donenfeld, Harry, 12–13, 39, 55
Doom Patrol, 211, 217
Dreaming, The, 214
Dr. Occult (character), 12
Duffy, Mary Jo, 180, 182

Eastern Color Printing, 11, 39, 76, 266n1
Easter Story, The, 203–204
EC Comics: Christian symbolism in, 80–84; Comics Code Authority and, 219; death of Max Gaines and, 49–50, 269n76; horror comics and, 155; *Mad* magazine and, 97–98; origins of, 39–40
Eerie, 52, 68, 118
Ehrman, Bart D., 147, 160
Eightball, 127
Eisner, Will, 19, 65, 230–231
Elvira, 158–159
Ennis, Garth: Christianity and, 188, 193, 224, 241; early career, 223; *Hellblazer* and, 222; *Preacher* and, 3, 102, 125, 222–227; *The Punisher* and, 245; Vertigo and, 188, 218, 243
Esposito, Mike, 160, 162
Eternal Truth, 114–116
Eve (Biblical figure): *The Bible: Eden* and, 254; *The Book of Genesis* and, 104; DC Comics and, 154–155, 157; *The Goddamned* and, 255; Marvel Comics and, 169; *Picture Stories from the Bible* and, 40–41; *The Sandman* and, 212, 214–215; Spire Christian Comics and, 139, 141, 146, 157, 202; *Testament* and, 250
evolution: *Binky Brown Meets the Holy Virgin Mary* and, 112; Chick Publications and, 120, 124, 129, 132; DC and, 154

Famous Funnies, 5, 11–12, 39, 76, 266n1
Fantasia (1940 film), 20
Fantastic Comics, 16

Fantastic Four: artists of, 68, 160, 182, 187; Mephisto and, 162–164; Satan and, 167; silver age era and, 152; superhero genre and, 205
Fatima... Challenge to the World, 71
Fay, William E., 33, 39
Feature Funnies, 12
Finck, Liana, 230
Firebrands of Christ, 71
Fitzgerald, Frances, 207
Flash Comics, 39, 47
Fleetway Publications, 223
Fleming H. Revell Company, 137
Flowers, Ebony, 230, 232, 234
Foster, Dorothy Fay, 33, 39
Four Horsemen, 251
Four Immigrants Manga, The, 230
Fox Feature Syndicate, 16, 53
Frakes, Margaret, 59
Francis, Brother of the Universe, 180–183, 199–200
fundamentalism, 124, 207, 261
Fun Home, 231
Funnies on Parade, 11, 39
Funny Animals, 114

Gaiman, Neil: Christianity and, 3, 188, 193, 225, 227, 243; *Hellblazer* and, 218; *The Sandman* and, 158, 164, 211–217, 248
Gaines, Maxwell Charles: career of, 39–40, 77, 268n60; death of, 49–50, 269m76; EC Comics and, 49–50, 97; "Narrative Illustration" article and, 77, 261–262; *Picture Stories from the Bible* and, 40–51, 80, 115, 148, 152, 230, 258, 261
Gaines, William, 49–50, 81
Gales, Father Louis A., 61
Gartland, Rev. Frank E., 59, 60
Gasnick, Roy, O.F.M., 180, 185
Geertz, Clifford, 251
Genesis, Book of, 102, 104, 154–157, 168, 255
Gerber, Steve, 170
Ghost Rider: Christianity and, 7, 171, 187, 215, 227, 253; Jesus Christ and, 169–170, 254; Satan and, 164–167, 180, 195, 210, 218, 254, 257, 280n32
Girlhood Days, 30
Goddamned, The, 255–260
God Is Dead, 3

God Nose, 100
God's Heroes in America, 71, 75
Graham, Billy, 6, 77
Grant, Steven, 183, 185
Green, Justin, 110–114, 149, 225, 232, 241
Green Arrow, 217
Green Lantern, 130, 190, 243–244
Gregg, Steve, 116
Grendel, 207–208, 210
Guéra, R. M., 255, 257

Hall, Charles E., 202–203
Hansi: The Girl Who Loved the Swastika, 138–139
Hartley, Al: *Archie* and, 142–146, 148; career of, 137–138; gender and, 144–146, 205; science and, 146–148, 154, 205; Spire Christian Comics and, 138–149, 157, 198, 200, 202, 224–225, 262; sports and, 52
Harvey Comics, 24, 27, 94, 190
Haunt of Fear, The, 49, 52, 81, 155
Hellblazer (see *John Constantine, Hellblazer*)
Hellboy, 208–210, 214, 227, 241
Hello, I'm Johnny Cash, 139
Hellstorm: Prince of Lies, 195
Hellstorm: Son of Satan, 247–249
Hendrix, John, 230
Herdling, Glenn, 198, 205
Heroes All: Catholic Action Illustrated, 63, 65, 68, 75, 235
Higgins, Violet Moore, 68
Holy Ghost Zapped Comix, 116–118
Holyoake, George, 85, 87
Holyoke Publishing, 27, 40
Holy Trinity, 8, 19, 266n7
Hot Stuff, 94–97, 99, 190, 210
House of Mystery, 22, 155–159, 187, 214, 254
House of Secrets, 155, 157–158, 187, 214

IDW (publisher), 230, 254
If The Devil Would Talk, 85–94, 96, 99, 118, 158
Illuminator, 196–199, 203–205, 210, 227
Image Comics (publisher), 253–254
Indigenous characters, 75–76
In His Steps, 200, 201–203, 205
In Love with Jesus, 71, 257
International Crime Patrol, 49

In the Presence of Mine Enemies, 138
Irvine, Alexander, 247–248
Isabella, Tony, 170, 175, 254
Iscariot, Judas, 35–36, 157, 159, 204, 254
Islam, 14, 211, 241
Is This Tomorrow, 93–94
It Ain't Me Babe, 108

Jackie Robinson, 72
Jackson, Jack, 100
Jacobs, Dale, 46, 67, 278n122
Jerusalem: Chronicles from the Holy City, 234–235
Jesus: The Man with the Miracle Touch, 190
Jesus Delivers, 127
Jesusfreak, 253–254, 261
Joan of Arc, 68
John Constantine, Hellblazer, 188, 218–222, 227, 241, 257
Joseph: The Kid Whose Dreams Came True, 190
Jude: The Forgotten Saint, 71
Justice League of America, 55, 152, 211

Kid Eternity (1946 series), 23
Kid Eternity (1991 series), 221, 241
King, 235–237
King Jr., Martin Luther, 72–75, 235–237
Kingstone Bible, The, 230
Kirby, Jack, 105, 206, 211
Kiyama, Henry, 230
Know Your Mass, 71, 85
Kominsky-Crumb, Aline, 114
Kubert, Joe, 153–155
Ku Klux Klan, 62, 84, 127, 135
Kull the Conqueror, 182
Kurtzman, Harvey, 230

Lake of Fire, 255, 257
Latinx characters, 72, 118, 123–124, 152
Latinx readers, 71–72
Lawson, Jim, 237
Lee, Stan, 68, 196
Lévi-Strauss, Claude, 2
Lewis, John, 75, 237, 239
LGBTQ+ characters: *Adventures of God* and, 259; Chick Publications and, 122–123, 132–133, 137; stereotypes and, 9
Lichtenstein, Roy, 39

Liebowitz, Jack S., 12, 39, 48
Life of Christ Visualized, The: as Biblical adaptation, 2, 35–38, 43, 45, 67, 203, 257, 262; as early Christian title, 30, 40, 51; pedagogic potential, 63; visual nature of, 32–35, 41, 43, 70, 139
Life of Esther Visualized, The, 39
Life of Joseph Visualized, The, 39
Life of Pope John Paul II, The, 180, 183–185, 187
Life of the Blessed Virgin Mary, The, 85
Lilith (Judaic figure), 212–214
Living Bible, The, 51
Loaded Bible, 7, 258–260
Lonsbury, Earl, 68
Lots "O" Fun Comics, 53–55
Lucifer, 217, 254, 258
Lynn, Gabriel, 61–65

Mace, David, 57–58
Mad, 97–98
Madam Satan (character), 20–23
Manousos, Rev. Demetrius, 85, 89
Mantlo, Bill, 171–174
March: Book One, 75, 237
Marston, William Moulton, 77
Martin Luther King and the Montgomery Story, 72–75, 235
Marvel Comics: artists, 52, 68, 130, 137–138, 143, 210; Biblical adaptations, 38, 76; Catholicism and, 180–187; Christian imagery and, 160, 162, 169–171, 187, 229–230, 254, 257; Comics Code Authority and, 207; comix and, 113; Nelson imprint, 195–205, 227, 262; Satan and, 158, 166–167; superhero genre and, 151–152, 164, 179, 245, 247; young readers and, 190, 196
Marvel Knights (imprint), 245, 247
Marvel MAX (imprint), 247–248
Marvels of Science, 51–52, 148, 235
Marvel Super Heroes Secret Wars, 179
Mary Wept over the Feet of Jesus, 230, 241–243, 260–261
materialism, 92–94
Maus, 114, 229, 231, 261
Mayer, Sheldon, 154–155
McDaniel, Scott, 203
McKean, Dave, 191–193

McLuhan, Marshall, 4, 13
McMartin preschool trials, 166
medium theory, 4
Mendes, Barbara, 108
Mephisto (character), 162–164, 166, 182, 280n32
Mephisto Vs., 163–164, 230, 257
Michelinie, David, 185
Mighty Thor, The, 171, 187
Mignola, Mike, 208–210, 214, 227, 241
Miniature Jesus, 251, 261–262
Moench, Doug, 171
Mongomery bus boycott, 72–73
Moore, Alan, 158, 189–190, 217–218, 284n57
Moran, Penny, 109–110
More Fun Comics, 2, 12, 14–16, 152, 244
Morrison, Grant, 190–193, 211, 220, 241, 259
Moses: The Man Who Talked to Bushes, 190
Mother Teresa of Calcutta, 180, 185–187, 199
Movie Comics, 40
Ms. Marvel, 241
Mulford, Montgomery, 40
Mumma, Win, 190
My Brother's Keeper, 139
Mystery Play, The, 220–221, 241

Nat Turner, 230, 237–239, 261
Negro Heroes, 72
Negro Romance, 72
New Fun Comics, 5, 12
New Mutants, The, 179
New Testament: *Adventures of Jesus* and, 100; DC Comics and, 155, 159; *Life of Christ Visualized* and, 30, 35–36, 38; Marvel Comics and, 169–170, 203–204; *Mary Wept Over the Feet of Jesus* and, 241; *Picture Stories from the Bible* and, 40, 43–48, 50, 98; *Saints* and, 239
New Testament Heroes, 39
Noah (Biblical figure), 41, 77, 129, 146, 154, 255
Noah's Ark, 139

Of Such Is the Kingdom, 71
Old Testament: Chick Publications and, 122; DC Comics and, 159; *The Goddamned* and, 255, 258; Marvel Comics and, 169; *Picture Stories from the Bible* and, 40–41, 46, 50, 98; *Sunday Pix* and, 76; Vertigo and, 248

Oral Roberts' True Stories, 77–79, 98
Orlando, Joe, 52, 155, 157
Our Family Catechism, 71
Our Lady of Fatima, 71

Pace, Richard, 259–260
Padre of the Poor, 71
Parables Jesus Told, 39
Paradise Lost, 20, 217
Parks, Rosa, 73
parochial school readership, 6, 58, 63–65, 98, 119, 254
Paul: Close Encounters of the Real Kind, 138, 255
Paulist Press, 182
Payne Foundation, 60, 166
Peanuts, 67
Pearson, Vee Quintal, 68, 75
Pekar, Harvey, 229
Pelc, Gene, 180, 183
Pep Comics, 20–22
Persepolis, 229, 231, 241
Pflaum, George A., 67–71, 80–81, 203, 255
Phantom Stranger, The, 22, 159, 193, 257, 279n19
Phillips, Jim, 115
Picture Stories from American History, 48
Picture Stories from Science, 48, 98, 148
Picture Stories from the Bible: advertising for, 50, 97–98; artwork of, 46–47, 68, 203; as Biblical adaptation, 10, 41–50, 65, 67, 70, 77, 204; as early Christian title, 13, 39, 51, 67, 257; comix and, 115; EC Comics and, 83; graphic novels and, 230–231; origins of, 40; pedagogic potential of, 63, 80, 258, 261; science and, 148
Picture Stories from World History, 48, 98
Pilgrim's Progress, 199–205
Planet Comics, 53
Pocket Comics, 23–27
Popular Comics, 5, 12
Postema, Barbara, 43
Power Man and Iron Fist, 182–183
Power Mark, 230
Preacher: blasphemy and, 223; Christian tropes and, 222–227, 241, 245, 253, 257–258, 261; faith and, 225, 232, 251, 262; representations of God and, 102, 125, 224–226

Prince Valiant, 5, 33
Prison to Praise, 118
Prize Comics, 97
Proposition Player, 251
pulp magazines, 12, 55, 210
Punisher, The, 183, 195, 245, 247
Punk Rock Jesus, 251–253, 258
purgatory, 20, 158, 244

Quesada, Joe, 247

racism: caricature and, 72, 75–76, 132; Chick Publications and, 130–133; Comics Code Authority and, 81, 206; EC Comics and, 50, 83–84; *God Nose* and, 100; *If the Devil Would Talk* and, 89; jungle comics and, 72, 271n34; Robert Crumb and, 100, 273n107; *Seduction of the Innocent* and, 59; white supremacy and, 50, 62
Real Hit Comics, 40
Red Iceberg, The, 98
Redondo, Nestor, 154
Revelation, Book of: Chick Publications and, 119, 147; DC and, 191; *Hellboy* and, 210; Marvel and, 177, 179–180; *Preacher* and, 222; Spire and, 139, 141
Richardson, Mike, 206, 208
Richie Rich, 27, 94, 190
Riddel, Mabel, 58
Rivera, Alberto, 133–136
Robbins, Trina, 9, 108–109, 113
Rothchild, D. Aviva, 204–205
Run Baby Run, 118
Rushkoff, Douglas, 248, 250–251, 258
Russell, Mark, 259–261

Sacco, Joe, 235
Sacred and Profane, 110, 113, 241
Saga of the Swamp Thing, 217–218
Said, Edward, 17
Saints, 230, 239–241, 262
Sammy Saved and Al Most, 114–116
Samson: The Kid Who Never Got a Haircut, 190
Samson, 16–20, 46
Sandman, The: Biblical figures and, 212–217; gender and, 212–214; genre and, 227; origins of, 211; religion and, 211, 248; Vertigo and, 217, 229, 245

Satan: Catechetical Guild and, 85–92; crime genre and, 27–29, 84–85; crossword puzzles and, 85; DC Comics and, 158, 160; Harvey Comics and, 23–26, 94–97; horror genre and, 23, 116; in literature, 20; Marvel Comics and, 162–167; as supervillain, 23–27, 254, 257; symbolism and, 21–22
satanism: Chick Publications and, 125, 127, 129, 131–132, 205; DC Comics and, 158; Halloween and, 125; Marvel Comics and, 164–167, 257; moral panic surrounding, 166, 257; Vertigo and, 220
Satrapi, Marjane, 229, 231
Savage Sword of Jesus Christ, 241, 259
Schulz, Charles, 67, 93
science: EC Comics and, 48, 98; role in Christian comics, 40, 51–52, 137, 144, 146–149, 154, 202, 205, 262; secularism and, 87; societal attitudes towards, 52
Screwtape Letters, The, 202–203, 205
Second Coming, 259–261
secularism: definition of, 87; *If the Devil Would Talk* and, 85, 87–94; religious affiliation and, 221
Seduction of the Innocent, 58–59, 79
Sensation Comics, 39, 47
Severin, Marie, 182–183, 199
Shade the Changing Man, 217
Shafer, Elizabeth, 220
Shooter, Jim, 170–171, 183, 254
Shuster, Joe, 12, 39, 115–116
Siegel, Jerry, 12, 14, 16, 19, 39
Silver Surfer, 68, 162, 199
Simonson, Louise, 204
Sinnott, Joe, 68, 70, 118, 182–183, 185
Slow Death Funnies, 108
Smith, Kevin, 245, 247
Smith, Wilfred Cantwell, 7, 18
Sonday Funnies Comic Corporation, 114
Son of Satan: Christian tropes and, 2, 167–168, 227; hell and, 164, 171, 180; satanism and, 187, 257
Source Point Press, 259
Spectre, The (character): DC Comics and, 13, 39, 158–159; God and, 19, 22, 152, 243–245; *More Fun Comics* and, 12, 14, 152; origins of, 14; spirituality and, 14–16, 46, 158–159, 193

Spiegelman, Art, 113–114, 229, 231, 261
Spire Christian Comics: adaptation and, 138, 200, 255; *Archie* titles, 58, 142–146, 148; celebrity biographies, 139, 180; children's titles, 139, 142, 146; Christian bookstores and, 119, 143, 190, 254; gender and, 144–146, 205; origins of, 137–138; race and, 202; science and, 146–148, 205; science fiction and, 139, 141–142; spirituality and, 108, 148, 198, 224–225, 262
Spirit, The, 19, 58, 65
sports, 52, 139, 148
Standard Publishing, 30, 39
Star Comics (imprint), 190
Story of David and Goliath, The, 77
Sunday Pix, 76–77, 98, 204, 272n50
Sunday school, 6, 30, 76, 98, 143, 232
Sunday School Standard, 30
Superman (character): *Batman: Holy Terror* and, 193; book burnings and, 58; *Lots "O" Fun Comics* and, 53, 55; religious allegories, 6, 12–14, 19, 245; superhero genre and, 20, 23, 36, 152, 190
Suspense Comics, 23, 27–30
Swaim, Kathleen M., 200

Tales from the Crypt: advertising for *Picture Stories from the Bible* in, 50, 97–98; Christian symbolism in, 81–82; EC Comics and, 49, 155
Tales from the Great Book, 76
Tales from the Heart, 195
Tales from the Heart of Africa: The Temporary Natives, 195
Tales of Horror, 84
Tallarico, Tony, 118
Talmud, 212, 215
Teacher and the Comics, The, 62–64
There's a New World Coming, 139, 141
Thomas Nelson (publisher), 196–205, 227, 262
Thompson, Craig, 230–233, 235
Timeless Topix, 63, 65, 76
Timely Comics, 20, 33, 76, 137
Töpffer, Rudolphe, 5, 230
Topix Comics, 65–67, 70, 76, 85, 98, 148
Top Shelf Productions, 231
Transmetropolitan, 221, 284n71
Treasure Chest of Fun and Fact: artists, 118–119, 182, 187; Comics Code Authority and, 80–81; educational purposes of, 76–77, 148, 185, 262; origins of, 67–70; readership of, 98, 185
Trejo, Danny, 120–121
Troubled Souls, 223
True Faith, 223, 241
Tullus, 76, 204–205
Tyndale House (publisher), 190

Uncanny X-Men, 177, 179, 195, 204

Vertigo Comics (imprint): Christian tropes in, 125, 195, 221–222, 227, 230, 243, 251, 253, 257; creators and, 220, 229, 245, 259, 262; origins of, 217–218; Satan and, 30, 160
V for Vendetta, 217
Vincent de Paul, 71
Voodoo, 84–85

Wagner, Matt, 206–207
Walking Dead, The, 259, 261
Walt Disney's Comics and Stories, 190
Warren Publications, 52, 68
Watchmen, 189, 231, 261
Web of Mystery, 84
Wein, Len, 157
Weird Fantasy, 49
Weird Science, 49, 52, 81
Weird Tales, 210
Wertham, Fredric, 58–60, 79–80, 97, 105
Western Publishing, 52, 189–190
What If . . . ? 198–199
Wheeler-Nicholson, Malcolm, 12, 14
Whitted, Qiana, 40, 50, 75, 84
Wilkie, David, 230
Wilshire, Mary, 203
Wilson, S. Clay, 99, 108, 110, 202
Wimmen's Comix, 6, 9, 108–110, 114
Woodring, Jim, 127–128
World Is His Parish, The, 71

X-Factor, 177–180, 187, 191, 230, 243

Yang, Gene Luen, 230, 239–241
Yoe, Craig, 115–116

Zap Comix, 99–105, 108–110, 114, 116, 202

About the Author

BLAIR DAVIS is a professor of media and popular culture in the College of Communication at DePaul University in Chicago. His books include *The Battle for the Bs: 1950s Hollywood and the Rebirth of Low-Budget Cinema*, *Movie Comics: Page to Screen/Screen to Page*, *Comic Book Movies*, and the award-winning *Comic Book Women: Characters, Creators, and Culture in the Golden Age*. He has written about comics and pop culture for *USA Today*, the *Washington Post*, the *Saturday Evening Post* and *Ms.* magazine and has comics-related essays in numerous anthologies, including *Comics and Pop Culture*, *Working-Class Comic Book Heroes*, and the Eisner Award–winning *The Blacker the Ink*. Davis serves on the editorial advisory board of the journal *Inks*, for which he edited a roundtable on comics and methodology in its inaugural issue, and has served on the executive board of the Comics Studies Society. He appeared on two episodes of AMC's *James Cameron's Story of Science Fiction* and has been interviewed about comics and cinema for ABC-7, CBC, the *Chicago Tribune*, PRI, *USA Today*, *Voice of America*, and the *Wall Street Journal*.